If you're wondering why you should buy this new edition of *State and Local Politics: Government by the People*, here are 6 good reasons!

1. New Introduction previews the broad themes of the book and helps students step back from the details to understand the bigger picture. Organized around the Course Learning Objectives, it summarizes the important overall concepts students should master by the end of the course. A comprehensive **Course Exam**, appearing at the end of the text, allows students to test their mastery of the course material as a whole.

2. Chapter Learning Objectives are more fully integrated into the chapters, providing stronger pedagogical guidance for navigating the chapter content. Objectives are also used to structure end-of-chapter content, which includes a **Summary and Self-Test**, allowing students to assess their understanding of each objective.

3. New features are built around the framework of a government of, by, and for the people. **Of the People** boxes explore the diversity of Americans and assess how they compare to the global community; **By the People** boxes demonstrate nontraditional and accessible ways students can participate in government and public service; and **For the People** boxes remind students of the important accomplishments achieved by our government. These features help today's students see the relevance of government and the important role that they as citizens play in this country's present and future.

4. Being part of a government by the people requires consideration of differing points of view. **You Will Decide** boxes, updated with the latest in-the-news topics, explore questions that citizens and policy analysts alike wrestle with, like the advantages and disadvantages of a national presidential primary, or the need for restrictions on civil liberties during the war on terror, and then ask students to weigh options for resolving these issues.

5. The **visual program**, updated for currency and relevance, has also been developed to be more pedagogically effective in helping students build their study skills and get more out of the visuals. Photo captions include analysis questions designed to promote critical thinking and stimulate class discussion, and figures are accompanied by visual literacy questions that ensure students are accurately reading and assessing the data.

6. All chapters revised with an emphasis on anticipating areas of student confusion and revising explanations to address those areas of common difficulty. In particular, the discussion in Chapter 13 on bureaucratic agencies and in Chapter 17 on the public policy process have been revised and reorganized for greater clarity and comprehension.

PEARSON

ELECTORAL COLLEGE VOTES IN THE 2008 ELECTION

THE UNITED STATES
A political map showing the number of electoral votes per state

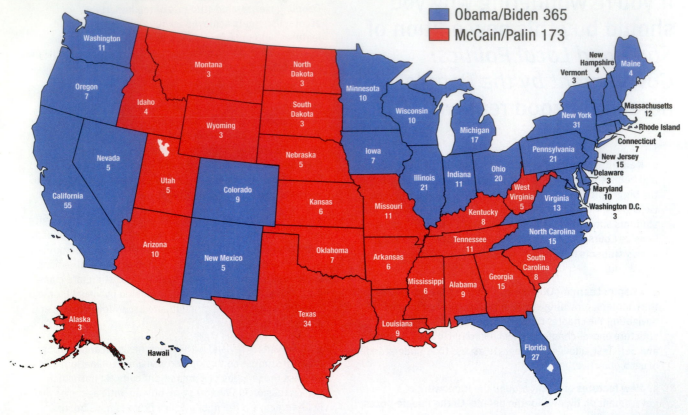

Obama/Biden 365
McCain/Palin 173

A political map with states drawn in proportion to the number of electoral votes

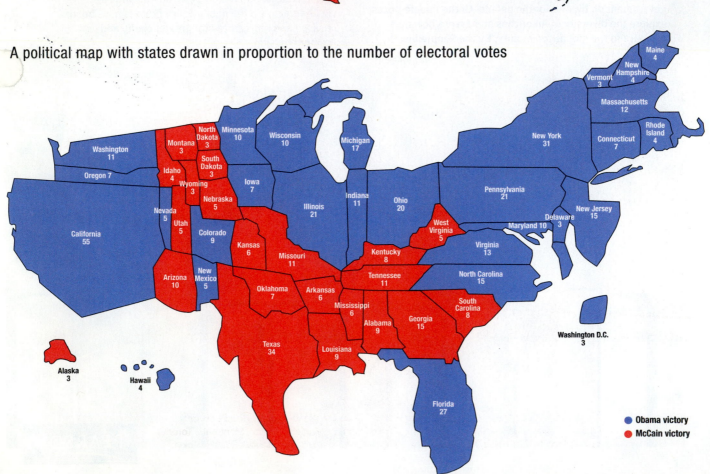

Obama victory
McCain victory

STATE AND LOCAL POLITICS: GOVERNMENT BY THE PEOPLE

DAVID B. MAGLEBY
Brigham Young University

PAUL C. LIGHT
New York University

CHRISTINE L. NEMACHECK
The College of William and Mary

Fifteenth Edition

Longman

Boston   Columbus   Indianapolis   New York   San Francisco   Upper Saddle River
Amsterdam   Cape Town   Dubai   London   Madrid   Milan   Munich   Paris   Montreal   Toronto
Delhi   Mexico City   São Paulo   Sydney   Hong Kong   Seoul   Singapore   Taipei   Tokyo

EXECUTIVE EDITOR:	Reid Hester
EDITORIAL ASSISTANT:	Elizabeth Alimena
DIRECTOR OF DEVELOPMENT:	Meg Botteon
ASSOCIATE DEVELOPMENT EDITOR:	Donna Garnier
SUPPLEMENTS EDITOR:	Corey Kahn
SENIOR MEDIA PRODUCER:	Regina Vertiz
SENIOR MARKETING MANAGER:	Lindsey Prudhomme
PRODUCTION MANAGER:	Bob Ginsberg
PROJECT COORDINATION, TEXT DESIGN, AND ELECTRONIC PAGE MAKEUP:	Integra Software Services, Inc.
COVER DESIGN MANAGER/COVER DESIGNER:	John Callahan
COVER ILLUSTRATION/PHOTO:	Michael Eudenbach/Aurora Photos
PHOTO RESEARCHER:	Teri Stratford
SENIOR MANUFACTURING BUYER:	Dennis J. Para
PRINTER AND BINDER:	RR Donnelley & Sons Company/Willard
COVER PRINTER:	Lehigh Phoenix

For permission to use copyrighted material, grateful acknowledgment is made to the copyright holders on p. 243, which are hereby made part of this copyright page.

Library of Congress Cataloging-in-Publication Data

Magleby, David B.
 Government by the people: state and local/David B. Magleby, Paul C. Light,
Christine L. Nemacheck.—2011 ed.
 p. cm.
Includes bibliographical references and index.
ISBN 978-0-205-00639-7
 1. United States—Politics and government—Textbooks. I. Light, Paul Charles.
II. Nemacheck, Christine L. III. Title.
JK276.G68 2011
320.473—dc22

MAGLEBY   2010045839

Longman
is an imprint of

1 2 3 4 5 6 7 8 9 10—DOW—13 12 11

www.pearsonhighered.com

ISBN-13: 978-0-205-00639-7
ISBN-10:   0-205-00639-6

BRIEF CONTENTS

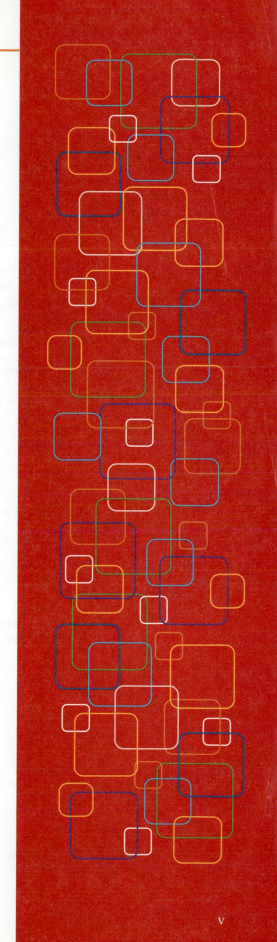

CONTENTS

COURSE
OBJECTIVES

PREFACE

This book is about the institutions and political forces that shape policy making and policy outcomes in state and local communities. To those of us who are students of American politics, states and their local government subdivisions are fascinating political laboratories that allow comparisons among different political systems and traditions. States vary in the powers given to governors, how their legislatures are structured, how judges are selected and reviewed, and how they operate in a host of policy areas, including how they impose taxes. The party system is much weaker in some regions of the country than in others. Stage legislatures in some of the smaller or rural states meet for just a few months a year, whereas in other states, they meet all year. The importance of interest groups and the media varies from state to state and from city to city. Generalizations are sometimes difficult, yet we try in this book to summarize what political scientists know about state and local politics and government.

State and local government and politics remain important not only to the residents of a particular state but to all Americans. A tax-cutting ballot initiative can spawn scores of similar votes in other states just as successful bonds to pay for highways and education can do the same. And as we learned from welfare reform, states can be catalysts for change on the national level and then central to its implementation. Those who want better government in their communities and states will be more likely to achieve it by doing something to make it happen. If government by the people is to be more than just rhetoric, citizens must understand state and local politics and be willing to form political alliances, respect and protect the rights of those with whom they differ, and be willing to serve as citizen leaders and citizen politicians. We hope this book will motivate you to appreciate that every person can make a difference, and that we should each work toward this end.

What's New in This Edition

The new edition of *State and Local Politics: Government by the People* builds on the long-standing reputation of this book for strong coverage of the foundations of American government that is accurate, accessible, and current. We have integrated the latest in scholarship on American politics and government, the 2010 midterm elections, recent Supreme Court appointments and decisions, and comparisons with countries around the world into a book that introduces you to the subject and the discipline of political science.

Building on the theme of the people in government, we examine government through a new set of features that we have named *Of the People*, *By the People*, and *For the People*. These features explore who the American people are, how they compare to people and cultures around the world, the ways they are engaging in their government, and the important accomplishments that have resulted.

Growing from the success of the previous edition, this edition expands on the framework of learning pedagogy to help you navigate each chapter's discussion, focus on the most important concepts, and understand American politics and government. After surveying American government and politics courses taught around the country, we developed a list of Learning Objectives—the concepts professors teaching this course most often want their students to understand—to shape and guide the development of this edition. Each part opens with a list of Course Objectives, which provides students with a big picture overview of the broad concepts they will encounter, giving them a better understanding of how to focus their reading and studying for each section. At the end of the book, they will be able to test their mastery of the course material as a whole through the comprehensive Course Exam. Paralleling this structure, each chapter opens with a list of Chapter Objectives, highlighting the learning goals for that chapter.

Chapter Objectives are called out in the text margins as the key concepts are discussed, and a summary and self-test at the end of each chapter provide students with a final check of their understanding of the chapter.

Chapter-by-Chapter Changes:

Chapter 1 uses the recent state regulations on texting while driving to introduce the chapter. The discussion of federalism has been expanded to compare the advantages and disadvantages of a federal system of government in the United States. Analysis of the centralist and decentralist arguments has been reorganized and clarified. A new feature shows students how to track and monitor distribution of funds from the national stimulus package.

Chapter 2 begins with an example of the current budget challenges faced by California. This and other new examples in the chapter illustrate how the economy and even international relations affect governments at all levels. The chapter has a new section on how individuals can influence state and local governments.

Chapter 3 has been updated to include a timely discussion of state constitutional efforts to deal with the question of same-sex marriage, one of the most hotly debated topics in politics today, and an excellent lens through which to analyze the importance of state constitutions. An expanded section on new judicial federalism addresses the important role state courts play in protecting individual liberties as they increasingly decide cases using protections in their own state constitutions rather than the U.S. Constitution.

Chapter 4 anticipates the reapportionment coming in 2011 and 2012 and provides a current and expanded discussion of the redistricting process. The chapter also explores the important agenda-setting role of ballot initiatives and referendums. With states experimenting with new ways to vote—by mail or electronically, for example—the chapter examines why these reforms were instituted and what has changed as a result of their adoption.

Chapter 5 places state legislatures in their historical context as predating the U.S. Constitution. The chapter explores similarities and differences between state legislatures and the U.S. Congress. One important similarity is a reliance on committees to do much of the work. New to this edition is information on how to contact your representative in the state legislature.

Chapter 6 has been updated to include results from the 2010 election in a broader analysis of the politics of becoming a governor. Although states vary in the power they give the governor, all governors have important formal and informal powers. For example, governors typically have the power to pardon criminals. As discussed in the new opener, former Illinois Governor Ryan exercised that power when he pardoned four death row inmates and commuted the sentence of all 167 death row inmates to life sentences.

Chapter 7 includes an updated and enhanced discussion of judicial elections and campaign contributions. State courts, like their federal counterparts, are becoming increasingly diverse, and this chapter also includes updated data on the presence of women and racial and ethnic minority judges on the state judiciary. The chapter also includes new discussions on the changing treatment of the death penalty in the states, the role of court monitoring groups, and efforts in some states to publicly fund judicial elections.

Chapter 8 taps into the controversy surrounding Arizona's immigration law by contrasting the responses of two county sheriffs to the new law. The impact of local differences in law and policy is also illustrated at the beginning of the chapter in a comparison of the different approaches local governments have taken in rules for posting bail for minor offenses. The chapter also presents an example of how people can make a difference in local zoning and school decisions.

Chapter 9 examines the broad sweep of policy making that occurs at the state and local levels. Using education as an example, the chapter includes a current examination of efforts by governments at all levels to improve public education. Of particular interest to college students is a section on higher education funding.

Chapter 10 includes an updated discussion of one of the consequences of the economic challenges faced by the United States in 2008–2011: the growing debt not only at the national level but in some states and many localities. There is also a renewed focus on lowering costs in local and state governments, exploring the challenges of adequately staffing government in a time of shrinking budgets.

Resources for Instructors

The **Instructors Manual and Test Bank** (ISBN: 0-205-11603-5) offers chapter overviews and outlines, teaching ideas, discussion topics, activity suggestions, and additional resources. The Test Bank contains over 100 questions per chapter in multiple-choice, true-false, short answer, and essay format. Questions address all levels of Bloom's taxonomy and are correlated to the Learning Objectives in the book. All questions have been reviewed for accuracy and effectiveness. **PowerPoint Presentations** (ISBN: 0-205-18906-7) include a lecture outline of the text, graphics rom the book, and quick check questions for immediate feedback on student comprehension. Available to qualified adopters through the Instructor Resource Center at http://www.pearsonhighered.com/educator.

State and Local Government and Politics Study Site provides an online set of practice tests, Web links, and flash cards organized by major topics and arranged according to the book's table of contents. www.pearsonhighered.com/stateandlocalgov.

A FOCUS ON
FOUNDATIONS . . .

Read by over one million students, this new edition of the classic *Government by the People* has been substantially rewritten and redesigned to assist you in your study of American government and politics.

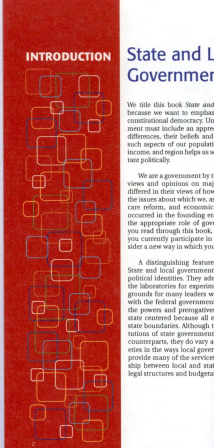

INTRODUCTION

State and Local Government

We title this book *State and Local Politics: Government by the People* because we want to emphasize the important role people play in our constitutional democracy. Understanding American politics and government must include an appreciation of the people, their similarities and differences, their beliefs and attitudes, and their behaviors. Examining such aspects of our population as race, ethnicity, gender, age, religion, income, and region helps us see how the diversity of our country is important politically.

We are a government by the people, but we are people with differing views and opinions on major issues of our day, just as the framers differed in their views of how our government should operate. Many of the issues about which we, as Americans, disagree today, such as health care reform, and economic policy mirror the kinds of debates that occurred in the founding era. They concern basic assumptions about the appropriate role of government and individual responsibility. As you read through this book, we challenge you to think about the ways you currently participate in our democratic system and perhaps consider a new way in which you might make your voice heard.

A distinguishing feature of American government is federalism. State and local governments help define our politics and shape our political identities. They administer most public programs, have been the laboratories for experiments in public policy, and are the proving grounds for many leaders who go on to serve at the national level. As with the federal government, the states have constitutions that detail the powers and prerogatives of government. Electoral competition is state centered because all elective offices in the United States honor state boundaries. Although the executive, legislative, and judicial institutions of state government have some similarities with their federal counterparts, they do vary across the states. There are even more varieties in the ways local governments are organized. Local governments provide many of the services... ship between local and state... legal structures and budgeta...

New! An Introduction identifies the **Big Picture** themes and explains the **Course Learning Objectives** for each set of chapters. These will give you a better understanding of how to focus your reading and studying for the section, and will help you to integrate concepts across chapters.

New! At the end of the book you'll be able to test your mastery of the course material as a whole through the comprehensive **Course Exam.**

COURSE EXAM

Part I Constitutional Principles

Chapter 1: American Federalism
Explain federalism in America, and analyze the relationship between the federal and state and local governments.

1. Define federalism and explain the ways governments at different levels can share power in different kinds of federalism.

2. Which one of the following is NOT an advantage of federalism?
   a. It checks the growth of tyranny.
   b. It encourages experimentation.
   c. It allows unity without uniformity.
   d. It encourages holding elected officials accountable through a division of power.
   e. It keeps government closer to the people.

3. What is the difference between delegated or express powers and implied powers? List some of both types.

   c. The devolution revolution should be defeated.
   d. Presidents Abraham Lincoln and Franklin Roosevelt had a correct understanding of the balance in power between the states and federal government.
   e. The national government is an agent of the people, not the states.

5. Which of the following is one of the three types of federal grants currently given?
   a. Welfare grant
   b. Income equalization grant
   c. Categorical-formula grant
   d. Revenue sharing grant
   e. Education grant

6. Historically, how had federalism been used to retain slavery, segregation, and discrimination? Provide arguments for and against retaining federalism given these patterns. Are there examples of states having laws today that treat people differently?

American Federalism

The relationship of the national government to the states has been the subject of intense debate since the founding.[1] In 1787, members of what would become the Federalist Party defended the creation of a strong national government, whereas the Antifederalists warned that a strong national government would overshadow the states. The great debate over which level of government best represents the people continues to rage.

State governments have often complained that the national government is either taking over their responsibilities or controlling too much of what they do. Yet, in policy areas such as civil rights, educational opportunities for people with disabilities, and handgun control, the states have been slow to respond to citizens, and the national government has taken steps to deal with these issues.

At the same time, states retain enormous authority under the Constitution to regulate life within their borders. Working with the local governments they create, states police the streets, fight fires, impose their own taxes, create most of the laws that govern their citizens, define the meaning of marriage, set the rules for elections and voter registration, run the public schools, and administer most of the programs to help the poor, even when the money for those programs comes from the national government.

In recent years, for example, states have become increasingly involved in regulating cell phone use and texting while driving. As the number of text messages sent in the United States increased from 57.2 billion in 2005 to more than 600 billion in 2008, states became increasingly concerned that texting was an even greater threat to safety than talking on cell phones. According to recent studies, drivers who are texting while driving are significantly more likely to drift out of their lane and look away from the cars in front of them. As a result, they are much more likely to be in life-threatening accidents than drivers who talk on cell phones, who themselves are already more likely to be in life-threatening accidents than those who keep their eyes on the road and hands on the wheel.[2] As with talking on cell phones, younger drivers are much more likely to text than older drivers.

The pressure to pass new laws banning texting while driving increased in 2009, when British television began running a public service advertisement showing the grizzly results of a fictitious accident. The four-minute advertisement is graphic, bloody, and terrifying. It is so disturbing that viewers must be 18 to watch the film on YouTube, although anyone can watch a 2009 *Today Show* story about the film, also available on YouTube.

States are reacting to the threat by passing new laws to ban texting while driving. By the end of 2009, 18 states were already imposing stiff fines for texting while driving under a general ban on distracted driving, and some were suspending the driver's license of anyone caught texting on the road. Delaware, Indiana, Kansas, Maine, Mississippi, and West Virginia now prohibit texting while driving for drivers with learning permits or probationary licenses, while Missouri prohibits texting while driving for anyone under age 21.

Enforcement is the problem with such bans. Police cannot be everywhere watching every possible violation, and text messaging is particularly hard to spot. This is why state-sponsored education campaigns built around the kind of intense messages in the British television advertisement may be the only way to frighten drivers away from the practice. Under the Constitution, it is mostly up to the states to figure out both what to do about texting while driving and how to enforce the laws they make.

7

& CHAPTER OUTLINE
CHAPTER LEARNING OBJECTIVES

Defining Federalism
1.1 Interpret the definitions of federalism, and assess the advantages and disadvantages of the American system of federalism.

The Constitutional Structure of American Federalism
1.2 Differentiate the powers the Constitution provides to national and state governments.

The National Courts and Federalism
1.3 Assess the role of the national courts in defining the relationship between the national and state governments, and evaluate the positions of decentralists and centralists.

The National Budget as a Tool of Federalism
1.4 Analyze the budget as a tool of federalism, and evaluate its impact on state and local governments.

The Politics of Federalism
1.5 Evaluate the current relationship between the national and state governments and the future challenges for federalism.

& CHAPTER OUTLINE
CHAPTER LEARNING OBJECTIVES

Defining Federalism
1.1 Interpret the definitions of federalism, and assess the advantages and disadvantages of the American system of federalism.

CHAPTER SUMMARY

1.1 Interpret the definitions of federalism, and assess the advantages and disadvantages of the American system of federalism.

A federal system is one in which the constitution divides powers between the central government and lower-level governments such as states or provinces. But, over time, there has been support for different balances between state and government power such

Each chapter begins with a **Chapter Outline** that breaks down larger subjects into important subparts and previews the topics to come. **Chapter Learning Objectives** help you identify the kinds of learning you will be expected to do with each chapter. We also integrate the Chapter Learning Objectives throughout the chapter and return to them at the end of the chapter in a short **Chapter Summary**. This closely knit pedagogical system helps you navigate through chapter discussions and demonstrate that you have mastered the concepts.

CHAPTER SELF-TEST

1.1 Interpret the definitions of federalism, and assess the advantages and disadvantages of the American system of federalism.

1. Match each term with its appropriate definition:

a. Dual federalism

b. Cooperative federalism

c. Marble cake federalism

d. Competitive

i. The power of the national government is limited in favor of the broad powers reserved to the states

ii. All levels of government are engaged in a variety of policy areas, without rigid divisions between governmental jurisdictions

iii. Local governments, state governments, and the national government offer various "packages" of taxes and services, and citizens can choose which package they like best

iv. A system that requires intergov-

a. A unitary state

b. A cooperative federalist state

c. A confederation

d. A territorial union

3. Federalism affords five benefits benefit along with a sentence

1.2 Differentiate the powers the provides to national and sta

4. Determine whether the followi to the national government, re shared by both:

a. Power to establish courts

b. Power to tax citizens and bus

c. Express powers stated in the

d. Power to oversee primary a education

e. Inherent powers to present a

To assist you in preparing for exams and make your learning experience more effective, we have prepared a **Chapter Self-Test** of multiple choice and essay questions. Before you take an exam, take this practice test to make sure you understand the chapter.

GOVERNMENT...

These features demonstrate how a government of, by, and for the people is put into practice, and highlight the important role of the people in our government.

OF THE PEOPLE
America's Changing Face

In important ways, the people of the United States today are much more diverse than at any previous time. This feature explores the impact of the ever-increasing level of diversity in the American political landscape, including how race and gender are changing the way the American government works. These unique boxes are designed to reflect the concerns and experiences of ethnic and minority groups in American politics.

Of the People
AMERICA'S CHANGING FACE

Where Americans Come From and Where They Live

The United States is a nation of immigrants who have arrived from many parts of the world. Throughout the decades, the portrait of immigrants has been changing from mostly white to mostly minority. In 2008, for example, 38 million Americans, or 12.5 percent, were foreign born, consisting of 16 million naturalized citizens, 10 million long-term visitors, and 12 million undocumented immigrants. The number of unauthorized, or illegal, immigrants has fallen somewhat in recent years due to the economic recession, which has depressed employment opportunities.

Many foreign-born residents live in the nation's largest cities. The New York City–area population includes more than 5 million foreign-born residents, while Los Angeles includes another 4.5 million; Miami, slightly more than 2 million; Chicago, 1.6 million; and San Francisco, 1.3 million. Although the inner cities host a majority of foreign-born residents, there has been recent movement of immigrants to the suburbs and some movement toward certain areas of the country such as the southwest.

The changing face of America brings great diversity in all aspects of life, from schools to farm fields and small businesses. It enriches the quality of life through the mix of new cultures and old and can often be a source of innovation in how the economy operates. Diversity also brings complaints about the national government's effort to close its borders to illegal immigrants. Some groups complain that illegal immigrants take jobs that should go to U.S. citizens, whereas others worry about the costs associated with high-poverty rates. Governments at all levels must reconcile these complaints with our history of welcoming immigrants from all around the world.

QUESTIONS

1. How are foreign-born citizens from different regions of the world different from each other?

2. Why do you think foreign-born citizens tend to live in our nation's largest cities?

3. How do foreign-born citizens contribute to the nation's quality of life?

The Statue of Liberty symbolizes America's long tradition of welcoming immigrants to its shores. The inscription at the base of the statue reads: "Give me your tired, your poor, Your huddled masses yearning to breathe free, The wretched refuse of your teeming shore. Send these, the homeless, tempest-tost to me, I lift my lamp beside the golden door!"

Other areas 10%
Asia 9%
Other Latin America 11%
Europe

Other areas 7%
Europe 13%
Asia 27%
Mexico 30%
Other Latin America 23%

2007

...ographic Trends in Metropolitan America," Washington, D.C.:

Of the People
THE GLOBAL COMMUNITY

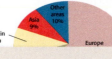

Global Opinion on the Role of Government

State and local governments are on the front lines of most programs for helping the needy. They provide much of the money and/or administration for unemployment insurance for the jobless, health care clinics and hospitals for the poor, school lunch programs for hungry children, and homeless shelters. Although many U.S. citizens see poverty firsthand as volunteers for local charities such as food pantries, some have doubts about how much government should do to help poor people who cannot take care of themselves. According to the Pew Global survey, citizens of other nations vary greatly on the question.

These opinions reflect very different social and economic conditions in each country. Japan has a culture of self-reliance that puts the burden on individuals to help themselves, while Nigeria continues to suffer from some of the highest poverty rates in the world. In this regard, U.S. citizens tend to mirror the Japanese—they want government to help the less fortunate but also want the less fortunate to help themselves. As a general conclusion, citizens of wealthier nations think poor people should take advantage of the opportunities that already exist in their economies, whereas citizens of poor nations believe that government should be more aggressive in providing support.

This does not mean wealthier nations are uncaring toward citizens in need, but it does suggest that they sometimes view

of race, gender, or circumstance have the same opportunity to participate in politics, self-government, and the economy. Most Americans want to help the less fortunate, but only when they are truly needy, not when they fail because they will not help themselves.

QUESTIONS

1. What are the advantages of having the government provide services for the poor? What are the advantages of relying on individual citizens to seize opportunities for themselves?

2. Why might more wealthy nations be more likely to believe that individuals ought to take care of themselves and not rely on the state?

3. Which level of government might be most effective in providing services to the poor?

Agreement with the statement:
It is the responsibility of the (state or government) to take care of the very poor people who can't take care of themselves.

70
60
50
40
30
20
10
0
Britain China India Japan Mexico Nigeria United

OF THE PEOPLE
The Global Community

speaks to the increasingly global context of American politics, examining public opinion from around the world on political issues and institutions. The experiences and opinions of people in other countries can both impact and provide insight into our own political system and culture.

By the People
MAKING A DIFFERENCE

Monitoring the National Stimulus Package

In early 2009, Congress and President Barack Obama passed a nearly $800 billion spending package designed to stimulate the national economy. The number of unemployed Americans was rising fast, small businesses were closing, consumers were spending less, sales of new and old homes alike had fallen, and the economy was in the worst recession in decades. Under the stimulus, states were given nearly $260 billion to invest in projects that would put unemployed Americans back to work and restart the economy.

Much of this money was designed to support highway construction, new building projects, and scientific research but has been difficult to track. According to ongoing monitoring by the national government and outside groups, thousands of small companies are still receiving national dollars for a broad mix of projects.

Citizens can track the spending as a form of public service—the more they pay attention to propublica.org, pick an individual county in that state, and see every project funded by the stimulus. Once citizens pick a project, they can visit the project and see what is actually happening. If the project is not even under way, citizens can report the inaction to the federal government through recovery.gov.

Colleges and universities have received a sizable amount of stimulus money. By early 2010, Florida's Alachua County had received more than $100 million. As home of the University of Florida, much of the money ended up in university research projects. According to the propublica.org list, the university received support for nearly 150 separate projects and student programs, while Santa Fe Community College received more than a dozen grants to support students with Pell Grants.

CRITICAL THINKING QUESTIONS

1. Why is monitoring the stimulus spending a form of public service?

For the People
GOVERNMENT'S GREATEST ENDEAVORS

Supporting the States in Achieving National Goals

Throughout the decades, the national government has given state and local governments a long list of responsibilities for implementing national programs, such as health care for the poor, highway construction, and waste-water treatment. These programs involve important national goals for creating a healthy society and economy.

Most of these programs carry large amounts of national dollars, which allow the national government to set minimum standards for those who get unemployment insurance, public assistance, and medical care. National funds also offset state spending on both the administrative and program costs of achieving the national goals profiled throughout this book. But the national government relies on the states for the implementation of these programs.

Homeland security is a case in point. Following the 9/11 terrorist attacks on the World Trade Center and Washington, D.C. in linked to the national government through computer systems that contain the names of terrorist suspects and are often first at the scene of suspected terrorist acts such as the 2008 bombing of a Jewish center in New York City. The national government provides large amounts of funding to improve state and local defenses against terrorist attacks.

All totaled, the national government will spend nearly $600 billion in 2010 helping states achieve its broad goals for improving the quality of life in the United States, including $20 billion on transportation, $21 billion on education and job training, $43 billion on health care for the poor and substance abuse programs, and $36 billion on food and nutrition programs.* Although much of this money comes with tight restrictions on which citizens and projects qualify for funding, this spending indicates how much the national government is willing to invest in helping states help their citizens.

The national government works with state and local governments to ensure that airports are safe from terrorism. Baggage and passenger screeners are national government employees, but they work closely with local airports.

collectively on problems like airport security? What are the disadvantages?

2. Why might the national government prefer working in cooperation with state

ACKNOWLEDGMENTS

The writing of this book has profited from the informed, professional, and often critical suggestions of our colleagues around the country. This and previous editions have been considerably improved as a result of reviews by the following individuals, for which we thank them all:

Scott Adler, *University of Colorado*
Wayne Ault, *Southwestern Illinois College–Belleville*
Paul Babbitt, *Southern Arkansas University*
Thomas Baldino, *Wilkes University*
Barry Balleck, *Georgia Southern University*
Robert Ballinger, *South Texas College*
Jodi Balma, *Fullerton College*
Jeff Berry, *South Texas College*
Cynthia Carter, *Florida Community College–Jacksonville, North Campus*
Leonard Champney, *University of Scranton*
Mark Cichock, *University of Texas at Arlington*
Alison Dagnes, *Shippensburg University*
Paul Davis, *Truckee Meadows Community College*
Ron Deaton, *Prince George's Community College*
Robert DeLuna, *St. Philips College*
Anthony Di Giacomo, *Wilmington College*
Richardson Dilworth, *Drexel University*
Rick Donohoe, *Napa Valley College*
Art English, *University of Arkansas, Little Rock*
Alan Fisher, *CSU–Dominguez Hills*
Bruce Franklin, *Cossatot Community College of the University of Arkansas*
Eileen Gage, *Central Florida Community College*
Richard Glenn, *Millersville University*
David Goldberg, *College of DuPage*
Nicholas Gonzalez, *Yuen DeAnza College*
Charles Grapski, *University of Florida*
Billy Hathorn, *Laredo Community College*
Max Hilaire, *Morgan State University*
James Hoefler, *Dickinson College*
Justin Hoggard, *Three Rivers Community College*
Gilbert Kahn, *Kean University*
Rogan Kersh, *Syracuse University*
Todd Kunioka, *CSU–Los Angeles*
La Della Levy, *Foothill College*
Jim Lennertz, *Lafayette College*
John Liscano, *Napa Valley College*
Amy Lovecraft, *University of Alaska–Fairbanks*
Howard Lubert, *James Madison University*
Lowell Markey, *Allegany College of Maryland*
Larry Martinez, *CSU–Long Beach*
Toni Marzotto, *Towson University*
Michael McConachie, *Collin County Community College*
Brian Newman, *Pepperdine University*

Adam Newmark, *Appalachian State University*
Randall Newnham, *Penn State University–Berks*
Keith Nicholls, *University of South Alabama*
Sean Nicholson-Crotty, *University of Missouri–Columbia*
Richard Pacelle, *Georgia Southern University*
William Parente, *University of Scranton*
Ryan Peterson, *College of the Redwoods*
Robert Rigney, *Valencia Community College–Osceola Campus*
Bren Romney, *Vernon College*
Jack Ruebensaal, *West Los Angeles College*
Bhim Sandhu, *West Chester University*
Gib Sansing, *Drexel University*
Colleen Shogan, *George Mason University*
Tom Simpson, *Missouri Southern*
Linda Simmons, *Northern Virginia Community College–Manassas Campus*
Dan Smith, *Northwest Missouri State University*
Jay Stevens, *CSU–Long Beach*
Lawrence Sullivan, *Adelphi University*
Halper Thomas, *CUNY–Baruch*
Jose Vadi, *CSU–Pomona*
Avery Ward, *Harford Community College*
Shirley Warshaw, *Gettysburg University*
Ife Williams, *Delaware County Community College*
Margie Williams, *James Madison University*
Christy Woodward-Kaupert, *San Antonio College*
Chris Wright, *University of Arkansas–Monticello*
Martha Burns, *Tidewater Community College*
David Caffey, *Clovis Community College*
Ann Clemmer, *University of Arkansas at Little Rock*
Ellen Creagar, *Eastern Wyoming College*
Robert Locander, *Lone Star College North Harris*
Sean Mattie, *Clayton State University*
Jerry Murtagh, *Fort Valley State University*
Tally Payne, *Casper College*
Mark Peplowski, *College of Southern Nevada*
Geoff Peterson, *University of Wisconsin–Eau Claire*
Dennis Pope, *Kean University*
Jonathan Reisman, *University of Maine at Machias*
Sean Savage, *Saint Mary's College*
Carolyn Schmidt, *Florida Community College Jacksonville*
Kevin Sims, *Cedarville University*
Melanie Young, *University of Nevada Las Vegas*

State and Local Politics: Government by the People began in 1948 when two young assistant professors, James MacGregor Burns of Williams College and Jack W. Peltason of Smith College, decided to partner and write an American government text. Their first edition had a publication date of 1952. Their aim was to produce a well-written, accessible, and balanced look at government and politics in the United

States. As authors have become a part of this book, they have embraced that objective. Tom Cronin of Colorado College and David O'Brien of the University of Virginia have been coauthors and made important contributions to the book. As the current authors of *State and Local Politics: Government by the People,* we are grateful for the legacy we have inherited.

Writing the book requires teamwork—first among the coauthors who converse often about the broad themes, features, and focus of the book and who read and rewrite each other's drafts; then with our research assistants, who track down loose ends and give us the perspective of current students; and finally with the editors and other professionals at Pearson Longman. Important to each revision are the detailed reviews by teachers and researchers, who provide concrete suggestions on how to improve the book. Our revision of the chapters on state and local government especially benefited from the tremendous input of Tom Carsey at the University of North Carolina. We are grateful to all who helped with this edition.

Research assistants for the current edition of *State and Local Politics: Government by the People* are Rebecca Eaton, Jeff Edwards, Bret Evans, Maren Gardiner, Eric Hoyt, David Lassen, Virginia Maynes, Haley McCormick, Kristen Orr, and Case Wade of Brigham Young University.

We also express appreciation to the superb team at Longman, especially Political Science Editor Eric Stano, who has been wonderfully supportive. Donna Garnier, our Development Editor, kept us on schedule and added helpful insights all along the way. We also appreciate the work Bob Ginsberg for production, Heather Johnson at Elm Street Publishing for page layout, Teri Stratford for photo research, and John Callahan for cover design.

We also want to thank you, the professors and students who use our book, and who send us letters and email messages with suggestions for improving *State and Local Politics: Government by the People.* Please write us in care of the Political Science Editor at Pearson Longman, 51 Madison Avenue, New York, NY 10010, or contact us directly:

David B. Magleby Distinguished Professor of Political Science and Dean of FHSS, Brigham Young University, Provo, UT 84602, david_magleby@byu.edu

Paul C. Light Paulette Goddard Professor of Public Service at New York University and Douglas Dillon Senior Fellow at the Brookings Institution, pcl226@nyu.edu

Christine L. Nemacheck Alumni Memorial Distinguished Associate Professor of Government at The College of William & Mary, Williamsburg, VA 23187, clnema@wm.edu

ABOUT THE AUTHORS

David B. Magleby is nationally recognized for his expertise on direct democracy, voting behavior, and campaign finance. He received his B.A. from the University of Utah and his Ph.D. from the University of California, Berkeley. Currently Distinguished Professor of Political Science, Senior Research Fellow at the Center for the Study of Elections and Democracy, and Dean of the College of Family, Home and Social Sciences at Brigham Young University (BYU), Professor Magleby has also taught at the University of California, Santa Cruz, and the University of Virginia. He and his students have conducted statewide polls in Virginia and Utah. For the 1998–2008 elections, he has directed national studies of campaign finance and campaign communications in competitive federal election environments involving a consortium of academics from nearly 80 universities and colleges in 38 states. This research is summarized in seven edited books. In addition, he is coeditor of a long-standing series of books on financing federal elections. In partnership with colleagues, he has been studying the implementation of new voting technology, work funded in part by the National Science Foundation. He has been a Fulbright Scholar at Oxford University and a past president of Pi Sigma Alpha, the national political science honor society. Magleby is the recipient of many teaching awards, including the 1990 Utah Professor of the Year Award from the Council for the Advancement and Support of Education and the Carnegie Foundation, the 2001 Rowman & Littlefield Award for Innovative Teaching in Political Science, and several department and university awards. At BYU, he served as chair of the Political Science Department before being named dean. He is married to Linda Waters Magleby. They are the parents of four and grandparents of one.

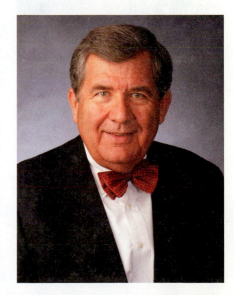

Paul C. Light is the Paulette Goddard Professor of Public Service at New York University's Wagner School of Public Service. He received his B.A. from Macalester College and his Ph.D. from the University of Michigan. Professor Light has a wide-ranging career in both academia and government. He has worked on Capitol Hill as a senior committee staffer in the U.S. Senate and as an American Political Science Association Congressional Fellow in the U.S. House of Representatives. He has taught at the University of Virginia, University of Pennsylvania, and Harvard University's John F. Kennedy School of Government. He has also served as a senior adviser to several national commissions on federal, state, and local public service. He is the author of 15 books on government, public service, and public policy. Light's current research focuses on government reform, Congress, the presidency, and social entrepreneurship. His latest books are *A Government Ill Executed* (Harvard University Press, 2008) and *The Search for Social Entrepreneurship* (Brookings Institution Press, 2008). He was the founding director of the Brookings Institution's Center for Public Service and continues his research on how to invite Americans to serve their communities through public service. His work has been funded by the Douglas Dillon Foundation, the Pew Charitable Trusts, and the David and Lucille Packard Foundation, among many others. He is also an expert on preparing government, charitable organizations, and private corporations for natural and human-made disasters, and he was a recognized leader in the response to Hurricane Katrina in 2005. He has testified before Congress more than a dozen times in the last five years.

Christine L. Nemacheck is the Alumni Memorial Distinguished Associate Professor of Government at The College of William & Mary. She received her B.A. from the University of Michigan and her Ph.D. from The George Washington University. Professor Nemacheck has previously taught at Iowa State University. Her research focuses on judicial selection and the role of the courts in a separation-of-powers system. Her book, *Strategic Selection: Presidential Selection of Supreme Court Justices from Herbert Hoover through George W. Bush* was published in 2007. Other work on judicial selection has appeared in political science and law review journals. Her research, which is primarily archival, has been funded by numerous grants and awards from presidential library foundations. Nemacheck has received a number of awards for her teaching and research activity, including the Alumni Fellowship Award for excellence in teaching at The College of William & Mary, a Coco Faculty Fellowship, and she was named a Dean's Distinguished Lecturer in 2010. She is the coeditor of the Pi Sigma Alpha Undergraduate Journal of Politics, which will be housed at The College of William & Mary through the spring 2013 semester.

GOVERNMENT BY THE PEOPLE

State and Local Government

We title this book *State and Local Politics: Government by the People* because we want to emphasize the important role people play in our constitutional democracy. Understanding American politics and government must include an appreciation of the people, their similarities and differences, their beliefs and attitudes, and their behaviors. Examining such aspects of our population as race, ethnicity, gender, age, religion, income, and region helps us see how the diversity of our country is important politically.

We are a government by the people, but we are people with differing views and opinions on major issues of our day, just as the framers differed in their views of how our government should operate. Many of the issues about which we, as Americans, disagree today, such as health care reform, and economic policy mirror the kinds of debates that occurred in the founding era. They concern basic assumptions about the appropriate role of government and individual responsibility. As you read through this book, we challenge you to think about the ways you currently participate in our democratic system and perhaps consider a new way in which you might make your voice heard.

A distinguishing feature of American government is federalism. State and local governments help define our politics and shape our political identities. They administer most public programs, have been the laboratories for experiments in public policy, and are the proving grounds for many leaders who go on to serve at the national level. As with the federal government, the states have constitutions that detail the powers and prerogatives of government. Electoral competition is state centered because all elective offices in the United States honor state boundaries. Although the executive, legislative, and judicial institutions of state government have some similarities with their federal counterparts, they do vary across the states. There are even more varieties in the ways local governments are organized. Local governments provide many of the services most important to citizens. The relationship between local and state governments is influenced by different legal structures and budgetary policies.

COURSE LEARNING **OBJECTIVES**

CHAPTER 1 American Federalism

Explain federalism in America, and analyze the relationship between the federal and state and local governments.

Federalism is a system of government in which power is divided between a central government and subdivisional governments; in the United States, those subdivisions are referred to as states. Under a system of federalism, neither the national government nor the states depend on the other for power, and neither government can usurp the other's authority. Instead, the power for each is derived from the people, and in our case, their views as represented in the Constitution.

Although the Constitution describes the authority that belongs to the national government and the states, not everyone agrees on what the document means and the appropriate balance of power. Some argue for a more limited national government in favor of greater power for the states, whereas others prefer a stronger central government. Supreme Court cases have defined many aspects of the relationship between the national and state governments, and amendments to the Constitution have also affected this relationship. Over time, depending on conditions in the country and the parties in government, national and state power has ebbed and flowed.

CHAPTER 2 State and Local Politics

Identify the range of policy programs administered by state and local governments, and analyze the influences on state and local politics.

Most government programs, including those funded in part by federal programs, are administered by state and local governments. The range of policy issues dealt with by state and local governments is broad and important. As a result, interest groups are organized and active at the state and local levels. Because of the closer proximity of local and state government and the tradition in many localities and states of more direct citizen participation, there is a perception that state and local governments are more responsive to the people. Other factors that impact local government are the political structure, the local traditions, the social structure, and the local economy.

CHAPTER 3 State Constitutions

Compare and contrast the U.S. Constitution with state constitutions.

State constitutions are often patterned after the U.S. Constitution in providing both a separation and sharing of powers among the legislative, executive, and judicial branches. They differ from each other and from the U.S. Constitution in some of the ways they structure these branches. State constitutions are typically longer and more detailed than the U.S. Constitution. Constitutional change occurs by different means, ranging from wholesale change at a constitutional convention to specific amendments, which in some states may be proposed by a petition process and then voted on by the people.

CHAPTER 4 Parties and Elections in the States

Assess the importance of parties and elections at the state level.

States are where the action is in American campaigns and elections. Presidential, congressional, gubernatorial, and legislative elections all have substantial state components. State laws determine who may vote, the means by which people vote, how nominees are selected, and which candidates may appear on ballots. Political parties are organized around the units of competition, which are most typically state and local elections. The strength of parties varies across states.

CHAPTER **5** State Legislatures

Describe the functions of state legislatures, and evaluate their responsiveness to the people.

With the exception of Nebraska's unicameral and nonpartisan legislature, all other state legislatures are bicameral and organized along party lines. State legislatures, like Congress, rely on committees, staff, and seniority in doing business. Most legislators are white, middle-aged, and male. Voters and the courts have attempted to make legislatures more representative and responsive by requiring that legislative districts have equal numbers of people and, in some states, by enacting term limits. In approximately half of the states, voters may effectively veto legislation through the popular referendum or initiative process.

CHAPTER **6** State Governors

Explain how governors use their formal and informal powers to influence public policy.

The executive branch in state government often includes several elected office holders, including the governor, lieutenant governor, secretary of state, attorney general, and state treasurer. Although the formal powers of governors differ across states, governors typically have appointment, budgetary, veto, and pardon powers. Governors also have informal powers and substantial visibility in their states. The power of governors has grown in recent years.

CHAPTER **7** Judges and Justice in the States

Describe the judicial system at the state level, and evaluate the differences across the states in judicial selection and sentencing.

Although the names given to particular courts vary by state, states generally have trial courts, appellate courts, and a court of last resort. Judges are selected or elected by different means in different states. The justice system includes lawyers who serve as prosecutors, defenders, and judges; citizens who serve as jurors; and state employees who serve as corrections officials. States differ in their sentencing practices and use of incarceration as they attempt to find a balance in protecting the rights of the accused and the victim.

CHAPTER **8** Local Governments and Metropolitics

Identify the functions of local governments, including counties, cities, towns, and special districts.

Local governments are typically agents of state governments with limited independence. The size, population density, structure, and role of county governments vary dramatically. Some counties are effectively like large cities, whereas others are largely administrative structures to manage state and federal policies. Cities can also be very different from each other, but share in common such aims as economic development and providing services like public safety and sanitation. Suburbs, which may or may not be incorporated with the nearby city, have been fast growing and increasingly share the same challenges as cities. Mayors are the most visible leader of cities.

CHAPTER **9** Making State and Local Policy

Evaluate the importance of state and local governments in implementing policy.

State and local governments are essential in implementing policy in such areas as health care, education, welfare, and transportation. The ability of states to implement policy is dependent on revenue, which comes from grants or transfers from the federal government, and from taxes at the state and local level. Revenue shortfalls have forced state govern-ments to scale back spending in recent years. In higher education, for example, this has often resulted in increasing students' tuition. Rising costs of providing services, especially health care, have also constrained state and local governments. States influence national policy by taking the lead in areas such as health care (Massachusetts) and the environment (California).

CHAPTER **10** Staffing and Financing State and Local Governments

Describe the challenges for state and local governments in organizing resources, raising funds, and managing expenditures.

Most of state spending is on education and health. The revenue to pay for these and other services comes from taxes, user fees, and transfers from other levels of government. Some states utilize sales, income, or excise taxes, but states vary in how much they tax the people and businesses in their state. States generally are prohibited from deficit spending, so they must either adjust taxes or spending to keep their budgets balanced. Much of the spending by state and local governments goes to pay for public employees. Hoping to reduce costs, states have increasingly privatized the delivery of services.

American Federalism

The relationship of the national government to the states has been the subject of intense debate since the founding.[1] In 1787, members of what would become the Federalist Party defended the creation of a strong national government, whereas the Antifederalists warned that a strong national government would overshadow the states. The great debate over which level of government best represents the people continues to rage.

State governments have often complained that the national government is either taking over their responsibilities or controlling too much of what they do. Yet, in policy areas such as civil rights, educational opportunities for people with disabilities, and handgun control, the states have been slow to respond to citizens, and the national government has taken steps to deal with these issues.

At the same time, states retain enormous authority under the Constitution to regulate life within their borders. Working with the local governments they create, states police the streets, fight fires, impose their own taxes, create most of the laws that govern their citizens, define the meaning of marriage, set the rules for elections and voter registration, run the public schools, and administer most of the programs to help the poor, even when the money for those programs comes from the national government.

In recent years, for example, states have become increasingly involved in regulating cell phone use and texting while driving. As the number of text messages sent in the United States increased from 57.2 billion in 2005 to more than 600 billion in 2008, states became increasingly concerned that texting was an even greater threat to safety than talking on cell phones. According to recent studies, drivers who are texting while driving are significantly more likely to drift out of their lane and look away from the cars in front of them. As a result, they are much more likely to be in life-threatening accidents than drivers who talk on cell phones, who themselves are already more likely to be in life-threatening accidents than those who keep their eyes on the road and hands on the wheel.[2] As with talking on cell phones, younger drivers are much more likely to text than older drivers.

The pressure to pass new laws banning texting while driving increased in 2009, when British television began running a public service advertisement showing the grizzly results of a fictitious accident. The four-minute advertisement is graphic, bloody, and terrifying. It is so disturbing that viewers must be 18 to watch the film on YouTube, although anyone can watch a 2009 *Today Show* story about the film, also available on YouTube.

States are reacting to the threat by passing new laws to ban texting while driving. By the end of 2009, 18 states were already imposing stiff fines for texting while driving under a general ban on distracted driving, and some were suspending the driver's license of anyone caught texting on the road. Delaware, Indiana, Kansas, Maine, Mississippi, and West Virginia now prohibit texting while driving for drivers with learning permits or probationary licenses, while Missouri prohibits texting while driving for anyone under age 21.

Enforcement is the problem with such bans. Police cannot be everywhere watching every possible violation, and text messaging is particularly hard to spot. This is why state-sponsored education campaigns built around the kind of intense messages in the British television advertisement may be the only way to frighten drivers away from the practice. Under the Constitution, it is mostly up to the states to figure out both what to do about texting while driving and how to enforce the laws they make.

In 2009, a small city in Britain began running a graphic four-minute television advertisement about the dangers of texting while driving. Many U.S. states have passed or are considering legislation banning the practice. ■ *What are some of the potential difficulties for drivers when the regulation of texting while driving is handled on a state-by-state basis?*

In this chapter, we first define federalism and its advantages and disadvantages. We then look at the constitutional basis for our federal system and how court decisions and political developments have shaped, and continue to shape, federalism in the United States. Throughout, you should think hard about how you influence the issues you care about, even in your local city council or mayor's office. The Constitution clearly encourages, and even depends on, you to express your view at all levels of government, which is why action in a single state can start a process of change that spreads to other states or the national government.

Defining Federalism

Scholars have argued and wars have been fought over what federalism means. One scholar recently counted 267 definitions of the term.[3]

Federalism, as we define it, is a form of government in which a constitution distributes authority and powers between a central government and smaller regional governments—usually called states, provinces, or republics—giving to both the national and the regional governments substantial responsibilities and powers, including the power to collect taxes and to pass and enforce laws regulating the conduct of individuals. When we use the term "federalism" or "federal system," we are referring to this system of national and state governments; when we use the term "federal government," here and in the other chapters of the book, we are referring to the national government headquartered in Washington, D.C.

The mere existence of both national and state governments does not make a system federal. What is important is that a *constitution divides governmental powers between the national government and smaller regional governments,* giving clearly defined functions to each. Neither the central nor the regional government receives its powers from the other; both derive them from a common source—the Constitution. No ordinary act of legislation at either the national or the state level can change this constitutional distribution of powers. Both levels of government operate through their own agents and exercise power directly over individuals.

Constitutionally, the federal system of the United States consists of only the national government and the 50 states. "Cities are not," the Supreme Court reminded us, "sovereign entities." This does not make for a tidy, efficient, easy-to-understand system; yet, as we shall see, it has its virtues.

federalism

A constitutional arrangement in which power is distributed between a central government and subdivisional governments, called states in the United States. The national and the subdivisional governments both exercise direct authority over individuals.

There are several different ways that power can be shared in a federal system, and political scientists have devised terms to explain these various kinds of federalism. At different times in the United States' history, our system of federalism has shared power based on each of the below interpretations.

■ *Dual federalism* views the Constitution as giving a limited list of powers—primarily foreign policy and national defense—to the national government, leaving the rest to sovereign states. Each level of government is dominant within its own sphere.

■ *Cooperative federalism* stresses federalism as a system of intergovernmental relationships in delivering governmental goods and services to the people and calls for cooperation among various levels of government.

■ *Marble cake federalism* conceives of federalism as a mixed set of responsibilities in which all levels of government are engaged in a variety of issues and programs, rather than a layer cake, or dual federalism, with fixed divisions between layers or levels of government.[4]

■ *Competitive federalism* views the national government, the 50 states, and the thousands of local governments as competing with each other over ways to put together packages of services and taxes.[5]

■ *Permissive federalism* implies that, although federalism provides "a sharing of power and authority between the national and state government, the states' share rests on the permission and permissiveness of the national government."[6]

■ *New federalism,* championed by former presidents Richard M. Nixon (1969–1974) and Ronald Reagan (1981–1989), presumes that the power of the federal government is limited in favor of the broad powers reserved to the states.

Alternatives to Federalism

Among the alternatives to federalism are **unitary systems** of government, in which a constitution vests all governmental power in the central government. The central government, if it so chooses, may delegate authority to constituent units, but what it delegates, it may take away. China, France, the Scandinavian countries, and Israel have unitary governments. In the United States, state constitutions usually create this kind of relationship between the state and its local governments.

At the other extreme from unitary governments are **confederations,** in which sovereign nations, through a constitutional compact, create a central government but carefully limit its authority and do not give it the power to regulate the conduct of individuals directly. The central government makes regulations for the constituent governments,

unitary system
A constitutional arrangement that concentrates power in a central government.

confederation
A constitutional arrangement in which sovereign nations or states, by compact, create a central government but carefully limit its power and do not give it direct authority over individuals.

State and local governments are responsible for policing the streets but not for enforcing federal laws. Nevertheless, they often work with national agencies such as the Federal Bureau of Investigation, Drug Enforcement Administration, or the Immigration and Customs Enforcement Bureau. ■ *What are some of the benefits of federal, state, and local law enforcement agencies working together against crime?*

Of the People

THE GLOBAL COMMUNITY

Global Opinion on the Role of Government

State and local governments are on the front lines of most programs for helping the needy. They provide much of the money and/or administration for unemployment insurance for the jobless, health care clinics and hospitals for the poor, school lunch programs for hungry children, and homeless shelters. Although many U.S. citizens see poverty firsthand as volunteers for local charities such as food pantries, some have doubts about how much government should do to help poor people who cannot take care of themselves. According to the Pew Global survey, citizens of other nations vary greatly on the question.

These opinions reflect very different social and economic conditions in each country. Japan has a culture of self-reliance that puts the burden on individuals to help themselves, while Nigeria continues to suffer from some of the highest poverty rates in the world. In this regard, U.S. citizens tend to mirror the Japanese—they want government to help the less fortunate but also want the less fortunate to help themselves. As a general conclusion, citizens of wealthier nations think poor people should take advantage of the opportunities that already exist in their economies, whereas citizens of poor nations believe that government should be more aggressive in providing support.

This does not mean wealthier nations are uncaring toward citizens in need, but it does suggest that they sometimes view poverty as the fault of the poor. In the United States, these opinions reflect the importance of equality of opportunity as a basic social value, meaning that all individuals regardless of race, gender, or circumstance have the same opportunity to participate in politics, self-government, and the economy. Most Americans want to help the less fortunate, but only when they are truly needy, not when they fail because they will not help themselves.

CRITICAL THINKING QUESTIONS

1. What are the advantages and disadvantages of having the government provide services for the poor?

2. Why might more wealthy nations be more likely to believe that individuals ought to take care of themselves and not rely on the state?

3. Which level of government might be most effective in providing services to the poor?

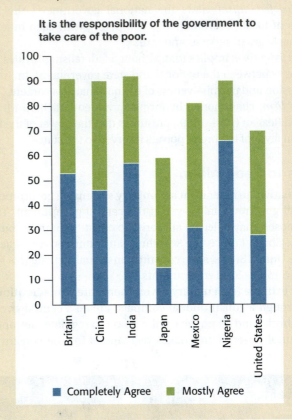

It is the responsibility of the government to take care of the poor.

Completely Agree ▪ Mostly Agree

---

but it exists and operates only at their direction. The 13 states under the Articles of Confederation operated in this manner, as did the southern Confederacy during the Civil War.

There is no single model for dividing authority between the national and smaller regional governments of the other nations. Indeed, even in the United States, we have seen shifts in the balance of federal-state power throughout our history. Some countries have no federal system at all, whereas others have different variations of power sharing between the national and smaller regional governments.

For example, Britain's government is divided into three tiers: national, county, and district governments. County and district governments deliver roughly one-fifth of all government services, including education, housing, and police and fire protection. As a rule, most power is reserved for the central government on the theory that there should be "territorial justice," which means that all citizens should be governed by the same laws and standards. In recent years, however, Great Britain has devolved substantial authority to Scotland, Wales, and Northern Ireland.

Why Federalism?

In 1787, federalism was a compromise between centrists, who supported a strong national government, and those who favored decentralization. Confederation had proved unsuccessful. A unitary system was out of the question because most people were too deeply attached to their state governments to permit subordination to central rule. Many scholars think that federalism is ideally suited to the needs of a diverse people spread throughout a large continent, suspicious of concentrated power, and desiring unity but not uniformity. Yet, even though federalism offers a number of advantages over other forms of government, no system is perfect. Federalism offered, and still offers, both advantages and disadvantages for such a people.

Advantages of Federalism

Federalism Checks the Growth of Tyranny Although in the rest of the world federal forms have not always prevented tyranny (Germany's federal constitution did not, for example, prevent Hitler from seizing power in the 1930s), U.S. citizens tend to associate federalism with freedom.[7] When one political party loses control of the national government, it is still likely to hold office in a number of states and can continue to challenge the party in power at the national level. To the framers, who feared that a single interest group might capture the national government and suppress the interests of others, this diffusion of power was an advantage. There are now nearly 90,000 governments in the United States, including one national government, 50 state governments, and thousands of county, city, and town governments, as well as school boards and special districts that provide specific functions from managing hospitals or parks to mosquito control.[8] (See Figure 1–1 for the number of governments in the United States.)

Federalism Allows Unity Without Uniformity National politicians and parties do not have to iron out every difference on every issue that divides us, whether the issue is abortion, same-sex marriage, gun control, capital punishment, welfare financing, or assisted suicide. Instead, these issues are debated in state legislatures, county courthouses, and city halls. Information about state action spreads quickly from government to government, especially during periods when the national government is relatively slow to respond to pressing issues.

Federalism Encourages Experimentation As Justice Louis Brandeis once argued, states are "laboratories of democracy." If they adopt programs that fail, the negative effects are

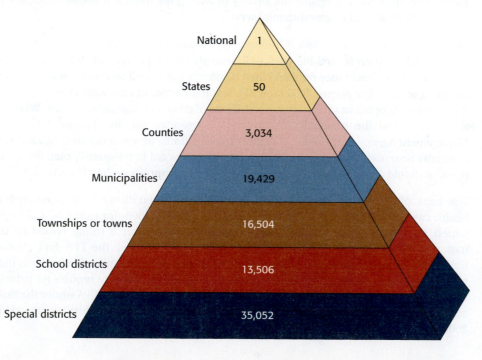

National: 1
States: 50
Counties: 3,034
Municipalities: 19,429
Townships or towns: 16,504
School districts: 13,506
Special districts: 35,052

FIGURE 1–1 **Number of Governments in the United States, 2009.**
■ *How do the levels and numbers of governments in the United States help to prevent tyranny?*

SOURCE: U.S. Census Bureau, *Statistical Abstract of the United States*, www.census.gov/prod/2006pubs/07statab/stlocgov.pdf.

There are thousands of special districts in the United States that are responsible for providing specific services, such the Metropolitan Mosquito Control District in Minnesota. ■ *What are the advantages and disadvantages of dividing control of government services into local and special districts?*

limited; if programs succeed, they can be adopted by other states and by the national government. Georgia, for example, was the first state to permit 18-year-olds to vote; Wisconsin was a leader in requiring welfare recipients to work; California moved early on global warming; and Massachusetts created one of the first state programs to provide health insurance to all its citizens. Not all innovations, even those considered successful, become widely adopted.

Federalism Provides Training and Creates Opportunities for Future National Leaders   Federalism provides a training ground for state and local politicians to gain experience before moving to the national stage. Presidents Jimmy Carter, Ronald Reagan, Bill Clinton, and George W. Bush previously served as governor of the respective states of Georgia, California, Arkansas, and Texas. In addition, three governors and one mayor ran for the Republican Party nomination for president in 2008, and another governor, Alaska's Sarah Palin, was selected as the Republican vice presidential candidate.

Federalism Keeps Government Closer to the People   By providing numerous arenas for decision making, federalism provides many opportunities for Americans to participate in the process of government and helps keep government closer to the people. Every day, thousands of U.S. adults serve on city councils, school boards, neighborhood associations, and planning commissions. Federalism also builds on the public's greater trust in government at the state and local levels. The closer the specific level of government is to the people, the more citizens trust the government.

Disadvantages of Federalism

Dividing Power Makes It Much More Difficult for Government to Respond Quickly to National Problems   There was a great demand for new efforts on homeland security after the September 11, 2001, terrorist attacks, and the national government created a new Department of Homeland Security in response. However, the department quickly discovered that there would be great difficulty coordinating its efforts with 50 state governments and thousands of local governments already providing fire, police, transportation, immigration control, and other governmental services.

The Division of Power Makes It Difficult for Voters to Hold Their Elected Officials Accountable   When something goes well, who should voters reward? When something goes wrong, who should they punish? When Hurricane Katrina hit New Orleans and the surrounding areas in late August 2005 (and Rita less than a month later near Houston), many thousands of people lost their homes and billions of dollars in damage was done. Who was responsible? Did the national government and agencies like the Federal Emergency Management Agency (FEMA) drop the ball on relief efforts, or was it the state or local government's responsibility? Did the mayor and/or governor fail to adequately plan for such a crisis, or should the national government have had more supplies on hand in advance?

The Lack of Uniformity Can Lead to Conflict   States often disagree on issues such as health care, school reform, and crime control. In January 2008, for example, California joined 15 other states in suing the national government over a ruling issued by the national Environmental Protection Agency (EPA). For decades, the EPA had allowed California to enact tougher air quality restrictions through higher mileage standards than required by the national Clean Air Act (first enacted in 1970). A similar request for permission to raise mileage standards was rejected in 2008, however, by the EPA under the Bush administration. The Obama Administration eventually approved California's request in 2009 and extended the higher mileage standards to all states.

Of the People

Where Americans Come From and Where They Live

The United States is a nation of immigrants who have arrived from many parts of the world. Throughout the decades, the portrait of immigrants has been changing from mostly white to mostly minority. In 2008, for example, 38 million Americans, or 12.5 percent, were foreign born, consisting of 16 million naturalized citizens, 10 million long-term visitors, and 12 million undocumented immigrants. The number of unauthorized, or illegal, immigrants has fallen somewhat in recent years due to the economic recession, which has depressed employment opportunities.

Many foreign-born residents live in the nation's largest cities. The New York City–area population includes more than 5 million foreign-born residents, while Los Angeles includes another 4.5 million; Miami, slightly more than 2 million; Chicago, 1.6 million; and San Francisco, 1.3 million. Although the inner cities host a majority of foreign-born residents, there has been recent movement of immigrants to the suburbs and some movement toward certain areas of the country such as the southwest.

The changing face of America brings great diversity in all aspects of life, from schools to farm fields and small businesses. It enriches the quality of life through the mix of old and new cultures, and can often be a source of innovation in how the economy operates. Diversity also brings complaints about the national government's effort to close its borders to illegal immigrants. Some groups complain that illegal immigrants take jobs that should go to U.S. citizens, whereas others worry about the costs associated with high-poverty rates. Governments at all levels must reconcile these complaints with our history of welcoming immigrants from all around the world.

CRITICAL THINKING QUESTIONS

1. How are foreign-born citizens from different regions of the world different from each other?

The Statue of Liberty symbolizes America's long tradition of welcoming immigrants to its shores.

2. Why do you think foreign-born citizens tend to live in our nation's largest cities?

3. How do foreign-born citizens contribute to the nation's quality of life?

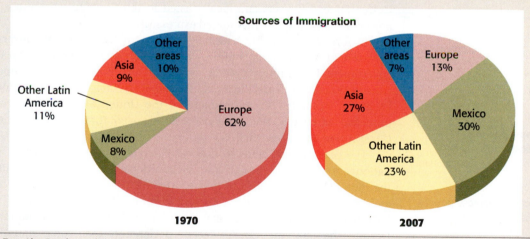

Sources of Immigration

1970
- Other areas 10%
- Asia 9%
- Other Latin America 11%
- Mexico 8%
- Europe 62%

2007
- Other areas 7%
- Europe 13%
- Mexico 30%
- Other Latin America 23%
- Asia 27%

SOURCE: William H. Frey, Alan Berube, Audrey Singer, and Jill H. Wilson, "Getting Current: Recent Demographic Trends in Metropolitan America," Washington, D.C.: The Brookings Institution, 2009.

Variation in Policies Creates Redundancies and Inefficiencies The rules for environmental regulation, labor laws, teacher certification, gun ownership laws, and even the licensing requirements for optometrists vary throughout the 50 states, and this is on top of many federal regulations. Companies seeking to do business across state lines must learn and abide by many different sets of laws, while individuals in licensed professions must consider whether they face recertification if they choose to relocate to another state. One of the obstacles to health care reform debated throughout 2009 in Congress is the fact that each state has a different set of regulations for health insurance companies.

The Constitutional Structure of American Federalism

LEARNING **OBJECTIVE**

1.2 Differentiate the powers the Constitution provides to national and state governments.

The division of powers and responsibilities between the national and state governments has resulted in thousands of court decisions, as well as hundreds of books and endless speeches to explain them—and even then the division lacks precise definition. Nonetheless, it is helpful to have a basic understanding of how the Constitution divides these powers and responsibilities and what obligations it imposes on each level of government.

The constitutional framework of our federal system is relatively simple:

1. The national government has only those powers delegated to it by the Constitution (with the important exception of the inherent power over foreign affairs).
2. Within the scope of its operations, the national government is supreme.
3. The state governments have the powers not delegated to the central government except those denied to them by the Constitution and their state constitutions.
4. Some powers are specifically denied to both the national and state governments; others are specifically denied only to the states or to the national government.

Powers of the National Government

The Constitution explicitly gives legislative, executive, and judicial powers to the national government. In addition to these **delegated powers,** such as the power to regulate interstate commerce and to appropriate funds, the national government has assumed constitutionally **implied powers,** such as the power to create banks, which are inferred from delegated powers. The constitutional basis for the implied powers of Congress is the **necessary and proper clause** (Article I, Section 8, Clause 3). This clause gives Congress the right "to make all Laws which shall be necessary and proper for carrying into Execution the foregoing Powers, and all other Powers vested . . . in the Government of the United States." (Powers specifically listed in the Constitution are also called **express powers** because they are mentioned expressly.)

In foreign affairs, the national government has **inherent powers.** The national government has the same authority to deal with other nations as if it were the central government in a unitary system. Such inherent powers do not depend on specific constitutional provisions but exist because of the creation of the national government itself. For example, the government of the United States may acquire territory by purchase or by discovery and occupation, even though no specific clause in the Constitution allows such acquisition.

The national and state governments may have their own lists of powers, but the national government relies on four constitutional pillars for its ultimate authority over the states: (1) the *national supremacy article,* (2) the *war power,* (3) the *commerce clause,* and especially (4) the *power to tax and spend* for the general welfare. These authorities have permitted a tremendous expansion of the functions of the national government. Despite the Supreme Court's recent declaration that some national laws exceed Congress's constitutional powers, the national government has, in effect, almost full power to enact any legislation that Congress deems necessary, so long as it does not conflict with the provisions of the Constitution designed to protect individual rights and the powers of the states. In addition, Section 5 of the Fourteenth Amendment, ratified in 1868, gives Congress the power to enact legislation to remedy constitutional violations and the denial of due process or equal protection of the laws.

The National Supremacy Article   One of the most important constitutional pillars is found in Article VI: "This Constitution, and the Laws of the United States which shall be made in Pursuance thereof; and all Treaties made . . . under the Authority of the United States, shall be the supreme Law of the Land; and the Judges in every State shall be bound thereby; any Thing in the Constitution or Laws of any State to the Contrary notwithstanding." All officials, state as well as national, swear an oath to support the Constitution of the United States. States may not override national policies; this restriction also applies to local units of government because they are agents of the states.

delegated (express) powers
Powers given explicitly to the national government and listed in the Constitution.

implied powers
Powers inferred from the express powers that allow Congress to carry out its functions.

necessary and proper clause
The clause in the Constitution (Article I, Section 8, Clause 3) setting forth the implied powers of Congress. It states that Congress, in addition to its express powers, has the right to make all laws necessary and proper to carry out all powers the Constitution vests in the national government.

inherent powers
The powers of the national government in foreign affairs that the Supreme Court has declared do not depend on constitutional grants but rather grow out of the very existence of the national government.

National laws and regulations of federal agencies *preempt* the field, so that conflicting state and local regulations are unenforceable. States must abide by the national government's minimum wage laws, for example, but are allowed to set the minimum wage higher if they wish.

The War Power   The national government is responsible for protecting the nation from external aggression, whether from other nations or from international terrorism. The government's power to protect national security includes the power to wage war. In today's world, military strength depends not only on the presence of troops in the field but also on the ability to mobilize the nation's industrial might and apply scientific and technological knowledge to the tasks of defense. As Charles Evans Hughes, who became chief justice in 1930, observed: "The power to wage war is the power to wage war successfully."[9] The national government is free to create "no-fly" zones only for its military aircraft both within and across state borders, for example, and may use any airports it needs during times of war or peace.

The Power to Regulate Interstate and Foreign Commerce   Congressional authority extends to all commerce that affects more than one state. Commerce includes the production, buying, selling, renting, and transporting of goods, services, and properties. The **commerce clause** (Article I, Section 8, Clause 1) packs a tremendous constitutional punch; it gives Congress the power "to regulate Commerce with foreign Nations, and among the several States, and with the Indian Tribes." In these few words, the national government has found constitutional justification for regulating a wide range of human activity because few aspects of our economy today affect commerce in only one state and are thus outside the scope of the national government's constitutional authority.

The landmark ruling of *Gibbons* v. *Ogden* in 1824 affirmed the broad authority of Congress over interstate commerce. The case involved a New York state license that gave Aaron Ogden the exclusive right to operate steamboats between New York and New Jersey. Using the license, Ogden asked the New York state courts to stop Thomas Gibbons from running a competing ferry. Although Gibbons countered that his boats were licensed under a 1793 act of Congress governing vessels "in the coasting trade and fisheries," the New York courts sided with Ogden. Just as the national government and states both have the power to tax, the New York courts said they both had the power to regulate commerce.

commerce clause
The clause in the Constitution (Article I, Section 8, Clause 1) that gives Congress the power to regulate all business activities that cross state lines or affect more than one state or other nations.

The national military has the power to set restrictions on airspace so that it can fly anywhere across the country without approval of state or local governments.
■ *Why does the national government have the final say on national security issues?*

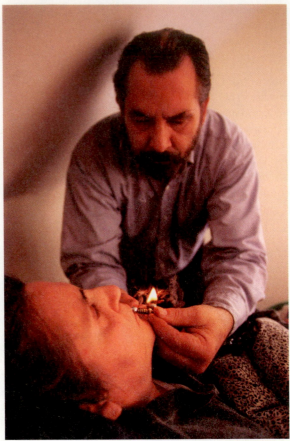

Though many states allow the use of medicinal marijuana, the Supreme Court decided that the national government could regulate its use in the states as a form of interstate commerce. ■ *Why did the Obama administration choose not to exercise this power to prohibit marijuana sales in states such as California that have legalized its use?*

federal mandate
A requirement the national government imposes as a condition for receiving federal funds.

Gibbons appealed to the Supreme Court and asked a simple question: Which government had the ultimate power to regulate interstate commerce? The Supreme Court gave an equally simple answer: The national government's laws were supreme.[10]

Gibbons v. *Ogden* was immediately heralded for promoting a national economic common market, in holding that states may not discriminate against interstate transportation and out-of-state commerce. The Supreme Court's brilliant definition of "commerce" as *intercourse among the states* provided the basis for national regulation of "things in commerce"[11] and an expanding range of economic activities, including the sale of lottery tickets,[12] prostitution,[13] radio and television broadcasts,[14] and telecommunications and the Internet.

The Power to Tax and Spend Congress lacks constitutional authority to pass laws solely on the grounds that they will promote the general welfare, but it may raise taxes and spend money for this purpose. For example, the national government lacks the power to regulate education or agriculture directly, but it does have the power to appropriate money to support education or to pay farm subsidies. By attaching conditions to its grants of money, the national government creates incentives that affect state action. If states want the money, they must accept the conditions.

When the national government provides the money, it determines how the money will be spent. By withholding or threatening to withhold funds, the national government can influence or control state operations and regulate individual conduct. For example, the national government has stipulated that federal funds should be withdrawn from any program in which any person is denied benefits because of race, color, national origin, sex, or physical handicap. The national government also used its "power of the purse" to force states to raise the drinking age to 21 by tying such a condition to federal dollars for building and maintaining highways.

Congress frequently requires states to provide specific programs—for example, provide services to indigent mothers and clean up the air and water. These requirements are called **federal mandates.** Often the national government does not supply the funds required to carry out "unfunded mandates" (discussed later in the chapter). Its failure to do so has become an important issue as states face growing expenditures with limited resources.

Powers of the States

The Constitution *reserves for the states all powers not granted to the national government,* subject only to the limitations of the Constitution. Only the states have the **reserve powers** to create schools and local governments, for example. Both are powers not given exclusively to the national government by the Constitution or judicial interpretation, so that states can exercise these powers as long as they do not conflict with national law.

The national and state governments also share powers. These **concurrent powers** with the national government include the power to levy taxes and regulate commerce internal to each state.

In general, states may levy taxes on the same items the national government taxes, such as incomes, alcohol, and gasoline, but a state cannot, by a tax, "unduly burden" commerce among the states, interfere with a function of the national government, complicate the operation of a national law, or abridge the terms of a treaty of the United States. Where the national government has not preempted the field,

Under national pressure, states have raised the drinking age to 21. States are also under pressure to monitor drunk driving more aggressively.

TABLE 1–1	The Constitutional Division of National and State Powers	
Examples of Powers Delegated to the National Government	**Examples of Powers Reserved for State Governments**	**Examples of Concurrent Powers Shared by the National and State Governments**
Regulate trade and interstate commerce	Create local governments	Impose and collect taxes and fees
Declare war	Police citizens	Borrow and spend money
Create post offices	Oversee primary and elementary education	Establish courts
Coin money		Enact and enforce laws
		Protect civil rights
		Conduct elections
		Protect health and welfare

states may regulate interstate businesses, provided these regulations do not cover matters requiring uniform national treatment or unduly burden interstate commerce.

Who decides which matters require "uniform national treatment" or what actions might place an "undue burden" on interstate commerce? Congress does, subject to the president's signature and final review by the Supreme Court. When Congress is silent or does not clearly state its intent, the courts—ultimately, the Supreme Court—decide whether there is a conflict with the national Constitution or whether a state law or regulation has preempted the national government's authority.

Constitutional Limits and Obligations

To ensure that federalism works, the Constitution imposes restraints on both the national and the state governments. States are prohibited from doing the following:

1. Making treaties with foreign governments
2. Authorizing private persons to interfere with the shipping and commerce of other nations
3. Coining money, issuing bills of credit, or making anything but gold and silver coin legal tender in payment of debts
4. Taxing imports or exports
5. Taxing foreign ships
6. Keeping troops or ships of war in time of peace (except for the state militia, now called the National Guard)
7. Engaging in war

In turn, the Constitution requires the national government to refrain from exercising its powers, especially its powers to tax and to regulate interstate commerce, in such a way as to interfere substantially with the states' abilities to perform their responsibilities. But politicians, judges, and scholars disagree about whether the national political process—specifically the executive and the legislature—or the courts should ultimately define the boundaries between the powers of the national government and the states. Some argue that the states' protection from intrusions by the national government comes primarily from the political process because senators and representatives elected from the states participate in congressional decisions.[15] Others maintain that the Supreme Court should limit the national government's power and defend the states.[16]

On a case-by-case basis, the Court has held that the national government may not command states to enact laws to comply with or order state employees to enforce national laws. In *Printz* v. *United States,* the Court held that states were not required to conduct instant national background checks prior to selling a handgun.[17] Referring broadly to the concept of dual federalism discussed early in this chapter, the Supreme Court said that the national government could not "draft" local police to do its bidding. But as previously discussed, even if the national government cannot force states to enforce certain national laws, it can threaten to withhold its funding if states do not comply with national policies, such as lowering the minimum drinking age or speed limit.

reserve powers
All powers not specifically delegated to the national government by the Constitution. The reserve power can be found in the Tenth Amendment to the Constitution.

concurrent powers
Powers that the Constitution gives to both the national and state governments, such as the power to levy taxes.

The U.S. Supreme Court ruled that the national government cannot demand that states enforce the national law requiring handgun dealers to run background checks on potential buyers. States are free, however, to use a national registry of criminals in doing background checks, which almost all do. ■ *Should the national government extend gun control laws to flea markets, where guns are still sold without first checking the national registry? Under what authority could these laws be imposed?*

full faith and credit clause
The clause in the Constitution (Article IV, Section 1) requiring each state to recognize the civil judgments rendered by the courts of the other states and to accept their public records and acts as valid.

extradition
The legal process whereby an alleged criminal offender is surrendered by the officials of one state to officials of the state in which the crime is alleged to have been committed.

interstate compact
An agreement among two or more states. Congress must approve most such agreements.

The Constitution also obliges the national government to protect states against *domestic insurrection.* Congress has delegated to the president the authority to dispatch troops to put down such insurrections when the proper state authorities request them.

Interstate Relationships

Three clauses in the Constitution, taken from the Articles of Confederation, require states to give full faith and credit to each other's public acts, records, and judicial proceedings; to extend to each other's citizens the privileges and immunities of their own citizens; and to return persons who are fleeing from justice.

Full Faith and Credit
The **full faith and credit clause** (Article IV, Section 1), one of the more technical provisions of the Constitution, requires state courts to enforce the civil judgments of the courts of other states and accept their public records and acts as valid.[18] It does not require states to enforce the criminal laws or legislation and administrative acts of other states; in most cases, for one state to enforce the criminal laws of another would raise constitutional issues. The clause applies primarily to enforcing judicial settlements and court awards.

Interstate Privileges and Immunities
Under Article IV, Section 2, individual states must give citizens of all other states the privileges and immunities they grant to their own citizens, including the protection of the laws, the right to engage in peaceful occupations, access to the courts, and freedom from discriminatory taxes. Because of this clause, states may not impose unreasonable residency requirements, that is, withhold rights to American citizens who have recently moved to the state and thereby have become citizens of that state.

Extradition
In Article IV, Section 2, the Constitution asserts that, when individuals charged with crimes have fled from one state to another, the state to which they have fled is to deliver them to the proper officials on demand of the executive authority of the state from which they fled. This process is called **extradition.** "The obvious objective of the Extradition Clause," the courts have claimed, "is that no State should become a safe haven for the fugitives from a sister State's criminal justice system."[19] Congress has supplemented this constitutional provision by making the governor of the state to which fugitives have fled responsible for returning them.

Interstate Compacts
The Constitution also requires states to settle disputes with one another without the use of force. States may carry their legal disputes to the Supreme Court, or they may negotiate **interstate compacts.** Interstate compacts often establish interstate agencies to handle problems affecting an entire region. Before most interstate compacts become effective, Congress has to approve them. Then the compact becomes binding on all signatory states, and the federal judiciary can enforce its terms. A typical state may belong to 20 compacts dealing with such subjects as environmental protection, crime control, water rights, and higher education exchanges.[20]

The National Courts and Federalism

LEARNING OBJECTIVE

1.3 Assess the role of the national courts in defining the relationship between the national and state governments, and evaluate the positions of decentralists and centralists.

Although the political process ultimately decides how power will be divided between the national and the state governments, the national court system is often called on to umpire the ongoing debate about which level of government should do what, for whom, and to whom. The nation's highest court claimed this role in the celebrated case of *McCulloch* v. *Maryland.*

McCulloch v. Maryland

In *McCulloch* v. *Maryland* (1819), the Supreme Court had the first of many chances to define the division of power between the national and state governments.[21] Congress had established the Bank of the United States, but Maryland opposed any national bank and levied a $10,000 tax on any bank not incorporated in the state. James William McCulloch, the cashier of the bank, refused to pay on the grounds that a state could not tax an instrument of the national government.

Maryland was represented before the Court by some of the country's most distinguished lawyers, including Luther Martin, who had been a delegate to the Constitutional Convention. Martin said the Constitution did not expressly delegate to the national government the power to incorporate a bank. He maintained that the necessary and proper clause gives Congress only the power to choose those means and to pass those laws absolutely essential to the execution of its expressly granted powers. Because a bank is not absolutely necessary to the exercise of its delegated powers, he argued, Congress had no authority to establish it. As for Maryland's right to tax the bank, the power to tax is one of the powers reserved to the states; they may use it as they see fit.

Equally distinguished counsel, including Daniel Webster, represented the national government. Webster conceded that the power to create a bank is not one of the express powers of the national government. However, the power to pass laws necessary and proper to carry out Congress's express powers is specifically delegated to Congress. Although the power to tax is reserved to the states, Webster argued that states cannot interfere with the operations of the national government. The Constitution leaves no room for doubt; when the national and state governments have conflicts, the national government is supreme.

Speaking for a unanimous Court, Chief Justice John Marshall rejected every one of Maryland's contentions. He summarized his views on the powers of the national government in these now-famous words: "Let the end be legitimate, let it be within the scope of the Constitution, and all means which are appropriate, which are plainly adapted to that end, which are not prohibited, but consist with the letter and spirit of the constitution, are constitutional."

Having established the presence of *implied national powers,* Marshall then outlined the concept of **national supremacy.** No state, he said, can use its taxing powers to tax a national instrument. "The power to tax involves the power to destroy.... If the right of the States to tax the means employed by the general government be conceded, the declaration that the Constitution, and the laws made in pursuance thereof, shall be the supreme law of the land, is empty and unmeaning declamation."

It is difficult to overstate the long-range significance of *McCulloch* v. *Maryland* in providing support for the developing forces of nationalism and a unified economy. If the contrary arguments in favor of the states had been accepted, they would have strapped the national government in a constitutional straitjacket and denied it powers needed to deal with the problems of an expanding nation.

National Courts and the Relationship with the States

The authority of national judges to review the activities of state and local governments has expanded dramatically in recent decades because of modern judicial interpretations of the Fourteenth Amendment, which forbids states to deprive any person of life, liberty, or property without *due process of the law.* States may not deny any person the *equal protection of the laws,* including congressional legislation enacted to implement the Fourteenth Amendment. Almost every action by state and local officials is now subject to challenge before a federal judge as a violation of the Constitution or of national law.

Preemption occurs when a national law or regulation takes precedence over a state or local law or regulation. State and local laws are preempted not only when they conflict directly with national laws and regulations but also when they touch on a field in which the "federal interest is so dominant that the federal system will be assumed to preclude enforcement of state laws on the same subject."[22] Examples of federal preemption include laws regulating hazardous substances, water quality, clean air standards, and many civil rights acts, especially the Civil Rights Act of 1964 and the Voting Rights Act of 1965.

Throughout the years, federal judges, under the leadership of the Supreme Court, have generally favored the powers of the national government over those of the states. Despite the Supreme Court's recent bias in favor of state over national authority, few would deny the Supreme Court the power to review and set aside state actions. As Justice Oliver Wendell Holmes of the Supreme Court once remarked, "I do not think the United

national supremacy
A constitutional doctrine that whenever conflict occurs between the constitutionally authorized actions of the national government and those of a state or local government, the actions of the national government prevail.

preemption
The right of a national law or regulation to preclude enforcement of a state or local law or regulation.

States are responsible for registering voters, but the national government is responsible for assuring that state registration rules are Constitutional. ■ *How and why might state voter registration rules vary from state to state? Does this highlight a strength or weakness of federalism?*

States would come to an end if we lost our power to declare an Act of Congress void. I do think the Union would be imperiled if we could not make that declaration as to the laws of the several States."[23]

The Supreme Court and the Role of Congress

From 1937 until the 1990s, the Supreme Court essentially removed national courts from what had been their role of protecting states from acts of Congress. The Supreme Court broadly interpreted the commerce clause to allow Congress to do whatever Congress thought necessary and proper to promote the common good, even if national laws and regulations infringed on the activities of state and local governments.

In the past 15 years, however, the Supreme Court has signaled that national courts should be more active in resolving federalism issues.[24] The Court declared that a state could not impose term limits on its members of Congress, but it did so by only a 5-to-4 vote. Justice John Paul Stevens, writing for the majority, built his argument on the concept of the federal union as espoused by the great Chief Justice John Marshall, as a compact among the people, with the national government serving as the people's agent.

The Supreme Court also declared that the clause in the Constitution empowering Congress to regulate commerce with the Indian tribes did not give Congress the power to authorize national courts to hear suits against a state brought by Indian tribes.[25] Unless states consent to such suits, they enjoy "sovereign immunity" under the Eleventh Amendment. The effect of this decision goes beyond Indian tribes. As a result—except to enforce rights stemming from the Fourteenth Amendment, which the Court explicitly acknowledged to be within Congress's power—Congress may no longer authorize individuals to bring legal actions against states to force their compliance with national law in either national or state courts.[26]

Building on those rulings, the Court continues to press ahead with its "constitutional counterrevolution"[27] and return to an older vision of federalism from the 1930s. Among other recent rulings, in *United States* v. *Morrison,* the Court struck down the Violence Against Women Act, which had given women who are victims of violence the right to sue their attackers for damages.[28] Congress had found that violence against women annually costs the national economy $3 billion, but a bare majority of the Court held that gender-motivated crimes did not have a substantial impact on interstate commerce and that Congress had thus exceeded its powers in enacting the law and intruded on the powers of the states.

By the People

Monitoring the National Stimulus Package

In early 2009, Congress and President Barack Obama passed a nearly $800 billion spending package designed to stimulate the national economy. The number of unemployed Americans was rising fast, small businesses were closing, consumers were spending less, sales of new and old homes alike had fallen, and the economy was in the worst recession in decades. Under the stimulus, states were given nearly $260 billion to invest in projects that would put unemployed Americans back to work and restart the economy.

Much of this money was designed to support highway construction, new building projects, and scientific research but has been difficult to track. According to ongoing monitoring by the national government and outside groups, thousands of small companies are still receiving national dollars for a broad mix of projects.

Citizens can track the spending as a form of public service—the more they pay attention to the projects, the more the states pay attention to them. One way to monitor the spending is to pick a project and see what is actually happening. The first step in this monitoring is to find the project through Web sites such as recovery.gov or propublica.org. Citizens can click on a specific state at propublica.org, pick an individual county in that state, and see every project funded by the stimulus. Once citizens pick a project, they can visit the project and see what is actually happening. If the project is not even under way, citizens can report the inaction to the federal government through recovery.gov.

Colleges and universities have received a sizable amount of stimulus money. By early 2010, Florida's Alachua County had received more than $100 million. As home of the University of Florida, much of the money ended up in university research projects. According to the propublica.org list, the university received support for nearly 150 separate projects and student programs, while Santa Fe Community College received more than a dozen grants to support students with Pell Grants.

CRITICAL THINKING QUESTIONS

1. Why is monitoring the stimulus spending a form of public service?
2. What is the effect of visiting a project to see if it is working?
3. Does simply visiting the stimulus Web sites make any difference in telling Congress and the president that someone is watching?

University of Florida students conduct research with funds from the federal stimulus package.

These Supreme Court decisions—most of which split the Court 5 to 4 along ideological lines, with the conservative justices favoring states' rights—have signaled a shift in the Court's interpretation of the constitutional nature of our federal system. It is a shift that has been reinforced with the most recent Supreme Court appointments made by Presidents Bush and Obama. Chief Justice John Roberts and Justice Samuel Alito, each appointed by President George W. Bush, tend to favor the states, while justices Sonia Sotomayor and Elena Kagan, Obama appointees, tend to side with the national government.

The Great Debate Continues: Centralists Versus Decentralists

From the beginning of the Republic, there has been an ongoing debate about the "proper" distribution of powers, functions, and responsibilities between the national government and the states. Did the national government have the authority to outlaw slavery in the territories? Did the states have the authority to operate racially segregated schools? Could Congress regulate labor relations? Does Congress have the power to regulate the sale and use of firearms? Does Congress have the right to tell states how to clean up air and water pollution?

Today, the debate continues between **centralists,** who favor national action, and **decentralists,** who defend the powers of the states and favor action at the state and local levels on such issues as environmental and gun regulation.

centralists
People who favor national action over action at the state and local levels.

decentralists
People who favor state or local action rather than national action.

The Decentralist Position   Among those favoring the decentralist or **states' rights** interpretation were the Antifederalists, Thomas Jefferson, the pre–Civil War statesman from South Carolina John C. Calhoun, the Supreme Court from the 1920s to 1937, and, more recently, Presidents Ronald Reagan and George H. W. Bush, the Republican leaders of Congress, former Chief Justice William H. Rehnquist, and current Justices Antonin Scalia and Clarence Thomas.

Most decentralists contend that the Constitution is basically a compact among sovereign states that created the central government and gave it limited authority. Thus the national government is little more than an agent of the states, and every one of its powers should be narrowly defined. Any question about whether the states have given a particular function to the central government or have reserved it for themselves should be resolved in favor of the states.

Decentralists believe that the national government should not interfere with activities reserved for the states. Their argument is based on the Tenth Amendment, which states: "The powers not delegated to the United States by the Constitution, nor prohibited by it to the States, are reserved to the States respectively, or to the people." Decentralists insist that state governments are closer to the people and reflect the people's wishes more accurately than the national government does.

Decentralists have been particularly supportive of the **devolution revolution,** which argues for returning responsibilities to the states.[29] In the 1990s, the Republican-controlled Congress gave states more authority over some programs such as welfare, and President Clinton also proclaimed, "The era of big government is over." However, he tempered his comments by adding, "But we cannot go back to the time when our citizens were left to fend for themselves," and despite its dramatic name, the revolution has fallen short of the hoped-for results.

Instead of a devolution revolution, the national government has actually grown stronger during the past decade. The national government has passed a number of laws that give states specific responsibilities in defending homeland security, including the implementation of national criteria for issuing driver's licenses. It has also ordered states not to sell any citizen's personal information to private companies, ended state regulation of mutual funds, nullified state laws that restrict telecommunication competition, and gave the national judiciary the power to prosecute a number of state and local crimes, including carjacking and acts of terrorism.

states' rights
Powers expressly or implicitly reserved to the states.

devolution revolution
The effort to slow the growth of the national government by returning many functions to the states.

Decentralists believe that education should be a state responsibility. However, because the national government provides money to the states, it has the power to impose strings on how the money is spent.
■ *What are some of the arguments for greater or less federal government involvement in public education?*

The Centralist Position The centralist position has been supported by presidents, Congress, and the Supreme Court. Presidents Abraham Lincoln, Theodore Roosevelt, Franklin Roosevelt, and Lyndon Johnson were particularly strong supporters, and the Supreme Court has generally ruled in favor of the centralist position.

Centralists reject the idea of the Constitution as an interstate compact. They view it as a supreme law established by the people. The national government is an agent of the people, not of the states, because it was the people who drew up the Constitution and created the national government. They intended that the national political process should define the central government's powers and that the national government be denied authority only when the Constitution clearly prohibits it from acting.

Centralists argue that the national government is a government of all the people, whereas each state speaks for only some of the people. Although the Tenth Amendment clearly reserves powers for the states, it does not deny the national government the authority to exercise all of its powers to the fullest extent. Moreover, the supremacy of the national government restricts the states because governments representing part of the people cannot be allowed to interfere with a government representing all of them.

The National Budget as a Tool of Federalism

Congress authorizes programs, establishes general rules for how the programs will operate, and decides whether room should be left for state or local discretion and how much. Most important, Congress appropriates the funds for these programs and generally has deeper pockets than even the richest states. Federal grants are one of Congress's most potent tools for influencing policy at the state and local levels.

Federal grants serve four purposes, the most important of which is the fourth:

1. To supply state and local governments with revenue
2. To establish minimum national standards for such things as highways and clean air
3. To equalize resources among the states by taking money from people with high incomes through federal taxes and spending it, through grants, in states where the poor live
4. To attack national problems but minimize the growth of federal agencies

Types of Federal Grants

The national government currently gives states three types of grants: *categorical-formula grants*, *project grants*, and *block grants* (sometimes called *flexible grants*). From 1972 to 1986, the national government also gave states a share of national tax revenues through *revenue sharing*. The program was terminated in an effort to reduce rising national budget deficits.

Categorical-Formula Grants The national government provides grants for specific purposes, such as promoting homeland security. By definition, these grants are distributed to the states based on population. Many categorical-formula grants require state governments to provide at least some of the total funding, often on a matching basis. Categorical-formula grants are tightly monitored to ensure that the money is spent exactly as directed. There are hundreds of grant programs, but two dozen, including Medicaid, account for more than half of total categorical-formula spending.

Project Grants The national government supports states through project grants for specific activities, such as scientific research, highway construction, and job training. Project grants are generally restricted to a fixed amount of time and can only be spent within tight guidelines. Many university-based medical schools rely on project grants to support their efforts to cure life-threatening diseases such as cancer and heart disease.

LEARNING **OBJECTIVE**

1.4 Analyze the budget as a tool of federalism, and evaluate its impact on state and local governments.

For the People
GOVERNMENT'S GREATEST ENDEAVORS

Supporting the States in Achieving National Goals

Throughout the decades, the national government has given state and local governments a long list of responsibilities for implementing national programs, such as health care for the poor, highway construction, and waste-water treatment. These programs involve important national goals for creating a healthy society and economy.

Most of these programs carry large amounts of national dollars, which allow the national government to set minimum standards for those who get unemployment insurance, public assistance, and medical care. National funds also offset state spending on both the administrative and program costs of achieving the national goals profiled throughout this book. But the national government relies on the states for the implementation of these programs.

Homeland security is a case in point. Following the 9/11 terrorist attacks on the World Trade Center and Washington, D.C. in 2001, the national government launched what President George W. Bush called the "war on terrorism." Local police departments are essential partners in the effort. They are

linked to the national government through computer systems that contain the names of terrorist suspects and are often first at the scene of suspected terrorist acts such as the 2008 bombing of a Jewish center in New York City. The national government provides large amounts of funding to improve state and local defenses against terrorist attacks.

All totaled, the national government will spend nearly $600 billion in 2010 helping states achieve its broad goals for improving the quality of life in the United States, including $20 billion on transportation, $21 billion on education and job training, $43 billion on health care for the poor and substance abuse programs, and $36 billion on food and nutrition programs.* Although much of this money comes with tight restrictions on which citizens and projects qualify for funding, this spending indicates how much the national government is willing to invest in helping states help their citizens.

CRITICAL THINKING QUESTIONS

1. What are some of the advantages of national and local governments working

The national government works with state and local governments to ensure that airports are safe from terrorism. Baggage and passenger screeners are national government employees, but they work closely with local airports.

collectively on problems like airport security? What are the disadvantages?

2. Why might the national government prefer working in cooperation with state governments?

3. How is airport security a form of marble cake federalism? How is it a form of cooperative federalism?

*SOURCE: U.S. Census Bureau, The 2010 Statistical Abstract: National Data Book, Table 419 (Washington, D.C.: U.S. Census Bureau, 2010).

Block Grants   Block grants are broad grants to states for specific activities, such as public assistance, child care, education, social services, preventive health care, and health services. By definition, these blocks of funding are provided with very few requirements attached. States have great flexibility in deciding how to spend block grant dollars, but unlike programs such as national unemployment insurance that are guaranteed for everyone who qualifies for them, block grants are limited to specific amounts set by the national government.

The Politics of Federal Grants

Republicans "have consistently favored fewer strings, less federal supervision, and the delegation of spending discretion to the state and local governments."[30] Democrats have generally been less supportive of broad discretionary block grants, instead favoring more detailed, federally supervised spending. The Republican-controlled Congress in the 1990s gave high priority to creating block grants, but it ran into trouble when it tried to lump together welfare, school lunch and breakfast programs, prenatal nutrition programs, and child protection programs in one block grant.

The battle over national versus state control of spending tends to be cyclical. As one scholar of federalism explains, "Complaints about excessive federal control tend to be followed by proposals to shift more power to state and local governments. Then, when problems arise in state and local administration—and problems inevitably arise when any organization tries to administer anything—demands for closer federal supervision and tighter federal controls follow."[31]

The Americans with Disabilities Act of 1990 required state and local governments to improve access to buildings and public transportation for people with disabilities. The law covers all public colleges and universities. ■ *Why is enforcing the Americans with Disabilities Act so costly for state and local governments?*

Unfunded Mandates

Fewer federal dollars do not necessarily mean fewer federal controls. On the contrary, the national government has imposed mandates on states and local governments, often without providing federal funds. State and local officials complained about this, and their protests were effective. The Unfunded Mandates Reform Act of 1995 was championed by then-House Republican Speaker Newt Gingrich as part of the GOP's Contract with America. The act was considered part of what commentators called the "Newt Federalism."

The law requires Congress to evaluate the impact of unfunded mandates and imposes mild constraints on Congress itself. A congressional committee that approves any legislation containing a federal mandate must draw attention to the mandate in its report and describe its cost to state and local governments. If the committee intends any mandate to be partially unfunded, it must explain why it is appropriate for state and local governments to pay for it.

At least during its first 15 years, the Unfunded Mandates Reform Act has been mostly successful in restraining mandates.[32] According to the National Conference of State Legislatures, the national government has enacted only 11 laws that impose unfunded mandates. Three of these unfunded mandates involved increases in the minimum wage that apply to all state and local employees.

The Politics of Federalism

The formal structures of our federal system have not changed much since 1787, but the political realities, especially during the past half-century, have greatly altered the way federalism works. To understand these changes, we need to look at some of the trends that continue to fuel the debate about the meaning of federalism.

The Growth of National Government

Throughout the past two centuries, power has accrued to the national government. As the Advisory Commission on Intergovernmental Relations observed in a 1981 report, "No one planned the growth, but everyone played a part in it."[33]

LEARNING **OBJECTIVE**

1.5 Evaluate the current relationship between the national and state governments and the future challenges for federalism.

DECIDE Should the No Child Left Behind Act Be Renewed?

Early in 2002, President George W. Bush signed the No Child Left Behind Act into law, thereby creating one of the most significant mandates ever imposed on the states. Although primary and secondary education has long been considered an almost exclusive responsibility of state and local governments, the No Child Left Behind Act required states to create a new system of standardized testing for every public school. States could either implement the new mandate or lose their federal funding, which amounts to approximately 10 percent of all school budgets.

Under the No Child Left Behind Act, schools were required to adopt a number of separate reforms for improving student achievement. Students in grades three through eight were to be tested each year in reading and math, while students in high school were to be tested at least once in reading, math, and

science. Based on the test results, schools were also required to show academic progress or risk the possibility of losing national funds.

Like many national laws, however, the No Child Left Behind Act is not permanent. It must be renewed every five years, which means that it can be changed. As they gain more experience with the act, parents and teachers will have more influence over the future of the tests and report cards that now govern their schools. Despite the five-year time limit, the law had not been formally reauthorized by September 2010, but continued to operate under a temporary extension.

What do you think? Should the No Child Left Behind Act be renewed? What arguments would you make for or against such an idea?

THINKING IT THROUGH

Parents and teachers already seem to agree that the No Child Left Behind Act created two problems that may need congressional attention.

First, some parents and teachers complain that instead of inspiring schools to focus on reading, math, and science, the act may encourage them to "teach to the test"—to prep students on how to take tests in reading, math, and science. There is no question, for example, that primary school students now spend enormous amounts of time practicing for the annual reading and math tests or that teachers are being encouraged to produce the highest scores possible, even if that occasionally means giving students extra practice on the test instead of instruction on basic skills. There have also been several highly publicized scandals in which schools cheated on the tests.

Second, parents and teachers worry that the national government has not provided enough funding to make the law work. Failing public schools cannot be improved simply by giving parents the right to remove their children, if only because they may not be able to find a better school. Moreover, new programs such as mentoring, afterschool tutoring, and summer school cost money that is often in short supply in large, urban school districts. These districts may also have much higher proportions of students who speak English as a second language, which can lead to lower test scores.

Despite these concerns, the act is almost certain to be renewed. Even though some say it focuses on testing, not learning, No Child Left Behind has created significant pressure for higher performance. The question is how its provisions might be changed to increase success.*

Actor Matthew McConaughey volunteers for Teach for America, a program that helps public schools by training young college graduates to spend two years teaching low-income students.

Critical Thinking Questions

1. What changes do you recommend when Congress and the president renew the No Child Left Behind Act?

2. Why does the support of teachers and parents matter to renewal of the No Child Left Behind Act?

3. Does the act ask too much of state and local governments given that the national government supplies only 10 percent of all school funding?

4. Should the national government be involved in issues like public education to make sure all states act the same way?

---

* Laura S. Hamilton et al., "Passing or Failing? A Midterm Report Card for 'No Child Left Behind,'" *RAND Review*, 31 (Fall 2007), pp. 16–25.Laura S. Hamilton et al., "Passing or Failing? A Midterm Report Card for 'No Child Left Behind,'" *RAND Review*, 31 (Fall 2007), pp. 16–25.

This shift occurred for a variety of reasons. One is that many of our problems have become national in scope. Much that was local in 1789, in 1860, or in 1930 is now national, even global. State governments could supervise the relationships between small merchants and their few employees, for instance, but only the national government can supervise relationships between multinational corporations and their thousands of worldwide employees, many of whom are organized in national unions.

As the economy grew rapidly during the early nineteenth century, powerful interests made demands on the national government. Business groups called on the government for aid in the form of tariffs, a national banking system, subsidies to railroads and the merchant marine, and uniform rules on the environment. Farmers learned that the national government could give more aid than the states, and they too began to demand help. By the beginning of the twentieth century, urban groups in general and organized labor in particular were pressing their claims. Big business, big agriculture, and big labor all added up to big government.

The growth of the national economy and the creation of national transportation and communications networks altered people's attitudes toward the national government. Before the Civil War, citizens saw the national government as a distant, even foreign, entity. Today, in part because of television and the Internet, most people know more about Washington than they know about their state capitals, and they know more about the president and their national legislators than about their governor, their state legislators, or even the local officials who run their cities and schools.

The Great Depression of the 1930s stimulated extensive national action on welfare, unemployment, and farm surpluses. World War II brought federal regulation of wages, prices, and employment, as well as national efforts to allocate resources, train personnel, and support engineering and inventions. After the war, the national government helped veterans obtain college degrees and inaugurated a vast system of support for university research. The United States became the most powerful leader of the free world, maintaining substantial military forces even in times of peace.

Although economic and social conditions created many of the pressures for expanding the national government, so did political claims. Once established, federal programs generate groups with vested interests in promoting, defending, and expanding them. Associations are formed and alliances are made. "In a word, the growth of government has created a constituency of, by, and for government."[34] The national budget can become a negative issue for Congress and the president if it grows too large, however. With the federal budget deficit rising rapidly in 2010, the Obama Administration was forced to back away from some of its largest spending programs and promise greater restraint.

The politics of federalism are changing, however, and Congress is being pressured to reduce the size and scope of national programs, while dealing with the demands for homeland security. Meanwhile, the cost of entitlement programs such as Social Security and Medicare are rising because there are more older people and they are living longer. These programs have widespread public support and to cut them is politically risky. "With all other options disappearing, it is politically tempting to finance tax cuts by turning over to the states many of the social programs…that have become the responsibility of the national government."[35]

The Future of Federalism

During recent decades, state governments have undergone a major transformation. Most have improved their governmental structures, taken on greater roles in funding education and welfare, launched programs to help distressed cities, expanded their tax bases by allowing citizens to deduct their state and local taxes from the national income tax, and assumed greater roles in maintaining homeland security and in fighting corporate corruption.

After the civil rights revolution of the 1960s, segregationists feared that national officials would work for racial integration. Thus, they praised local government, emphasized the dangers of centralization, and argued that the protection of civil rights was not a proper function of the national government. As one political scientist observed, "Federalism has a dark history to overcome. For nearly 200 years, states' rights have been asserted to protect slavery, segregation, and discrimination."[36]

Today, the politics of federalism, even with respect to civil rights, is more complicated than in the past. The national government is not necessarily more sympathetic to the claims of minorities than state or city governments are. Rulings on same-sex marriages and "civil unions" by state courts interpreting their state constitutions have extended more protection for these rights than has the Supreme Court's interpretation of the U.S. Constitution. Other states, however, are passing legislation that would eliminate such protections, and opponents are pressing for a constitutional amendment to bar same-sex marriages.

The national government is not likely to retreat to a more passive role. Indeed, international terrorism, the wars in Afghanistan and Iraq, and rising deficits have substantially altered the underlying economic and social conditions that generated the demand for federal action. In addition to such traditional challenges as helping people find jobs and preventing inflation and depressions—which still require national action—combating terrorism and surviving in a global economy based on the information explosion, e-commerce, and advancing technologies have added countless new issues to the national agenda.

Most American citizens have strong attachments to our federal system—in the abstract. They remain loyal to their states and show a growing skepticism about the national government. Yet, evidence suggests the anti-Washington sentiment "is 3,000 miles wide but only a few miles deep."[37] The fact is that we are pragmatists: We appear to prefer federal–state–local power sharing and are prepared to use whatever levels of government are necessary to meet our needs and new challenges.[38]

Federalism can be a source of great reward for the people, especially when it allows states to lead the nation in creating new programs to address problems such as global warming and health care access. If the people cannot move the national government toward action, they can always push their state and local governments. By giving them different leverage points to make a difference, the Constitution guarantees that government *is* by the people.

Federalism can also be a source of enormous frustration, especially when national and state governments disagree on basic issues such as civil rights and liberties. This is when the people need to step forward not as citizens of their states but as citizens of the nation as a whole. Even as they influence their state and local governments, the people must understand they have a national voice that often needs to be heard.

CHAPTER **SUMMARY**

1.1 Interpret the definitions of federalism, and assess the advantages and disadvantages of the American system of federalism.

A federal system is one in which the constitution divides powers between the central government and lower-level governments such as states or provinces. But, over time, there has been support for different balances between state and government power such as the shift from dual federalism to marble cake federalism. The federal system in the United States does protect us from tyranny, permit local variation in policy, and encourage experimentation, but it comes at the cost of greater complexity, conflict, and difficulty in determining exactly which level of government is responsible for providing which goods and services that citizens might demand.

1.2 Differentiate the powers the Constitution provides to national and state governments.

The Constitution provides three types of powers to the national and state governments: delegated powers to the national government, reserve powers for the states, and concurrent powers that the national and state

governments share. Beyond delegated powers, the national government also has implied powers under the necessary and proper clause and inherent powers during periods of war and national crisis.

The national government's power over the states stems primarily from several constitutional pillars: the national supremacy clause, the war powers, its powers to regulate commerce among the states to tax and spend, and its power to do what Congress thinks is necessary and proper to promote the general welfare and to provide for the common defense. These constitutional pillars have permitted tremendous expansion of the functions of the national government.

1.3 Assess the role of the national courts in defining the relationship between the national and state governments, and evaluate the positions of decentralists and centralists.

The national courts umpire the division of power between the national and state governments. The Marshall Court, in decisions such as *Gibbons* v. *Ogden* and *McCulloch* v. *Maryland,* asserted the power of the national government over the states and promoted a national economic common market. These decisions also reinforced the supremacy of the national government over the states.

Today, debates about federalism are less often about its constitutional structure than about whether action should come from the national or the state and local levels. Recent Supreme Court decisions favor a decentralist position and signal shifts in the Court's interpretation of the constitutional nature of our federal system.

1.4 Analyze the budget as a tool of federalism, and evaluate its impact on state and local governments.

The major instruments of national intervention in state programs have been various kinds of financial grants-in-aid, of which the most prominent are

categorical-formula grants, project grants, and block grants. The national government also imposes federal mandates and controls activities of state and local governments by other means.

1.5 Evaluate the current relationship between the national and state governments and the future challenges for federalism.

The national government has grown dramatically throughout the past 200 years. Its budget dwarfs many state budgets combined. As it has grown, the national government has asked states to do more on its behalf. States have pressed back against the national government, however, and continue to fight for their authority to use powers that are reserved for them under the Constitution.

CHAPTER **SELF-TEST**

1.1 Interpret the definitions of federalism, and assess the advantages and disadvantages of the American system of federalism.

1. Match each term with its appropriate definition:

a. Dual federalism	i. The power of the national government is limited in favor of the broad powers reserved to the states
b. Cooperative federalism	ii. All levels of government are engaged in a variety of policy areas, without rigid divisions between governmental jurisdictions
c. Marble cake federalism	iii. Local governments, state governments, and the national government offer various "packages" of taxes and services, and citizens can choose which package they like best
d. Competitive federalism	iv. A system that requires intergovernmental support to deliver goods and services to the people
e. Permissive federalism	v. Limited powers are given to the national government, while the rest are retained by the states; the Supreme Court resolves disputes between the two
f. New federalism	vi. Power is shared between the state and national governments, but the national government determines what powers are given to the states

2. Canada has a central government in Ottawa, the nation's capital, along with ten provinces and three territories, each of which has its own government. According to Canada's constitution, both the provinces and the central government have powers to tax and regulate individual citizens. Which type of government best describes Canada?

a. A unitary state
b. A cooperative federalist state
c. A confederation
d. A territorial union

3. Federalism affords five benefits to its citizens. List each benefit along with a sentence or two that describes it.

1.2 Differentiate the powers the Constitution provides to national and state governments.

4. Determine whether the following powers are delegated to the national government, reserved for the states, or shared by both:
a. Power to establish courts
b. Power to tax citizens and businesses
c. Express powers stated in the Constitution
d. Power to oversee primary and elementary education
e. Inherent powers to present a united front to foreign powers

5. In one paragraph, explain the national supremacy article and discuss its consequences for state and local governments.

6. Create a diagram showing the relationships among *express, implied, inherent, reserved,* and *concurrent* powers.

1.3 Assess the role of the national courts in defining the relationship between the national and state governments, and evaluate the positions of decentralists and centralists.

7. In a few sentences, discuss the "constitutional counter-revolution" instigated by Chief Justice William Rehnquist and continued by Chief Justice John Roberts.

8. Discuss *McCulloch* v. *Maryland* and the reasons for its importance to federalism.

9. Write a persuasive essay appraising whether the balance of governmental power should lean more toward either

the national government or the states. Note the main arguments of both centralists and decentralists, and then refute the arguments of the side you disagree with.

1.4 Analyze the budget as a tool of federalism, and evaluate its impact on state and local governments.

10. Give an example of a program funded by (1) a *categorical-formula grant*, (2) a *project grant*, and (3) a *block grant*.

11. Identify which of the following is an example of a *federal mandate*:
    a. The New York state legislature passes a law requiring all New York school teachers to spend ten hours a year learning new teaching techniques.
    b. Congress passes a law requiring all coal plants in the United States to reduce their carbon emissions by 30 percent by 2015.
    c. The Supreme Court upholds a law requiring teenage women to get parental permission before having an abortion.

d. The Federal Emergency Management Agency sends funds from the national government to help clean up after a tornado.

12. Explain why unfunded mandates can cause problems.

1.5 Evaluate the current relationship between the national and state governments and the future challenges for federalism.

13. Write an essay that explains the reasons for the growth of the national government since the founding and that outlines the pressures that exist today that encourage further expansion of the national government.

14. Analyze the arguments for and against turning over to the states many of the economic and social programs that have become the responsibility of the national government, and write a persuasive essay that advocates one of these positions.

Answers to selected questions: 1. a. i; b. iv; c. ii; d. iii; e. vi; f. v. 2. b 4. a. both; b. both; c. national; d. states; e. national 11. b

---

mypoliscilab™ EXERCISES

Apply what you learned in this chapter on MyPoliSciLab.

📖—**Read** on **mypoliscilab.com**

    eText: Chapter 1

✔—**Study** and **Review** on **mypoliscilab.com**

    Pre-Test
    Post-Test
    Chapter Exam
    Flashcards

👁—**Watch** on **mypoliscilab.com**

    Video: The Real ID
    Video: Water Wars
    Video: Proposition 8

❋—**Explore** on **mypoliscilab.com**

    Simulation: You Are a Federal Judge
    Simulation: You Are a Restaurant Owner
    Comparative: Comparing Federal and Unitary Systems
    Timeline: Federalism and the Supreme Court
    Visual Literacy: Federalism and Regulations

KEY **TERMS**

federalism, p. 8	**commerce clause,** p. 15	**national supremacy,** p. 19
unitary system, p. 9	**federal mandate,** p. 16	**preemption,** p. 19
confederation, p. 9	**reserve powers,** p. 16	**centralists,** p. 21
delegated (express) powers, p. 14	**concurrent powers,** p. 16	**decentralists,** p. 21
implied powers, p. 14	**full faith and credit clause,** p. 18	**states' rights,** p. 22
necessary and proper clause, p. 14	**extradition,** p. 18	**devolution revolution,** p. 22
inherent powers, p. 14	**interstate compact,** p. 18	

ADDITIONAL **RESOURCES**

FURTHER READING

SAMUEL H. BEER, *To Make a Nation: The Rediscovery of American Federalism* (Harvard University Press, 1993).

MICHAEL BURGESS, *Comparative Federalism Theory and Practice* (Routledge, 2006).

CENTER FOR THE STUDY OF FEDERALISM, *The Federalism Report* (published quarterly by Temple University; this publication notes research, books and articles, and scholarly conferences).

CENTER FOR THE STUDY OF FEDERALISM, *Publius: The Journal of Federalism* (published quarterly by Temple University; one issue each year is an "Annual Review of the State of American Federalism"; Web site is www.lafayette.edu/~publius).

TIMOTHY J. CONLAN, *From New Federalism to Devolution: Twenty-Five Years of Intergovernmental Reforms* (Brookings Institution Press, 1998).

DANIEL J. ELAZAR AND **JOHN KINCAID,** EDS., *The Covenant Connection: From Federal Theology to Modern Federalism* (Lexington Books, 2000).

NEIL C. MCCABE, ED., *Comparative Federalism in the Devolution Era* (Rowman & Littlefield, 2002).

PIETRO NIVOLA, *Tense Commandments: Federal Prescriptions and City Problems* (Brookings Institution Press, 2002).

JOHN T. NOONAN, *Narrowing the Nation's Power: The Supreme Court Sides with the States* (University of California Press, 2002).

WILLIAM H. RIKER, *The Development of American Federalism* (Academic Press, 1987).

DENISE SCHEBERLE, *Federalism and Environmental Policy: Trust and the Politics of Implementation* (Georgetown University Press, 2004).

KEVIN SMITH, ED., *State and Local Government, 2008–2009* (CQ Press, 2008).

CARL VAN HORN, ED., *The State of the States*, 4th ed. (CQ Press, 2008).

WEB SITES

www.OPM.gov The national government's Web site for all information on the civil service system. It contains the Factbook of basic demographic information on every federal employee.

www.USAjobs.gov The national government's Web site listing all available jobs. Also provides application information and online application forms.

www.USASpending.gov The national government's summary of all spending activity. Includes charts and graphs on overall spending trends and amounts of funding dedicated to specific programs.

www.ourpublicservice.org The Partnership for Public Service Web site. The Partnership is dedicated to improving the national government's workforce.

www.govexec.com The Web site for *Government Executive* magazine. The magazine provides a news stream on current news affecting the national bureaucracy.

State and Local Politics

On May 19, 2009, voters in California went to the polls for a special election. Like nearly every state, California's budget was running large deficits ($25 billion) because of the national economic recession. The Democratically controlled legislature had passed a budget in February 2009, which Republican Governor Arnold Schwarzenegger had signed, that contained several proposals to manage this crisis. However, that budget depended on voters approving constitutional amendments on how the state collects and distributes revenue. Thus, voters could endorse the actions of their elected officials or effectively scuttle the deal. This was literally government by the people. By overwhelming margins, voters defeated every proposed change except the largely symbolic one that prohibited the state from giving pay raises to the governor, legislators, or other state officials.

For those unfamiliar with California politics, this outcome might seem bizarre. Serious repercussions were at stake for the state—state workers faced unpaid furloughs or being fired; school teachers at every level faced larger classes, pay freezes or reductions, and substantial layoffs; and many government services, particularly those directed at California's neediest citizens, faced drastic cuts or elimination. From this crisis, a Democratic legislature and a Republican governor had crafted a deal that neither side loved, but that both sides could live with—the kind of political compromise that voters supposedly want when they complain about partisan bickering leading to gridlock. How could voters say "No" so emphatically to this compromise?

Those more familiar with California's political history, however, would tell you that this simply marked the most recent in a long line of ballot initiatives that have effectively tied the hands of state officials in dealing with budgetary matters. In 1978, for example, voters approved Proposition 13, which capped state property tax rates and required future increases in any state tax to receive a two-thirds majority in both legislative chambers. Voters have used other initiatives to tie a fixed percentage of the budget to education spending (1988). Add to this a 1933 provision requiring that a two-thirds majority in both chambers in the state legislature is needed to pass a budget, and you are left with a system where elected officials have little room to maneuver and where minorities can block nearly all attempts to change the fiscal situation.

The situation in California is not entirely unique, as states across the country face similar budgetary problems. However, no two states face exactly the same situation, and no two states have exactly the same set of rules and institutions in place to deal with policy problems. Some states have very professional state legislatures, whereas others have legislatures that meet part time and lack professional staff support. Some states have voter initiatives, while others do not. Some governors have strong veto and line-item veto powers, while others do not. Thus, a full understanding of the United States' political system requires exploring this variation across the states and how that shapes the way states respond to the very real policy problems facing their citizens.

Who Governs?

State and local governments flourished long before there was a national government. Indeed, the framers of our Constitution shaped the national government largely according to their practical experience with colonial and state governments. What happens today in state and local governments continues to influence the policies of the national government, and the national government and its policies have an important impact on local

LEARNING OBJECTIVE

2.1 Contrast the functions of federal, state, and local governments, and evaluate the theories of decision-making in local governments.

and state governments. The federal government, 50 state governments, and the more than 89,000 cities, counties, towns, villages, school districts, water control districts, and other local governments all interact to govern and make policy for the country.

The Role of State and Local Governments

The national government has become the driving force behind the nation's economic strength and security. It assumes major responsibility for protecting civil rights, fighting inflation and unemployment, regulating economic sectors, funding scientific research, and subsidizing weaker sectors of the economy. The national government also operates some of the nation's largest social programs, such as Social Security, Medicare, student loans and grants, and various forms of food and nutritional assistance. It funds recovery efforts after natural disasters, it dominates issues of international trade and relations, and it exercises exclusive authority over matters of war and peace.

However, many of the critical domestic and economic issues facing the United States are confronted by state and local officials. State and local governments make most of the decisions about how schools are run, where roads and bridges are built, how land is used, and what social services are provided and to whom. They regulate our driving, our occupations, and our families (through marriage and divorce laws, among others). They decide, for the most part, what constitutes criminal behavior and how it should be charged, tried, and punished, and they have custody of more than 91 percent of the nation's nearly 2.4 million prison and jail inmates.[1]

State and local governments administer most of our laws and domestic programs, including many programs funded by the federal government. Through Medicaid and related programs, state governments provide health care coverage for approximately half of all poor children and a quarter of all poor adults, and, with federal assistance, they finance half of all nursing home expenditures and more than one-third of all births.[2] They pay for 79 percent of the total costs of building and maintaining our public highway system, and they are responsible for building and maintaining most of our bridges, water and sewage systems, and other elements of our nation's infrastructure.[3] State and local colleges and universities educate nearly three of every four students enrolled in higher education.[4]

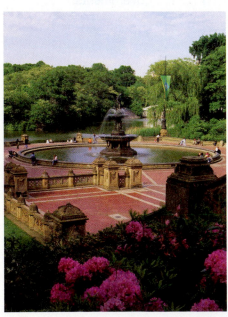
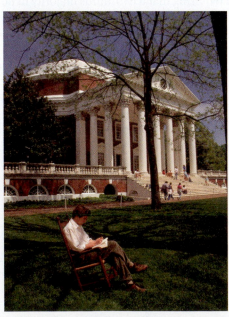

Some of the most beautiful buildings and parks in the United States were built with the support of state and local governments, including Central Park in New York City, the University of Virginia's original campus, and Pasadena City Hall. ■ *Are you surprised by the amount and variety of services provided by state and local governments? Why or why not?*

State and local governments are a very large part of our economy. The nation's more than 89,000 state and local governments spent slightly more than $2 trillion in 2008, which equals approximately 14 percent of the United States' gross domestic product (GDP).[5] (GDP is a good measure of the size of the country's economy; it measures the total market value of all final goods and services produced in the nation.) That is less than the federal government's expenditures of nearly $3 trillion in 2008, which were approximately 21 percent of GDP that year. State and local expenditures as a percentage of national GDP have steadily grown during the last 30 years, while federal spending has held steady or slightly declined,[6] although the massive federal spending in 2009 and 2010 in response to the recession runs counter to this trend. The critical point to remember is that state and local government spending combined has nearly the same total impact on our country's economy as does that of the national government.

State and local governments employ more than 19 million people, which is slightly more than seven times the 2.7 million civilians the federal government employs.[7] This ratio has increased in recent decades as the federal government has downsized, while state and local governments have grown. Most state and local employees work in education (10.9 million), hospitals (1.1 million), police protection (997,000), and corrections (743,000).[8] In fact, from 2001 onward, state and local governments have employed more workers than the entire manufacturing sector.

As these many functions suggest, state and local governments deal more directly with the average person than the national government does. The points at which people come into contact with government services and officials most often relate to schools, streets and highways, parks and playgrounds, police and fire protection, zoning, and health care—activities that are typically managed by state and local officials. However, even in these areas, the mix of national, state, and local programs and responsibilities is such that it is often hard to isolate what each level of government is doing. State and local employees are the face of government for many of us—but that face may be responsible for complying with rules and carrying out programs established by multiple levels of government.

Who Has the Power?

Every government system is part of a larger social system. Each one operates in the context of a particular economic system, class structure, racial and religious differences, political party structure, and set of lifestyles. The diversity of social systems surrounding state and local governments, along with their complex interconnections with each other and the federal government, affect how these many different state and local governments recognize problems, manage conflict, make decisions about what actions to take, and benefit some people and institutions and not others.

How can we grasp the complex operations and problems of so many state and local governments? We can do so by focusing on the core components of democratic governance: *citizen participation, liberty, constitutional checks and balances, representation,* and *responsible leadership.* Further, we can address several questions that throw light on all these problems: *Who governs?* How much influence or control is in the hands of the business community? Does political power gravitate toward a small number of people? If so, who are these people? Do they work closely together, or do they oppose each other? Do the same people or factions shape the agenda for public debate and dominate all decision making? Or do some sets of leaders decide certain questions and leave other questions to other leaders or influences?

In 1924, two sociologists from Columbia University, Robert and Helen Lynd, decided to study a typical U.S. city as though they were anthropologists. For two years, they lived in Muncie, Indiana—at that time, a city of 38,000 residents. They asked questions and watched how people made their living, raised their children, used their leisure time, and joined in civic and social associations. The Lynds reported that despite the appearance of democratic rule, a social and economic elite actually ran things.[9] Their work stimulated studies in all kinds of communities to find out whether

DECIDE Should States Exercise Authority over Climate Change Policies?

Many states have struggled over what, if anything, they should do to combat climate change, particularly because the federal government has done little in recent years to address or even recognize the problem.

In late 2007, the federal government denied a request from California to permit the state to implement its own law aimed at reducing greenhouse gas emissions from motor vehicles. The California law was stricter than relevant federal laws, and the federal law allowed California to set antipollution standards stronger than those of the federal government, if the federal Environmental Protection Agency (EPA) gave its approval. At least 16 other states were expected to adopt California's standards if the EPA granted the state a "waiver."

However, the head of the EPA denied California's request. He argued that it was better to adopt a unified federal standard than a state-by-state approach. A lobbyist for automobile manufacturers agreed and said that a "patchwork quilt of inconsistent and competing fuel economy programs at the state level would only have created confusion, inefficiency, and uncertainty for automakers and consumers."

What do you think? Should states be allowed to create stricter laws to help regulate climate change? What arguments would you make for and against such an idea?

THINKING IT THROUGH

This question raises many issues about who ought to govern efforts in the United States to deal with climate change. Those who support state discretion say global warming has different effects on different localities. California may be especially vulnerable because of its reliance on snowpack for water storage, its long coastline, its agricultural industry, and its severe air-quality problems. By contrast, some northern inland states may see gains from climate change—for instance, by having longer warm seasons for agriculture and recreation. Also, although the economies of some states, such as Michigan, depend on industries such as motor vehicle manufacturing that would be greatly affected by the proposed regulations, the economies of other states, such as California, are not so dependent on them.

Others claim that allowing California and other states to write their own emissions laws means some groups (such as motor vehicle manufacturers) are poorly represented in political processes even though they are strongly affected by the state's decisions. If every state set its own standards, it would make producing cars more expensive and distributing cars across states more complicated, which may lead to California regulations becoming the national standard. These opponents argue that such regulations should be made at the national level, where policy decisions are more likely to reflect the wider, more pluralistic array of competing interests found in the United States as a whole. In response, advocates for state control may say that this pluralism at the federal level contributes to political gridlock and the absence of vigorous and effective policies.

California's state government has played a leading role in climate change and other environmental issues, in part because its environmental problems are so severe. This picture shows Los Angeles.

Critical Thinking Questions

1. Should states have discretion over environmental policies, or should the federal government have exclusive control over efforts to deal with this global issue? Why?

2. If states dominated climate change policies in the United States, which groups or interests do you think would be advantaged, and which would be disadvantaged, when compared with a situation in which the federal government dominated policies?

power is concentrated in the hands of a few people, is dispersed among many, or operates in some other way.

Relying on a mix of research methods, social scientists since the Lynds' time have studied patterns of power in communities and arrived at a variety of findings. Floyd Hunter, a sociologist who analyzed Atlanta in the 1950s, found a relatively small and stable group of top policy makers drawn largely from the business class. This elite group operated through secondary leaders who sometimes modified policy, but the power of the elite was almost always important.[10] Clarence Stone's seminal study of Atlanta, *Regime Politics*, reaffirmed much of what Hunter first uncovered.[11] In contrast, Robert Dahl and his graduate students at Yale University studied New Haven, Connecticut, and concluded that although some people had a great deal of influence, there was no permanent group of elites. Instead, they found shifting coalitions of leaders who sometimes disagreed among themselves but who kept in mind what the public would accept when making decisions.[12]

Rule by a Few or Rule by the Many?

One group of investigators, chiefly sociologists such as Hunter, have been concerned with **social stratification** in the political system—how politics is affected by divisions among socioeconomic groups or classes in a community. These social scientists assume that political influence is a function of social stratification. They try to find out who governs particular communities by asking various citizens to identify the people who are most influential. Then they study those influential people to determine their social characteristics, their roles in decision making, and the interrelations among them and between them and the rest of the citizens. Using this technique, they find that the upper socioeconomic groups make up the **power elite.** Elected political leaders are subordinate to that elite, and the major conflicts within the community are between the upper and the lower socioeconomic classes.

In contrast, other investigators argue that the evidence of a power elite is merely a reflection of the research methods used by those scholars and the assumptions they made about social stratification. Instead of studying the activities of those thought to have "clout," these critics insist, we should study how decisions are actually made.

Researchers conducting *community power* studies that analyze the making of decisions usually find a relatively open, pluralistic power structure. Some people do have more influence than others, but that influence is shared among many people and tends to be limited to particular issues and areas. For example, those who decide how the public schools are run may have little influence over economic policies. These studies also find that, in the fight for influence, competing elites often appeal to the public, especially voters, and thus draw larger groups into local politics. Importantly, these studies find that local governments tend to be nonresponsive to those groups of citizens who are not engaged at all in local politics—those who are uninformed, apathetic, and do not vote.[13] Furthermore, scholars have also noted that political activism by citizens alone may not be enough to get local governments to respond to their needs. Rather, it often takes full political incorporation of representatives from the group to generate meaningful policy change.[14]

social stratification
Divisions in a community among socioeconomic groups or classes.

power elite
A group composed of community, business, and other leaders who determine public policy or block changes in policy without themselves necessarily holding office.

Members of Dover C.A.R.E.S. (Citizens Actively Reviewing Educational Strategies) in Dover, Pennsylvania, examine a list of school board candidates. The group formed in response to the school board's decision to require biology teachers to read a statement in class saying that Darwin's theory of evolution is not fact and that alternate theories exist, including "intelligent design."
■ *Who should be responsible for determining what is taught in schools? What are the arguments for or against citizen groups, school boards, or local governments making these decisions?*

Comparing power elite and community power studies highlights the fact that how we ask questions often influences the answers we get. If we ask highly visible and actively involved citizens for their opinions of who is powerful, we find they often name a small number of people as the real brokers of power. But if we study dozens of local events and decisions, we typically find that a variety of people are active, usually different people in different policy areas—a theory called **pluralism.**

Other studies of local politics suggest that local values, traditions, and the structure of governmental organizations affect which issues get on the local agenda.[15] Tobacco, mining, or steel interests may be so dominant in some areas that tax, regulation, environmental, or job safety policies are kept off the local policy agenda for fear of offending the "powers that be." Those "powers" may indeed go to great lengths to prevent what they deem to be adverse policies. Defenders of the status quo can mobilize power resources in such a way that nondecisions may be more important than decisions. In effect, these researchers tell us not only to study who governs but also to study the procedures and rules of the game. They urge us to determine which groups or interests would gain and which would lose if certain decisions are not made or even seriously considered.[16]

On many economic policy matters, local corporations and business elites have input. Studies of cities in Michigan and Georgia, employing refined and contextual analyses of political decision making, concluded that business elites are indeed important but are not necessarily the controlling factor in city governance:

> There is, then, no controlling hand in community politics. No conspiracy of business and government exists. Business interests do not invariably dominate government policy even where a single industry dominates the community. However, the giant industrial companies do provide the backdrop against which the public policy process operates in the industrial city. They are always there, seldom intervening in specific policy matters but never far from the calculations of policy makers.[17]

In summary, studies of states and communities reveal that political power is often highly unequal, and that local traditions, institutions, and social and economic factors frequently constrain what state and local governments can do. However, the studies also find pluralism and change, as different elites dominate different issues at different times. Also, conflicts often spill out and engage larger publics when competing elites seek to gain allies and legitimacy for their positions.

Influences on State and Local Governments

LEARNING OBJECTIVE

2.2 Analyze the activities and influence of interest groups and lobbyists at the state and local levels.

Because state and local governments are powerful institutions in the United States, it is important to understand what affects their actions. Similar to the federal level, individuals, parties, interest groups, elections, the beliefs and skills of political leaders, and media coverage can exert significant influence over state and local governments, although their importance varies greatly across different governments and types of government actions.

Who Are the Constituents?

Every state and local community is different. A town of 1,800 residents in rural Nebraska and a city of millions such as New York City present their elected leaders with very different opportunities and obstacles. California has more than 36 million residents, whereas 29 states have fewer than 5 million each. It is not only a question of size, either—many states and cities serve tremendously diverse populations, whereas others have populations that are much more homogeneous. For example, the population of Asian descent in California alone exceeds the total population of more than 26 states. States and localities also show tremendous differences in how urbanized they are, what industries they have, what natural resources they have, and what geographic

pluralism
A theory of government that holds that open, multiple, and competing groups can check the asserted power of any one group.

Of the People

The Growing Diversity of State Populations

The U.S. Census Bureau estimates for 2008 showed significant changes in both the number and location of minority residents. The percentage of whites declined from 76 percent of the population in 1990 to 66 percent in 2008, whereas the percentage of Hispanics increased from 9 to 15 percent, African-Americans from 12 to 13 percent, and Asian–Pacific Islanders from 3 to 4.5 percent. Nearly 2 percent of residents refer to themselves as members of two or more races.

The growing minority population in the United States is not equally distributed across the states and cities. Approximately three-quarters of all Hispanics live in the West or South, accounting for a quarter of the population in the West and 12 percent of the population in the South. In turn, more than half of all African-Americans live in the South, making up 20 percent of the total population; whereas half of the Asian–Pacific Islander population live in only three states (California, New York, and Hawaii), and two-fifths of all Native Americans live in the West.

Although Hispanics are counted as a single minority group, nearly 60 percent of Hispanics identified themselves in the 2000 census as Mexican, 10 percent as Puerto Rican, and 4 percent as Cuban. Similarly, the Asian–Pacific Islander population includes Asian Indians, Chinese, Filipinos, Japanese, Koreans, Native Hawaiians, and Samoans; Native Americans include members of American Indian tribes, including Cherokee, Navajo, Latin American Indian, Choctaw, Sioux, and Chippewa—as well as Eskimo.

CRITICAL THINKING QUESTIONS

1. As racial and ethnic "minority" groups become majorities in more and more states, do you expect these changes to increase or decrease political divisions in the United States?

2. What kinds of public policies might be most affected by the growing diversity of state populations?

Top Ten States by Minority Population in 2008	
Hawaii	75%
New Mexico	58%
California	58%
Texas	53%
Nevada	43%
Maryland	42%
Georgia	42%
Arizona	42%
Mississippi	41%
New York	40%

SOURCE: U.S. Census Bureau, *Statistical Abstract of the United States: 2010* (U.S. Government Printing Office, 2010), Table 19, http://www.census.gov/compendia/statab/2010/tables/10s0019.pdf.

advantages and obstacles they face. They also have different political cultures and political histories that influence politics.[18] And, as this and the remaining chapters will make clear, they all operate within a different set of political institutions. All of this diversity provides the backdrop for how politics and policy making unfolds across states and localities.

The Maze of Interests

A wide range of organized special-interest groups are typically very important at the state and local levels. Even industrial Rhode Island has farm organizations, and rural Wyoming has trade unions. Influential economic pressure groups and political action committees, organized to raise and disburse campaign funds to candidates for public office, operate in the states much as they do nationally. They try to build up the membership of their organizations, they lobby at state capitols and city halls, they educate and organize voters, and they support their political friends in office while opposing their enemies. They also face the same internal problems all groups face: maintaining unity, dealing with subgroups that break off in response to special needs, and balancing democracy with discipline.

One great difference, however, is that group interests can be concentrated and highly influential in states and localities, whereas their strength tends to be diluted in the national government. No single industry or business runs things in Washington, D.C., but in some states and localities, certain interests dominate because they represent the social and economic majorities of the area or because many people rely on a particular industry or corporation for their jobs and livelihood.

The range and variety of these groups give politics in each individual state its own special flavor, excitement, and challenge: auto unions and manufacturers in Michigan, corn and hog farmers in Iowa, gas and oil companies in Texas and Louisiana, tobacco farmers in North Carolina and Virginia, poultry growers and processors in Arkansas, Microsoft in Washington State, the banking and finance industries in Delaware and New York, wineries in California, and tourism in Utah. If there is one group that is present in nearly every state and locality, it is the various public school teachers' unions and associations.

Differences among groups and group representation are often reflected in state policies. State cigarette tax rates vary widely, from $2.70 per pack in New Jersey to $0.07 per pack in South Carolina.[19] Lower cigarette taxes are found among other southeastern and border states, such as Virginia, North Carolina, Tennessee, and Kentucky, where smoking is more common and tobacco farming is economically and politically significant. High cigarette taxes are found among states in the Northeast and Northwest, where neither of these conditions is true.[20]

Still, we should not exaggerate the power of interest groups. Because all groups have internal divisions, we have to be cautious about lumping all workers, all businesspeople, all teachers, or all Hispanics together. The union movement is sometimes sharply divided among truckers, building trades people, machinists, and auto workers. The business community is often divided between big industrial, banking, and commercial firms on the one hand and small merchants on the other. Hispanic voters with different family backgrounds—some more closely associated with Cuba, some with Puerto Rico, and some with Mexico—may also express very different political preferences.

Business interests are inevitably active in city and county politics and policy making. As one study of Atlanta found, the business elite is rarely a passive or reluctant partner in setting local priorities. "Atlanta's postwar political experience is a story of active business-elite efforts to make the most of their economic and organizational resources in setting the terms on which civic cooperation occurs."[21] Businesses everywhere depend on local governments for parking facilities, good roads and transportation, safety, urban renovations, and much more. Business elites become active in long-range community planning, are keenly interested in who gets elected, and are ever watchful of changes in taxes.

Another type of interest group intimately concerned with public policy is the professional association. States license barbers, beauticians, architects, lawyers, doctors,

Boston's "Big Dig" completely changed the way drivers got around the city by burying a major highway in a 3.5-mile tunnel under downtown. It was the largest urban construction project in modern history, cost $14.6 billion, and took 30 years to complete.
■ *What interest groups are likely active in planning and executing projects like this one?*

teachers, accountants, dentists, and many other occupational groups. At the statehouse, you will find lobbying representatives from the Beauticians Aid Association, the Funeral Directors and Embalmers Association, the Institute of Dry Cleaning, and the Association of Private Driver-Training Schools. Such lobbies are naturally interested in the nature of the regulatory laws and the makeup of boards that do the regulating. Stiffening licensing requirements for physicians will decrease the supply of new doctors, for example, and thereby raise the incomes of those in practice. Bar associations, for the same reason, closely monitor licensing standards for the legal profession and the appointment of state and local judges.

Today, other groups of citizens are also likely to organize to influence decisions in the state capital: those who are pro-life and those who are pro-choice; those who support laws permitting same-sex marriages and those who oppose such unions; those who want to keep illegal immigrants out of their state and businesspeople who rely on such workers; and those who want more wind farms to reduce reliance on nonrenewable energy and those who oppose them as damaging blights on our coasts and mountains. Environmental and antismoking groups; animal rights activists; and prison guards are also well organized. Antitax groups have also been common and have re-emerged as part of the so-called "Tea Party" movement that began in 2009.

Lobbyists at the Statehouse

Many businesses, especially large corporations, employ lobbyists, public relations specialists, political consultants, or law firms to represent them.[22] For a fee, lobbyists push desired bills through the legislature or block unwanted ones. This kind of activity again raises the question of who has clout or who governs. Clearly, those who can hire skilled lobbyists and other experts to shape the public agenda often wield more influence than unorganized citizens, who rarely follow state and regional governmental decision making. Public interest, religious, senior citizen, and other groups also have lobbyists, many of whom are not highly paid.

Lobbyists are present in every state capital, and they are there to guide through the legislature a small handful of bills their organization wants passed or to stop those their organization wants defeated.[23] Some observers believe that lobbyists have freer rein in state legislatures than they do in the U.S. Congress. Although there is little direct evidence either for or against this claim, there are a few reasons why we might assume it to be true. Compared with most members of Congress, state legislators typically have few professional staff and have shorter electoral careers, so they may rely more on lobbyists for information about public policies, problems, and political risks and opportunities. Also, lobbying regulations in most states are more relaxed than at the federal level.[24] Media coverage of state politics is often weak and spotty in many states, especially when compared with the attention focused on national politics in Washington, D.C.

Some of these factors may be changing. In response to some prominent scandals,[25] several legislatures enacted comprehensive financial disclosure laws, and today, most state governments are more open, professional, and accountable than in the past.[26] Now five states ban lobbyists from contributing to campaigns at any time, and 22 states prohibit contributions during a legislative session. Four states ban gifts of any sort to state officials—this is

The Cape Wind energy company has proposed building a wind farm in Nantucket Sound off the coast of Massachusetts. Interest groups, most notably the Alliance to Protect Nantucket Sounds, have fought to stop this project, citing environmental concerns. ■ *Should interest groups and lobbyists at the state level have the same regulations as those at the federal level? Why or why not?*

sometimes called the "no cup of coffee" rule—and approximately half of the states prohibit gifts to public employees above a certain monetary value, ranging from $3 (Iowa) to $500 (Texas).[27]

We have already noted that some states have diverse populations and economies, while others have a more limited range of central interests. In most states, many organizations compete, and in no state does only one organization control legislative politics. Political scientist Diane Blaire writes, "It is still true that ordinarily those with greater economic resources, greater numbers, and higher status have far more impact than those who lack these attributes. Nevertheless, an increasingly complex economy has produced many more actors in the political system, and especially when there is division among the economic elite, some of the lesser voices can be heard."[28]

Not to be overlooked is the growing number of groups and media outlets that view themselves as "watchdogs" of the public policy process. State PIRGs (Public Interest Research Groups, often staffed by students or recent college graduates), the League of Women Voters, Common Cause, and various citizens' groups regularly monitor state politics for questionable fund-raising or lobbying practices. Their "watchdog" efforts are sometimes aided by reporters who cover state capitals.

Participation Patterns in Local Government

LEARNING OBJECTIVE

2.3 Assess the level and consistency of involvement of the major participants in local communities.

Citizens feel closer to local governments than to the more remote national government in Washington, D.C. When the public was surveyed regarding its confidence in different governments in 2006, 69 percent of the respondents said they had a "great deal" or a "fair amount" of trust in local governments, compared with 65 percent for state governments, and only 54 percent for the federal government.[29] These numbers have all dropped more recently. A 2009 Gallup poll showed only 51 percent trusted state governments a "great deal" or a "fair amount."[30] A 2010 report by the Pew Center on the States demonstrated public confidence in the national government had reached all-time lows, with fewer than one in four Americans saying they can trust the government in Washington.[31]

Nonetheless, citizens generally take less interest in, vote less often in, and are less informed about their local governments than about the national government. Although decisions about where to locate a garbage dump or a prison or how to deal with police brutality can arouse considerable attention, most of the time, local governments are preoccupied with relatively noncontroversial routine matters, such as keeping the roads in shape, providing fire and police services, attracting businesses that can create more jobs, or applying for state and federal financial assistance. In addition, the news media devotes considerably more time and resources to reporting on national news events and national political leaders than they do state and local issues.

Local communities want to keep their tax rates down and promote their cities as "nice places" in which to live, work, and raise families. Mayors and city officials generally try to avoid controversy and criticism that will divide a community. Although they do not always succeed, they go to considerable lengths to be reasonable and work for the good of the community. Few aggressively seek to alter the status quo. They do not, as a rule, try to promote equality by redistributing various resources to needier citizens. **Redistributive policies** are programs to shift wealth or benefits from one segment of the population to another, usually from the rich to the poor. Local officials tend to believe that this is the task of national or state authorities—if they think it should be done at all. Typically, they say their communities do not have the funds for such programs. They might add, "Go see the governor," or "Go talk to your member of Congress." This may be good advice because various

redistributive policies
Governmental tax and social programs that shift wealth or benefits from one segment of the population to another, often from the rich to the poor.

programs (educational loans, unemployment compensation, disability assistance, and so on) explicitly designed to help the less fortunate are administered at the state or federal level.

Neighborhood groups sometimes become engaged in protecting their neighborhoods and petitioning for improvements. One concern that often activates them is the possibility that "undesirable" facilities may be located in their neighborhood, such as drug treatment clinics, prisons, dumps, or homeless shelters. Although attendance at local government meetings is usually low, the announcement of a landfill or a prison construction project often stimulates the reaction that local officials call NIMBY, an acronym for "Not In My Back Yard!" This response can have the perverse effect of forcing facilities such as airports to remain in densely populated areas because it is too difficult to find alternative sites for them. Of course, sometimes the need for economic development trumps concerns about possibly undesirable facilities. For example, when President Obama announced a plan for sending military detainees held by the U.S. government at its Guantanamo Bay facility to an underutilized facility in Thomson, Illinois, local officials touted the nearly 3,000 jobs the move was expected to create for the local community.[32] Illinois's governor, Pat Quinn, reportedly suggested the move, knowing that region of his state faced an unemployment rate of more than 10 percent at the time.

The Role of Local Media

Most communities have only one newspaper (and associated Web site), and in small communities it is often only published once a week. Some newspapers and local radio and television stations do a good job of covering city and county politics, but this is the exception rather than the rule. Reporters assigned to cover local politics are often inexperienced, yet they provide the only news that citizens get about their city council or zoning board. Even the best of them have difficulty conveying the full complexities of what is going on in a column or two of newsprint.

Some local newspapers enjoy a cozy relationship with elected local officials. Sometimes, the owners or editors are social friends or golfing buddies of local officials. Friendships and mutual interests develop, and close scrutiny of what goes on in city hall takes a back seat to city boosterism. In effect, "newspapers boost their hometown, knowing that its prosperity and expansion aid their own. Harping on local

When Illinois Governor Quinn suggested housing Guantamano detainees at the Thomson Correctional Center's maximum security prison, he touted the jobs it would create. However, residents exhibited the "not in my backyard" reaction, opposing the proposal. ■ *How should state and local officials balance the inevitable trade-offs involved with any economic development policy?*

faults, investigating dirty politics, revealing unsavory scandals, and stressing governmental inefficiencies only provide readily available documentary material to competing cities."[33]

Editors and station managers recognize that their readers, viewers, or listeners are more interested in state or national news, and especially in sports, than in what is going on at municipal planning meetings or county commission sessions. Also, although we have dozens of ways to find out about Congress and the White House, we usually have fewer sources for stories about the mayor or sheriff or school board. Many local newspapers have gone out of business in recent decades, and the remaining papers and local TV stations often ignore local political and economic issues. Some local governments have established Web sites to make information more accessible to residents, but the quality of the sites varies greatly, and many are not very useful in helping citizens understand and participate in local government.[34]

Grassroots Apathy

Voter turnout in local elections is substantially lower on average than turnout in most state and national elections. Much of the difference in turnout stems from the fact that a large number of local governments hold elections separate from state and federal elections; turnout is much higher when cities and other local governments hold their elections at the same time when voters select governors or presidents. Also, many local elections are uncontested, and voting turnout is lower when no competition exists for some of the races on a particular ballot.[35]

Voter apathy about local politics may also depress turnout. Charter revision and taxation often galvanize only those directly affected by the new taxes or regulations. Even New England town meetings have difficulty getting people to participate—despite the fact that decisions made at these meetings have major consequences for local tax rates and the quality of the schools, the police force, and the parks and recreational areas. Thomas Jefferson once proclaimed the town meeting to be the noblest, wisest instrument yet devised for the conduct of public affairs, but today, most towns find that only a very small percentage of the population has the time, interest, or ability to participate in local government meetings.[36]

Although apathy may be widespread under most circumstances, issues emerge from time to time that draw intense public interest—and that increases participation in local governments. For instance, one study of Massachusetts town meetings found that although only 4 percent of citizens reported they attended all annual meetings during the previous five years, nearly three out of four citizens attended at least one of the meetings during the five-year period—probably meetings that dealt with controversial issues.[37] This level of participation would be high by national standards. Sometimes, local political processes even see citizen protests—mass demonstrations, economic boycotts, and even civil disorders—that make demands on government. People become politically active when certain issues become intense, especially issues they think will affect their families, property, and deeply held values, such as severe cuts in school budgets, sharp increases in taxes, the building of an "undesirable" facility (such as a "big box" store or extensive housing for low-income families). Most of the time, large groups of citizens may constitute less of a real, concrete presence in local government decision making than a threat to mobilize if and when officials make unpopular choices.

Civic Initiatives in Communities

Because participation at the local level is more limited, the impact an individual can have is likely even greater than at the state or national level. States such as Oregon and Minnesota seem to encourage a climate of innovation and civic enterprise, and a wider look at the United States finds buoyant, optimistic, creative problem solvers in nearly every corner of the nation. The Internet may make it easier for these "innovators" to network and share ideas.

By the People

Holding State Governments Accountable

We all want our state governments to perform well and operate efficiently, but how can we measure their performance and track their progress? The Government Performance report produced by the Pew Center on the States and *Governing* magazine graded all 50 states in how their governments manage themselves in four key areas: people, information, money, and infrastructure. States receive performance grades of A through F in each area, plus an overall grade. You can find the most recent report here: http://www.pewcenteronthestates.org/uploadedFiles/Grading-the-States-2008.pdf.

How does your state stack up compared to others? The overall national average was a B-. Three states—Utah, Virginia, and Washington—received the highest grade awarded (A-) for their innovations to manage

information about state services, retain state workers, and budget for short- and long-term needs. For example, Alabama has a single Web site where citizens can go to find information on all of the social services provided by the state (http://camellia.alabama.gov/default.aspx), and Washington produces six-year budget forecasts that are widely available and updated every quarter. States receiving low grades did not manage their resources well or lacked sufficient communication and transparency. Some state workers in Rhode Island are still working on typewriters rather than computers, and New Hampshire, which received the lowest grade awarded (a D+) ."has such weak data-sharing systems that it doesn't know how much it spends each month."*

States differ in how they manage their operations. However, studies like this of

the best and worst practices employed by states show citizens how their states are performing, and they provide opportunities for states to learn from each other. Find out whether your state makes the grade. Knowing what areas your state excels in and what areas it needs to improve is the first step to getting involved and making a difference.

CRITICAL THINKING QUESTIONS

1. How should citizens measure government performance? How do the factors we use reflect our priorities for government performance?

2. What can citizens do to encourage stronger and more efficient performance from their government?

* Pew Center on the States, "Grading the States, 2008" p. 27. http://www.pewcenteronthestates.org/uploadedFiles/Grading-the-States-2008.pdf.

Enterprising local activists have advocated and implemented cost-saving energy programs, environmental cleanup campaigns, recycling and solar energy initiatives, job training centers, AIDS prevention efforts, housing for the elderly, tutoring for the illiterate, housing for the poor, and hundreds of other problem-solving and opportunity-enhancing community efforts.[38] In almost every case, they create partnerships with elected officials at city hall, sometimes with the Urban League or Chamber of Commerce, and often with local foundations and business corporations.

Sometimes, it takes a tragedy to get community groups mobilized. Such an event happened in Boston when gang members burst into the funeral of a young man. "In the presence of the mourners, the gang killed one of those in attendance," writes the Reverend Eugene Rivers of the Azusa Christian Community:

> That brazen act told us we had to do more. Now. That young man's death galvanized us, and soon the Ten Point Coalition was reaching out to at-risk youth. Our mission was to pair the holy and the secular, to do whatever it took to save our kids. The black churches worked hand-in-hand with the schools, courts, police, and social service agencies. We called on anyone and everyone who had the means to help our children. We formed programs for teens, neighborhood watches, and patrols...We established ourselves in the neighborhood, standing on the same street corner where the drug dealers once stood. We tracked down the thieves, dealers, and gangs. We tried to give people a chance, but if they wouldn't take it, we staked our claim and ran them out of our neighborhood.[39]

The aftermath of the devastation produced by hurricanes Katrina and Rita in 2005 to the Gulf Coast also revealed the importance of community groups. Local governments varied greatly in their effectiveness in dealing with the disasters, but the consensus among close observers was that "nonprofit, community-based, and faith-based organizations as well as individual volunteers...responded to the rebuilding challenge beyond all expectation."[40]

Debates persist about how to solve social, economic, and racial problems in our large metropolitan areas. Some people contend that government cannot undertake this task and that private initiatives will be more effective. Others insist that state and local governments are best suited to deal with these challenges. Still others believe that imaginative public–private collaboration is needed to fashion the strategies and mobilize the resources needed to revive cities and bring about greater opportunity. Whatever the merits of such contending interpretations, it is clear that neighborhood organizations and spirited civic renewal are critical to the vitality of local government.[41]

Challenges for State and Local Governments

LEARNING **OBJECTIVE**

2.4 Evaluate the challenges facing state and local governments.

Most states and communities are confronting difficult times. People want better schools, a clean environment, and safe roads and bridges. Many of our inner-city governments and school systems are in financial distress. The cycle of poverty in many inner cities remains one of the greatest threats to the economic health of the country. Cities, though, usually cannot raise enough funds through local taxes to create jobs and to provide adequate educational opportunities and housing. Federal and state initiatives have attempted to create economic opportunities for inner-city residents. Community development banks, "empowerment zones," Head Start, charter schools, and national service (AmeriCorps) programs have all been tried in an attempt to bring residents of depressed inner cities into the economic mainstream. However, these efforts have been inadequate, and support for them must compete with other demands on financially pressed states and localities. Meanwhile, federal officials are proposing cuts in many of the domestic programs that aid state and local governments.[42]

The following central issues in state and local communities command the attention of the country. They vary depending on location, of course, but these urgent challenges are part of the unfinished business of a government by the people:

■ *People want more services but at the same time would like to see their taxes cut.* Voters in many states and communities have enacted spending limits that constrain growth in public budgets, yet state and local governments struggle with many long-run problems in raising revenues to pay for programs the public demands—problems such as shifts to Internet purchasing and the consumption of services rather than goods, trends that make it harder for state and local governments to collect sales taxes. On the spending side, states are further squeezed by hard-to-control increases in costs, such as health care and energy prices and pensions for retired government workers.[43]

■ *Intense political divisions over new immigrants exist in many communities.* As our nation has become more diverse, most U.S. citizens have learned to appreciate the strength that comes from multiple cultures and races, and many of our businesses have come to rely on immigrant labor, both legal and illegal. However, in many communities where foreign-born residents have settled in large numbers, longtime residents have resented the changing racial, linguistic, and ethnic composition of their communities and have pushed state and local officials to stem or even reverse the growth of immigrants. New immigration laws passed in Arizona in 2010 reignited a national debate on how all levels of government might address this problem.

■ *Much of the nation's infrastructure needs to be repaired or rebuilt.* The collapse of the Interstate 35W bridge in Minneapolis in 2007 and the failure of the levees in New Orleans in 2005 highlight the poor conditions of many of the nation's roads, highways, bridges, dams, levees, water and sewage systems, and other elements of our infrastructure. But the enormous cost of

Not all citizens are apathetic. These young people are spending their free time rehabilitating a community center. ■ *What, if any, responsibility do you think citizens have to their community?*

For the People

Improving Access to Information

Sometimes, the hardest part of interacting with a government is knowing where to start. States are using the Internet to help make that first step easier. States have made tremendous strides in providing their citizens with more information about their state's government and access to government agencies and officials. The state of Nebraska provides a good example. The official Web site of the state, http://www.nebraska.gov/, provides users with instant access for citizens, businesses, education, those relocating to the state, and tourists. From the main page, users can check on the status of their income tax refund, renew their license plates, or apply for financial aid to any of the state's colleges and universities. Citizens can also search the campaign contribution records for all public officials or track the use of federal funds received as part of the American Recovery and Reinvestment Act of 2009 (the federal stimulus program).

Another innovation is the link to what the state calls the Reference Desk, which advertises, "When you just can't find the answers…we can help." This link takes you to the Government Information Services of the Nebraska Library Commission. Among the features on this Web page is a live chat window where you can ask a librarian on staff any question you have, and the librarian will help you track down an answer. Inquiring with the Reference Desk about the history of the program generated a response within about two minutes reporting that the service has been available since 2006 and that it gets used daily. Efforts like this demonstrate how at least some states go the extra mile to try to serve their citizens.

CRITICAL THINKING QUESTIONS

1. In a state where citizens have easy access to information about government, which groups or interests do you think would be advantaged, and which would be disadvantaged?

2. How might the development of a Web site like Nebraska's help state and local governments address some of the current challenges they face that are discussed in this chapter?

---

repairs or replacements is well beyond the current fiscal capacities of state and local governments.

- *The costs of corrections and prisons have skyrocketed in recent years,* driven by the rapid growth of prison populations as well as the costs of caring for an aging population of prisoners. In 2007, nearly 7 percent of state expenditures went to corrections.[44] Many states are trying to cut costs with new policies and programs, including stronger efforts to divert inmates to rehabilitation facilities; "good-time" credits to low-risk offenders, who would then be allowed to shorten their prison terms; shorter sentences at the discretion of judges; more effective systems of parole and probation; and greater use of privately run (and often out-of-state) prison facilities.

- *Poverty in the inner cities persists.* We have extremes of rich and poor within metropolitan regions, and many feel that wealthier suburbs often turn their backs on the problems and poverty of the older cities. Indifference to these inequalities and lack of opportunities undermine a sense of community and fairness—and limit the nation's capacity to develop a skilled and internationally competitive workforce.

- *We need to guarantee the best possible education for all our young people.* Parents are demanding better education and more parental involvement. Communities have been experimenting with educational choice and competition, school vouchers, charter schools, expanded hours, and prekindergarten programs. Improving the public schools is necessary, but their resources and the salaries of teachers are often too low to attract and retain the best-qualified educators. Many states also object to the federal No Child Left Behind program as a costly and ineffective way of using standardized tests to improve the accountability and quality of schools.

- *Environmental regulation, land use, and recycling are also major challenges at the local level.* Every city and state wants economic growth and economic opportunities for its workers and businesses, but many forms of economic development impose costs in terms of the quality of air, water, landscapes, and health. Local officials face tough decisions about the need to balance economic and environmental concerns. Governors of both political parties are trying to formulate laws to combat global

Harlem Children's Zone (www.hcz.org) is a non-profit organization that runs education programs designed to engage families and communities in the development and education of children. ■ *What are the pros and cons of organizations like this providing services instead of the public school district doing so?*

warming—by promoting renewable sources of energy, by creating multistate agreements to cut emissions from power plants, and by adopting California's greenhouse-gas limits for cars.

■ *Health care costs and delivery are challenges to all levels of government.* Health care costs have been rising rapidly for several years, while at the same time, citizens have faced greater obstacles to gaining access to care. Some states have responded by developing programs to cover the growing number of uninsured. Massachusetts succeeded in enacting its attempt at universal health insurance, and now it is trying to put this complicated system into effect. In the meantime, the uninsured often fail to get adequate health care, and many turn to emergency rooms in local public hospitals, which in turn seek funding from local and state governments. It remains to be seen how the reforms adopted at the national level in 2010 will affect the states.

Our political system does not rely exclusively on one level of government to take up these formidable challenges. If leadership is lacking at the federal level for a time, it may be found in at least some of our state and local governments, as citizens bring their concerns to whichever governments are willing to hear them and take action. As former governor of New York Nelson A. Rockefeller said in 1962, "By providing several sources of political strength and creativity, a federal system invites inventive leadership—on all levels—to work toward genuine solutions to the problems of a diverse and complex society."[45]

CHAPTER **SUMMARY**

2.1 Contrast the functions of federal, state, and local governments, and evaluate the theories of decision-making in local governments.

Although the federal government has enacted a large number of major domestic programs, state and local governments face many of the most critical domestic and economic issues facing the United States. State and local governments also administer most public

programs, including those funded in large part by the federal government. Finally, most interactions between citizens and government involve employees of state and local governments.

Studies of states and communities have investigated how formal government institutions, social structure, economic factors, and local traditions interact to create a working political system. Some studies find that a power elite dominates, whereas community power studies find pluralism and diverse interest groups competing for influence over a range of policy areas. These different findings may reflect in part differences in research methods.

2.2 Analyze the activities and influence of interest groups and lobbyists at the state and local levels.

Special-interest groups operate in every state and locality, but their composition and influence vary a great deal, and the politics of some states and localities are dominated by a small number of major, usually economic interests. In some ways, the types of interest groups found at the state and local levels are similar to what we find at the national level, as are their activities and paths to influence. But the influence of groups is often greater at the state and local levels, as there is often less competition between diverse groups and as legislators typically have fewer sources of alternative information.

2.3 Assess the level and consistency of involvement of the major participants in local communities.

Although local governments command more public trust and are widely viewed as "closer to the people" than the national government, voting and other forms of participation at the local level are low. Nonetheless, local civic action often does occur, and it frequently produces innovative and flexible approaches to problems in education, the environment, crime and violence, and recovery from natural disasters.

2.4 Evaluate the challenges facing state and local governments.

State and local governments face severe challenges now and in the near future—in raising sufficient revenues, resolving conflicts over recent immigrants, rebuilding infrastructure, paying the costs of a fast-growing prison population, alleviating urban poverty, providing quality education, solving environmental problems, and ensuring that all residents have access to good-quality and affordable health care.

CHAPTER **SELF-TEST**

2.1 Contrast the functions of federal, state, and local governments, and evaluate the theories of decision-making in local governments.
1. Match the following functions with the appropriate level of government—either national or state and local.
   a. Hospitals
   b. Highways
   c. Universities
   d. Social Security
   e. Regulating the economy
   f. Elementary, middle, and high schools
2. Which of the following accurately defines *social stratification?*
   a. Direct democracy in small communities
   b. The division of government leaders into specialized policy areas
   c. The division of people in a community by social or economic class
   d. The fiscal relationship between local, state, and federal governments
3. List and briefly explain at least three theories about who actually has power in communities.
4. Write a paragraph suggesting three reasons why some responsibilities are best left to the national government, while others are best met by state and local government. Use examples in your answer.

2.2 Analyze the activities and influence of interest groups and lobbyists at the state and local levels.

5. Give three examples of state and local interest groups, and show how state and local government policies affect them.
6. In a paragraph, suggest why lobbyists and interest groups might be more effective at the state and local level than at the national level.

2.3 Assess the level and consistency of involvement of the major participants in local communities.
7. Which is closest to the size of typical turnout in local-only elections?
   a. Less than 20 percent
   b. 20 to 40 percent
   c. 40 to 60 percent
   d. More than 60 percent
8. In an essay, explore the reasons why citizens are typically apathetic toward their local government. Suggest two or three ideas that would help solve this problem.

2.4 Evaluate the challenges facing state and local governments.
9. List three areas of government spending in which costs have risen dramatically during the last few years.
10. Which of the following states has successfully enacted a program to provide its citizens with universal health insurance?
    a. Florida
    b. Kansas
    c. California
    d. Massachusetts

11. Select one of the challenges facing state and local government and, in one paragraph, argue which level of government—local, state, or national—is best equipped to face the challenge.

12. Write a short essay identifying which of the current challenges facing state and local governments deserves the most attention. Explain how emphasizing it will best help the U.S. people and why the other challenges are less important.

Answers to selected questions: 1. a. state & local, b. state & local, c. state & local, d. national, e. national, f. state & local; 2. c; 7. a; 10. d

---

mypoliscilab EXERCISES
Where participation leads to action!

Apply what you learned in this chapter on MyPoliSciLab.

📖—**Read** on **mypoliscilab.com**

eText: Chapter 2

✔—**Study** and **Review** on **mypoliscilab.com**

Pre-Test
Post-Test
Chapter Exam
Flashcards

👁—**Watch** on **mypoliscilab.com**

Video: L.A. Billboards
Video: California Teachers Stage Sit-Ins

✳—**Explore** on **mypoliscilab.com**

Comparative: Comparing State and Local Governments
Visual Literacy: Explaining Differences in State Laws

KEY TERMS

social stratification, p. 37
power elite, p. 37

pluralism, p. 38
redistributive policies, p. 42

ADDITIONAL RESOURCES

FURTHER READING

PETER L. BERNSTEIN, *Wedding of the Waters: The Erie Canal and the Making of a Great Nation* (Norton, 2005).

BUZZ BISSINGER, *A Prayer for the City* (Random House, 1997).

FRANK J. COPPA, *County Government* (Praeger, 2000).

E. J. DIONNE JR., ED., *Community Works: The Revival of Civil Society in America* (Brookings Institution Press, 1998).

ROBERT S. ERIKSON, GERALD C. WRIGHT, AND **JOHN P. McIVER,** *Statehouse Democracy: Public Opinion and Policy in the American States* (Cambridge University Press, 1993).

LARRY N. GERSTON AND **TERRY CHRISTENSEN,** *Recall! California's Political Earthquake* (Sharpe, 2004).

STEPHEN GOLDSMITH, *The Twenty-First Century City* (Regnery, 1997).

VIRGINIA GRAY AND **RUSSELL HANSON,** EDS., *Politics in the American States: A Comparative Analysis,* 9th ed. (CQ Press, 2007).

VALERIE C. JOHNSON, *Black Power in the Suburbs* (State University of New York Press, 2002).

ANDREW KARCH, *Democratic Laboratories: Policy Diffusion Among the American States* (University of Michigan Press, 2007).

V. O. KEY, JR., *Southern Politics in State and Nation* (Alfred A Knopf, 1949; reprinted by the University of Tennessee Press).

PAUL E. PETERSON, *The Price of Federalism* (Brookings, 1995).

DOUGLAS W. RAE, *City: Urbanism and Its End* (Yale University Press, 2003).

ALAN ROSENTHAL, *The Third House: Lobbyists and Lobbying in the States,* 2d ed. (CQ Press, 2001).

JON C. TEAFORD, *The Rise of the States* (Johns Hopkins University Press, 2002).

SUSAN W. THRANE AND TOM PATTERSON, *State Houses: America's 50 State Capitol Buildings* (Boston Mills Press, 2005).

JOSEPH F. ZIMMERMAN, *The New England Town Meeting: Democracy in Action* (Praeger, 1999).

ROBERT DAHL, *Who Governs: Democracy and Power in an American City* (Yale University Press, 1961).

WEB SITES

www.pewcenteronthestates.org/ The Pew Center for the States non-profit organization conducts research on state government performance and numerous state policy issues.

www.statelocalgov.net/ State and Local Government on the Net provides a directory of official state, county, and city government websites.

www.loc.gov/rr/news/stategov/stategov. html Library of Congress State Government Page provides information and government publications from all 50 states.

http://sppq.sagepub.com The official website of the academic journal *State Politics and Policy Quarterly*, which publishes research articles on state politics.

www.governing.com/ *Governing Magazine* provides news articles and analysis of political and policy issues facing the states.

State Constitutions

Charters or Straitjackets?

On May 1, 1991, three couples filed a lawsuit against the state of Hawaii challenging the state's law that limited marriage to opposite-sex couples. Hawaii's state Supreme Court ruled that such a law would be presumed to be unconstitutional unless the state could show it has a compelling interest in barring same-sex marriages and that it could do so without unnecessary abridgments of citizens' rights. This ruling triggered a firestorm of political and media attention. Certainly, same-sex marriage was (and remains) a controversial topic, but why would folks in the rest of the country be so concerned about how Hawaii's Supreme Court interpreted Hawaii's state constitution? The reason centers on what is called the "Full Faith and Credit" clause of the U.S. Constitution, which generally requires every state to recognize the "public Acts, Records, and judicial Proceedings" of every other state. In other words, those opposed to same-sex marriage were concerned that if Hawaii legalized it, all others would have to treat any same-sex couple lawfully married in Hawaii as lawfully married if or when they came to any other state to visit, work, or reside.

The national government responded by passing the so-called Defense of Marriage Act (DOMA) in 1996. This act defined marriage with regard to federal law as between one man and one woman, and it granted states the authority to refuse to recognize same-sex marriages performed in other states. There have been several challenges to DOMA in the federal court system, but so far, it has been upheld and the U.S. Supreme Court has yet to accept an appeal of one of these cases for review.

On November 18, 2003, the Massachusetts Supreme Judicial Court ruled that discriminating against same-sex marriages violated the state constitution. That ruling has survived several attempts to amend the state's constitution to ban same-sex marriage. Since that time, four other states: New Hampshire, Connecticut, Iowa, and Vermont, along with Washington, D.C., have legalized same-sex marriages. Same-sex marriages were legal in California for a short time under a state supreme court ruling, but voters passed Proposition 8 in the 2008 election to amend the state's constitution to ban them. There is a case in the federal court system, *Perry v. Schwarzenegger*, seeking to overturn this ban. In August of 2010, a federal judge ruled that Prop 8 violated the U.S. Constitution, but the Ninth Circuit Court of Appeals ordered no change in the policy pending an appeal.

Except for DOMA, and now *Perry v. Schwarzenegger*, virtually the entire battle surrounding same-sex marriage has been fought in the states, and the major battleground has centered on state constitutions. Does a state's constitution permit the legislature to ban or approve same-sex marriage? Can the state's constitution be amended to either permit or ban such marriages? Since all of this began back in 1991, the U.S. Supreme Court has yet to review a case or rule on the constitutionality of same-sex marriage bans, although some experts believe the *Perry v. Schwarzenegger* case may make it that far.

What the history of same-sex marriage makes clear is that state constitutions (a) can play a central role in defining meaningful rights for citizens and (b) vary a great deal from one state to another. Take a look at your state's constitution and see what sorts of rights and restrictions it contains that differ from the U.S. Constitution. Constitutions are foundational documents that establish the basic scope and structure of a government. They both empower governments to take actions and limit the actions they can take. Our U.S Constitution holds a revered place in our country's history and culture, but our state constitutions do not generally enjoy the same iconic status. On a trip to your state capitol, you are unlikely to find the state constitution "displayed [like] the federal Constitution, in a setting similar to a Shinto shrine."[1] Still, our state constitutions are powerful documents that affect our government and our lives as citizens in more ways than we typically realize.

In this chapter, we examine the roots of state constitutions and some of the reasons for constitutional rigidity. Then, we look at methods of amending state constitutions, ending with a few case studies of states that have tried, for the most part unsuccessfully, to adopt new constitutions.

The Roots of State Constitutions

The first state constitutions were outgrowths of colonial charters. Massachusetts and New Hampshire can boast of charters still in effect that are older than the federal Constitution. Virginia added a bill of rights to its constitution in 1776—13 years before the national one was proposed by Congress. In 1787, the framers of the U.S. Constitution drew heavily on their experience with these state charters. "What is the Constitution of the United States but that of Massachusetts, New York, and Maryland!" remarked John Adams, who drafted the Massachusetts Constitution in 1779. "There is not a feature in it," he said, "which cannot be found in one or the other."[2]

Subject only to the broad limitations of the U.S. Constitution, the people of each state are free to create whatever kind of republican government they wish. All state constitutions are similar in general outline (see Figure 3–1). A state constitution typically

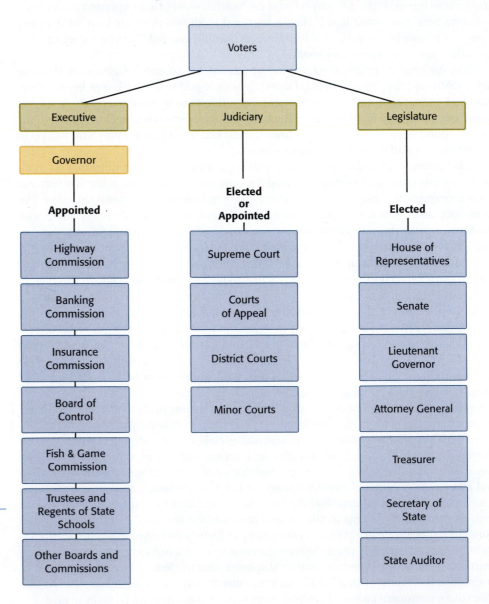

FIGURE 3–1 Government Under a Typical State Constitution.

■ *How does this figure help explain why state constitutions are typically so much longer than the U.S. Constitution?*

By the People

Exploring Your State Constitution

Although state constitutions are generally not permitted to restrict rights beyond the U.S. Constitution, they routinely provide for additional rights for their citizens beyond those included in the U.S. Constitution. Although the Equal Rights Amendment barring discrimination based on gender was never added to the U.S. Constitution, 22 state constitutions include at least partial guarantees of equal rights based on sex.

These provisions have been used by state supreme courts to expand the rights of women beyond those provided for in the U.S. Consti-tution. For example, the Colorado Supreme Court in 1988 ruled that an insurance policy that excludes coverage for pregnant women but is otherwise comprehensive constituted a violation of Colorado's Constitution.* Of course, there is considerable variance in the wording of individual state equal rights provisions. Montana's expressly includes the actions of government as well as private individuals while five states—Virginia, Colorado, Illinois, Hawaii, and New Hampshire—limit the scope of their equal rights protections to only the actions of governments.

What rights regarding gender discrimination does your state's constitution provide, and how does your state's constitution compare to those of other states? Several Web sites make it easy for you to find out. At Cornell University Law School's Legal Information Institute (LII), you can find constitutions, statutes, and legislative information by state, and you can also search state statutes by topic at http://www.law.cornell.edu/statutes.html#state. Knowing what rights are provided by your state constitution will help you become a more informed participant in political debate and a better protected citizen.

CRITICAL THINKING QUESTIONS

1. What do you think about the notion that the rights citizens enjoy in this country depend at least in part on the state in which they happen to reside?

2. Why would states differ in the constitutional rights they provide?

* Linda J. Wharton. "State Equal Rights Amendments Revisited: Evaluating Their Effectiveness in Advancing Protection Against Sex Discrimination." *Rutgers Law Journal* 36 (2004–2005): 1201–1294.

---

consists of a preamble, a bill of rights, articles providing for the separation of powers, a two-house legislature, an executive branch, and an independent judiciary with the power of judicial review. It will also have a description of the form and powers of local units of government, an article on how to amend the constitution, and miscellaneous provisions dealing with election procedures, corporations, railroads, finances, education, and other specific topics.

The bills of rights in state constitutions are, in general, similar to the federal Bill of Rights, although they sometimes use different language. However, the bills of rights in many state constitutions go beyond the protections the federal government offers, covering more recently emerging protections, such as the right to an equal public education and the rights of crime victims. Fourteen states adopted the Equal Rights Amendment even though it was never ratified to become part of the U.S. Constitution. (See the box, By the People: Exploring Your State Constitution.)

State constitutions contain more details than the U.S. Constitution does. They have to deal with a much wider range of functions, educational provisions, and criminal codes than the U.S. Constitution, which created a national government of intentionally limited powers to deal with a limited range of functions.[3] Thus, state constitutions often include articles with statute-like details that concern specific substantive policies. As a result, state constitutions are longer than the U.S. Constitution, which has only 7,400 words. The median state constitution has approximately 26,000 words,[4] ranging from the 9,200 words of New Hampshire's to the 365,000 words of Alabama's. Alabama's Constitution is nearly 40 times as long as the U.S. Constitution.

Constitutions as Straitjackets

The earliest state constitutions granted authority to the legislatures without much restriction on how they should exercise it. However, after many legislatures gave special privileges to railroads, canal builders, and other business interests, reform groups began to insist on certain controls in state constitutions. In time, state constitutions became encrusted with layer on layer of procedural detail.

Although most state constitutional provisions deal with matters of significance, some deal with subjects more appropriate for legislative statute. California's much-amended constitution (more than 500 amendments since it was adopted in 1879) goes into great detail about the internal organization of various departments.[5] The South Dakota Constitution declares that providing hail insurance is a public purpose and authorizes the legislature to levy a tax to do so.[6] The Alabama Constitution authorizes the legislature to indemnify peanut farmers for losses incurred as a result of *Aspergillus flavus* (a fungus) and freeze damage in peanuts.[7]

What does this mean for democratic government? It means that state constitutions—intended as charters of self-government—are often like straitjackets imposed on the present by the past. Some outdated provisions do no harm, but others are roadblocks to effective government. For example, fixed salaries do not reflect changing economic conditions, and a rigidly organized administrative structure is incapable of adjusting to new needs. When a constitution allocates revenues, elected officials are deprived of discretion to deal with budget difficulties as they arise. Under such conditions, the legislature cannot act, and the constitution must be amended or provisions interpreted to reflect contemporary circumstances.

Because state constitutions are long and often specific, they require more frequent amendment and revision[8] (see Figure 3–2). Louisiana has had 11 constitutions; Georgia has had ten; South Carolina, seven; and Alabama, Florida, and Virginia, six.[9] Only 19 states have their original constitution. The average state constitution is more than 100 years old and has been amended approximately 140 times, with Alabama's leading the way at more than 800 adopted amendments.[10]

The New Judicial Federalism Amendments are one way to alter constitutions. But another device for constitutional change is **judicial interpretation,** whereby judges modify a constitutional provision by giving a new interpretation of its meaning. One reason for the growing length of some constitutions is that amendments are often required to *reverse* judicial interpretations. In addition, some sections of state constitutions have been invalidated by federal action, especially in the areas of civil rights and suffrage.

In what is called **new judicial federalism,** state constitutions have taken on greater importance than in the past. For decades, state judges tended to look only to the U.S. Constitution and Bill of Rights and how the U.S. Supreme Court interpreted these documents. But since the 1970s, as the Supreme Court has become more conservative, some state

judicial interpretation
A method by which judges modify the force of a constitutional provision by reinterpreting its meaning.

new judicial federalism
The practice of some state courts using the bill of rights in their state constitutions to provide more protection for some rights than is provided by the Supreme Court's interpretation of the Bill of Rights in the U.S. Constitution.

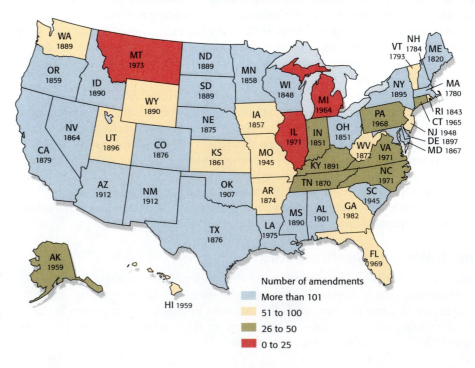

FIGURE 3–2 Amending State Constitutions.

■ *What factors might influence how often a state's constitution is amended?*

NOTE: Dates indicate year state constitution was ratified.

Number of amendments
- More than 101
- 51 to 100
- 26 to 50
- 0 to 25

For the People

Providing for Quality Education in the States

Every state provides for some level of public education in its constitution. In fact, 36 of the 37 states in the United States in 1868 already had provisions in their state constitutions regarding public education.* Several states have interpreted their state's constitution to define access to public education as a fundamental right for their state's citizens. In contrast, the U.S. Supreme Court has expressly rejected the argument that access to public education is a fundamental right protected by the Fourteenth Amendment.[†]

Some state courts have even gone so far as to declare state education funding systems that allow for large discrepancies in funding between schools or that simply underfund the school system as a whole as unconstitutional. For example, early in 2010, a judge in Washington state ruled that the state's low level of funding failed to meet its constitutional obligation to make "ample provision" for the education of all children residing within the state a "paramount duty."[††] In this particular case, the plaintiffs and their supporters cited the lack of textbooks, overcrowding, dilapidated and inadequate facilities, and the extensive use of class time for activities associated with fund-raisers as evidence that the state had failed to meet its constitutional obligation.[$] In his decision, Judge Erlick ordered the state to determine the actual cost of providing basic education and then to adequately fund it through stable and reliable sources.

Cases like this one in Washington show the value of state constitutions and the protections they can provide beyond those provided for by the national government. Students in Washington state stand to benefit to the tune of an additional $1 billion a year for better educational resources due entirely to the state's constitution and how judges in Washington have interpreted it.

CRITICAL THINKING QUESTIONS

1. As the national government begins playing a bigger role in providing for public education, should we consider amending the U.S. Constitution to provide for a right to public education? What might be the pros and cons of such an amendment?

2. Do the differences among states in the rights and protections they offer conflict with the national constitutional provisions designed to provide all citizens with equal protection under the law?

---

* Steven Calabresi and Sarah E. Agudo. "Individual Rights Under State Constitutions When the Fourteenth Amendment Was Ratified in 1868: What Rights Are Deeply Rooted in American History and Tradition?" *Texas Law Review* 87 (November 2008), No. 1.

[†] *San Antonio Independent School District* v. *Rodriguez* (1973).

[††] Linda Shaw, "King County Judge Rules That State Isn't Providing Enough Money for Schools," *The Seattle Times,* February 4, 2010, http://seattletimes.nwsource.com/html/localnews/2010981329_webschoollawsuit05m.html.

[$] *McCleary* v. *State of Washington*, No. 07-2-02323-2 SEA.

---

supreme courts have been relying on their own state constitutions and state bills of rights in overruling state laws and the actions of state and local officials. Recall that although states must provide citizens the minimum protection guaranteed by the U.S. Constitution, they can and sometimes do provide even more in areas such as equal protection and privacy. Based on the U.S. Constitution, the U.S. Supreme Court has allowed governments to adopt sobriety checkpoints for drivers,[11] random drug testing of public employees,[12] and restrictions on minors who seek abortions.[13] However, these rulings do not force states to adopt such policies. In fact, several state supreme courts have ruled that such policies are unconstitutional violations of privacy provisions included in their own state's constitution.

This trend takes its inspiration from the U.S. Supreme Court, which sent clear messages to state supreme court judges that they are free to interpret their own state constitutions to allow greater protections for citizens against government action than the U.S. Constitution does. The U.S. Supreme Court and the U.S. Constitution set the floor, not the ceiling, for the protection of rights.[14] As a result, some state judges are now using their constitutions to require state legislatures to provide better schools for children living in poor neighborhoods, build low-income housing, provide public financing of abortions for poor women, and regulate business enterprises to protect the environment.[15]

When state judges rely on their own state constitutions to protect rights beyond those required by the U.S. Constitution, they do so at some political peril. Many such rulings protect minorities and/or run counter to popular opinion and current state law. Because most state judges depend on voter approval to keep their office, making unpopular rulings risks voter backlash. This risk has increased now that the U.S. Supreme Court requires state judges who wish to escape its review of their decisions to make it clear that they have decided a case on adequate and independent state constitutional grounds.[16]

Amending State Constitutions

Amendments to state constitutions may be proposed by state legislatures, citizen-initiated ballot petitions, or constitutional conventions. After an amendment has been proposed, it must be ratified. In all states except Delaware, where the legislature can ratify as well as propose amendments, ratification is by the voters. In most states, an amendment becomes part of the constitution when approved by a majority of those who actually vote on it. In a 2003 special election in New Mexico, voters approved by only 195 votes constitutional amendments that created a cabinet-level secretary of education and authorized more spending for public education.[17] In some other states—such as Minnesota—approval by a majority of all those voting in the election is required. This provision makes ratification more difficult because some people who vote for candidates do not vote on amendments. In recent years, state voters have typically adopted approximately 75 percent of all constitutional amendments proposed by legislatures, but voter approval increased in 2006, when 85 percent of the amendments proposed by legislatures were adopted.[18] That figure dropped to only 60 percent in 2008.[19]

Legislative Proposals

All states permit their legislatures to propose constitutional amendments; in fact, this is the most common method. Although provisions vary, the general practice is to require the approval by a supermajority, usually two-thirds or three-fifths, of each chamber of the legislature. Some states, however, permit proposal of an amendment by a simple majority in two successive legislatures.

A legislature may appoint a **revision commission** to make recommendations for constitutional change that, except in Florida, have no force until acted on by the legislature and approved by the voters. The legislature creates a commission of a relatively small number of people—some selected by the governor and some by the legislature—and charges it with presenting proposals for constitutional revision. A commission is less expensive than a full-blown constitutional convention, does not require initial voter approval, and gives the legislature final control of what is presented to the electorate.

California, for instance, turned to a revision commission to overcome its budgetary gridlock after its senate rejected a 1992 proposal asking voters whether they wanted a constitutional convention (the first in 113 years). California's constitution has been so frequently amended to require certain expenditures that approximately 85 percent of the state's annual revenues are allocated before the governor and legislature even start working on the budget! Eventually, if this trend were to continue, *all* state revenues could be allocated in this way, and there might be no state funds available for programs such as higher education and health care.[20] A 23-member revision commission was created in 1993 to examine the budget process and the configuration of state and local duties. Two years later, the commission made its recommendations. However, the legislature failed to act on any of them, in part because it was an election year. Also, because the state senate was Democratic and the state assembly Republican, it proved impossible to work out any compromise.

Constitutional commissions are, in fact, infrequently used. Utah is the only state that had such a commission in operation in 2004.[21] Voters in three states—Connecticut, Hawaii, and Illinois—voted on whether to call constitutional conventions in their states in 2008, but more than 60 percent of voters in all three states said no.[22] The recommendations of revision commissions are also seldom implemented quickly, perhaps because the commissioners have not been responsive to political currents or are not representative of broad enough interests. Still, a commission may be less partisan and more resistant to single-interest groups than either the legislature or a convention. Mississippi has tried, so far unsuccessfully, to use a commission for changing its 1890 constitution, which was designed to keep African Americans out of the political process.[23]

Nonetheless, Florida, Virginia, and Louisiana have used the commission procedure to bring about significant constitutional change. Utah's Constitutional Revision Commission is a permanent body, required by law to submit recommendations for constitutional revision to the legislature 60 days before each regular session.[24] It has initiated revisions

revision commission
A state commission that recommends changes in the state constitution for action by the legislature and vote by the voters.

relating to the rights of crime victims as well as to changes in revenue and taxation. Florida has a Taxation and Budget Reform Commission that is called into session every ten years. Unlike other such commissions, in addition to making recommendations to the legislature, it may propose constitutional amendments directly to the voters. In 1998, the commission recommended nine amendments; Florida voters approved eight of them.

Initiative Petitions

At the end of the nineteenth century, revelations of corruption diminished the prestige of state governments, especially state legislatures. From this disillusionment and the Progressive Movement came a variety of reforms. Among them was the **constitutional initiative petition,** a device that permits voters to place specific constitutional amendments on the ballot by petition. Eighteen states allow amendments to their constitutions to be proposed by initiative petitions.

The number of signatures required on petitions varies from 4 to 15 percent of either the total electorate or the number who voted in the last election.[25] Although it takes more signatures to propose a constitutional amendment than to place other kinds of initiatives on the ballot, "the higher threshold is no longer a significant impediment to well-financed special-interest groups."[26] Once the appropriate state official (attorney general or secretary of state) approves the precise wording of a petition, the amendment goes on the ballot at the next general election. (California allows initiatives to appear even on primary election ballots.)

In some states, initiative proposals are limited to *amending* the state constitution, not to *revising* it. The distinction between revision and amendment is that revision refers to a comprehensive change in the basic governmental plan, a substantial alteration in the basic governmental framework, or a substantial alteration of the entire constitution, rather than to a less extensive change in one or more of its provisions.[27] Some states exclude certain subjects from amendment by initiative. Massachusetts, for example, does not allow amendments by popular initiative that concern religion, the judiciary, or judicial decisions; that are restricted to a particular town, city, or political division; that appropriate money from the state treasury; or that restrict rights such as freedom of speech.

In recent years, voters have approved slightly more than a third of amendments proposed by initiative petitions. This figure compares with a slightly more than 75 percent approval rate for amendments proposed by state legislatures.[28] In 2008, 78 amendments were proposed to voters by their legislatures, and 52 were approved.

constitutional initiative petition
A device that permits voters to place specific amendments to a state constitution on the ballot by petition.

A citizen in Seattle stops to consider signing a petition to legalize marijuana. If the petition gets enough signatures, it can appear on the ballot for Oregon voters. ■ *Are there issues that should not be permitted to be considered by citizen initiative? Why?*

In contrast, only 29 amendments were proposed to voters through the citizen initiative process, and only 12 of them were approved.[29] A variety of factors may account for the lower adoption rate of initiative measures. Initiatives tend to be used for controversial issues that have already been rejected by the legislature and engender an organized opposition. Initiatives are also often proposed by narrow-based groups or by reform-minded elites who lack broad support for their views. Sometimes initiatives are proposed in order to launch educational campaigns rather than to actually win adoption.

Use of the initiative process is spreading among people who are anxious to limit the power of state and local governments. Since 1978, when California adopted Proposition 13 limiting property taxes, other states have followed suit. In addition, these "new reformers" have produced "a series of state constitutional amendments that, taken together, fundamentally altered the character and powers of state governments by limiting the tenure of governmental officials, reducing their powers, and transferring policy-making responsibilities to the people."[30] In addition, "the focus of constitutional initiatives ... has shifted from questions of governmental structure ... to questions of substantive policy," such as initiatives on tort liability, the rights of gays, affirmative action, and the rights of immigrants.[31]

Constitutional Conventions

Voters once loved state constitutional conventions: they held 144 in the nineteenth century. But the twentieth century produced only 63 constitutional conventions, and only one has been convened in the twenty-first century so far.[32] One scholar noted that calling conventions of the people is a uniquely American idea, emphasizing that legislators cannot be trusted and that the supreme power belongs to the people.[33]

Forty-one state constitutions authorize their legislature to submit the calling of a convention to the voters; the other states assume that the legislature has the power to do so. Fourteen state constitutions require the legislature to question voters about a convention at fixed intervals. For example, Missouri is required to submit the question to the voters every 20 years; Hawaii, every 9 years; and Michigan, every 16 years.

If the voters approve, the next step is to elect delegates. Some state constitutions contain elaborate procedures governing the number of delegates, the method of election, and the time and place of the convention. Others leave the details to the legislature. The way convention delegates are selected seems to affect the kind of document the convention proposes. Selection by nonpartisan, multimember districts is more likely to result in a reform convention that makes major changes than one in which political parties play a major role because the two major political parties generally resist changing any rules that might threaten their standing or influence.[34]

The chosen delegates usually assemble at the state capital, prepare a draft of the new constitution, and submit it to the voters. First, they have to make a difficult choice: Should they ask the voters to accept or reject the new constitution as a whole? Or to vote on each section separately?

The advantage of the first method is that each provision of a constitution ties in with another, and to secure all the advantages of revision, voters should adopt the entire document. The disadvantage is that those who oppose only a particular provision may vote against the entire constitution. Delegates may decide to submit separately a provision they know is controversial. Whichever method they choose, supporters of change must rally their forces to gain voter approval.

The Politics of Constitutional Revision

Constitutions are not a neutral set of rules perched above the world of everyday politics. Rather, they significantly affect who gets what from government. Changes can thus help or hinder various groups.

DECIDE

Should States Require a Supermajority to Approve a Constitutional Amendment?

Florida's constitution has been changed considerably since the state was first admitted to the Union in 1845. Constitutional changes were required when the state seceded from the Union in 1861, was readmitted to the Union in 1865, and grappled with Reconstruction. Yet the state's constitution has also been used to change public policy, through amendments that reduce class size in public schools or construct high-speed rail lines.

Legislators worried that amendments restricting legislative flexibility and straining the state's budget were passed too easily and pressed for a constitutional amendment that would make it more difficult for amendments to pass by raising the threshold of adoption from a simple majority, 50 percent plus one, to a supermajority, or 60 percent plus one. In 2006, this amendment received 58 percent of the vote and thus did not reach the threshold it establishes for future amendments.

What do you think? Should states require a supermajority to approve a constitutional amendment? What arguments would you make for and against such an idea?

THINKING IT THROUGH

Supporters of the amendment argued that Florida's Constitution was too easily changed. They were concerned that well-funded special-interest groups could advance their own narrow self-interests by posing as grassroots organizations, hiring people to gather signatures on petitions, and then bankrolling advertising campaigns that never told the full story about the consequences of a particular amendment. "A spot on the ballot can be purchased for $2 million and takes only six months of work," lamented Protect Our Constitution, Inc., a group formed to advocate for the amendment.*

Legislators also grumbled that amendments too often involved proposals they had already rejected as not in the state's best interest. The state needed to rely on representative democracy, they asserted, and allow the legislature to do its job. Requiring a higher threshold for adoption of a constitutional amendment would preserve the people's right to amend the constitution yet ensure that amendments reflected "the collective will of folks and not just a whim."†

Opponents responded that the supermajority requirements subverted democracy. It blocked the will of the people by allowing a minority to block the majority position. Moreover, they said, Florida needed direct democracy to check the abuse of representative democracy. A coalition of citizen groups that formed to fight against the amendment, Trust the Voters, alleged that the amendment was "nothing short of a power grab by a Legislature that is already unresponsive to popular will." Pointing out that all the money raised by Protect Our Constitution, Inc., came from major corporations and business interests, opponents charged that those supporting the amendment were the special interests and had far too much influence in the legislature. Amendments such as those that banned smoking in restaurants, raised the state minimum wage, and reduced class size reflected the public will and were necessary because the legislature had refused to enact them.

Critical Thinking Questions

1. Should states use a threshold greater than 50 percent plus one to determine whether the people have approved an amendment to the constitution? Why or why not?

2. In establishing the charter for the state government, should state constitutions strengthen direct democracy or rely more heavily on representative democracy?

---

* www.protectourconstitution.org/mx/hm.asp?id=home.
† Sen. Jim King (R-Jacksonville, Flor.), quoted in J. Taylor Rushing, "Amending State's Top Document Could Be Tougher," *(Jacksonville) Florida Times-Union*, September 22, 2006, p. B1.

There are generally two types of proposed amendments: those focused on streamlining or modernizing the constitution and those targeting specific policy issues rather than institutional reforms. Proponents of the first type generally find that people might favor such measures in the abstract, but only special-interest groups are likely to get invested in the debate and outcome, and they are more likely to oppose than to favor reform.[35] Supporters of the status quo thus have a systemic advantage: "To be successful, revision requires gubernatorial as well as legislative leadership.... An effective political campaign is essential.... Success at the polls is not assured. Constitutional revision can be a high-risk endeavor."[36] Amendments aimed at specific policy issues are often initially promoted by a more focused interest group or constituency with intense preferences. For example, same-sex marriage bans have often been based on a motivated group of citizens organized in favor of such bans working against a less-organized opposition. The following case studies illustrate the risky nature of constitutional revision.

Rhode Island Amends Its Constitution

Rhode Island's biennial constitutional convention began in 1984 and produced 14 separate propositions for amending its 1843 constitution. On November 4, 1986, voters approved 8 of the 14 provisions, rejecting attempts to increase compensation of state legislators, to provide for merit selection of judges, and to create a paramount right to life that would have banned abortions or public funding of them. The voters approved provisions strengthening free speech, due process, and equal protection rights, and expanding fishing rights and access to the shore; they also approved a statement that the rights protected by the Rhode Island Constitution are independent of the U.S. Constitution.[37]

The Rhode Island Constitution calls for voters to be asked every ten years whether they want to convene a constitutional convention. In November 1994, the voters rejected a convention by a vote of 173,693 to 118,545.[38] Despite this defeat, in November 2001, voters approved by a 2-to-1 margin a nonbinding ballot question calling for a constitutional convention focused on separation-of-powers issues. This was a response to a decision of the Rhode Island Supreme Court ruling that the Rhode Island Constitution allowed the state legislature to both make and execute state laws. After continued pressure from Common Cause and 30 other organizations, in 2003, Rhode Island's legislature approved a constitutional amendment strengthening the separation of powers and placed it on the 2004 ballot for voters' approval. State voters passed the separation-of-powers amendment by a 78 percent vote, and in 2005, the state's legislature began developing legislation implementing the new constitutional provisions.[39]

Changing the Hawaii Constitution

More than 800 proposals for constitutional changes were submitted to the Hawaii state constitutional convention of 1978. The League of Women Voters and other groups conducted extensive information and discussion meetings, and the convention held many public hearings on key issues. The 102 delegates met for nearly three months and eventually narrowed the proposals to 34 questions for the fall ballot.

The delegates endorsed a two-term limit for governor and lieutenant governor, moved to make Hawaii's party primaries more open by allowing voters to cast ballots without declaring party preference, and authorized the state legislature to provide partial public funding for election campaigns and to establish spending limits. The convention reflected concern over government spending by setting tougher overall debt and spending limits for the state. It also strengthened environmental safeguards and gave further constitutional and financial protection to the special status of native Hawaiians. In November 1978, 74 percent of the voters went to the polls and adopted all 34 amendments.

However, in 1986, Hawaiians narrowly rejected the periodic question of whether to call a convention. The decision was put to them again in 1996, and the vote was 163,869 in favor and 160,153 against, but 45,245 people left the question unanswered. Blank ballots were tallied as a no, in response to a decision of the state supreme court that the Hawaii Constitution required approval by a majority of all ballots cast. The Ninth U.S. Circuit Court of Appeals, which refused to order a new election, sustained this decision.

Since 1996, additional proposals for a convention have been backed by several interests, including those who wanted to ban same-sex marriage after learning of the Hawaii Supreme Court's ruling in 1993 suggesting that the current constitution would not support such a ban, those who wanted to impose term limits on state legislators, and those who wanted to limit the power of state courts to restrict police searches. Other groups, including the League of Women Voters, have argued that there is no compelling need for a constitutional convention and that these hot-button issues would dominate and polarize the delegates, hindering deliberative discussion about other equally important issues.

In November 2008, Hawaiian voters were asked again to decide whether the state should hold a constitutional convention. Controversial issues included rights and legal protections for native Hawaiians, same-sex marriage, public finance of election campaigns, and term limits. Typical of many drives for state conventions, the effort in Hawaii failed by nearly a 30 percentage-point margin.[40]

Of the People

Affirmative Action via State Amendment

Although most American adults believe everyone should be given an equal start in achieving a good education, job, housing, and so forth, they do not agree on how to remedy past discrimination. They are especially divided on affirmative action, which has sometimes been upheld by the U.S. Supreme Court due to the state's compelling interest in providing a diverse educational experience.

In 2006, Michigan voters spoke on the issue in the elections by enacting an amendment to their state constitution to "ban public institutions from using affirmative action programs that give preferential treatment to groups or individuals based on their race, gender, color, ethnicity, or national origin for public employment, education, or contracting purposes." The amendment also contained a specific list of public institutions affected by the ban, including the University of Michigan. Prior to 2006, the university had waged a long fight to consider diversity in admission decisions. In those battles, the U.S. Supreme Court struck down the university's point system for undergraduate admission that included awarding points to minorities, but it upheld the university's broader interest in including race as part of

evaluating diversity among its law school applicants.

The Michigan amendment banning affirmative action passed, 58 to 42 percent. Although it may not survive another Supreme Court challenge, the ban did reflect a statewide sentiment that all applicants should be treated the same and specifically rejected any preference in state job and university applications. Michigan voters were not saying that the demographics of state institutions should remain mostly white or male but rather that they did not want to give any group special status.

The vote itself reflected a division over just how important these programs aimed at increasing diversity were. According to exit polls of voters, the vote was clearly split on whether to end affirmative action in the state, with white men providing the most support for the amendment (see the table that follows).

The Michigan amendment echoes similar bans in California and Washington state but was much more specific. It is no surprise that nonwhite women expressed the greatest opposition to banning affirmative action because they are likely to be the most affected, but the University of Michigan was also intensely opposed. Like many colleges

and universities, Michigan has used a variety of tools to increase the number of minority students and made clear its intent to fight the ban through the federal court system. Michigan voters may want the face of American politics to continue changing but not if it involves affirmative action.

CRITICAL THINKING QUESTIONS

1. Why do you think there is opposition to affirmative action programs?

2. Should affirmative action programs in university admissions be treated differently from programs aimed at public employment or government contracts? Why or why not?

Proposition 2: Restrict Affirmative Action		
Vote by Race and Gender	Yes	No
White Men	70%	30%
White Women	59	41
Nonwhite Men	30	70
Nonwhite Women	18	82

SOURCE: www.cnn.com/ELECTION/2006/pages/results/states/MI/I/01/epolls.O.html.

Texas Keeps Its Old Constitution

Texas has a lengthy constitution adopted in 1876 and amended more than 430 times. The most recent effort to thoroughly revise it occurred in 1972, after political scandals brought in a new governor, Dolph Briscoe, and a reform-oriented state legislature. After pushing through a variety of reforms dealing with the ethics of officeholders, campaign practices, and registration of lobbyists, the legislature called an unusual convention of members of the legislature, rather than a specially elected body, to revise the constitution.

After 17 months, the legislator-delegates came up with a much revised and shortened document intended to modernize many obsolete governmental practices. The convention deadlocked, however, over whether to give constitutional status to the state's right-to-work law, which prohibits labor contracts that require union membership as a condition of employment, so this issue was referred to the voters. In the end, neither the AFL-CIO nor Governor Briscoe supported all the convention's recommendations. The governor was especially opposed to the proposal that legislative sessions be held annually, rather than every two years, because he thought yearly sessions would lead to higher taxes. Advocates of the revised constitution tried to salvage their work by offering voters substantial parts of the new charter as amendments to the existing constitution.

Conservatives praised the old constitution, claiming that it had served Texas well for 100 years. Progressives complained that it was elitist, permitted only the narrowest governmental objectives, and made real change nearly impossible. In November 1975,

63

The Alabama Citizens for Constitutional Reform (constitutionalreform.org) is promoting a new film that shows a re-enactment of Alabama's 1901 Constitutional Convention, based on actual transcripts, in which delegates openly discussed ways to disenfranchise black and poor white voters. ■ *Do you think the creation of the Alabama Citizens' Constitutional Commission was a good idea? What are the strengths and weaknesses of putting a group like this in charge of constitutional reform?*

amid charges and countercharges, Texas voters rejected the amendments by a 2-to-1 margin.[41] Since then, they have approved 143 amendments and rejected 33 but have not held another convention.

Alabama Considers a New Constitution

Alabama has had six constitutions. The most recent, written in 1901 and adopted in 1902, was "a document of the Old South,"[42] unashamedly designed to keep African Americans segregated in public schools and prevent them from voting or participating in governmental matters.[43] It has been amended more than 740 times and survived many attempts to modernize and replace it.

The issue of constitutional reform remains on the state's agenda. The 21-member independent commission, called Alabama Citizens for Constitutional Reform, has been pushing the idea for years[44] and proposed putting the question of holding a constitutional convention to a statewide vote.

Although one poll showed that 61 percent of Alabamans favored reform, in November 2002, that proposal was nonetheless defeated in the Alabama House of Representatives by a vote of 33 to 105.[45, 46] However, the Democratic and Republican candidates for governor that year both supported constitutional reforms and a statewide vote on the matter. Shortly after his inauguration in 2003, Governor Bob Riley established a 35-member Alabama Citizens' Constitutional Commission to propose constitutional reforms in several areas: strengthening the governor's line-item veto power, giving more home rule back to counties, requiring more than a simple majority of the legislature to raise taxes, changing provisions that earmark 90 percent of all tax revenues for specific purposes, eliminating racist provisions, and studying how the constitution might be shortened and reformed. Based on the commission's recommendations and Governor Riley's leadership, major revisions of the constitution were encapsulated into one amendment, which was resoundingly defeated. Despite the defeat, Governor Riley was praised for his political courage and leadership.

In 2004, the legislature pressed forward with one of the reform areas and proposed an amendment eliminating language in the constitution that requires segregated schools and poll taxes, which remain even though federal courts invalidated them more than 40 years ago. Opponents claimed that the proposed changes in language would have established a right to a public education, opening the door to activist judges demanding that taxes be raised to increase school spending.[47] Voters defeated the amendment by only 1,850 of the more than 1.3 million votes cast. Nonetheless, the issue has not died: Many in Alabama still want to call a convention to reform the constitution and are pushing to get the question placed on the ballot.[48]

The Future of State Constitutions

Unlike the federal Constitution, amended only 27 times in more than 220 years, most state constitutions are amended on a regular basis. Although no entirely new state constitution has been adopted since the 1980s, the process of constitutional amendment allows state governments and voters to modify and modernize constitutions to fit changing conditions. Nearly 1,100 amendments were proposed between 1998 and 2006, affecting nearly every state constitution. Many were limited in scope, concerning only local issues or specific state agencies. However, others affected states' bills of rights, broad finance and taxation issues, and electoral processes.[49]

State constitutions will continue to be modified as new issues arise and conditions change in the states. The recent trend to add bans on same-sex marriages to state constitutions is not exceptional. Indeed, it reflects the fact that voters are the ultimate judges of the meaning and content of their state's constitution, which rights the state will recognize, and which policies it will follow.

CHAPTER **SUMMARY**

3.1 **Compare and contrast the U.S. Constitution and state constitutions.**

Like the U.S. Constitution, state constitutions usually have a preamble, a bill of rights, and articles providing for a legislature, an executive branch, and an independent judiciary. State constitutions are longer and more detailed than the U.S. Constitution, and their bills of rights often include new and expanded rights not mentioned in the U.S. Constitution. In the past 20 years, state constitutions have become instruments for protecting and expanding rights in what is known as the new judicial federalism. Some state supreme courts have relied on their own state constitutions and bills of rights to provide their citizens greater protections than those found in the U.S. Constitution.

3.2 **Outline the processes used to amend state constitutions.**

State constitutions can be amended by voters' ratifying proposals submitted by the legislature, by popular

initiative petitions, or by constitutional conventions. Conventions tend to revise the entire constitution rather than amend only portions of it. The Progressive Movement advanced initiative petitions as a reform measure to control legislatures thought to be beholden to special interests. In recent decades, initiative petitions have become a popular means to amend state constitutions by people anxious to limit the power of state and local governments.

3.3 **Evaluate the states' recent attempts at constitutional revision.**

States rarely call full-blown constitutional conventions, as they expose current elected officials to substantial risk. Thus, most revisions of state constitutions happen via individual amendments proposed either by the legislature or directly by citizens. Citizen-led initiatives can produce an array of proposals, which often deal less with constitutional issues, such as fundamental rights or the basic structure of government, and more with very narrow policy questions.

CHAPTER **SELF-TEST**

3.1 **Compare and contrast the U.S. Constitution and state constitutions.**

1. Which of the following statements is true?
   a. The U.S. Constitution is longer than all state constitutions.
   b. The U.S. Constitution is shorter than all state constitutions.
   c. The U.S. Constitution is longer than some state constitutions and shorter than others.

2. In a few sentences, explain what is meant by referring to state constitutions as "straitjackets."
3. Imagine a judge serving in your state recently ruled that according to the state constitution, the government must provide a free college education to all of its residents. In one or two paragraphs, explain how this decision is an example of "new judicial federalism," and tell why it is or is not appropriate for judges to make rulings in such a way.

4. Decide whether state constitutions should be as specific as they are. Write a short essay (one to two paragraphs) explaining your decision and attempting to persuade a person who is unfamiliar with the issue.

3.2 Outline the processes used to amend state constitutions.

5. Explain the distinction between *amending* and *revising* a constitution.

6. List the three ways in which state constitutions can be amended. Which of these methods do you feel will provide the highest-quality amendments? In two or three paragraphs, defend your position and explain some shortcomings of the other methods.

7. In a few paragraphs, argue that states should have constitutional conventions more frequently than they currently do.

8. List some amendments more likely to be proposed by petition of the general population than by the legislature. Write a short paragraph arguing why states should or should not be able to propose amendments through petitions.

3.3 Evaluate the states' recent attempts at constitutional revision.

9. Write a few paragraphs comparing efforts at constitutional changes in two of the following states: Rhode Island, Hawaii, Texas, and Alabama. Give your opinion on how each case did or did not improve the state's constitution.

10. In one or two paragraphs, explain why state constitutions are amended much more frequently than the U.S. Constitution. Describe any major problems or benefits you see in the frequent amending of state constitutions.

Answers for selected questions: 1. b

 **EXERCISES**

Apply what you learned in this chapter on MyPoliSciLab.

📖 **Read** on **mypoliscilab.com**

eText: Chapter 3

✓ **Study** and **Review** on **mypoliscilab.com**

Pre-Test
Post-Test
Chapter Exam
Flashcards

✳ **Explore** on **mypoliscilab.com**

Simulation: You Are Attempting to Revise the California Constitution
Simulation: You Are Attempting to Revise the Texas Constitution

---

KEY **TERMS**

judicial interpretation, p. 56
new judicial federalism, p. 56

revision commission, p. 58
constitutional initiative petition, p. 59

ADDITIONAL **RESOURCES**

FURTHER READING

WILLI PAUL ADAMS, *The First American Constitutions: Republican Ideology and the Making of State Constitutions in the Revolutionary Era* (Rowman & Littlefield, 2001).

RICHARD J. ELLIS, *Democratic Delusions: The Initiative Process in America* (University Press of Kansas, 2003).

PAUL FINKELMAN AND **STEPHEN E. GOTTLIEB,** EDS., *Toward a Usable Past: Liberty Under State*

Constitutions (University of Georgia Press, 1991).

JENNIFER FREISEN, *State Constitutional Law* (Michie, 1996).

SANFORD LEVINSON, ED., *Responding to Imperfection: The Theory and Practice of Constitutional*

Amendment (Princeton University Press, 1995).

CHARLES LOPEMAN, *The Activist Advocate: Policy Making in State Supreme Courts* (Praeger, 1999).

ROBERT L. MADDEX, *State Constitutions of the United States,* 2d ed. (CQ Press, 2005).

G. ALAN TARR, *Understanding State Constitutions* (Princeton University Press, 2000).

G. ALAN TARR AND **ROBERT F. WILLIAMS,** *State Constitutions for the Twenty-First Century* (State University of New York Press, 2006).

ROBERT F. WILLIAMS, *State Constitutional Law: Cases and Materials* (Michie, 1993). See also the quarterly review *State Constitutional Commentaries and Notes,* published by the Edward McNail Burns Center for State Constitutional Studies at Rutgers University.

WEB SITES

www.greenwood.com/catalog/series/ Reference%2bGuides%2bto%2bthe% 2bState%2bConstitutions%2bof% 2bthe%2bUnited%2bStates.aspx The Greenwood Publishing Group has commissioned reference guides for the constitution of each state, written by an expert on the state.

www.constitution.org/ The Constitution Society Web site includes links to every state's constitution.

www.stateconstitutions.umd. edu/index.aspx The NBER/University of Maryland State Constitutions Project Web site includes search functions for the text of state constitutions.

Parties and Elections in the States

On May 6, 2008, voters in North Carolina and Indiana went to the polls to cast ballots in the presidential primaries. Three years earlier, Indiana had adopted laws requiring voters to provide valid identification (ID) before they would be allowed to vote. According to Indiana Public Law 109-2005, a valid ID is one that: (1) displays a photo, (2) displays your current name, (3) displays an expiration date that is current, and (4) was issued by the State of Indiana or the U.S. government. Student IDs could only be used if they met all four criteria, which automatically excluded students from private schools.

The law was adopted to limit potential voter fraud, but critics feared it would lead to many eligible voters being discouraged from voting or being turned away at the polls. On that day in May, news sources reported that several nuns were blocked from voting—they were in their 80s or 90s and did not have driver's licenses or up-to-date passports. Several students from private colleges were also turned away from the polls. Voters in North Carolina casting ballots that same day faced no such obstacles unless they had never voted before and had registered to vote by mail rather than in person. How can there be such differences between the two states? Doesn't the U.S. Constitution provide for equal voting rights for all citizens?

Actually, the U.S. Constitution and a series of U.S. Supreme Court decisions throughout the years have made it quite clear that states have the power to regulate the conduct of elections, even for national offices. As such, considerable variation exists across the states regarding when elections are held, how citizens cast ballots, how candidates qualify to get on the ballot, and who is eligible to vote. About one month before the Indiana primary, the U.S. Supreme Court, in *Crawford* v. *Marion County Election Board*, upheld the Indiana law as constitutional by a vote of 6 to 3.[1] The majority of the justices argued that the state's interest in preventing fraud was sufficient grounds for adopting the policy and that the identification requirement did not place an undue burden on voters. However, in 2009, an Indiana appeals court struck down the law, finding that it violated Indiana's constitution by not treating all voters equally. The appeal of this decision was heard by the Indiana Supreme Court on March 4, 2010 (*The League of Women Voters et al* v. *Todd Rokita*; you can watch video of the oral arguments online at https://mycourts.in.gov/arguments/default. aspx?view=detail&id=1007). At that hearing, the state supreme court set aside the appeals court ruling and agreed to take over the case. As we learned in the previous chapter, state constitutions can and often do provide for more broadly defined rights than does the U.S. Constitution.

These recent events in Indiana illustrate the central role that states play in conducting elections in the United States for offices at the local, state, and national levels. In this chapter, we focus on state elections in general, leaving detailed discussions of gubernatorial, state legislative, and judicial elections to subsequent chapters. As we will see, states have made very different decisions about how to manage elections and regulate participation, so "democracy" varies significantly across states. Though state differences are large and many problems remain, our state and local governments have seen major advances in democratic government in recent decades—in who is permitted to vote, in the ease of voting, in the openness of party primaries and caucuses to diverse voters, in the administration of elections, in the regulation of campaigns, and in the spread of party competition.

The Constitutional Context: State and Federal Roles in Regulating Elections

LEARNING OBJECTIVE

4.1 Compare and contrast the constitutional roles of state and federal governments in regulating elections.

Although we often speak of national elections for the U.S. Congress or the presidency, in fact there are no purely national elections in the United States. All elections for national offices are held by and within the states. Senate elections are statewide contests; elections to the House of Representatives are held within states and in districts drawn by the states, and even presidential elections are actually a set of statewide contests for electoral votes. The U.S. Constitution gives states the leading role in regulating the conditions under which elections for members of the U.S. Congress are held. Article I, Section 4, says, "The Times, Places and Manner of holding Elections for Senators and Representatives shall be prescribed in each State by the Legislature thereof; but the Congress may at any time by Law make or alter such Regulations, except as to the Places of choosing Senators."[2] The language regarding presidential elections also gives states a leading role: "Each State shall appoint, in such Manner as the Legislature thereof may direct, a Number of Electors."[3]

Nonetheless, the federal government also exercises considerable control over the circumstances under which national elections are held. As already noted, although Article I, Section 4, gives states the leading role in regulating congressional elections, it also gives the Congress the authority to "make or alter such Regulations." *The Federalist*, No. 59, defended this provision by arguing that, although state control over elections was preferable under most circumstances, the national government had to have the authority to intervene "whenever extraordinary circumstances might render that interposition necessary to its safety."[4] That is, control over elections was so important, giving states exclusive control would have made the national government's very existence vulnerable to state regulation. By sharing authority over elections, the original Constitution set up an ever-shifting tug-of-war between state variation and national standards.

The U.S. Constitution says little about state and local elections—the elections of governors, lieutenant governors, attorneys general, state legislators, mayors, city council members, and many other public officials. It seems to require only that states actually use and abide by elections, as some sort of popular sovereignty is implied by the clause in Article IV, which says "the United States shall guarantee to every State in this Union a Republican Form of Government."[5] As a result, states differ even more in the ways they regulate elections that fill state and local offices than in the laws they apply to congressional and presidential elections.

Amendments to the original Constitution maintained the primacy of states in regulating elections, although they placed constraints on how states could exercise that authority. The Fifteenth Amendment prohibits states from denying the franchise on the basis of "race, color, or previous condition of servitude." The Seventeenth Amendment requires that U.S. senators be chosen directly by a state's voters rather than its legislators. The Nineteenth Amendment guarantees women the right to vote. The Twenty-Fourth Amendment prohibits states from requiring voters to pay a poll tax. And the Twenty-Sixth Amendment prevents states from denying the vote to otherwise qualified persons age 18 or older.

These amendments do not necessarily represent triumphs of national over state powers to control elections because national action was often a culmination of state flexibility and innovation. For instance, the ratification of the Nineteenth Amendment in 1920 came after a half-century of change at the subnational level, which eventually forced national action. In 1869–1870, the Wyoming territory gave women the rights to vote and hold office, rights that continued after Wyoming became a state 20 years later. Soon afterward, Colorado, Utah, and Idaho also gave women equal political rights. Between 1910 and 1914, seven more states in the West and Midwest gave women full voting rights, followed by large states such as New York in 1917 and Michigan in 1918. By the end of 1918,

Women in several western states were given the right to vote and hold public office before they won the right to vote at the national level in 1920. ■ *What examples can you think of in how regulations for conducting elections differ across the states today?*

women had full voting rights in 15 states and partial rights (that is, they were eligible to vote in presidential elections only) in a dozen others.[6] Thus, when Congress considered the proposed Nineteenth Amendment, many members were understandably reluctant to vote against it and face the prospect of having to explain to female voters in their own districts why they thought women were unqualified to participate in the nation's politics. In this instance, then, as in others, shared state and national authority over elections created pathways for change that would not have been available if either the states or the federal government had exclusive control.

Elections at the State and Local Levels

LEARNING **OBJECTIVE**

4.2 Describe differences among the states in laws regulating voting, elections, and campaign finance, and assess federal influence on these regulations.

Each year, there are thousands of state and local elections. Europeans, used to voting for one or two candidates at the national and local levels and only once every two or three years, are flabbergasted to learn that we engage in so many elections. Selection of town and local officials in the late winter may be followed in the spring by **primary elections,** which are used to determine who will run in the general elections under the party labels. Actual officeholders are chosen in **general elections** in the fall. These elections may be interspersed with **special elections,** which are generally held to fill vacant offices or address one-time issues, or elections for school boards or to adopt school budgets. Some states allow for **recall elections,** which are used to throw unpopular officials out of office, as in California in 2003 when voters removed Gray Davis from the governorship and replaced him with Arnold Schwarzenegger.[7] Voters in all states but Delaware must ratify changes to the state constitution in a referendum, and approximately half the states allow public **initiatives** and **referendums** to be put on the ballot by petition. A public referendum occurs when enough citizens petition to hold an election to vote on a bill that has already been approved by the legislature. A public initiative allows citizens to petition to propose a law to be voted on in an election without requiring any action by the legislature. Just as bewildering to some observers is the number of offices we vote on, from president to probate judge, from senator to sheriff, from governor to noxious weed control superintendent. By contrast, Europeans elect only a handful of key officials, who in turn appoint career officials.

For the most part, control over this vast electoral process in the United States is *decentralized* in its rules and administration. States, for example, differ in the hours the polls are open, how close to the voting place campaigning may be conducted, and whether and when they require voters to register. Furthermore, many states delegate a number of responsibilities to county or other local governments. Such delegation was why voters in Palm Beach County, Florida had the infamous "butterfly" ballot in the 2000 presidential election while others did not (see Figure 4–1). Due to overriding federal legislation, some of the differences among the states in their electoral laws have diminished in recent years. Yet new differences open up as new options and issues emerge, such as mail-in ballots and extended voting periods. The remainder of this section discusses these differences as well as occasional federal efforts to reduce them.

Differences in Who May Vote

States determine, for the most part, who is eligible to vote—and their laws can exclude large numbers of people from the polls and create considerable variation in voting throughout the country. All states but Maine and Vermont, for example, prohibit prison inmates from voting. Most states also refuse to register citizens on parole or probation, and ten states permanently ban some or all convicted felons from voting (see the "You Will Decide" box).[8] Thirty-six states have a "mental competency" requirement for voter registration. States must keep accurate and up-to-date lists of registered voters and those ineligible to register. States could also extend the right to vote further, but most do not exercise this authority. If a state wanted to permit 16-year-olds to vote, it could do so—yet none has chosen that option.[9]

Voter registration rules are important because they can exclude or discourage people from participating in elections. All states except North Dakota require citizens to register

primary elections
Elections in which voters choose party nominees.

general elections
Elections in which voters elect officeholders.

special elections
Elections in which voters decide on ballot initiatives, vote on statewide constitutional changes or new constitutions, or elect a senator or representative to replace one who has died or resigned.

recall elections
A procedure for submitting to popular vote the removal of officials from office before the end of their term.

initiative
A procedure whereby a certain number of voters may, by petition, propose a law or constitutional amendment and have it submitted to the voters.

referendum
A procedure for submitting to popular vote measures passed by the legislature or proposed amendments to a state constitution.

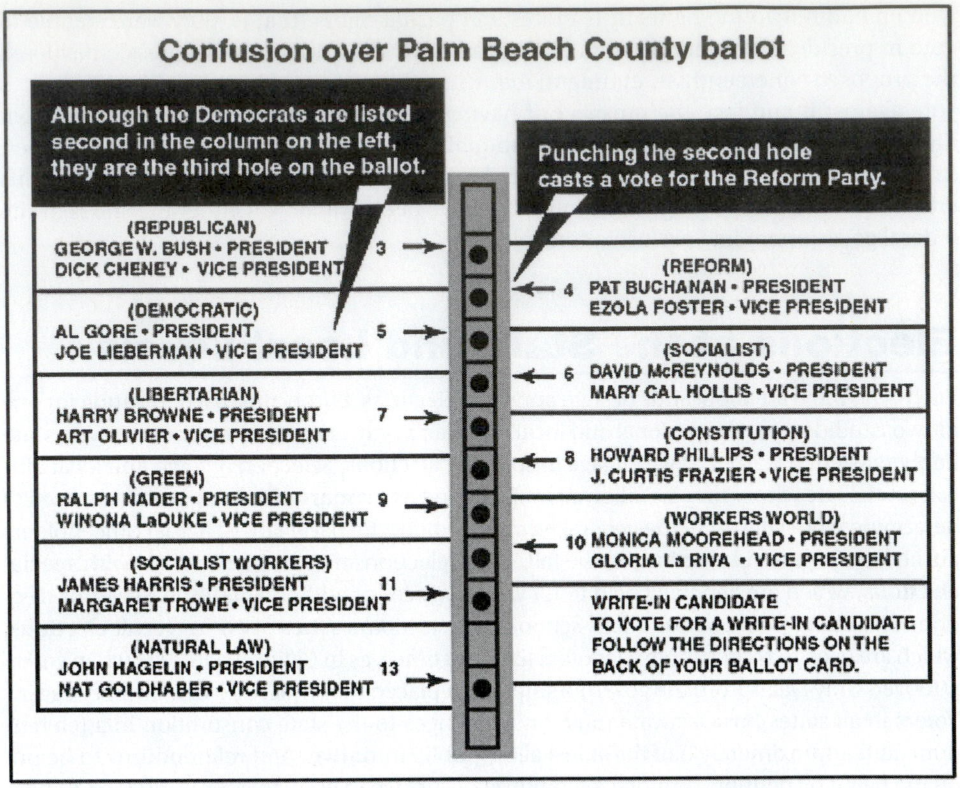

Confusion over Palm Beach County ballot

FIGURE 4–1 Sample Butterfly Ballot.
■ *What are some of the pros and cons of decentralized control over elections?*

before voting, and states vary greatly in how easy they make registration. More than 20 states require persons to live in a state or locality for one month before they can register or vote, but about the same number have no minimum residency period. Although most states require citizens to register as much as 30 days before the election in which they plan to vote, nine states allow citizens to register at the polls on election day. Voter turnout is generally higher in states where getting registered is easier. A common reason people do not register is that they have moved. Fifteen percent of U.S. citizens change their residence every year.[10] After moving, they may not realize they need to register at their new address until only a few days before the election, when it may be too late. Early registration deadlines may thus cause some people not to vote.

Voter registration became somewhat easier when Congress passed the National Voter Registration, or Motor Voter, Act in 1993. The Act tried to reduce disparities in voter registration throughout income groups by, among other things, requiring states to offer voter registration when people apply for or renew their driver's license, or when they visit government agencies offering public assistance benefits. The eight states that permit election day registration or do not require voter registration are exempt from the law.

What difference has Motor Voter made? During 2005 and 2006, nearly 21 million people registered through motor vehicle or other agencies, approximately 43 percent of total registrations in that period.[11] However, scholars suggest that many of those would likely have registered anyway and also that Motor Voter has had only a limited impact on reducing disparities in voter registration or subsequent turnout.[12] Also, many of these new registrants are registering as Independents. Motor Voter thus does not appear to have made much difference in party balance, contrary to expectations that it would result in a bias in favor of Democrats.[13]

Taken together, states' voter eligibility and registration rules can have important effects on **voter turnout,** which we typically measure as the percentage of a state's voting-age

voter turnout

The proportion of the voting-age public that votes.

population who actually vote in a particular election. (The U.S. Census Bureau annually estimates the voting-age population.) More restrictive voting registration laws may lower turnout, according to one study, by as much as 9 percent.[14]

Voter turnout may also be influenced by *voter identification laws,* which affect how registered voters can demonstrate to poll workers that they are who they say they are. The issue of voter identification received a push from a section of the federal Help America Vote Act of 2002 (HAVA), which attempted to combat fraud by requiring new registrants to show or prove identification, either when they registered or when they first showed up to vote. However, as discussed in the opener of this chapter, many states, such as Indiana, decided to go beyond these minimal requirements and demanded that all registrants identify themselves using strict criteria before casting a ballot in any election.

Although not much is known about the effects of strict voter identification requirements, early studies suggest that such requirements may depress voter turnout for registered voters, especially persons with little education and low incomes, perhaps because such individuals are less likely to own cars or travel and thus are less likely to have up-to-date driver's licenses or passports.[15] Now that the states have some flexibility on this issue, the debate over voter identification laws—and the trade-offs they suggest between preventing fraud and ensuring widespread and unbiased voter access—will probably be intense for several years into the future.

States' voter turnouts vary enormously, even for the same elections. In the 2008 presidential election, fewer than 50 percent of the voting-age population in four states—Hawaii, Texas, Arizona, and California—cast votes, whereas more than 65 percent voted in ten states.[16] Although registration and other voting rules affect these rates, many other factors affect turnout. States whose residents have individual characteristics associated with voting—such as being older and better educated—have higher turnout rates. States with more competitive elections also have higher rates, in part because such elections draw more public interest, though perhaps also because competitive elections spur candidates and parties to work harder to get voters to the polls.

Voter eligibility and registration laws may seem like mundane matters, but they have stirred some of the greatest controversies in the history of U.S. politics. Voter registration laws were at the heart of the struggle for civil rights in the South in the 1950s and 1960s. Southern states disenfranchised African American citizens by selectively enforcing poll taxes, literacy tests, and vouchers of "good character." Even attempting to register was dangerous for blacks in some parts of the South, sometimes resulting in severe harassment and death.

To combat disenfranchisement, President Lyndon Johnson pushed for and signed the Voting Rights Act of 1965 into law. The Act prohibited the denial or abridgment of the right to vote by means of literacy tests throughout the nation. It also contained special enforcement provisions aimed at parts of the country where discriminatory laws and administrative practices were prevalent. These mostly southern states and localities were prohibited from implementing any changes affecting voting unless the federal government reviewed the proposed changes and found them to be nondiscriminatory. The Act gave the federal government authority to monitor and review local elections, voter qualifications, and registration procedures.

The Voting Rights Act had an enormous effect on voter registration and participation. In Mississippi, registration among African Americans climbed from 6.7 percent in 1965 to 74.2 percent in 1988. In Alabama, it went from 19.3 percent in 1965 to 68.4 percent in 1988. Voting rates among black citizens also increased enormously, and southern politics became multiracial, with significant new competition between parties in many parts of the region.[17]

Students protested against literacy tests and other ways in which public officials prevented black citizens from voting in this 1962 demonstration in McComb, Mississippi.

DECIDE Should Former Felons Be Allowed to Vote?

All states except Maine and Vermont prohibit citizens in prison from voting, and most states also withhold voting rights from persons on parole or probation. Ten states permanently ban some or all ex-felons from voting, even those not on parole or probation. It is estimated that approximately 5.3 million Americans are not allowed to vote due to state laws restricting the voting rights of some felons.* However, some states are reconsidering such laws. Nebraska eliminated its lifetime ban

in 2006 in favor of one that ends two years after felons complete their sentences. In Iowa, the governor signed an executive order in 2005 restoring voting rights to felons who have completed their sentences.

What do you think? Should former felons be allowed to vote? What arguments would you make for and against such an idea?

THINKING IT THROUGH

One argument in favor of restoring voting rights to felons after they complete their prison sentences is that the voting bans affect too many people. The American Civil Liberties Union claims that hundreds of thousands of people are disenfranchised by Florida's ban on voting by former felons.[†] The United States' high rate of incarceration, including many people convicted of nonviolent crimes, reduces the vote for large parts of low-income and minority communities. Laws prohibiting former inmates from voting may, for instance, affect as many as 20 to 30 percent of African Americans in some states. Advocates for former inmates say state governments ought to stress their reintegration into society, not their permanent separation. Another reason not to withhold the vote is that the administration of such laws has had negative side effects. In Florida's 2000 elections, many black voters may have been wrongly prevented from voting by the former-felon ban, due to mistakes in identity.

On the other hand, some argue that the bans should stay. A Tennessee state representative said, "I don't believe we need

to have a voting bloc that comes out of prison angry at the sheriff's department . . . and angry at the prosecutor's office."[‡] One can also make the argument that simply because a law is badly administered—resulting in too many black voters disqualified—does not mean that the law itself is bad; instead, the law should be better implemented. The central difference, however, remains whether a convicted felon permanently forfeits the right to vote.

Critical Thinking Questions

1. Are there other arguments for or against laws that prevent U.S. citizens from voting after they have completed their prison terms?

2. What information or research would you need to make an appropriate decision on these arguments?

3. How is it fair that former felons may vote for president in one state but not in another?

---

* Estimate provided by The Sentencing Project, http://www.sentencingproject.org/template/page.cfm?id=133.
† See American Civil Liberties Union, "State Legislative and Policy Reform to Advance the Voting Rights of Formerly Incarcerated Persons: ACLU Policy Activities and Legislative Accomplishments: 2007," www.aclu.org/votingrights/exoffenders/statelegispolicy2007.html#text.
‡ Charisse Jones, "Rhode Island to Revisit Felons' Voting Rights," *USA Today*, May 31, 2006, www.usatoday.com/news/nation/2006-05-31-felons-voting-rights_x.htm.

Differences in How We Vote

As a result of widespread problems in election administration in 2000, Congress passed HAVA, which provided federal funds to help states replace punch cards, paper ballots, and lever voting machines. Since HAVA was enacted, big changes have occurred in the way citizens vote. In 2000, nearly half of all registered voters in the United States (49 percent) voted in counties that used lever machines, punch cards, or hand-counted paper ballots. Punch-card ballots can be subject to problems such as dangling or dimpled chads (the little pieces of paper voters punch out to make machine-readable holes) that do not clearly indicate the voter's intent.[18] Only 29 percent used optically scanned paper ballots, and 12 percent used electronic touchscreen machines. Eight years later in 2008, only 7 percent of registered voters voted in counties that used the older methods, while 56 percent used optically scanned ballots and 33 percent used electronic screens (see Figure 4–2).[19]

The spread of computerized voting prompted new debates about the accuracy and accountability of computerized voting machines. Unlike punch cards, optical scanners, and paper ballots, touchscreen voting machines do not permit an audit of the vote.[20] To deal with this accountability problem, many states require all of their voting machines to print paper ballots that they can check in case of problems in the electronic tally. Others use optical scan technologies, in which voters mark paper ballots that are then scanned,

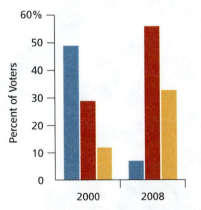

Percent of Voters

■ Used old technology (lever machines, punch cards, hand-counted ballots)
■ Used optically scanned paper ballots
■ Used electronic screens

FIGURE 4–2 Changes in Voting Technology, 2000 and 2008.

■ *How has the way we vote changed since 2000? What are some potential advantages and drawbacks of these changes?*

allowing quick and accurate tallies but still preserving a paper record. Yet even these systems—called a "voter-verified paper trail"—can malfunction or be tampered with.[21]

These changes reduced some of the uncertainty over vote counts. The biggest voting problem in 2004 was long lines at polling locations in several states. However, this was more the result of an insufficient number of voting machines and booths than a breakdown in voting technology. The 2006 elections appeared to be quite successful, with few reports of problems or controversies. Voting went smoothly in the 2008 elections as well, although some "early voters" (people who voted before election day, in states where that is allowed) stood in long lines.

There are still, however, many issues for voting systems in the future. The new technologies are harder and more expensive to maintain; local governments may not have the funds to keep them in good condition and will rely more on state and federal dollars.[22] Also, at least one study found that older, less-educated voters may make more mistakes than others when using various computerized voting or optical scanning machines.[23] So long as the nation relies on a highly decentralized system—often under-funded, staffed not by professionals but by partisan volunteers, and strained by intense party competition—problems and future changes are likely to occur.

A critical and often overlooked aspect of voting is poll workers. Poll workers implement the rules on who may and may not vote, manage the entire process of voting, and have a strong impact on citizens' experience at the polls. With the new voting technology, poll workers also manage the machines, explain their operation to voters, and at the end of the day ensure that they are properly stored. The competence of the poll worker is correlated to voters' overall satisfaction with the voting experience.[24]

State election ballots also vary widely and with important implications. Ballots are of two basic kinds. The **party column ballot** (also known as the *Indiana ballot*) is organized by parties, with the party name and symbol at the top of a column that lists all the party's candidates running for offices in that election. Typically, there is an option at the top of the ballot column that allows voters to cast votes for all candidates of that party. When voters choose this option, they cast a **straight ticket** vote. Voters may also have to work their way through any state constitutional amendments, referendums, and initiatives on the ballot.

Partly to discourage straight ticket voting, some states use the **office block ballot** (also known as the *Massachusetts ballot*), which lists all the candidates running for an office together in one block or on one screen, all those running for another office in another block/screen, and so on. Office block ballots encourage **split ticket** voting, or voting for candidates from more than one party. One consequence of computerized ballots will be a shift to office block formats. The sample ballot in Figure 4-3 allows the voter to either cast a straight ticket or to select each vote independently by office.

Voting by Mail and Absentee Ballot Modern technology makes it possible to vote by other means than appearing in person at a voting place on election day. Cities such as San Diego and Berkeley first experimented with holding *elections by mail*. The government mails voters a pamphlet that describes the questions to be decided in the election and gives instructions on how to complete the ballot and return it by mail. Voters sign the return envelope, and their signatures are compared against their signatures on the voter registration form. There have been no major problems administering local mail ballot elections, and the turnout has been higher than the norm for in-person special elections.[25]

In January 1996, Oregon voters elected a U.S. senator in a special election through the mail rather than in person. Oregonians had 20 days from the date the ballots were mailed to return them to county clerks, and two-thirds of those who received ballots returned them. In 1998, Oregon voters approved an initiative to conduct all elections by mail. Vote-by-mail elections have proved popular there and show little evidence of fraud.[26]

Nonetheless, opponents of the vote-by-mail system worry about fraud, and they worry that voters may be pressured to vote a certain way. One person in a household may try to direct the votes of others. Another problem is that supporters of a candidate may visit voters at home soon after the ballots are delivered and pressure people to vote on the spot,

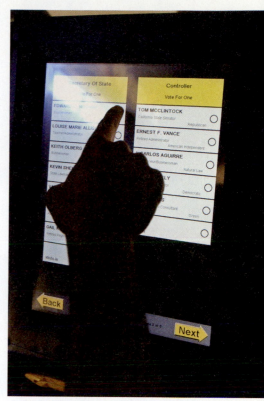

Touchscreen voting machines typically present candidates in office blocks, not party columns, and may thus discourage straight ticket voting.

party column ballot
A type of ballot that encourages party-line voting by listing all of a party's candidates in a column under the party name.

straight ticket
A vote for all of one party's candidates.

office block ballot
A ballot on which all candidates are listed under the office for which they are running.

split ticket
A vote for some of one party's candidates and some of another party's.

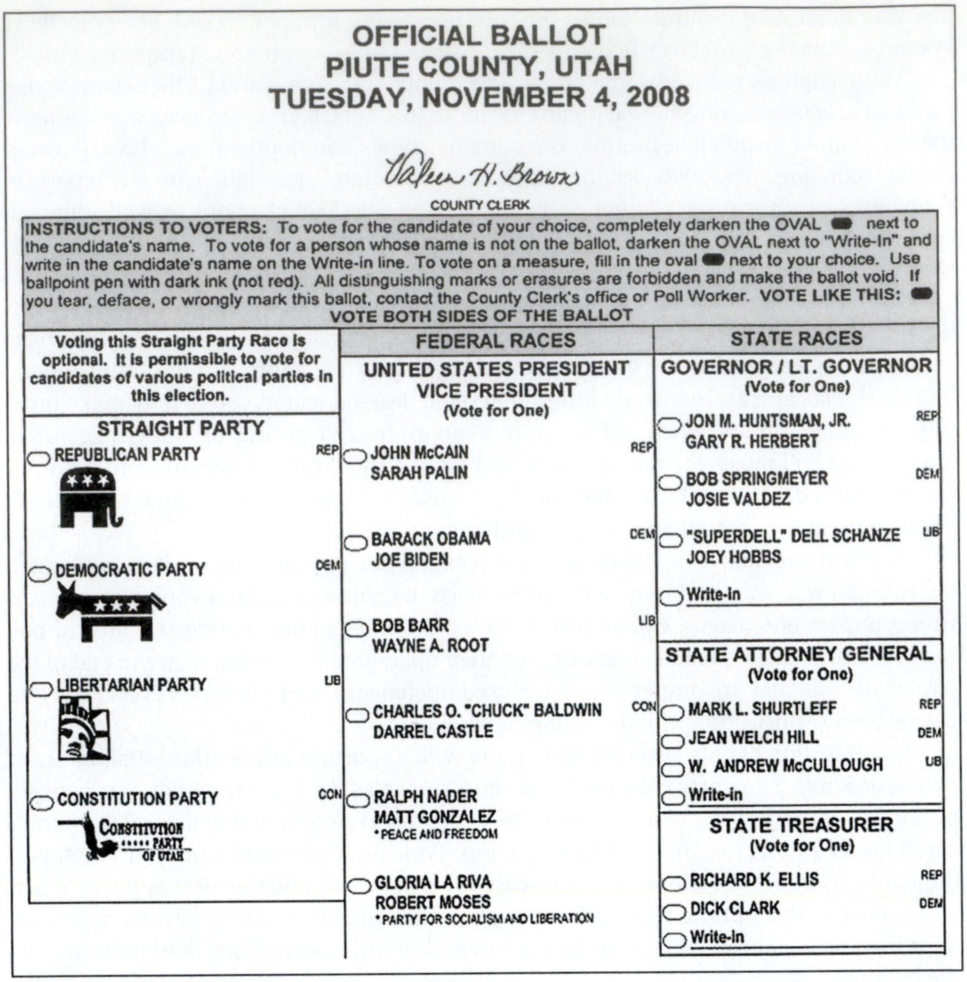

OFFICIAL BALLOT
PIUTE COUNTY, UTAH
TUESDAY, NOVEMBER 4, 2008

Valeen H. Brown
COUNTY CLERK

INSTRUCTIONS TO VOTERS: To vote for the candidate of your choice, completely darken the OVAL next to the candidate's name. To vote for a person whose name is not on the ballot, darken the OVAL next to "Write-In" and write in the candidate's name on the Write-in line. To vote on a measure, fill in the oval next to your choice. Use ballpoint pen with dark ink (not red). All distinguishing marks or erasures are forbidden and make the ballot void. If you tear, deface, or wrongly mark this ballot, contact the County Clerk's office or Poll Worker. VOTE LIKE THIS:
VOTE BOTH SIDES OF THE BALLOT

Voting this Straight Party Race is optional. It is permissible to vote for candidates of various political parties in this election.

STRAIGHT PARTY
- REPUBLICAN PARTY — REP
- DEMOCRATIC PARTY — DEM
- LIBERTARIAN PARTY — LIB
- CONSTITUTION PARTY — CON (Constitution Party of Utah)

FEDERAL RACES

UNITED STATES PRESIDENT
VICE PRESIDENT
(Vote for One)
- JOHN McCAIN / SARAH PALIN — REP
- BARACK OBAMA / JOE BIDEN — DEM
- BOB BARR / WAYNE A. ROOT — LIB
- CHARLES O. "CHUCK" BALDWIN / DARREL CASTLE — CON
- RALPH NADER / MATT GONZALEZ — *PEACE AND FREEDOM
- GLORIA LA RIVA / ROBERT MOSES — *PARTY FOR SOCIALISM AND LIBERATION

STATE RACES

GOVERNOR / LT. GOVERNOR
(Vote for One)
- JON M. HUNTSMAN, JR. / GARY R. HERBERT — REP
- BOB SPRINGMEYER / JOSIE VALDEZ — DEM
- "SUPERDELL" DELL SCHANZE / JOEY HOBBS — LIB
- Write-in

STATE ATTORNEY GENERAL
(Vote for One)
- MARK L. SHURTLEFF — REP
- JEAN WELCH HILL — DEM
- W. ANDREW McCULLOUGH — LIB
- Write-in

STATE TREASURER
(Vote for One)
- RICHARD K. ELLIS — REP
- DICK CLARK — DEM
- Write-in

FIGURE 4–3 **Sample ballot with straight party option**

■ *Why would the major parties prefer to keep the "straight party vote" option on the ballots? What interests might prefer solely office block ballots?*

perhaps offering to mail the ballot. However, supporters point to the higher turnout and lower costs in administering vote-by-mail elections. They also cite the absence of observed and documented fraud or abuse in vote-by-mail elections.

A less dramatic reform of election laws is the *absentee ballot.* In most of the country, voters may request a ballot by mail. In some states, voters must give an acceptable reason why they cannot reach the polls on election day, such as a planned trip or a physical disability (though these reasons are almost never verified). But in an increasing number of states—28 in 2008—voters may ask for and get an absentee ballot without giving any excuse or reason at all.[27] Absentee balloting is especially useful for initiative measures. In states such as California or Washington, where voters may face 20 or more complicated ballot questions, those who vote by absentee ballot can take their time researching and pondering how they are going to vote instead of deciding within the few minutes they have in a voting booth.

Increased ease in obtaining ballots has significantly expanded the rate of absentee voting in California. It has been used especially by Republicans to activate retirees and other voters who find it difficult to get to polling places. In Washington state, absentee ballots made up nearly 89 percent of all ballots in 2008.[28] Other forms of *early voting* have also spread widely in recent years. In 2008, 35 states permitted voters to cast their ballots in person several days before an election at several locations in each county, and only 4 of those states required voters to give an excuse for not showing up on election day.[29] Michael McDonald, a political scientist at George Mason University, estimates that nearly 32 million citizens cast early votes in 2008.[30]

Differences in Nomination Processes

State law establishes the process by which party nominees are selected. Most states use primary elections, but some permit the parties to nominate their candidates through a *caucus* or *convention*. In the caucus system, party delegates elected in local voting district meetings decide on the party nominee. In some states, a convention narrows the field to two candidates if no candidate gets a set percentage of delegate votes at the party convention.

The dynamics of winning a nomination in states with a caucus system are different from those in states with a primary. In a caucus system, having a grassroots organization or an intense appeal that can mobilize politically active, better-educated voters to attend a neighborhood meeting is essential for candidates. In the 2008 presidential primaries, Barack Obama did especially well in caucuses in part because, as one political scientist argued, "He's got a middle-class base. They're more likely to be turning out (for caucuses), and he's turning them out."[31] The state best known for the caucus system is Iowa, whose party caucuses yield the first decision in our presidential election system and are covered extensively by the media. In presidential elections, about a dozen states use some form of the caucus or convention system. For state offices, nearly all states use primaries or some combination of primaries and conventions.[32]

There are two kinds of party primaries. In a **closed primary,** only voters registered in a party may vote in that party's primary. Such a primary discourages **crossover voting**—allowing voters from outside the party to help determine the party's nominee—which is why partisans prefer closed primaries. In an **open primary,** any voter can participate in any party's primary. Candidates whose policy positions or leadership styles appeal to independent voters (those without party affiliation), or even to people who are registered or generally vote with the opposite party, are likely to benefit from open primaries. In the 2008 Republican presidential primaries, John McCain did particularly well in states with open primaries. In fact, he failed to get pluralities from Republican voters in the crucial primaries of New Hampshire and South Carolina, but he won both states because of his strong support among Independents choosing to vote in these open primaries.[33]

Louisiana has a unique system. All candidates, regardless of party, run in a single election. If no candidate gets a majority of the votes, a runoff election determines the winner between the two candidates with the most votes. It is not uncommon for both candidates in a runoff to be from the same party. Washington has a similar top-two primary system in place. Voters in California voted on June 8, 2010, on a ballot initiative that would create a similar system for primaries in their state. This proposal was supported by outgoing Republican Governor Arnold Schwarzenegger but opposed by both the Republican and Democratic parties of California. Voters approved the measure by a margin of 54 percent to 46 percent, which will go into effect for primaries held in 2012, assuming the measure survives expected legal challenges in the courts.

closed primary
A primary election in which only persons registered in the party holding the primary may vote.

crossover voting
Voting in another party's primary.

open primary
A primary election in which any voter, regardless of party, may vote.

These absentee ballots will be sent to voters in Missouri as an alternative to the conventional practice of going to the polls to vote. ■ *What are the advantages and disadvantages of widespread use of absentee ballots?*

Differences in the Timing and Frequency of Elections

Federal law sets the date of the presidential election as "the Tuesday next after the first Monday in November, in every fourth year," with similar language applying to elections for the House and Senate. States are free to determine the dates of all other elections, but for ease of administration, they usually consolidate gubernatorial and state general elections on the first Tuesday after the first Monday in November.

Two-thirds of the states elect governors in presidential midterm years, halfway between presidential elections; only 11 states hold their gubernatorial elections in presidential election years. Vermont and New Hampshire elect their governor every two years. Five states conduct their primary and general elections for governor, other state officials, and the state legislature in odd-numbered years, leaving the even-numbered years for federal elections.

Separating state elections from presidential or federal elections permits voters to focus more closely on state issues than if they had to vote for state and federal candidates at the same time. Separating elections also means state and local officials are less likely to be hurt by an unpopular presidential candidate at the top of the ticket. Of course, even in off-year elections, national political forces are sometimes strong enough to have a big impact on state and local elections. In the 1994 congressional elections, for instance, when Republicans mobilized around the conservative "Contract with America" and many voters reacted against unpopular policies and economic problems during the first years of the Clinton administration, Democrats in state governments were turned out of office in large numbers. A similar situation in the 2010 midterm elections saw even greater gains by the Republicans at the state level. Energized by tea party activists and supported with record spending made possible in part by the U.S. Supreme Court's ruling in *Citizens United* v. *Federal Election Commission* (2010), the GOP rode low approval of President Obama and the poor national economy to electoral success. The GOP emerged with control of at least 29 governorships, both legislative chambers in at least 25 states, and one chamber in another 5 states. Overall, Republicans captured about 700 seats in state legislatures, leaving them with an outright majority of state legislative seats nationally and the party's largest such majority since 1928. Still, the 1994 and 2010 elections were exceptional. Most off-year elections are not as strongly affected by national issues, though presidential evaluations and "coattails" generally remain.[34]

State law establishes the rules for local elections but often allows cities and towns some discretion in setting the dates of elections. Many municipal elections are held in the spring of odd-numbered years, again to avoid any positive or negative carryover from candidates running for federal or statewide office. Counties usually conduct their elections at the same time state officials are elected.

State governments can also hold *special elections* to vote on a ballot initiative, a statewide constitutional change or a new constitution, or to replace a U.S. senator who has died or resigned. Participation in special elections varies greatly, depending on what is being decided, but turnout is generally lower than in midterm general elections.

What are the consequences of holding so many elections at so many different times? One is that voters pick and choose which elections, if any, they participate in. Primaries ordinarily draw fewer voters than general elections, and sometimes the turnout is very low, less than 10 percent. General election turnout is also lower in nonpresidential years, and generally lower still if a state lacks a hotly contested race for governor or U.S. senator at the top of the ballot. Low turnout raises concerns about whether the voters who participate are representative of the general public.

Rallies designed to capitalize on Democratic President Obama's low approval ratings and the weak economy were held across the country leading up to the 2010 midterm elections. Republicans rode this wave of discontent to major electoral gains. ■ *What role should national political and economic conditions play in elections for state and local offices?*

Differences in What We Vote On

When we think about elections in the United States, we generally think about voting for candidates for a particular set of offices. However, citizens in many states and communities frequently face a range of other choices as well when they go to the polls. For example, approximately half of the states permit citizens to vote on initiatives and public referendums. Some states and many cities also have recall elections, and many localities use elections to gain approval for special projects or initiatives.

Voting on Ballot Questions   After California voters passed Proposition 13 in June 1978, which amended the state's constitution to cut property taxes and keep them low, ballot questions have become increasingly popular among the states. There are many types of ballot questions. Some, like Proposition 13, are citizen initiatives, which may be placed before the state's voters if proponents collect a minimum number of signatures from registered voters on a petition. Referendums are questions typically proposed by state legislatures. Both types of questions may be used to amend the state's constitution or to enact ordinary legislation. Each decade since the 1970s, more and more citizen initiatives have been placed on the ballot, and more have been approved. Since 1998, around 200 initiatives and referendums appear on state ballots every even-numbered year, two-thirds of which are generally legislative referendums.[35]

Conservative groups have used initiatives to reduce taxes, cut government spending, deny public benefits to immigrants, and restrict same-sex marriages. Liberal groups have backed them to increase taxes on tobacco, ban smoking in public places, expand Medicaid coverage, raise the minimum wage, and promote stem cell research. One concern about ballot questions is that voting may hinge on factors having little to do with the merits of the proposals.

Voters typically do not have much information about the proposals or their likely consequences, and many simply vote no. Others suffer from "ballot fatigue" when there are too many contests and questions on the ballot, and they refuse to vote on the questions at all.[36] Because voters typically have little information about the questions and their views are not deeply rooted in party affiliation, feelings toward an incumbent, or party appeal, there may also be greater opportunities for campaign advertising to shape public opinion on ballot questions.[37]

Because many initiatives are supported by well-funded interests and because a vote in one state can start a national movement on an issue, initiative campaigns can attract large sums of money. For example, more than $101 million was spent in California in the late 1990s on five initiatives that dealt with automobile insurance reform.[38]

Voting in Recall Elections   Recall elections permit citizens to attempt to remove elected public officials from office before the end of their term. Eighteen states permit the recall of at least some state-level officials.[39] Like initiatives and referendums, recalls require sufficient petition signatures from registered voters to meet a preestablished threshold. Recall elections have been relatively rare at the statewide level. For example, before the successful 2003 recall of Governor Gray Davis, there had been 31 unsuccessful attempts to recall California governors, none of which made it to the ballot.[40] Only one other governor in U.S. history has ever been recalled (Lynn Frazier in North Dakota in 1921). Although there were significant political problems in California at the time of the Davis vote, including large budget deficits, it has been argued that Davis was recalled largely because of negative views of his political character, which caused him to lose the goodwill and trust of voters.[41]

The 2003 California recall ballot consisted of two questions: the first asking whether to remove Governor Davis from office, the second asking who should replace him if he were recalled.[42] If a majority had voted no on the first question, the results of the second question would not have mattered. Because a majority voted yes on the first question, the person who got the most votes on the second question became the new governor. Other states divide the questions, first having an election to decide whether to recall the official. If a majority votes yes, a second election determines the replacement. Although still relatively rare, recall elections are more common and have been more likely to succeed for local elected officials.[43]

Voting on Bond Issues   Maybe the most common elections voters throughout the country are involved with that do not involve specific candidates revolve around bond issues.

For the People

Improving the Election Process

The chaos in the counting of ballots in Florida in the 2000 presidential election surprised many citizens, who assumed that vote counting was simple and precise. They were wrong. The problems were not isolated to Florida's clogged voting machines or poorly designed ballots. Ballots were misplaced in New Mexico; voting machines broke down in several states; people's names were incorrectly purged from voting lists; and long lines of people waiting to vote led to court challenges. In the weeks and months following the election, at least half the states launched efforts to study the problems and propose solutions. In addition, national commissions, advisory groups, and experts undertook extensive analyses of our voting procedures. How have governments responded?

In 2002, Congress passed the Help America Vote Act (HAVA). HAVA helped states replace antiquated punch-card and lever voting machines with optical scanners and video touchscreen systems. Many states also made it easier for voters to vote early. Thirty-two states now allow voters to vote early without needing to provide a reason for why they might not be able to vote on election day. The remaining 18 states have some form of absentee voting as well.* Other states make it possible to vote by mail, and Oregon has been conducting all of its elections by mail for a decade. HAVA has also led to improved voter registration lists, better trained poll workers, and improved information access for voters.

Of course, even changes designed to make it easier for us to vote come with controversy. The spread of touchscreen voting prompted new debates about the accuracy and accountability of computerized voting machines. How could election outcomes be checked and verified if electronic systems fail to provide a paper record? Other efforts targeted at reducing the potential for fraud by requiring stricter forms of identification might discourage some voters from participating. For years to come, states will debate how best to conduct elections, as elections are central to how our democracy works.

CRITICAL THINKING QUESTIONS

1. When it comes to regulating elections, should we be more concerned about maximizing participation or minimizing fraud?

2. What other aspects of the regulation of elections should be addressed by the states?

* Information available at http://www.ncsl.org/LegislaturesElections/ElectionsCampaigns/AbsenteeandEarlyVoting/tabid/16604/Default.aspx.

States, cities, school boards, and other governmental organizations routinely issue bonds as a way to raise funds for a project now that can be paid off gradually over time. When the government sells the bond to investors, it agrees to pay the purchaser back for the price of the bond plus some amount of interest. The money collected from selling the bonds is then used for some purpose, such as building a new school, expanding a highway, or something similar. In many cities throughout the country, city officials need the approval of voters before they can issue such bonds. Voter participation in such elections is frequently quite low, and information about the issues at hand is generally scarce.

Differences in Campaign Finance

By the early 1980s, nearly all states had campaign finance **disclosure laws.** Disclosure is a fundamental element of campaign finance regulation that asks candidates to file statements specifying who contributed money to their campaigns, and how much the individuals or organizations gave and when. Interest groups are often required to file reports on how they distribute their campaign contributions as well. By making public which individuals and interest groups support a candidate, disclosure laws help voters understand how a candidate may behave in office and help prevent corrupt relationships by making all potential connections public and open to investigation.

Contribution limits are also widespread among the states. These are intended to prevent politicians from relying on a small number of large contributors who might, as a result, exert undue influence. Approximately three-fourths of the states have enacted contribution limits for individual donors—usually limits on how much an individual may give to a particular candidate in a single election or year. All but six states restrict corporate contributions, and most also limit or ban direct contributions from unions.[44] Of course, this may change in the wake of the U.S. Supreme Court's 5-to-4 ruling in January of 2010 that the government may not ban political spending by corporations and unions in candidate elections.[45] This ruling immediately brought laws governing similar kinds of contributions into question in half of the states.[46] Businesses and labor organizations that want to give money to candidates must usually establish political action committees (PACs)—separate political agencies that raise money from employees or union members

disclosure laws

A requirement that candidates specify where the money came from to finance their campaign.

contribution limits

Limits on how much a single contributor may give to a candidate in an election or period of time.

according to clear rules and disclosure requirements. State contribution laws often resemble federal regulations, but some states (and a few cities) have much lower and stricter contribution limits than those allowed in federal elections, whereas five states have virtually no restrictions at all.[47]

Public financing laws aim to replace or supplement private donations with public dollars. The laws have several purposes: to reduce the potential for corruption in relationships between donors and elected officials; to give candidates who are not wealthy or who have no access to rich donors an opportunity to run strong campaigns; and to keep total campaign spending down. The two basic types of public financing programs for candidates are matching grants and flat grants. *Matching grant programs* provide funds to candidates in proportion to every qualifying private contribution the candidates raise and report. In New York City, for example, qualifying candidates for mayor, borough president, and city council seats receive $4 for every $1, up to $250, contributed by a New York City resident. In exchange for accepting public matching money, candidates agree to limit their total campaign spending. This clause is important because, under the U.S. Supreme Court's interpretation of the First and Fourteenth Amendments, involuntary **candidate expenditure limits** are unconstitutional infringements on free speech.[48] *Flat grant programs* provide funds to qualifying candidates in lieu of their raising additional private donations. In Maine, candidates qualify for public subsidies by raising a minimum number of $5 contributions from eligible voters in their state or district.[49] The idea behind this requirement is to determine which candidates are serious, with real voter support. After they raise this "seed money," candidates get a grant from the state to pay all the costs of their primary and general elections campaigns.[50]

Although there are few studies of the effects of public financing programs, evidence suggests they are more important in expanding opportunities to run for office and mounting competitive campaigns than in reducing the role of private contributors.[51] One reason is that private donors, whether individuals or organizations, have many other ways to become active in campaigns and politics, and many candidates who have access to a lot of private money usually forgo using public money. Another challenge for public financing laws is the chronic difficulty states face in raising sufficient public money to support the programs.[52] Maine's legislators, for example, borrowed large sums from the state's Clean Election Fund after the state's general revenues dropped.[53] Thus, although 16 states offer public funds to candidates, many of the programs have few resources to give to candidates, and serious candidates typically refuse to accept public money because the amounts are not sufficient to fund a strong campaign. Public financing has also been advocated for judicial elections as a way to insulate candidates from the potential influence of money from individuals, businesses, or groups that might have cases pending before the court. North Carolina's recent program in this area has been touted by supporters as a model for other states to follow.[54]

public financing laws
Laws authorizing grants of government funds to qualifying candidates for elective office, to be used in their campaigns.

candidate expenditure limits
Limits on how much money a candidate may spend in support of a campaign for elective office.

The Role of Political Parties

Although political parties are not mentioned in the U.S. Constitution, they are vital to our national government and to the functioning of the electoral system within the states. Parties organize electoral competition by recruiting and nominating candidates, function as the loyal opposition when out of power, unify and organize the electorate, and provide a link between the people and their government. Many state constitutions acknowledge their existence.

State parties are, in many ways, more important than national parties. Indeed, national parties, aside from their congressional campaign committees, are largely federations of autonomous state parties. The independence of state parties also helps explain why, for instance, Democratic voters in one state can be so different from those in another, and why Republicans from different states can come down on opposite sides of some major issues.

LEARNING OBJECTIVE
4.3 Outline the organization of state parties and their major functions with respect to elections, voters, and government.

Most states prescribe the organization of the state parties, the means by which their officers are elected, the nomination process for president and other offices, and the requirements that party candidates must meet to get on the ballot.[55] Election rules in general favor the two major parties over minor parties. Although Republican and Democratic candidates can count on being placed on the ballot, state laws typically require minor parties to garner a minimum number of votes in the previous election or submit a prescribed number of signatures of registered voters in order to appear on the ballot. States vary in the difficulty of ballot access for minor parties, depending on three factors: the number of signatures required, the time allowed to collect them, and whether signatures must be distributed across several counties. A handful of states, such as New York, make it easier for minor parties to get on the ballots by allowing them to cross-endorse major-party candidates for office. For example, a candidate for governor in New York might appear on the ballot twice—once as the Republican Party nominee and a second time as the Conservative Party nominee. The candidate's vote total will simply be the sum of the votes he or she gets regardless of which party line a voter marks. In a similar vein, Oregon adopted a system in 2009 that will allow candidates to list up to three political parties next to their names on the ballot.

Party Organization and Officers

Political party organizations have changed enormously throughout the last century, from urban machines dominated by political bosses who often did not serve in elective office, to modern organizations with professional staff able to provide extensive and often technical support to state party candidates.

An Earlier Era: Machines and Bosses   In the nineteenth century, political *machines* became established in a number of U.S. cities. Typically, one political party dominated the political life of the city, often by recruiting new immigrants as supporters and voters by offering them patronage jobs and social welfare benefits. For many years, the epitome of a political machine in the United States was Tammany Hall, the building where the Tammany Society (named after a Delaware Indian chief) met and ran New York City politics. Tammany Hall was closely identified with Democrats and was ruled by William Tweed, the boss of New York City politics.

A *boss* is a party leader who uses patronage, government contracts, and access to power to dictate policy. Some bosses, like Tweed, were never elected to office but rather were powers behind the scenes. Party bosses were common after the Civil War and well into the twentieth century. Other cities with powerful political machines and bosses were Los Angeles, Boston, Pittsburgh, Cincinnati, Philadelphia, Indianapolis, San Francisco, and Baltimore. Maybe the last real political machine boss was Chicago's Mayor Richard J. Daley. Daley, first elected mayor in 1955, served 21 years before his death. Reviled by some as corrupt, brutal, and racist,[56] he was also ranked by a group of historians as the sixth best mayor in American history.[57] His oldest son, Richard M. Daley, served as Chicago's mayor from 1989 to 2011.

The principal objective of the urban reform movement in the early twentieth century was to overthrow the bosses and political machines. Reformers advocated nonpartisan local elections, competitive bids for projects, and civil service in place of patronage. They achieved most of their goals, although it is not clear whether the power of political machines was reduced by these reforms or by other social and economic forces in play at the time.

Party Organizations Today   Although state party organizations vary greatly from one state to another, they differ in several ways from the old political machines. First, instead of being dominated by city bosses, political party organizations are typically under the influence of top state-elected officials, such as the governor or state legislative leaders. These elected officials usually play important, though often informal, roles in selecting the party chair. In all states, a *party chair* is elected by the party's central committee or delegates to a party convention. Other statewide party officers include the *vice chair*, who by state law or party bylaws often must be of the opposite gender from the party chair,[58] plus officers such as treasurer and secretary. Party leaders generally answer to a *central committee,* which consists of 20 or more persons elected or otherwise chosen for specified terms.

The state party chair is the spokesperson for the party, especially when the party does not control the governorship. He or she raises money for the party and its candidates. Because overt expressions of partisanship are thought to be unbecoming in elected officials, often the party chair defends the party and, when necessary, goes on the offensive against the opposition party.

Second, contemporary political parties are more likely to have large, paid, and professional staffs. They often provide assistance to candidates in raising campaign money, developing ads, obtaining and using data on voters and party activists, conducting polls, calling prospective voters to get them to vote, and many other activities. The day-to-day operations of the party are usually carried out by the party's *executive director,* a full-time employee who oversees the staff, assists the chair, coordinates the work of the central committee and other party officials, and serves as a liaison with the national organizations.[59]

Third, political parties do not rely as much as the political machines did on ethnic ties and the promise of material benefits, such as jobs and contracts, to motivate large numbers of people to work on campaigns and support the party's candidates and interests. Most activists are now likely to be motivated by policy or ideological goals or by strong support for a particular candidate. Although some party activists may hope for a job in a new administration if their candidate for governor wins, most party workers are more likely to support the party's candidates because of their positions on issues or because the candidate has considerable personal charisma.

At the local level, political parties are generally patterned after the state party organization. In some counties, party organizations are fully staffed and functioning, but in most, they are run by volunteers and are mostly inactive until just before an election. Local parties provide opportunities for ordinary citizens to become active in politics, a first step that can eventually lead to running for office. Some states, such as Minnesota, have congressional district parties as well.[60]

Although party bosses and strong party machines are a thing of the past, local politics is still organized on a partisan basis in many of our largest cities. Outside these cities, local politics is typically nonpartisan, with three-quarters of U.S. cities having nonpartisan elections.[61]

Party Activities in Elections

U.S. parties used to dominate electoral politics through control of the nomination process, the ballot itself, and political patronage. Beginning with the widespread use of primaries to nominate candidates in the 1960s, our system shifted to a more candidate-centered process. Candidates created their own campaign organizations, appealed directly to potential voters, raised their own funds, and pushed the parties into the background. Starting in the 1980s and accelerating in the 1990s, parties began to enjoy a resurgence as they dramatically improved their fund-raising skills and expanded the campaign services they could provide to voters and, as activists, realized that working within the parties might be an easier path to success than by trying to go around them. In some places, parties recruit candidates, register voters, and mobilize voters on election day.

Structure for Elections Our election system would function in quite a different way if we had no political parties to organize the competition. Parties narrow the field of candidates through a primary election or convention process, providing voters with fewer and more focused choices in the general election. Candidates must secure the support of fellow partisans to win a place on the ballot as the party's nominees for the offices they are seeking.

Candidate Recruitment State party officials often seek out candidates to run for office. Many offices go uncontested, especially as you go down the ballot. Party leaders thus often try to identify potential candidates, even if that candidate will be a "sacrificial lamb" because they want to maintain some presence in a district. The most common place to find potential candidates for state office is among former candidates, local officeholders, or by getting

Former governor Sarah Palin was a force for the Republican party in the 2010 primaries, and her support bolstered the campaigns of a number of Republican Congressional candidates. ■ *How might strong party affiliation in a primary become a disadvantage for a candidate in a general election?*

names from local groups generally supportive of the party, such as a chamber of commerce or teachers association.

Voter Registration   Helping register sympathetic voters is important to candidates, parties, and interest groups. These efforts are typically aimed at citizens they anticipate will vote for their preferred candidate. Interest groups with active voter registration efforts include organized labor, business groups, and groups concerned about the environment and abortion.

Political parties favor laws requiring voters to disclose their party preference at the time they register. This requirement permits parties in states with closed primaries to limit participation to registered party members. Party registration also creates voter registration lists, which parties find extremely useful for campaigning and fund raising. *List vending*—selling voter lists with addresses, phone numbers, and party preferences—is a multimillion-dollar industry. Finally, voter registration helps the parties in the redistricting process because state legislators, using party registration, voting, and other data, can draw new congressional and state legislative district boundaries in ways that give their party an advantage.

Voter Mobilization   Slightly more than three-quarters of eligible voters are registered, and of that number, only approximately two-thirds vote in presidential elections, meaning that *as few as half of the voting-age population bothers to vote* in a presidential election, and still fewer in midterm elections.[62] Turnout in the 2004 presidential election was heavier than in any election since 1968 but was still only 55 percent of the voting-age population. Only 36 percent of the voting-age population voted in the 2006 congressional midterm elections, and only 17 percent of the voting-age population in the 1998 state and local primaries.[63] Turnout for the hotly contested presidential election in 2008 reached 57 percent of the voting-age population.[64]

Elections are often decided by which party does better at turning out its supporters. Get-out-the-vote drives are therefore a major activity of candidates and parties. But what works? The best research has found that a "personal approach to mobilizing voters is generally more effective than an impersonal approach."[65] Door-to-door canvassing, for instance, or telephone calls from neighbors and friends are much more effective than automatically dialed, prerecorded messages. Where resources permit, the parties may even provide transportation to the polls or baby-sitting services.[66]

Campaign Resources   In better-organized states, parties provide extensive campaign funds and campaign help. They raise funds for their party organization and finance voter registration and mobilization efforts, often with the help of national parties.

Well-organized parties train the candidates they have recruited. Wisconsin and New York have strong state legislative campaign committees that distribute resources to candidates, as the national party committee does to congressional candidates.[67] In many states, the state parties provide in-kind contributions to candidates, such as polling data for state and local candidates, advice on campaign themes and strategies, and generic advertisements to use in several state legislative districts. In some states, parties have come to dominate the campaign finance system. For instance, various New Jersey state party organizations provided 59 percent of all contributions to state legislative candidates in the 2005 elections.[68]

Political parties also make direct campaign contributions to candidates in most states. Although they do not typically provide large amounts, their contributions can have an important electoral impact by concentrating resources in support of candidates in the small number of legislative districts where elections are expected to be most competitive. Such districts are typically "open seats," where no incumbent is running for

Registering to Vote

Because elections are the central institution of representative democracy, the best way to participate in your government is to get registered and vote. Getting registered is now easier than it has ever been. Every state government operates a Web site that contains information on how to register to vote. Numerous other Web sites provide similar information, such as Rock the Vote (http://www.rockthevote.com/), the National Register to Vote Web site (http://register-vote.com/), and the League of Women Voters (http://www.lwv.org/). The laws are different in every state. Also, the rules regarding whether college students can register in the place where they attend school versus where their home address is located also vary. Most states require that voters get registered 30 days before the election takes place, so you need to plan in advance.

Once you are registered, you will be assigned a voting precinct. When an election is held, a location within that precinct will be designated as your polling place. It might be a school or an office building, but it might also be an apartment lobby or a local church. Most state Web sites where you can register to vote will also inform you of your polling location, although if you register well in advance of the election, you may need to check for voting location at a date closer to the election. Again, the League of Women Voters sponsors a Web site that helps voters find their polling sites: http://www.vote411.org/pollfinder.php. Find out how to register in your state, where your polling location is, and when the next election is scheduled. What do you need to bring with you when you go to vote? Can you vote early? Participation in governing ourselves is a fundamental right in a representative democracy, and there is no easier way to exercise that right than getting registered and voting.

CRITICAL THINKING QUESTIONS

1. Why might states require voters to register in advance of an election? What are the pros and cons of having voters register weeks in advance compared with doing so on election day?

2. What are the arguments for making voter registration easier? Are there any arguments for making registration more difficult? How do you think voter registration requirements affect young voters?

---

office, or legislative districts where the incumbent is widely viewed as vulnerable. By contrast, interest groups and individual contributors often direct their funds toward incumbents, even when they face weak challengers or none at all.[69]

Parties and Voting Choices

Voters generally base their election decisions on three factors, listed in decreasing order of importance: political party identification, candidate appeal, and issues. In many local elections, because party labels are absent from the ballot, voters rely more on candidate appeal, issues, and factors such as incumbency, media endorsements, and name recognition.

Party Identification   Party identification is the most important predictor of voting behavior. Parties provide a label for candidates that guides voters in making decisions. Party labels are especially important in elections in which voters have little information about candidates, as in contests for attorney general, state senator, state representative, or county commissioner.

People who identify themselves as strong Democrats and strong Republicans are remarkably loyal to their party when voting for state and local offices. Independent-leaners have clear partisan preferences in the direction of one party or the other. Pure Independents have no party preference and are most inclined to vote for one party and then another with changing circumstances, but there are few Pure Independents in the total electorate, and their turnout rates are often low, particularly when there is not a presidential race taking place.[70]

Candidate Appeal   Although party identification is important, it is not decisive. Candidate appeal can be crucial. For example, in the 2003 California recall election, voters not only viewed Governor Gray Davis negatively[71] but viewed Arnold Schwarzenegger positively because of his success in business, the independence from special interests his personal wealth allowed, and his sponsorship of a ballot initiative that provided for afterschool programs.[72] In the 1998 Minnesota gubernatorial election, Reform Party candidate Jesse Ventura was elected largely because his style and approach

Three Iowa Supreme Court justices facing a retention election were defeated in 2010, the first time anyone had lost their seat on the Iowa bench since the current system began in 1962. All three were targeted by a conservative group called "Iowa for Freedom" because they were part of the Court's unanimous decision in 2009 that permitted same-sex marriages in Iowa. The group spent several million dollars on its campaign, most of which came from individuals and groups outside of Iowa. ■ *Should state Supreme Court Justices be held accountable to the electorate for their rulings?*

generated interest among voters, and a plurality preferred him over the established candidates in the major parties.

In state and local elections, name identification and the advantages of incumbency—such as campaign resources and the ability to point to constituent service—are important. Incumbency advantages at the state level have been especially high for executive offices—governors and attorneys general, for instance—but they have been large factors in state legislative races as well.[73] In primary elections, when all the candidates are from the same party, voters cannot use party affiliation to make their choices and must rely on candidate appeal, issues, and incumbency. They may also vote for the candidate they perceive has the best chance of winning the general election.[74]

Issue Voting Issues can be very important to the outcome of elections. Economic conditions are as important a factor in state and local elections as they are in national ones. William Weld, a Republican, was able to win his first Massachusetts gubernatorial election in 1990, despite the fact that Massachusetts is a very strong Democratic state, because the state's economy at the time was so bad. Former New Jersey Governor Christine Todd Whitman won election in part because her incumbent opponent had raised state taxes and she promised a 30-percent tax cut. Although issues are important in state and local elections, it is fair to say that they are probably less important than at the national level.[75] Research shows that gubernatorial candidates can affect the issues voters use to evaluate them on election day by what issues the candidates choose to stress during their campaigns.[76]

Judicial Elections Judicial elections in some states are partisan and resemble campaigns for other offices in intensity. More than $16 million was spent on television ads in state judicial campaigns in 2006, with candidates increasingly stating positions and using negative advertisements against their opponents on issues such as gay marriage, school vouchers, abortion, gun control, and school choice.[77] Many states used to regulate the conduct of judicial candidates to limit such behavior, but the U.S. Supreme Court, in *Republican Party* v. *White* (2002) ruled such restrictions unconstitutional. This ruling has fueled the trend toward judicial campaigns looking more like races for other offices. A lot of campaign money comes from corporations concerned about liability, environmental, and other economic regulatory issues. The trend toward expensive and divisive judicial elections has prompted criticism by good-government groups and efforts to extend the use of alternative means of selecting and retaining judges. We will take up this issue in greater detail in Chapter 7 when we discuss state courts and the judicial branch.

Nonpartisan Local Elections Arguing that political parties had little to contribute to the administration of local government, reformers during the first half of the twentieth century introduced nonpartisan elections. The two parties were, in effect, blocked from exerting an open influence on local politics.

Some observers contend that nonpartisan local elections make it more difficult for less-affluent and less-educated citizens to participate effectively. For such people, the party label serves to identify politicians who share their values and perspectives on government. Well-educated and wealthy voters know more about who is running and what they stand for, even without party labels. Nonpartisan elections sometimes help Republican candidates, especially in cities with populations of more than 50,000, because Republican voters tend to vote in low-turnout elections and are more likely to know which candidates are Republicans.[78] Others have found that there is not generally an advantage to Republican candidates in nonpartisan elections.[79]

Parties in State Government

Political parties are not only critical in conducting elections and campaigns; they also help organize our governmental institutions, particularly the state executive and legislative branches.

Parties in the Executive Branch Just as winning the presidency is the big prize at the national level, so is winning the governorship at the state level. The party that controls the governorship has the power to appoint executive department officials and some state judges. Governors are usually perceived as the state leaders of their party, and they establish the political agenda and help define the party for their state.

Governors usually campaign on behalf of their party, even when they are not on the ballot for reelection. Presidential candidates often seek the help of governors. In fact, presidential candidates are often former governors, as were four of the last six presidents. Governors raise money for campaigns as well as for the state party. They have wide latitude in appointing boards, commissions, judges, and state administrators, and they almost always take party affiliation and activity into account when making appointments.

Parties in the Legislature Like Congress, state legislatures (excluding Nebraska, which is nonpartisan) are organized largely along party lines. The *speaker of the house or assembly* and the *president of the senate* are elected by the majority party in most states. They preside over floor proceedings and make key assignments to standing committees and study committees. Most state legislatures have floor leaders, called *majority leaders* and *minority leaders* and majority and minority *whips*.

In most states, parties sit on different sides of the aisle in the legislative chambers and are separated in committee meetings as well. Committee chairs in most state legislatures go to members from the majority party in that chamber, and most committees have more members from the majority party than from the minority party. As a result, leaders of the majority party wield great power in deciding what bills are considered and ultimately passed in state legislatures. The **party caucus** is often important in state legislatures. The caucus is a meeting of party leaders and legislators to discuss party policy. Because some state legislatures meet for only a few months a year, the party caucus can help hammer out agreements rapidly.

Political parties also structure the decision making of state legislators when casting their votes on bills. In most states, when a legislative proposal is controversial and the outcome is close, most Democrats find themselves on one side of an issue with most Republicans on the other side.[80] Political scientists Gerald Wright and Brian Schaffner demonstrate the importance of party in state legislatures by comparing the unicameral in Nebraska, in which members are elected on a nonpartisan ballot, to the state senate in neighboring Kansas. The party affiliation of legislators clearly structures the coalitions formed in the Kansas Senate but plays little role in shaping how senators in Nebraska's state legislature behave.[81]

One area in which legislatures are predictably partisan is **redistricting.** Each decade, following the national census, state legislatures are constitutionally required to realign congressional and state legislative district boundaries to make them equal in population and reflect population changes. In a series of decisions in the 1960s, the U.S. Supreme Court required states to equalize the population size within state legislative districts just as they are required to do for districts for the U.S. House of Representatives.[82] Previously, it was common for districts to follow other established boundaries, such as county lines. Industrialization and the resulting concentration of population in urban centers meant that many states had some urban legislative districts that included ten times as many voters as several rural districts. This forced **reapportionment**—the reallocation of legislative seats based on population—shifted power to urban areas and helped create pressure to modernize state legislatures.[83]

The redistricting following the 2000 census was especially important because the two parties were so evenly divided in numbers of legislative chambers controlled, that is, the upper and lower houses in 49 states, and the single unicameral in Nebraska. However, the 2006 elections altered this balance by shifting control of many state legislatures toward the Democratic Party. Going into the 2008 elections, the Democrats controlled 57 chambers, the Republicans 39, and two were tied.[84] Of course, redistricting will occur again following the 2010 census. Going into the 2010 elections, Democrats controlled both

party caucus
A meeting of the members of a party in a legislative chamber to select party leaders and develop party policy. Called a *conference* by the Republicans.

redistricting
The redrawing of congressional and other legislative district lines following the census, to accommodate population shifts and keep districts as equal as possible in population.

reapportionment
The redistribution of seats in a legislature. In the United States, this occurs in order to equalize the size of populations within legislative districts and happens as part of the redistricting process.

With the election of Governor Mary Fallin, Republicans control the governership and both legislative houses in Oklahoma for the first time ever.

two-party state
A state in which the two major parties alternate in winning majorities.

one-party state
A state in which one party wins all or nearly all of the offices and the other party receives only a small proportion of the popular vote.

chambers in 27 states, Republicans in only 8 states, with 14 states having split control (and Nebraska being nonpartisan).[85] The elections in 2010 dramatically reversed party control of state legislatures. Republicans emerged with control of both chambers in at least 25 states and one chamber in another 5 states. This shift will give Republicans an opportunity to use redistricting to solidify their electoral gains.

The way district lines are drawn can help or hurt a party. When one party controls both houses and the governorship or has a veto-proof majority in the legislature, the majority party can do what it wants with district boundaries, so long as it keeps the districts equal in population and respects the rights of racial minorities. For instance, Democratic legislators may try to pack as many Republican voters as possible in a small number of districts so that the remaining districts in the state have majorities of Democratic voters. The importance of state redistricting to the national parties is so great that the parties are establishing and funding special organizations devoted to influencing state redistricting processes.[86] Where power is divided between the parties, redistricting that protects incumbents is often the result.

Although, traditionally, it has been the practice to redistrict only once per decade, usually right after the decennial census data become available, redistricting may become more frequent and sensitive to shifts in party control of the state legislatures. In 2003, Texas replaced a congressional districting plan that a state court had drawn up the previous year with one much more favorable to Republicans. The new plan was challenged in court, eventually reaching the Supreme Court, which upheld the constitutionality of most of the second plan, overturning only one district's boundaries that were held to dilute Hispanic votes in violation of the Voting Rights Act.[87] However, a similar attempt to replace a court-drawn plan in Colorado was struck down by the state supreme court because the state constitution allowed redistricting only once a decade.[88]

In five states, commissions rather than the legislatures do the redistricting. Commissions tend to be more neutral and often create districts that are more competitive. This was the case in Arizona with the last redistricting. Arizona's new congressional district, the First District, had nearly equal numbers of registered Democrats and Republicans and was seen as a toss-up by political prognosticators. The Republican candidate has won this district most years, but three times with less than 55 percent of the vote, and the Democrat won in 2008.

Party Balance and Imbalance

LEARNING **OBJECTIVE**

4.4 Assess how party competition has changed in recent decades.

We can classify state politics according to how the parties share public offices. In a **two-party state,** the Republican and Democratic parties can each regularly assemble winning majorities. Two-party states include Indiana, Michigan, and Missouri. In a **one-party state,** one party wins all or nearly all the offices, and the second party usually receives only one-third or less of the popular vote. One-party Republican states currently include Utah, Idaho, and Kansas. Massachusetts and Rhode Island are examples of Democratic one-party states. It is possible for Democrats to win in Utah, and the same is true for Republicans in Massachusetts, but the more predictable tendency is for state voters to support the predominant party. Of course, the classic examples of one-party dominance of states in the United States are the Democratic party dominance that characterized southern states from the end of Reconstruction into the 1970s and 1980s.[89]

Since the end of World War II, there has been an accelerating trend toward two-party politics. The Democratic Party lost its previously solid support in the South as more and more white southerners moved to the Republican Party. Since the mid-1970s, the number of Republicans in southern state legislatures has increased from approximately 12 percent to nearly 50 percent in 2008.[90] In the 2008 elections, the South was the only region of the country where Republicans gained state legislative seats.

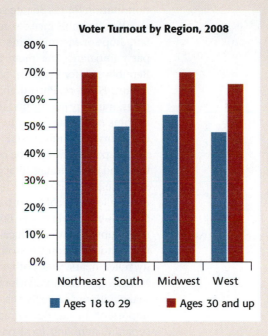

Youth Voting

Numerous reports following the 2008 presidential election credited a strong turnout among young voters as pivotal to Barack Obama's victory. Using data from the U.S. Census Bureau, the Center for Information and Research on Civic Learning and Engagement reported that approximately 51 percent of those under 30 years old voted, equivalent to approximately 22 million voters nationwide.* This marked an increase of 2 percentage points over the 2004 presidential election and a full 12 percentage points compared with 2000. Of course, turnout among older voters remained substantially higher in 2008 compared with younger voters (67 percent to 51 percent), but many wondered if 2008 signified a new and sustained high level of participation among younger citizens.

Higher turnout was not uniform across all younger voters. Among younger citizens, women were more likely to vote than were men (55 percent compared with 47 percent). African American youth turnout reached 58 percent, compared with 52 percent among non-Hispanic whites, with Asian and Latino voting rates at approximately 41 percent each. A major division among young people is whether they have attended college or not. While 62 percent of those who have attended at least some college voted, only 36 percent of those with no college experience did so.

Most important for this chapter, there were substantial differences across the states in terms of youth turnout. Youth turnout in Minnesota, Iowa, and New Hampshire exceeded 60 percent, whereas less than 40 percent of young people voted in Hawaii, Arkansas, Utah, and Texas. Although a variety of factors may explain these differences across states, a critical factor is whether or not states allow for election day registration (EDR). Youth voting was a full 9 percentage points higher in states with EDR compared with states without it. Early voting options, the distribution of sample ballots and polling place information, and no-excuse absentee balloting also appear to increase turnout among young voters.

CRITICAL THINKING QUESTIONS

1. Why are young people less likely to vote than older voters? Which of these factors could be affected by reforms to election laws and practices?

2. What might be the consequences for the policies different states adopt if youth voter participation rates are substantially different from one state to the next?

Voter Turnout by Region, 2008

Region	Ages 18 to 29	Ages 30 and up
Northeast	54%	70%
South	50%	66%
Midwest	54%	70%
West	48%	66%

■ Ages 18 to 29   ■ Ages 30 and up

---

* The Center for Information and Research on Civic Learning and Engagement, Youth Voting (http://www.civicyouth.org/?page_id=241), their Presidential Election fact sheet (http://www.civicyouth.org/PopUps/FactSheets/FS_youth_Voting_2008_updated_6.22.pdf), and their State Election Law Reform and Youth Voter Turnout fact sheet (http://www.civicyouth.org/PopUps/FactSheets/State_law_and_youth_turnout_Final.pdf) provide all the information for this section.

Republican gains have also been evident in contests for governor and president. Since 1966, all southern states have elected a Republican governor at least once, and in 2010, Republican governors led seven southern states. In terms of the popular vote for president, since 1964, the only Democratic candidate for president to win more than 4 of the 11 former Confederate states was Jimmy Carter in 1976, who at the time was governor of Georgia. In 2000 and 2004, all 11 former Confederate states went to George W. Bush. Democrat Barack Obama won three southern states in 2008, although three other southern states (Arkansas, Louisiana, and Tennessee) increased their support for the Republican ticket between 2004 and 2008.

Outside the South, there has also been a gradual spread of two-party politics, with the rise of Democratic strength in the formerly solid Republican states of Iowa, Maine, and New Hampshire. Democrats had been losing strength in parts of the Rocky Mountain area, though they gained four House seats, two Senate seats, and three governorships in these states in the 2004 and 2006 elections. Democrats gained another six House seats and two Senate seats in 2008. Democrats have also been winning most seats in Congress in the Northeast and Pacific Coast states.

What are the consequences of party balance? When parties and their candidates compete vigorously, they are more likely to be sensitive to public opinion, for the loss of even a fraction of the voters can tip the scales to the other side in the next election. Party competition may lead opposing candidates to compete for the middle ground on issues, at least the middle ground in their particular districts. Strong party competition may also generate more service to constituents by legislators.

In a one-party state, party imbalance may have a serious effect on the account-ability that is part of electoral competition. Voters do not participate as much as they do in two-party contests, and voters who do cannot rely on party labels to help them differentiate between candidates. Competition that otherwise would occur *between* the major parties occurs among factions *within* the majority party. The most important con-tests in some states such as Massachusetts are generally not between Democrats and Republicans but among Democrats in the primary; the same is true for Republicans in Utah. In these intraparty fights, personalities dominate the campaign. This was evident in 2010, when incumbent U.S. Senator Bob Bennett was defeated in his bid for the GOP nomination for his Senate seat by a coalition of conservatives and Tea Party supporters.

If party imbalance disorganizes the dominant party, it pulverizes the minority party. With faint hope of winning, minority party leaders do not put up much of a fight. Extreme forms of party imbalance are more commonly found in cities and towns than at the state level. Republicans, for instance, hardly ever carry Chicago; Boston; Washington, D.C.; Baltimore; Albany; Hartford; Pittsburgh; and many other cities throughout the industrial North. In such cases, minority parties find it difficult to raise money for campaigns and persuade people to become candidates. They have no state or local patronage to give out. Volunteers are slow to come forward. Young people wishing to succeed in politics drift into the dominant party. The second party is likely to be concerned only with national politics, where it may win an elec-tion, and the patronage that could come its way if its candidate wins the White House.

The great differences in party balance across state and local governments remind us that while we talk of a two-party system in the United States, the reality is we have more than 50 distinct party systems. Because parties are organized to compete for elective office, par-ties adapt to state and local political cultures, which vary enormously due to differences throughout the country in economic conditions, social classes, race, ethnicity and national-ity, religion, and many other factors. The resulting differences across state parties and party systems give rise to divisions within each of the major parties when the "national" parties make nationwide decisions, such as whom to nominate for presidential elections. But it is important for our democracy that these differences are expressed forcefully by the many separate state and local parties throughout the country, as they typically represent real differences in citizens' opinions. Thus, state political parties straddle between the varied (and often changing) opinions and circumstances of each state's citizens and the imperative to make national decisions regarding leadership and government policies in the federal government. As such, state parties help to ensure that when national decisions are made, those decisions are responsive to a wide range of citizen viewpoints.

CHAPTER **SUMMARY**

4.1 Compare and contrast the constitutional roles of state and federal governments in regulating elections.

In the United States, there are no national elections, only state elections. Even the presidential election is a set of 51 different elections to choose electors, who will in turn cast their ballots for president. The U.S. Constitution gives states the lead role in determining the conditions under which elections for U.S. senators and representatives are held, although it also author-izes the national government to make or alter those

regulations. States have even more authority to regulate elections to state and local governments. Amendments to the U.S. Constitution have generally extended access to the vote.

4.2 Describe differences among the states in laws regulating voting, elections, and campaign finance, and assess federal influence on these regulations.

States are primarily responsible for defining who may vote, conditions under which they may register, when elections will be held (other than elections to national offices), how voting occurs, how party nominees are chosen, and which candidates appear on the ballot. Unlike the federal government, most states have some provisions for direct forms of democracy, including citizen initiatives, referendums, or recall elections. States have also developed a wide variety of campaign finance regulations; some impose virtually no restrictions other than disclosure requirements, whereas other states and some cities have extensive regulations on private money combined with public financing programs. States share authority over election law with the federal government, which has sometimes imposed constraints on state election laws.

4.3 Outline the organization of state parties and their major functions with respect to elections, voters, and government.

Contemporary political parties are often dominated by top state officeholders who have extensive professional staff. Political parties play important roles in candidate recruitment, voter registration, voter mobilization, and fund raising, and they provide a link between people and government. Voters usually vote along party lines, although candidate characteristics and issues also influence them. Parties are also important to the operation of most state legislatures. The governor is the head of his or her party. Governors consider party loyalty when appointing people to executive and judicial openings.

4.4 Assess how party competition has changed in recent decades.

States vary in whether the two parties are competitive. In one-party states, elections are generally won by one party, whereas in two-party states, the parties often alternate in holding power. More states have become competitive in recent years.

CHAPTER **SELF-TEST**

4.1 Compare and contrast the constitutional roles of state and federal governments in regulating elections.

1. True or false: "The presidential election is the only purely national election in the United States."
   a. True
   b. False
2. Match the following Constitutional articles and amendments to their results:

a. Article I	i. States must have a republican form of government.
b. Article IV	ii. States may not deny voting rights on the basis of race.
c. Fifteenth Amendment	iii. Senators are elected by each state's people rather than by its legislators.
d. Seventeenth Amendment	iv. Each state may decide its own way of electing senators and representatives, but Congress can intervene if it wants.

4.2 Describe differences among the states in laws regulating voting, elections, and campaign finance, and assess federal influence on these regulations.

3. In a paragraph, identify three or four factors that influence voter turnout and explain how each increases or decreases it.
4. States are making it increasingly easy for people to vote, such as through vote-by-mail, absentee ballots, and pre-election day voting. In a paragraph, discuss the benefits and potential problems of these measures.

5. In two or three sentences, explain why strong supporters of the Republican and Democratic parties prefer closed primaries to open primaries.
6. In one or two paragraphs, suggest two reasons for campaign finance disclosure laws, and discuss the effects of these laws.

4.3 Outline the organization of state parties and their major functions with respect to elections, voters, and government.

7. In one or two sentences, describe the tools used by political machines to maintain their power.
8. In a few sentences, delineate three differences between the old political machines and today's political parties.
9. Which proportion of the voting-age population has turned out to vote for recent presidential elections?
   a. Approximately 35 percent
   b. Approximately 55 percent
   c. Approximately 75 percent
   d. Approximately 90 percent
10. In an essay, describe how the political parties help mobilize voters, simplify voting choices, and provide resources to candidates. Also, suggest how local elections might be different without political parties.

4.4 Assess how party competition has changed in recent decades.

11. List three areas of the country that have seen major shifts in party competition, and describe those shifts.
12. In a paragraph, list and discuss three problems that arise when one party dominates state politics.

Answers to selected questions: 1. b (False; there is no truly national election); 2. a. iv, b. i, c. ii, d. iii; 9. b

 **EXERCISES**

Apply what you learned in this chapter on MyPoliSciLab.

📖⊸ **Read** on **mypoliscilab.com**

eText: Chapter 4

👁⊸ **Watch** on **mypoliscilab.com**

Video: New Ballots Bring New Complications in New York
Video: Green Party Candidates Stay on Ballot

✔⊸ **Study** and **Review** on **mypoliscilab.com**

Pre-Test
Post-Test
Chapter Exam
Flashcards

KEY **TERMS**

primary elections, p. 71
general elections, p. 71
special elections, p. 71
recall elections, p. 71
initiative, p. 71
referendum, p. 71
voter turnout, p. 72
party column ballot, p. 75

straight ticket, p. 75
office block ballot, p. 75
split ticket, p. 75
closed primary, p. 77
crossover voting, p. 77
open primary, p. 77
disclosure laws, p. 80
contribution limits, p. 80

public financing laws, p. 81
candidate expenditure limits, p. 81
party caucus, p. 87
redistricting, p. 87
reapportionment, p. 87
two-party state, p. 88
one-party state, p. 88

ADDITIONAL **RESOURCES**

FURTHER READING

R. MICHAEL ALVAREZ AND **THAD E. HALL,** *Electronic Elections: The Perils and Promises of Digital Democracy* (Princeton University Press, 2008).

R. MICHAEL ALVAREZ, THAD E. HALL, AND **SUSAN HYDE,** EDS., *Election Fraud: Detection, Prevention, and Consequences* (Brookings Institution Press, 2008).

EARL BLACK AND **MERLE BLACK,** *Politics and Society in the South* (Harvard University Press, 2005).

BRUCE E. CAIN, TODD DONOVAN, AND **CAROLINE J. TOLBERT,** EDS., *Democracy in the States: Experiments in Election Reform* (Brookings Institution Press, 2008).

THOMAS M. CARSEY, *Campaign Dynamics: The Race for Governor* (University of Michigan Press, 2000).

JEFFREY E. COHEN, ED., *Public Opinion in State Politics* (Stanford University Press, 2006).

GARY W. COX AND **JONATHAN N. KATZ,** *Elbridge Gerry's Salamander: The Electoral Consequences of the Reapportionment Revolution* (Cambridge University Press, 2002).

THOMAS E. CRONIN, *Direct Democracy: The Politics of Initiative, Referendum, and Recall* (Replica Books, 2000).

LARRY N. GERSTON AND **TERRY CHRISTENSEN,** *Recall! California's Political Earthquake* (Sharpe, 2004).

V. O. KEY, JR., *Southern Politics in State and Nation* (Knopf, 1949; reprinted by University of Tennessee Press).

NORMAN R. LUTTBEG, *The Grassroots of Democracy* (Lexington Books, 1999).

DAVID B. MAGLEBY, *Direct Legislation: Voting on Ballot Propositions in the United States* (Johns Hopkins University Press, 1984).

L. SANDY MAISEL, *American Political Parties and Elections: A Very Short Introduction* (Oxford University Press, 2007).

MARK MONMONIER, *Bushmanders and Bullwinkles: How Politicians Manipulate*

Electronic Maps and Census Data to Win Elections (University of Chicago Press, 2001).

DANIEL SMITH AND **CAROLINE TOLBERT,** *Educated by Initiative: The Effects of Direct Democracy on Citizens and Political Organizations in the American States* (University of Michigan Press, 2004).

JON WINBURN, *The Realities of Redistricting: Following the Rules and Limiting Gerrymandering in State Legislative Redistricting* (Lexington Books, 2008).

LINDA WITT, KAREN M. PAGET, AND **GLENNA MATTHEWS,** *Running as a Woman: Gender and Politics in American Politics* (Free Press, 1994).

WEB SITES

www.democrats.org/local.html Links to the 50 state Democratic parties.
our.gop.com/app/render/go.aspx? **xsl=search.xslt&searchTerm=*:*&** **searchFilter=SearchObjectType:OUR.**

GOP.COM_STATES Links to the 50 state Republican parties.

www.nass.org/ This is the site for the National Association of Secretaries of State. The secretary of state in most states is the top official who oversees the conduct of elections in the state.

elections.gmu.edu/ This site for the United States Elections Project, hosted by Professor Michael McDonald at George Mason University, contains information on recent national and statewide elections.

www.ncsl.org/default.aspx?tabid=16580 This site for the National Conference of State Legislatures Ballot Initiative Database can be searched for information on any statewide ballot initiative that has been held.

State Legislatures

A lthough state legislatures play a vital role in state politics and policy making, they are not simply smaller versions of the U.S. Congress. State legislators face unique challenges related to the nature and resources of their positions. In addition, the experience of a state legislator can vary dramatically from state to state, as does the number of people legislators in different states represent. Some California state legislators represent more people than another state's U.S. Representative.

In some states, being a legislator can be a full-time job. These state legislatures pay good salaries, have numerous support staff and resources, meet year-round, and attend to a robust scope of activities. State legislators in California, Michigan, New York, and Pennsylvania earn annual salaries of nearly $80,000 or more. Many other states pay members poorly, provide little staff, and only meet part-time. Legislators in Maine, Mississippi, Nebraska, North Carolina, and Texas, among others, make less than $15,000 per year. In Vermont, legislators make $625 per week when the legislature is in session, which is typically for about 16 weeks from January through April. In contrast, the legislature in California has more than 2,000 staff members assisting the legislators, while members in Vermont share a common pool of around 20 clerks and 15 lawyers.[1] These states with part-time legislatures embody the ideal of the "citizen" legislature—a body of representatives who are not full-time career politicians but are instead part-time legislators serving as citizen representatives.

Another difficulty faced by legislators is balancing the need to represent the sometimes narrow interests of their districts with responding effectively to all of the major policy issues that affect residents of the entire state. State legislators decide on issues from taxes to health care to education to economic development, but they still cannot forget about the neighbors and local businesses in their own district that are holding them accountable. Former state legislator Ralph G. Wright was the Speaker of the House in Vermont for a record-setting ten years before being defeated for reelection in 1994. Wright reflects, "I got beat that November [because] I had forgotten my roots. Montpelier [the state capital] had become more important than my district, and like an army that outruns its supply line, I had outrun my reservoir of good will back home."[2] Thus, service as a state legislator is both broadly important for the entire state and deeply personal and local.

Faced with difficult tasks, few resources, and varying levels of professionalism, why would anyone want to serve in a state legislature? Wright suggests that people serve in legislatures like Vermont's for many reasons, but at least part of the draw is the desire to be part of the great "game" of politics: to be where the action is and to be in a place where you can effect some good for others. Serving in a state legislature can be an opportunity for average citizens to have a bigger impact on the policies that affect their own communities.

This chapter will examine state legislatures in greater detail by asking what they do, how they are organized, and how they have adapted to a much more complex world. As they have grown into more professional bodies, state legislatures are claiming a greater role in the workings of government and are becoming important partners in both state policy and federal action.

The Legislative Branch

State legislatures existed long before the Continental Congress was formed in 1776. They exerted great power under the Articles of Confederation and were reluctant to give up their power to either the national government or their own governors. Most states had relatively weak executives, and several had no executive at all. Although state legislatures

CHAPTER **OUTLINE**
CHAPTER LEARNING
OBJECTIVES

The Legislative Branch

5.1 Explain how state legislatures are organized, and describe state legislators and their responsibilities.

Influences on State Legislators

5.2 Identify the factors that influence state legislators' voting decisions.

Modernization and Reform

5.3 Evaluate recent changes in state legislatures.

Drawing Legislative District Lines

5.4 Analyze the controversies over redistricting.

Direct Legislation: Policy Making by the People?

5.5 Evaluate the debate regarding the methods of direct democracy available to some states.

LEARNING **OBJECTIVE**

5.1 Explain how state legislatures are organized, and describe state legislators and their responsibilities.

today do not dominate state policy making the way they did in 1787, they do play a vital role in state politics and policy.

State legislatures make laws and modify and approve budgets. They strive to solve problems and provide services without raising taxes or creating larger bureaucracies. They make or modify policies by balancing conflicting political pressures, while forging compromises among political factions, interest groups, or different parts of the state. Legislatures also perform countless constituency services and, along with the governor and the courts, help keep state agencies accountable to both the laws and the citizens.

The 50 state legislatures share many characteristics—all states except Nebraska have a two-house **bicameral legislature.** Nebraska has a one-house **unicameral legislature.**[3] The larger chamber is generally called the *house of representatives*, or in a few states, the *assembly* or *house of delegates*. It contains as few as 40 members in Alaska and as many as 400 in New Hampshire; the average number is about 100. In all but five states, representatives serve two-year terms; in Alabama, Louisiana, Maryland, Mississippi, and North Dakota, they serve four years. The smaller chamber, known as the *senate*, is typically composed of approximately 40 members who serve four-year terms, though senators in 11 states serve only two-year terms.[4]

How Are Legislatures Organized?

State legislatures look very much like the U.S. Congress. A *speaker*, usually chosen by the majority party, presides over the lower house. In many states, speakers have more power to control proceedings than their national counterpart has. For example, most state speakers have the right to appoint committees and thus play a key role in determining policy. However, their power varies greatly: Speakers in West Virginia, New Hampshire, Arizona, and more than a dozen other states have strong formal powers,[5] whereas Speakers in Alaska, Mississippi, Hawaii, and Wyoming have minimal powers.[6] In 25 states, lieutenant governors preside over the senate, though they are usually mere figureheads; in other states, the majority party in the senate chooses its presiding officer, the *president of the senate*.[7]

As in the U.S. Congress, the committee system prevails. Every state has a series of standing, or permanent, committees as well as some temporary or ad hoc committees. In several states, such as Maine and Massachusetts, *joint committees* can speed up legislative action. However, state legislative committees usually do not have the same power over bills as their national counterparts: Some still lack adequate professional staffs, the seniority system is not as closely followed as in Congress, and turnover is usually higher, especially where term limits have taken effect. Still, legislators themselves report that committees play an important part in legislative decision making in nearly every state legislative chamber.[8]

Every legislature has committees on education, transportation, agriculture, and energy or natural resources. Most also have important committees on rules, appropriations, and taxes (sometimes called the Ways and Means Committee). The number of standing committees varies widely across states. The lower houses of states including Colorado, Maryland, and Rhode Island have ten or fewer standing committees, whereas the lower houses of Illinois, Mississippi, North Carolina, Texas, and Wisconsin have 40 or more standing committees.[9] Legislators generally specialize and become experts on one or two substantive matters, such as education, crime, taxation, or the budget process.

Legislatures differ in the way members interact and conduct legislative politics—differences that stem from historical or ethnic traditions, or from regional divisions or differences. Here is how one expert on state politics viewed some of the more distinctive characteristics shaping state politics in the United States:

> In New York professional politics, political wheeling and dealing and frantic activity are characteristic. In Virginia, one gets a sense of tradition, conservatism, and gentility.... Louisiana's politics are wild and flamboyant. By contrast, moderation and caution are features of Iowa. A strong disposition of compromise pervades Oregon, with politicians disposed to act as brokers and deal pragmatically rather than dogmatically. In Kansas, hard work, respect for authority, fiscal prudence, and a general conservatism and resistance to rapid social change are pervasive features of the state environment. Indiana is intensely partisan. Wyoming is mainly individualistic, and Ohio is fundamentally

bicameral legislature
A two-house legislature.

unicameral legislature
A one-house legislature.

conservative. In Hawaii, the relatively recent political dominance of Japanese and the secondary status of Chinese, native Hawaiians, and Haoles (whites) makes for tough ethnic politics. Yankee Republicans used to run Massachusetts, but now the Irish dominate. Their personalized style, which blends gregariousness and political loyalty, results in a politics of the clan. Mormonism of course dominates Utah.[10]

Who Serves in the State Legislature?

Like members of the U.S. Congress, most state legislators run for reelection and win. Indeed, nearly 95 percent of incumbents who seek reelection succeed. Approximately one-third of state legislative elections are uncontested, especially in smaller, one-party states and in the South.[11] Although 67 percent are contested, only about 25 percent of state legislative elections are closely contested—with "closely" defined as the winner receiving 60 percent of the votes or less.[12] An incumbent seeking reelection has many advantages over a challenger: name recognition, better access to campaign funds, experience in running campaigns, and a record of helping constituents with problems.

Despite this apparent advantage, in an incumbent's mind, there is seldom such a thing as a "safe district" and a sure reelection. "Whatever their margins of victory in prior elections, however 'safe' their district may appear to the analyst, incumbents know that lightning can strike....They have seen colleagues relax their efforts and subsequently lose their seats. They live in perpetual danger of casting a roll-call vote that upsets their constituency or mobilizes a key interest group to seek their defeat."[13]

Personal Profile   The typical U.S. state legislator is a 53-year-old white male, well-educated and well-off, often a business executive or lawyer of Anglo-Saxon origin who has had some type of previous political experience—not always elective—at the city or county level. Some have worked as staff members in the legislature or in state government.[14] Most have held some type of local party position and have been active in political campaigns. Surprisingly, approximately one-third were born in some other state, a reflection of our increasingly mobile population.

State legislators tend to have more education and higher incomes than other citizens in their states. They are usually hard-working, public-spirited citizens who believe that being in the legislature is a good opportunity for service. Yet state legislators enjoy less prestige than members of Congress, especially in states that have large legislatures. Discouraged by modest salaries and long hours, many serve a few terms and then either retire voluntarily or run for higher office. As one one-termer explained, "A great deal in the political process does not—repeat, does not—involve the glamorous policy issues. Most of the work is sheer routine and hardly awe-inspiring."[15] And some leave because term limits in their states prevent more than two or three terms.

Party Affiliation   After the 2008 elections, Democrats had an edge over Republicans in the state legislatures. Democrats occupied 3,023 of the 5,411 House seats, whereas Republicans occupied 2,356; similarly, Democrats held 1,020 of the 1,971 Senate seats, whereas Republicans held 893. Only 70 of the nation's state legislators consider themselves Independents or nonpartisan, including all 49 members of Nebraska's unicameral legislature.[16] As a result of the 2008 election, Democrats controlled both houses in 27 states, the Republicans held both houses in 14 states, and 8 states had divided control.

Occupation   Business owners or managers has surpassed lawyers in recent years as the largest occupational group in most state legislatures. Business owners or managers account for approximately 18 percent of state legislators nationwide, with lawyers down to 15 percent. There has been an increase in those who consider themselves full-time legislators, from about 3 percent in 1976 to slightly more than 16 percent in 2007. There has also been a slight increase as well of teachers, homemakers, retirees, and students.[17] Because legislators must have flexible schedules, the job often attracts retired people and those whose businesses or professional practices have been so successful that they can afford to take time off. Real estate and insurance dealers and sales representatives are also commonly found. The number of farmers continues to fall, declining from about 10 percent of state legislators in 1976 to nearly 5 percent in 2007. This has

Congresswoman Hilda L. Solis was the first Latina elected to the California State Senate. In 2009, she was named U.S. Secretary of Labor.

Of the People

AMERICA'S CHANGING FACE

Diversity in the Statehouse

In the late 1960s, state legislatures were dominated by white men and often had the look of a "good old boys' club." This has begun to change in recent years, and there is more diversity in legislatures now than at any time previously.

Diversity in State Legislatures, 2009

Male: 5,594 (76%)
Female: 1,788 (24%)

White: 6,350 (86%)
African American: 628 (8.5%)
Latino: 242 (3.3%)
Asian: 85 (1.2%)
Native American: 77 (1%)

The largest growth has occurred among women. In 1971, only 4.5 percent of state legislators were female, whereas today, that number has reached 24 percent. In four states—Colorado, Minnesota, New Hampshire, and Vermont—more than 35 percent of legislators are women. The states with the largest number of African American legislators include Georgia, Maryland, and Mississippi. The largest numbers of Hispanic legislators reside in New Mexico, Texas, and California. More than half of all Asian legislators serve in Hawaii, and more than a quarter of all Native American legislators serve in Oklahoma.

Although scholarly research is a bit mixed, diversity appears to have both procedural and substantive consequences for how state legislatures operate. Several state legislatures have well-organized and influential black caucuses that help shape legislation. Some research suggests that female legislators may have somewhat different policy preferences than their male counterparts, and that women may also practice a more consensus-oriented politics. Evidence also suggests that female and minority citizens feel more efficacious toward government when they see members of their own group serving in office. Such *descriptive representation*, as it is called, allows some citizens to feel like they have an advocate representing their perspective on political issues facing the state.

CRITICAL THINKING QUESTIONS

1. How important is it for the legislature to reflect the demographic makeup of its population? How well does your state legislature reflect your state's demographic makeup?

2. Does descriptive representation have consequences for how your state legislature operates? Do you think it should?

SOURCE: National Conference of State Legislatures, "Legislator Demographics," http://www.ncsl.org/default.aspx?tabid=14850.

---

resulted from redistricting shifting power away from rural areas and a decline in the number of farms and farmers in the population (see Figure 5–1).

Prospects Many state legislators go on to fill other elected offices. About half of the members of the U.S. Congress in 2008 were former state legislators—229 of the 435 members of the House of Representatives and 40 of the 100 U.S. senators.[18] Many statewide elected officials are also former state legislators.

What State Legislators Do

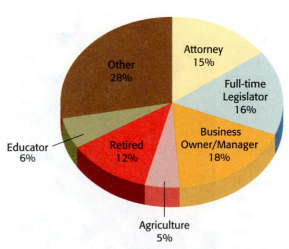

FIGURE 5–1 Professions of State Legislators.

■ *Why do you suppose only 16% are full-time legislators?*

SOURCE: National Conference of State Legislatures.

The nation's 7,382 state legislators engage in many of the same lawmaking and oversight activities as members of the U.S. Congress: They enact laws that create state parks; specify salaries for state officials; draw up rules governing state elections; fix state tax rates; set workers' compensation policies; determine the quantity and quality of state correctional, mental health, and educational institutions; and oversee welfare programs. State legislators approve all appropriations and thereby confirm or modify a governor's proposed budget. In most states, they are also responsible for overseeing the administration of public policy. Although they do not administer programs directly, legislators determine through hearings, investigations, audits, and the budgetary process whether programs are being carried out according to legislative intentions. Bill passage rates vary greatly from state to state, depending on a variety of factors, including procedural necessities, constitutional requirements, and local culture. Figure 5–2 outlines the steps in passing state laws.

State legislatures perform various functions within the larger federal system, such as ratifying proposed amendments to the U.S. Constitution, calling for a constitutional convention to propose an amendment to the U.S. Constitution, and approving interstate compacts on matters affecting state

98

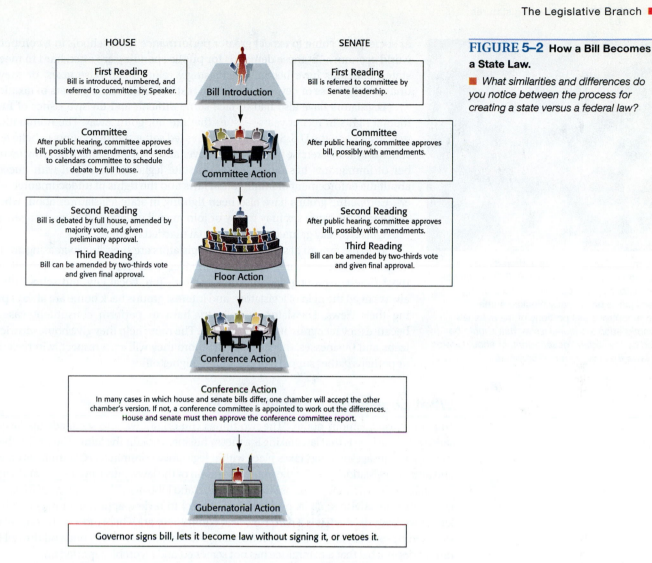

HOUSE

SENATE

First Reading
Bill is introduced, numbered, and referred to committee by Speaker.

Bill Introduction

First Reading
Bill is referred to committee by Senate leadership.

Committee
After public hearing, committee approves bill, possibly with amendments, and sends to calendars committee to schedule debate by full house.

Committee Action

Committee
After public hearing, committee approves bill, possibly with amendments.

Second Reading
Bill is debated by full house, amended by majority vote, and given preliminary approval.

Third Reading
Bill can be amended by two-thirds vote and given final approval.

Floor Action

Second Reading
After public hearing, committee approves bill, possibly with amendments.

Third Reading
Bill can be amended by two-thirds vote and given final approval.

Conference Action

Conference Action
In many cases in which house and senate bills differ, one chamber will accept the other chamber's version. If not, a conference committee is appointed to work out the differences. House and senate must then approve the conference committee report.

Gubernatorial Action

Governor signs bill, lets it become law without signing it, or vetoes it.

FIGURE 5–2 How a Bill Becomes a State Law.

■ *What similarities and differences do you notice between the process for creating a state versus a federal law?*

policies and their implementation. Each state's constitution prescribes the procedures its legislatures must follow and sets limits on the rate of taxation, the kinds of taxes, the subjects that may be taxed, and the purposes of taxation. State legislatures participate in amending their states' constitutions by proposing amendments for voter ratification (see Chapter 2). Legislatures also have authority to impeach and try state officials, and they confirm or reject individuals nominated by governors for executive and judicial posts.

State legislators help translate public wants and aspirations into laws and regulations. In addition to their lawmaking functions, they also try to be ombudsmen—to listen, learn, and find solutions to problems. Invariably, state legislators wind up doing a lot of favors: getting a merchant a license to sell lottery tickets, persuading a state agency to look into safety standards at the local hospital, pushing for funds to repair county roads, arranging for a campaign supporter to be appointed to the state labor commission, and so on. State legislators are accessible. Citizens and students can almost always contact their legislators directly and communicate with them in person, by telephone, or via e-mail.

The agenda of issues that legislators confront varies over time and from state to state. Some budget issues have severely challenged many states' legislatures in recent years. Rapid increases in health care costs and the growing number of people without health insurance have made it very difficult for state legislatures to slow government spending in this area. Public demands for state spending have also been strong for the building and repair of roads and highways; for environmental protection, particularly as the federal government has cut back its support for such functions; for correctional facilities, as more criminals have been given lengthy sentences; and for primary and secondary education,

State Senator Russell Pearce authored Arizona's immigration reform legislation, SB1070, which has been criticized for encouraging racial profiling. A federal judge has already blocked some of the more controversial portions of the state law.

■ *Is immigration a national issue, that should be handled by the federal government, or should states adopt laws that they deem appropriate?*

as society has come to expect greater performance from schools in a competitive world economy. Yet these demands for public spending are often hard to meet, as state politicians have become increasingly reluctant to raise taxes, or they are unable to because of new constitutional restrictions on their powers of taxation.

Legislators have also had to face some difficult and divisive issues of fundamental rights in recent years—issues that are not going away. The nomination of new justices on the U.S. Supreme Court has led some state legislators to believe that states may now exercise greater control over access to abortions. The growing number of immigrants has put pressure on state legislatures to deal with questions about the enforcement of immigration laws and the rights of undocumented workers. Competing groups have also been fighting in state legislatures about whether couples of the same sex may marry or join in civil unions and enjoy some or all of the rights typically granted to heterosexual married couples.

With the growth of state functions, legislators are spending increasing amounts of time on casework or constituency services. Constituent relations are often the most time-consuming aspect of a legislator's job. Local city and school officials always need the help of legislators, and interest groups back home are always pressing their views. Legislators usually try hard to perform constituent casework because they recognize its political value. The more help they give home-district citizens and businesses, they reason, the more they will earn respect, win reelection, or perhaps gather support for election to higher office.

What Legislative Committees Do

To paraphrase a famous quote, "The two things you do not want to see made are laws and sausages." The idea is that lawmaking is a messy business not for the faint of heart. The bulk of legislative "sausage-making" takes place within legislative committees. Committees consider and amend legislation, oversee the implementation of the laws, interview judges, and serve as the major access point for citizens, interest groups, and lobbyists. The functions of a legislative committee are advisory; all its proposals are subject to review, approval, or rejection by the legislative body of which it is a part. However, committees are where most of the critical decisions, compromises, and details of proposed legislation are hammered out, and the full body rarely adopts a bill that a committee has not screened and favorably reported on.

Committees vary in power and influence from state to state. In less populous states, committees are pale shadows of their counterparts in the U.S. Congress because of short sessions, limited staffing, and turnover of both staff and legislators. In other states, however, their influence has increased in recent decades. Committees process and shape hundreds or even thousands of bills and resolutions every year.[19] In many of the more professionalized legislatures, they may also meet between sessions of the legislature, conducting hearings and preparing for the next session.

The committee system allows members to concentrate their energies on specific areas of governmental operations. Over time, legislative committees and their members develop extensive knowledge about particular activities and provide their colleagues with greatly valued information about the content and desirability of proposed bills. Because it is impossible for everybody to be an expert on all aspects of state government, properly staffed and run committees can evaluate the merits and faults of a proposed law more effectively than any individual legislator can.

So just how powerful are committees? It is hard to tell because most committees are controlled by the majority party in a chamber, and committee members are appointed by chamber leaders. Thus, separating the power of committees from the power of parties and chamber leaders is difficult. Still, surveys show that the vast majority of state legislators believe that committees are important centers of power in the legislature.[20] Another way scholars look for evidence of committee power is by considering how many bills die in committees, arguing that killing bills is evidence of committees exercising *gatekeeping power*—the power to prevent proposals from being considered or passed by the entire chamber.[21]

Contacting Your Representative

State legislators generally work very hard to represent the view of their constituents. However, they often have very limited information on exactly how their constituents feel about a given issue. They do not have the time or resources for extensive public opinion polling, and a surprisingly small number of citizens contact their representatives directly to express their views. In fact, most of the letters, phone calls, and e-mails legislators receive come from organized efforts by interest groups. Thus, when legislators do get a genuine contact from a constituent, they are often eager to respond. This is where you come in.

Every state legislature operates a Web site for both its upper and lower house. They are easy to find using an Internet search of your state's name and the term "legislature." You can also find them on the following NCSL Web site, which provides links to chambers in all 50 states: http://www.ncsl.org/?tabid=17173. Now, find your own state representatives in both the upper and lower chamber of your state's legislature. What are their names, occupations, and party affiliations? On what committees do they serve, or what bills are they currently sponsoring?

You can write your representatives a personal letter or e-mail expressing your views on an issue currently under consideration by the legislature. This might be something your representative has sponsored, something under consideration in one of their committees, or just an issue that is of concern to you. Most legislators want to hear from their constituents. As a follow-up, keep track of how long it takes your representative to respond, whether that response looks like it came directly from him or her or from a staff person, and whether it specifically addresses the issue you mentioned or looks more like a generic "thank you for contacting me" letter. Compare your experience with your classmates, and discuss what this implies for the quality of representation you are receiving.

CRITICAL THINKING QUESTIONS

1. Why do you think legislators respond to personal letters and e-mails from individuals? What is their motivation?

2. How do you think the responses you might get from legislators would be affected by whether they serve in a professional or part-time legislature, whether they face term limits or not, or whether you are a member of the same political party as your legislators or not? Why might these factors matter?

Influences on State Legislators

State legislators are influenced by many of the same factors that affect members of the U.S. Congress, including legislators' personal ideology and policy positions and the views of their constituencies.

LEARNING OBJECTIVE

5.2 Identify the factors that influence state legislators' voting decisions.

Political Parties

Except in Nebraska, candidates for state legislatures are nominated by political parties in primaries or by party conventions and caucuses, and they are elected *as party members*. Although the official party organization is sometimes not a dominant influence in recruiting state legislative candidates, a candidate nonetheless has to go through the party to gain the nomination. Figure 5–3 shows the current party control of the state legislatures.

The role of political parties in the governance of legislatures and in policy making varies widely from state to state. Gerald Wright and Tracy Osborn report that party unity—the degree to which members of the same party vote together on bills and differently from members of the other party—varies substantially across states.[22] In fact, party unity scores in many state legislative chambers exceed those observed in the U.S. House of Representatives. Legislators in California, Washington, Colorado, Minnesota, Wisconsin, and Texas are among the most polarized, whereas those from Oregon, Louisiana, Rhode Island, and West Virginia are among the least polarized.[23]

In nearly every state where there are two active parties, the political party selects legislative leaders and assigns members to committees. **Party caucuses**—meetings of all the members of one party in the chamber—also distribute campaign funds to their members and to specifically targeted districts.

The party caucus is a principal instrument for legislative decision making in about half the states, including Colorado, Delaware, Idaho, Montana, California, and Utah. In states where a party holds a slim majority of the seats in a legislative chamber, representatives are more likely to feel pressure to "toe the party line" than where a party commands a large majority.[24] Similarly, legislators are more likely to vote with their party in states where the political party plays an important role in recruiting and nominating candidates.

party caucus
A meeting of the members of a party in a legislative chamber to select party leaders and develop party policy.

FIGURE 5–3 **Party Control of State Legislatures, 2011**
After the 2010 elections, at least eighteen legislative chambers switched from Democratic control to Republican control. ■ *How would public policy making under a single-party state legislature differ from policy making in a state legislature under split control?*

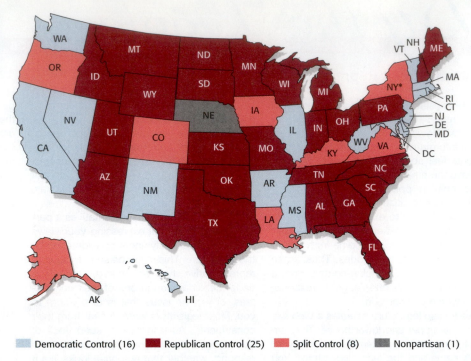

Democratic Control (16)　Republican Control (25)　Split Control (8)　Nonpartisan (1)

*Based on projections as of mid-November 2010.

In legislatures in which a single party has had long-standing dominance or control, as used to be true in most southern states, parties are less important in conducting and shaping legislative business. However, the re-emergence and success of the Republican party in the South was accompanied by a strengthening of parties both inside and outside legislative chambers.

Interest Groups

Interest groups are a significant and growing source of influence on state legislatures. One group of scholars concludes, based on surveys of public officials and political scientists, that interest groups have a dominant impact in Alabama, Florida, Hawaii, and Nevada, whereas they are weakest in Kentucky, Michigan, Minnesota, South Dakota, and Vermont.[25] Teacher organizations, trade associations, labor groups, trial attorneys, taxpayer associations, insurance, mining, real estate, road builders, and banking interests are often the most visible single-interest groups. In states with a dominant major economic interest, such as agriculture, mining, lumbering, or fishing, legislators pay close attention to the needs of that interest, regardless of whether the group employs lobbyists.

Most state interest groups use lobbying as a major tool of influence. **Lobbying** is attempting to influence the decisions of public officials, especially legislators. The right to lobby is secured by the First and Fourteenth Amendments to the Constitution, which protect the right of the people to petition the government for redress of grievances. State constitutions provide similar protections.

Anyone can try to influence how a state legislator votes. States usually define a professional **lobbyist** as someone paid to influence legislators on behalf of a client or clients. States now require lobbyists to register annually, either with the secretary of state's office or with an election or lobbyist commission. In most states, lobbyists must pay a fee for lobbying. The more populated states register thousands of lobbyists.

Most lobbyists are regular employees of corporations, unions, or trade associations. Many are members of law firms; others are former state employees. Effective lobbyists are specialists in both subject matter and legislative procedure. They know the schedule of general hearings, committee meetings, floor debates, and social events. They also know as much as possible about the legislators, their electoral support, their values, their hobbies, and who has their "ear." Lobbyists live by two important rules: First, remember that it is a lot easier to kill a bill than to pass it. And second, have no permanent allies and no permanent enemies. Today's opponent may be your supporter on the next issue for which you are lobbying.[26]

lobbying
Engaging in activities aimed at influencing public officials, especially legislators, and the policies they enact.

lobbyist
A person who is employed by and acts for an organized interest group or corporation to influence policy decisions and positions in the executive and legislative branches.

Some of the most effective lobbyists are retired state legislators. They not only have good contacts with their former colleagues but also know where the leverage points are in the legislative process. "If you happen to know the four people on a certain senate committee," said one Colorado legislator, "it's pretty damn easy to kill a bill."[27]

Lobbyists have two sources of influence: information and campaign resources. Information is usually the key ingredient in gaining or losing a vote. Effective lobbyists typically explain how the sometimes complicated laws or proposals are likely to affect the businesses, institutions, and individuals in a legislator's own district. Although the popular impression of lobbyists suggests that they will say and do anything to win, that is generally not true. A lobbyist who wants a long career must protect his or her reputation for dealing honestly with legislators. If a lobbyist tricks, misleads, or lies to a legislator, or does something that embarrasses a legislator or gets a legislator in hot water with his or her constituents, word will spread quickly that the lobbyist in question cannot be trusted.

In addition, interest groups are usually major financial backers of incumbent legislators, and in return, the lobbyists for those groups get unusual access. As the costs of state legislative races climb, so does the dependence of legislators, legislative leaders, and political parties on organized interests.[28]

Illegal use of lobbying techniques, primarily bribery, has been found in some states. Scandals have been exposed in Arkansas, Arizona, Kentucky, Massachusetts, New Mexico, and South Carolina, among others, in recent years. Still, bribery is not a widespread problem in most states. Writing about his own experiences in the Vermont Senate, Frank Smallwood observed that as a rule, most of the lobbyists "were articulate, hard-working, and extremely well-informed in their particular areas of expertise. This last attribute—information—represented their chief weapon and gave them real clout. As far as I could find out, the lobbyists didn't offer legislators any money or other direct inducements, at least, they never offered me anything, not even a sociable drink. Instead they relied on information."[29]

In recent years, states have sought to regulate lobbying activities, conflicts of interest, and the financing of political campaigns. For example, several states have enacted laws that prohibit contractors or executives from their companies from contributing to officials who could influence state contracts. In addition to adopting this pay-to-play law, Connecticut also bans campaign contributions from the children and spouses of candidates.[30] At the beginning of his term in 2008, Governor Bobby Jindal pushed through the Louisiana legislature a package of tough ethics rules, including financial disclosure, restrictions on lobbyist spending, and prohibitions on state-financed or disaster-related contracts with legislators and executive branch officials.[31]

Laws that control lobbying and campaign contributions are difficult to enforce. First Amendment rights severely limit a government's ability to regulate lobbying activities.[32] There are two schools of thought on lobbyist regulations. One says that creating more complex and difficult lobbying and campaign-funding regulations merely drives the process further away from the public eye to the advantage of those with the resources and skills needed to navigate the rules. The other school of thought is embodied in a quote by former Texas Governor Anne Richards, who said, "I'm all for…reform…just to slow things down. If you can create an atmosphere in which you got to learn new tricks to cheat…" it at least makes moneyed interests work harder.[33]

Constituents

Usually the greatest influence on legislators comes from the people who elect them, their constituents. Former state legislator John E. Brandl says state legislators understand that on election day, their constituents who are grateful for favors received "are more apt to express positive sentiments on the ballot than those not receiving benefits from the capitol.… A former colleague of mine in the Minnesota House of Representatives seemed bewildered when he heard the suggestion that his first responsibility as a legislator might not be to look out for his district but rather to be concerned for the good of the whole state. 'Nobody who thinks like that could ever get elected from my district,' he maintained."[34]

Still, if state legislators are elected to represent the people and their views at the statehouse, few lawmakers think they should merely mirror or "re-present" the views of their district's constituents. Most legislators like to consider themselves **trustees** of their

trustee
An official who is expected to vote independently, based on his or her judgment of the circumstances; one interpretation of the role of a legislator.

Promoting Trust in Government

Of importance to a constitutional democracy is that citizens understand what their governments are doing and have trust in their leaders. The National Conference of State Legislatures (NCSL) launched a program several years ago to promote civics education and citizen participation in order to foster greater trust. The program includes the "America's Legislators Back to School Program," in which more than 1,200 legislators reach out to more than 1 million students every year through classroom visits. NCSL has also produced several public service announcements targeted at young people designed to "tackle cynicism and common misconceptions about representative democracy." NCSL has partnered with other organizations to produce a nonpartisan television effort called "American Democracy Television," which also targeted school-aged children. Finally, NCSL has organized the "Democracy in America" seminars designed to provide training and support for teachers.

All these programs are designed to provide more information about how representative government in the states works and how citizens can get involved. Programs like this put a human face on government, making it easier for young people to relate to the political process and see a role for themselves in it. More information about the program, several additional documents, and video clips of the public service announcements can be found online here: http://www.ncsl.org/default.aspx?tabid=15390.

CRITICAL THINKING QUESTIONS

1. What kinds of activities or events do you think would influence the level of trust or cynicism young people might have toward government in their state? What kinds of things would work? What kinds of things would likely fail or even backfire?

2. Are teachers or representatives in your state participating in these "back-to-school" programs? What role should they have in promoting democratic values and trust in government?

constituents, claiming to rely on their own conscience or on their considered judgments in making decisions. Legislators who view themselves as **delegates,** by contrast, adhere more closely to instructions from their constituents. Not surprisingly, the trustee role is not only more popular among legislators, but it is also easier and more realistic to practice. Given the complexity of government and the difficulty of finding out where citizens stand on a wide variety of issues, the trustee role is a more workable one in the day-to-day decision making of a legislator during legislative sessions. Only on issues of keen local interest do legislators tend to assume the role of a trustee.

Learning from Other Governments

Another aspect of state politics that often fuels legislation is action taken by other states. Legislators frequently ask their staffs, "What is California, Minnesota, or Oregon doing on

delegate
An official who is expected to represent the views of his or her constituents even when personally holding divergent views; one interpretation of the role of a legislator.

this problem?" They are always on the lookout for innovative tax, educational, or welfare policies implemented elsewhere and keenly interested in how their state compares with others—on sales taxes, teenage driving privileges, high school dropout rates, air quality, the minimum wage, or federal monies coming to the state. The press often uses such rankings in headlines and editorials.

The National Conference of State Legislatures, a nonpartisan professional organization funded by all 50 state legislatures, acts as an effective clearinghouse for new ideas (www.ncsl.org). With approximately 180 staff members located mainly in Denver, Colorado, it distributes studies to legislators across the country. A rival yet smaller and more conservative group, the American Legislative Exchange Council, has developed in recent years (www.alec.org). The Council of State Governments (www.csg.org) and the State Legislative Leaders Foundation (www.sllf.org) are two groups that also help serve state legislative leaders.

Actions taken by the federal government also influence state laws and regulations. During the past 30 years, states have accepted federal grants for many programs, such as Medicaid and primary and secondary education. In exchange, they must dedicate state funding to the programs and meet certain federal requirements. The need to allocate state money and structure state-administered programs to meet these federal requirements is a sore point for many state legislators.

Finally, just as states sometimes serve as laboratories for other states and the national government, local governments sometimes serve as laboratories for the states. For example, many cities banned smoking in restaurants before most states considered taking such action. Local governments have also been innovators in policies as diverse as public education and public funding of elections.

Modernization and Reform

As states are asked to take on increasing responsibility, their legislatures face greater pressure to modernize, which has also changed how legislators act. According to state legislative scholar Alan Rosenthal, "Earlier, leaders were truly in command, and power was tightly held. Partly as a consequence of modernization and reform, legislatures have been democratized. Resources are more broadly distributed, and the gap between leaders and other legislators is narrower."[35]

State legislatures in the past were criticized as inefficient, ineffective, poorly staffed, scandal-ridden, secretive, sexist, unrepresentative, and often dominated by rural interests. Most had little or no staff and high rates of turnover among members. They were often run by factions that could not be held accountable, and parliamentary procedures and inadequate committee systems either prevented action or served narrow or specially favored interests. Legislators had to rely primarily on information from lobbyists or the governor's office.

Given the goals of members, the demands of groups, and the heavy workload, deliberation gives way to expediency. Members frequently are unwilling to say no to their colleagues, lest their colleagues say no to them. They also are averse to saying no to constituents, lest their constituents withdraw support. The process has become porous; much seeps through that probably should not. Standing committees do not screen the wheat from the chaff as diligently as they might.[36]

Most state legislatures have adopted internal reforms to address these shortcomings. Legislatures typically now have longer annual sessions, expanded and more competent staffs, more effective committee systems, streamlined procedures such as automated bill status and statute retrieval systems, higher salaries, and modern information systems.[37] In 1979, for example, state legislatures had 16,930 permanent staffers; by 1996, the number had climbed to 27,882, where it has held steady up through 2009.[38]

Legislatures have also become more sensitive to new technologies. Every legislature now has a colorful Web site with detailed information about the workings of the lawmaking body. Hawaii has a fully equipped and staffed "public access room," making it easy for citizens to lobby their state legislators.[39] Michigan, Missouri, Utah, Virginia, and Washington were scored by the Pew Center for the States as best in applying data and technology to measure the effectiveness of government services, to make decisions,

LEARNING OBJECTIVE
5.3 Evaluate recent changes in state legislatures.

DECIDE Should Legislators Be Paid Higher Salaries?

The idea of a citizen legislature, an assembly populated by ordinary citizens who meet periodically to discuss the needs of their community and decide how they should address them, is appealing to many. Idaho boasts that the success of the state's legislative chamber in guiding the state is due to its citizen legislators. "Farmers and ranchers, businessmen and business-women, lawyers, doctors, salespeople, loggers, and teachers" are in session for only three months each year. Their part-time status, the state asserts, enables them to "maintain close ties to their communities and a keen interest in the concerns of the electorate."*

In citizen legislatures, politics is not supposed to be a career, and elected officials are expected to work only part time.

Compensation for these state legislatures reflects this belief. In states with less professional legislatures, members spend approximately half their time on the job, and their compensation, including salary, per diem, and any other expense payments averages $15,984 a year. In states with professional legislatures, however, members work full time or close to it, and their higher compensation, averaging $68,599, allows them to make a living as a state legislator without having another source of income.**

What do you think? Should states provide higher compensation for their legislators? What arguments would you make for and against such an idea?

THINKING IT THROUGH

Raising legislative salaries is almost always a contentious issue in the states. The public tends to be skeptical of salary increases, doubtful that they are warranted, and inclined to believe that legislators enact them out of self-interest. Opponents of higher salaries argue that professional politicians do not necessarily do a good job, and they point to problems in a state with a professional legislature as evidence in favor of citizen assemblies. Debating a salary hike in Arizona, ultimately denied by the voters, Republican Senator Robert Blendu moaned, "Look at California—they're professional politicians and they've run that state into oblivion."†

Proponents of higher salaries counter that legislators work more hours than people realize, even in states with acknowledged part-time legislators. When the legislature is not in session, members attend meetings, work on legislation, and help their constituents. The work is complicated and demanding, especially as the federal government has given more responsibilities to the states and as citizens have come to expect more from their state governments. If legislators do not do this work, power is likely to shift to other government offices, such as the governorship and administrative agencies.

When compensation to legislators is low, proponents continue, the assembly resembles a citizen's body in name only. Many people cannot afford to serve in the legislature, and the opportunity is limited to those who are retired or independently wealthy, or whose occupations provide sufficient flexibility that they can leave their jobs for several months at a time. "No one goes into politics to get rich," notes former Massachusetts State Senator Tom Birmingham. "But you can't have a system where only the rich get into politics."‡

Critical Thinking Questions

1. What are the strengths and weaknesses of a citizen legislature, and how do they compare with the strengths and weaknesses of a professional legislature?

2. Is higher compensation for legislators likely to foster a more diverse and representative body? Why or why not?

* www.legislature.idaho.gov/about/citizenlegislature.htm.
** "NCSL Backgrounder: Full- and Part-Time Legislature," updated January 2008, National Conference of State Legislatures, 204.131.235.67/programs/press/2004/backgrounder_fullandpart.htm.
† Phil Riske, "Arizona Lawmakers Seek 50% Salary Hike—Again," *Arizona Capitol Times*, September 29, 2006.
‡ Tom Birmingham, quoted in Karen Hansen, "Legislator Pay: Baseball It Ain't," *State Legislatures* (July–August 1997), p. 20.

and to communicate with their citizens.[40] In short, amateur, part-time state legislatures are much less common now than a few decades ago. The new professionalism reflects a determination on the part of most legislators—especially the leaders—to take charge of their own branch as a major player in shaping state public policy.

The movement to encourage full-time professional legislatures with substantial staffs, however, has not been universally praised. In fact, in recent years, some political scientists and some citizens have contended that we were better off when we had part-time citizen-legislators. The groundswell in the early 1990s to enact term limits was in many ways a voters' protest against professionalized legislators who appeared to be making their job of representation into a career.

Legislative Term Limits: Problem or Solution?

Although the complexity of state problems may well require professional legislators who devote full-time attention to legislative issues, this professionalism "runs counter to the traditional theory of American politics in which citizens come together, conduct the public's business, and return to their other occupations."[41] In the 35 states without term limits, many legislators have served for a very long time—and hence are perceived by some as less connected to the people they represent.

Term limits were the most talked-about legislative "reform" in the 1990s. Reform began in 1990 when voters in California, Colorado, and Oklahoma approved the first term-limit restrictions through citizen-instigated ballot initiatives. Two years later, another 11 states enacted voter initiatives along the same lines. Several more approved term-limit provisions of some type, but voters in three states rejected them. In addition, state legislators in Utah and Louisiana voted to impose term limits on themselves. State supreme courts in five states—Massachusetts, Nebraska, Oregon, Washington, and Wyoming—have struck down term limits as unconstitutional. Note, however, that in 2000, four years after their court nullified voter-approved limits, Nebraskans voted to reinstate them. In 2004, voters in Arkansas and Montana rejected ballot measures that would have relaxed term limits.

There is some evidence that the term-limit movement has run out of energy. In 2002, Idaho legislators repealed term-limit provisions that voters had approved on several occasions. Term-limit supporters complained that this legislative repeal constituted "a slap in the face to all Idaho voters. The arrogance of the Legislature to repeal an issue that has been supported by four separate votes is unconscionable."[42] But Idaho legislative leader Bruce Newcomb responded that term limits won approval only because out-of-state money influenced the votes: "We were a cheap state to buy; it was not in the public interest....There was never a real debate....They had no opposition."[43] In 2003, the Utah legislature followed suit, repealing the limits it had imposed on itself only five years earlier.[44] Oregon voters in 2006 rejected an attempt to reinstate term limits after a court ruling had struck them down, and in 2007, Maine lengthened term limits from four to six terms.[45]

Nevertheless, term-limit provisions exist in 15 states (see Table 5–1). These limit state legislators to service of 6 to 12 years. In some states, lawmakers are barred from serving in the same office beyond a set number of years. In nine other states, they must skip one term (more in some states) before running again. In 2002, for example, 71 percent of Michigan's

TABLE 5–1 | Term Limits in the States

State	Year Enacted	House Limit (years)	House Year of Impact	Senate Limit (years)	Senate Year of Impact	Popular Vote in Favor
Maine	1993	8	1996	8	1996	67.6%
California	1990	6	1996	8	1998	52.2
Colorado	1990	8	1998	8	1998	71.0
Arkansas	1992	6	1998	8	2000	59.9
Michigan	1992	6	1998	8	2002	58.8
Florida	1992	8	2000	8	2000	76.8
Missouri*	1992	8	2002	8	2002	75.0
Ohio	1992	8	2000	8	2000	68.4
South Dakota	1992	8	2000	8	2000	63.5
Montana	1992	8	2000	8	2000	67.0
Arizona	1992	8	2000	8	2000	74.2
Oklahoma	1990	12	2004	12	2004	67.3
Nevada†	1996	12	2008	12	2008	70.4
Louisiana	1995	12	2007	12	2007	76.0
Nebraska‡	2000	8	2008	—	—	55.8

* Because of special elections, term limits became effective in 2000 for eight current members of the House and one senator in 1998.
† The Nevada Legislative Council and attorney general have ruled that Nevada's term limits cannot be applied to legislators who were elected in the same year that term limits were passed (1996). They first apply to persons elected in 1998.
‡ Nebraska has a unicameral legislature.

■ *During what period of time were most term limits enacted, and how many years on average were legislators limited to serving? Do you support or oppose term limits?*

SOURCE: National Conference of State Legislatures, "The Term-Limited States," www.ncsl.org/programs/legman/about/states.htm.

legislators were forced out of office under term limits. The California statute goes even further. It slashed legislative staffs, curbed legislative pensions, limited the number of terms legislators could serve, and prohibited legislators from ever running again for the legislature.

Thus far, term limits have not changed the general profile of state legislators.[46] Yet, term limits have serious consequences for state legislative activity. In a comprehensive study, political scientist Thad Kousser finds that the gains produced by "a higher level of professionalism" are wiped out by term limits.[47] Kousser argues that this gets at the fundamental question of whether we want professional politicians as our representatives. In California, novice lawmakers now chair committees and hold leadership positions, and signs there and elsewhere suggest that term limits discourage legislative cooperation, decrease institutional expertise, and generally weaken legislatures relative to governors, bureaucrats, and lobbyists. It takes several years for new legislators to become acquainted with rules, procedures, and regulations; to jettison politicians just as they begin to feel comfortable, confident, and knowledgeable is to lose a wealth of accumulated experience.

redistricting
The redrawing of congressional and other legislative district lines following the census to accommodate population shifts and keep districts as equal as possible in population.

gerrymandering
The drawing of legislative district boundaries to benefit a party, group, or incumbent.

malapportionment
Having legislative districts with unequal populations.

LEARNING **OBJECTIVE**

5.4 Analyze the controversies over redistricting.

Drawing Legislative District Lines

State legislatures are required by their state constitutions, by federal laws, and by court rulings to draw district boundaries for both their state legislature and U.S. House of Representative seats after each population census to ensure that each district represents essentially the same number of voters. The 2010 census will once again trigger this mandatory redistricting of congressional and state legislative lines. However, most states are free to redraw district boundaries more frequently, and several have done so in recent years either for political reasons or in response to court orders.

Redistricting is the action of a state legislature or other body in redrawing legislative electoral district lines. About a dozen states delegate these responsibilities to independent redistricting or reapportionment commissions. In Alaska, the governor's office draws the legislative districts. Most legislatures consider these once-a-decade responsibilities so important, however, that they are unwilling to turn over control of the task to anybody else.

Drawing legislative district boundaries has always been controversial, in large part because redistricting decisions are made by partisan majorities in legislatures. The highly political nature of the undertaking is usually reflected in the results. "Redistricting is the political equivalent," says one observer, "of moving the left field fence for a right-handed pull hitter. By changing the boundaries, redistricting helps some, hurts others—and leaves just about everyone else scrambling."[48] Computers and mapping software have made the politics of redistricting even more precise and sophisticated.

In 2003, Republicans in the Texas state legislature introduced a redistricting plan designed to help the party gain a majority of the state's seats in the U.S. House for the first time since Reconstruction. Democratic legislators tried to block the plan by leaving town, preventing the legislature from being able to vote. These eleven Democratic state senators spent a month in Albuquerque, New Mexico. Eventually one returned, the plan was passed, and the Republicans succeeding in winning a majority of Texas's U.S. House seats in 2004. ■ *Should redistricting be affected by partisanship? Should elected officials use the chamber's rules to block legislation that will otherwise pass?*

Drawing district boundaries to benefit a party, group, or incumbent is called **gerrymandering.** The term was first used in 1811 to describe a strange, salamander-shaped legislative district drawn in northeastern Massachusetts when Elbridge Gerry was governor. A district does not need to be odd in shape, however, to be gerrymandered.

As a result of huge differences in population among the districts, state legislative districts used to face problems of **malapportionment.** State legislatures for decades had given rural and small-town voters more votes in the legislature than they were entitled to based on population alone. In Georgia, for instance, the 1960 reapportionment gave the largest county, with 556,326 inhabitants, no more representation than the three smallest counties, whose *combined* population was 6,980.[49] City officials complained bitterly that small-town and farmland-dominated legislators were unsympathetic to their problems and had different legislative priorities.

No matter how much they protested, people who were underrepresented in the state legislatures made little progress. Legislators from small towns and farm areas naturally did not wish to reapportion themselves out of jobs, and their constituents did not wish to lose their influence. Even though the failure of state legislatures to reapportion often violated express provisions of state constitutions and raised serious questions under the U.S. Constitution, state and federal judges took the position that issues having to do with legislative districting were "political questions" and outside the scope of judicial authority.

Finally, the U.S. Supreme Court stepped in. In 1962, in *Baker* v. *Carr,* the Court held that voters have standing to challenge legislative apportionment and that the federal courts should consider such questions. Arbitrary and capriciously drawn districts deprive people of their constitutional rights of representation, and federal judges may take jurisdiction over such cases.[50]

One Person, One Vote

In *Wesberry* v. *Sanders* (1964), the U.S. Supreme Court announced that "as nearly as practicable one man's vote in a congressional election is to be worth as much as another's."[51] The Court extended this principle to representation in the state legislatures, although it subsequently modified this decision to allow for somewhat larger population discrepancies among state legislative districts than for congressional districts.

In *Reynolds* v. *Sims* (1964), the Court held that "the fundamental principle of representative government in this country is one of equal representation for equal numbers of people, without regard to race, sex, economic status, or place of residence within a state." In the Court's view, this principle should be applied to both the more numerous house of the state legislature, which was usually based on population, *and* to the state senate, where representation was often based on area, such as the county. Defenders of this pattern had argued that as long as the more numerous chamber represented population, the senate could represent geographical units. Looking at the federal system embodied in the U.S. Constitution, they said: Isn't representation in the U.S. Senate based on area? Although many thought this a compelling argument, a majority of the Court did not. Chief Justice Earl Warren explained: "Legislators represent people, not trees or acres. Legislators are elected by voters, not farms or cities or economic interests.... The right to elect legislators in a free unimpaired fashion is a bedrock of our political system."[52]

The Supreme Court has been especially strict about how states draw districts for the U.S. House of Representatives. A state legislature must justify any variance from absolute equality by showing that it made a good-faith effort to come as close as possible to the standard. The Supreme Court is, however, less insistent on absolute equality for state legislative districts. Thus, in 1983, the Court upheld a Wyoming plan that allocated at least one state legislative seat per county, saying that Wyoming's policy was rational and appropriate to the special needs of that sparsely populated state.[53] This ruling was a rare exception to the general principle of allowing at most a 10 percent deviation between state legislative districts. The "reapportionment revolution" triggered by U.S. Supreme Court cases like *Baker* v. *Carr* (1962) and *Reynolds* v. *Sims* (1964) produced a seismic shift in state legislatures, more so than any reform adopted since the end of Reconstruction.[54]

New Rules for Redrawing the Districts

Even though the one-person, one-vote principle is firmly established, many issues affecting the nature of legislative representation continue to be hotly debated. In northern metropolitan areas, for instance, the general pattern has been for the center city to be Democratic and the outlying suburbs Republican. If legislative district lines in these areas are drawn like spokes from the center city to the suburbs, fewer Republicans will probably be elected than if district lines are drawn in concentric circles.

In recent decades, African Americans and Hispanics have begun to charge that state legislatures have an obligation under the Voting Rights Act of 1965 to redraw legislative districts to avoid dilution of the influence of minorities at the ballot box. They have gone to court to force legislators to create **majority-minority districts.** These are districts in which the majority of residents come from a minority population. The goal of creating such districts produced an otherwise unlikely coalition between Republican and African American legislators in many states. That is because creating a district that is majority African American generally also results in a district that is overwhelmingly Democratic. This leaves fewer Democratic voters in neighboring districts, which increases the chances for electoral victory for Republicans in those neighboring districts. The U.S. Supreme Court, however, has put restraints on implementation of the Act. The Court has held that although legislatures may take race into account in drawing state and federal legislative district lines and must act to avoid diluting the voting strength of minorities, a legislature violates the constitutional rights of white voters if race becomes the overriding motive.[55]

A case can be made that most state legislative elections offer little meaningful competition. Whether legislative party leaders or redistricting commissioners, those who carve up legislative districts every ten years do so primarily with the intent to protect incumbents or create districts that at least leave their party no worse off than it was before. The Supreme Court has ruled that partisan gerrymandering can be challenged in court as a violation of the Constitution. However, the Court did not find that a particularly controversial redistricting plan in Texas was an unconstitutional gerrymander, and it has not yet stated a standard by which to judge exactly what would make a gerrymander unconstitutional.[56]

Direct Legislation: Policy Making by the People?

LEARNING **OBJECTIVE**

5.5 Evaluate the debate regarding the methods of direct democracy available to some states.

Many states provide citizens with the power to create legislation through the initiative and referendum. This "direct democracy" movement began with populist reformers in Utah in 1900 and spread quickly to Oregon in 1902, Montana in 1904, Maine and Michigan in 1908, and Arizona and Colorado in 1910. Of the nearly 2,200 initiatives the public has placed on the ballot in the 24 states that allow this form of direct democracy, nearly 1,100 have been in five states: Oregon, California, Colorado, North Dakota, and Arizona.

Reformers had good reason to bypass their legislatures in the early 1900s—legislatures in several states were either incompetent or under the domination of political machines. For example, the Southern Pacific Railroad's political machine in California had dominated the selection of state legislators, governors, and U.S. senators for years.[57] The Progressives placed enormous trust in the wisdom of the people, assuming that voters would inform themselves about issues and make responsible decisions on a variety of policy questions put before them.

Initiative

The **initiative** permits a designated minimum number of voters to propose a law or constitutional amendment by petition. It becomes law if approved by a majority of the voters at a subsequent election, although Florida voters recently approved an initiative to require all subsequent initiatives to receive 60 percent of the vote to earn passage. As noted above, 24 states, mostly in the West, authorize the making of laws by means of the initiative petition (see Figure 5–4).

In some states, the *direct initiative* applies to constitutional amendments and to legislation; in others, it can be used only for one or the other. Thus, in Florida, voters can use

majority–minority district
A legislative district created to include a majority of minority voters; ruled constitutional as long as race is not the main factor in redistricting.

initiative
A procedure whereby a certain number of voters may, by petition, propose a law or constitutional amendment and have it submitted to the voters.

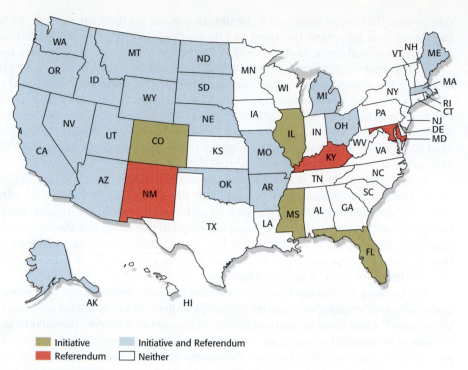

FIGURE 5–4 Citizen-Initiated Initiative and Referendum at the State Level.

■ *What parts of the country are more likely to allow citizen initiative and referendum? How does that relate to the overall political culture of those states?*

Initiative ▪ Initiative and Referendum
Referendum ▪ Neither

the direct initiative only to change the state constitution, whereas in Idaho, they can apply it only to statutory lawmaking. In a state that permits the direct initiative, any individual or interest group may draft a proposed law and file it with a designated state official, usually the secretary of state. Supporters have only to secure a certain number of signatures (between 2 and 15 percent of the vote total from the last election) to place the measure on the next general election ballot. Only California permits initiatives on primary election ballots.

The *indirect initiative* exists in a few states, including Alaska, Maine, and Massachusetts. After supporters have collected a certain number of petition signatures, the state legislature has an opportunity to act on the measure without altering it; if approved, the law simply goes into effect. If not, the proposed legislation is placed on the ballot, although in some states, additional signatures are required first.

Referendum

A **referendum** permits citizens to vote on, and possibly overturn, recently passed laws. More broadly, referendums can be on legislatively proposed amendments to a state's constitution. A majority vote is required to overturn legislatively approved laws. Every state except Delaware requires the referendum for the ratification of constitutional amendments.

Legislation may be subject to mandatory or optional referendums. The *mandatory referendum* calls for a waiting period, usually 60 to 90 days, before legislation goes into effect. If during this period, a prescribed number of voters sign a referendum petition requesting that the act be referred to the voters, the law does not go into effect unless a majority of voters give their approval at the next election. The *optional referendum* permits the legislature, at its discretion, to provide that a measure shall not become law until approved by voters at an election. This type is more common.

Although statewide initiatives and referendums get the most attention, the same processes also flourish at the local level in many states. Nearly 90 percent of cities have some form of referendum process.[58] The annual volume of measures presented to voters in school districts, cities, and counties runs to several thousand and covers a wide range of issues: bonds for school buildings, fluoridation of water, banning of glass bottles, restrictions on nuclear power facilities, and approval or rejection of convention facilities or sport stadiums.

The Debate Over Direct Democracy

Citizens have turned to the initiative process to try to regulate handguns in California, to protect moose in Maine, to encourage the death penalty in Massachusetts, to approve the

referendum
A procedure for submitting to popular vote measures passed by the legislature or proposed amendments to a state constitution.

sale of wine in grocery stores in Colorado, to abolish daylight saving time in North Dakota, to limit inhumane treatment of pregnant pigs in large hog production operations, and in several states, to allow marijuana to be used for specific medicinal purposes.

Voters approved 58 percent of the 174 ballot propositions considered across 37 states in 2008.[59] The highest profile issue associated with initiatives in 2008 continued to be same-sex marriage, where voters in Arizona, California, and Florida all approved bans on same-sex marriage. More than $85 million was spent by opponents and supporters combined in the California contest alone.[60] Also interesting in 2008, voters approved 15 of 16 statewide bond issues, authorizing their states to borrow more than $13.5 billion even as the economy was clearly already in decline.

In 2010, nearly 200 propositions will be on the ballot. Voters in Colorado will decide on tax and borrowing issues that could reduce the state's general fund by 25 percent. Voters in California will decide if the state should legalize personal marijuana use, if the current two-thirds majority needed to pass a budget in the legislature should be reduced to a simple majority, and if authority for redistricting should be returned to the legislature. Florida voters will decide if any changes made by local governments to their comprehensive land use plans must be approved by voters.

The initiative process has become a powerful tool used by interest groups, politicians, and ideologues, becoming what one author calls "a veritable fourth branch of government" in some states.[61] A vote on an issue in a single state can propel an issue onto the national agenda because of the widespread media attention given to some controversial initiatives.[62] Interest groups have set state policy by means of the initiative and have used it to reduce local government options in taxing, zoning and planning, and related matters. "One reason for this tendency to take on matters that were previously local and decide them at the statewide level is interest group efficiency. It is easier to restrict local taxing powers, strike local rent control laws, and eliminate ordinances protecting gays and lesbians by mobilizing a single statewide vote" rather than by campaigning to reverse or defeat local initiatives.[63]

The results of direct democracy have been mixed. Historically, direct legislation by initiative has resulted in progressive victories on many consumer and economic issues and conservative victories on social issues. Direct democracy has clearly had a con-siderable impact on state taxes and spending, especially in states that have enacted budget and tax limits. These measures have pleased many conservatives, upset liberals, and made life difficult for governors and state legislators. Political scientists, law professors, and lawmakers are often critical of direct legislation.[64] Critics of the initiative and the referendum believe that the Progressives who advocated direct legislation were overly optimistic regarding the abilities of citizens and naively idealistic in thinking that these mechanisms would be safe from manipulation by special interests. Only well-organized interests can gather the appropriate number of signatures and mount the required media campaigns to gain victory. Critics of direct democracy argue that special interests have in fact taken over the process in California, Oregon, and elsewhere.[65] Political consulting firms, for a price, will gather signatures and put nearly anything you want on the ballot. Deceptive pitches are sometimes made to get people to sign petitions. It takes a small fortune to do this, and only well-organized, well-financed, single-interest groups can afford it.[66]

Still another problem with the initiative process is that it can be used to target minorities, as California's limitations on illegal immigrants in 1994 and affirmative action in

Concerned that voters were lacking quality information on issues going through the initiative process, voters in Oregon formed the Citizens' Initiative Review. A panel of residents reviews the proposed ballots and writes a "Citizens' Statement" detailing their key findings, which is published in Oregon's official Statewide Voter's Pamphlet.

■ *What downside to direct democracy is this panel responding to? Should this solution be adopted in other states?*

1996 did. Similarly, Colorado's controversial Measure 2 in 1992 repealed local ordinances prohibiting discrimination against gays and lesbians and barred the future adoption of such provisions. How far can the majority go in using the initiative process against minorities? The courts have generally reversed part or all of discriminatory initiatives that were successful at the polls, yet such reversals put the courts in the awkward position of opposing a vote of the people. Critics also contend that initiatives and the campaigns around them tend to oversimplify complex policy problems, leaving voters with insufficient information to make informed choices and an inadequate appreciation for the consequences of their choice.

Viewed from another perspective, most of the perceived flaws of the populist processes of direct democracy are also the flaws of democracy. When we vote in an election, we often wish we had more information about issues and candidates. Delegates at constitutional conventions or national party conventions frequently have similar misgivings when they are forced to render yes-or-no votes on complicated issues. So, too, members of state legislatures—especially in the frantic days near the end of their sessions—yearn for more information, more clarity about consequences, and more discussion and compromise than time will permit.

Political scientists Daniel Smith and Caroline Tolbert find that participation in direct democracy also stimulates greater voter turnout, civic engagement, and political efficacy among citizens, and that their impact appears to be greatest at times when no national competitive race is present to stimulate voters.[67] They also note that political parties have seized on initiatives as a means to energize their supporters, divide their opponent's base of support, and raise contributions to the party. Thus, both citizens and political elites are learning political lessons from the initiative process.

Voters throughout the country say citizens ought to have the right, at least occasionally, to vote directly on policy issues. In surveys, both voters and nonvoters say they would be more likely to become interested in politics and vote if some issues appeared along with candidates on their ballots.[68] Californians, who have had to deal with more ballot issues than voters in any other state, continue to say that statewide ballot propositions elections are overall "a good thing for California" (74 percent), even as they acknowledge limits to their own grasp of the process.[69]

The legislative process is never perfect. Even with larger professional staffs, hearings, new technologies, bicameralism, and other distinctive features of constitutional democracy, mistakes are made and defective bills are enacted into law in our legislatures. The Supreme Court has overturned hundreds of laws passed by state legislatures as unconstitutional, and state legislatures often spend much of their time amending or otherwise improving measures they passed in previous years. As a practical matter, however, voters should be at least as skeptical and questioning of the initiative and referendum process as they already are of their state legislators.

CHAPTER **SUMMARY**

5.1 Explain how state legislatures are organized, and describe state legislators and their responsibilities.

All states except Nebraska have a bicameral legislature. In each chamber, the top leadership, including a speaker of the house, is usually selected by the majority party. State legislatures also have committees that focus on certain issue areas, and legislators tend to specialize in areas important to them. A typical state legislator is middle-aged, white, male, and has more education and a higher income than citizens of his or her state. State legislatures have become more diverse in recent decades. Legislators pass policy, provide oversight of how programs are administered, and perform constituency service, working with the resources and institutional structures provided.

5.2 Identify the factors that influence state legislators' voting decisions.

State legislators use many of the same tools for making decisions as members of the U.S. Congress. Political parties are very important in states with competitive party systems. Interest group and constituent concerns weigh heavily for all legislators. Legislators also pay attention to the recommendations of their colleagues, actions taken by other states, and expectations of the federal government.

5.3 Evaluate recent changes in state legislatures.

As a result of legislative reform efforts, most states now have longer annual sessions, larger and more competent staffs, open-meeting laws, and a variety of electronic-age information systems. As they have become more professionalized, they have also had more impact in a variety of policy areas, such as the environment, education, and crime control. Still, most are not as fully professionalized as is the U.S. Congress. Voters in many states are instating term limits as a way of keeping their representatives accountable, ensuring turnover in state legislatures, and encouraging the notion of citizen representation.

5.4 Analyze the controversies over redistricting.

Redistricting is redrawing the lines of legislative electoral districts to reflect changes in the population and conform with Supreme Court rulings regarding one person, one vote. Because political careers can be ruined by redrawn boundaries, redistricting is never easy. Major controversies have arisen over partisan and racially motivated drawing of legislative district lines, and the federal courts are increasingly asked to establish guidelines that will limit such outcomes.

5.5 Evaluate the debate regarding the methods of direct democracy available to some states.

Some states permit voters to place proposed laws or amendments to their state's constitution on the ballot by collecting enough signatures from eligible citizens. Other states allow the legislature to place proposals on the ballot before voters. Supporters of direct democracy like having citizens directly participate in governing themselves. It allows voters to break logjams that might occur in the state government, and it also allows citizens to place limits on state governments that legislatures themselves are unlikely to adopt (like term limits or caps on spending). Opponents argue that the initiative process can be manipulated by small groups with a lot of money, that complex issues are not well suited to simple solutions, and that citizen initiatives sometimes tie the hands of elected officials too much.

CHAPTER **SELF-TEST**

5.1 Explain how state legislatures are organized, and describe state legislators and their responsibilities.

1. In a short essay, describe the typical state legislator including gender, race, age, profession, and political experience. How do you think these demographic factors influence the actions of state legislatures as a whole? Is that result good for the U.S. population? Why or why not?

2. Which is often the most time-consuming aspect of a state legislator's job?
   a. Campaigning
   b. Tending to constituent relations
   c. Attending committee meetings
   d. Researching and writing legislation

3. In a short essay, describe three responsibilities of state legislatures. Consider how they interact with federal and other areas of government, specifically in terms of budgets.

5.2 Identify the factors that influence state legislators' voting decisions.

4. Write a paragraph explaining why retired state legislators are often the most effective lobbyists.

5. In a short essay, describe how lobbyists, interest groups, and party caucuses influence a state legislator's voting decision. Consider the specific desires and influence of each group.

5.3 Evaluate recent changes in state legislatures.

6. Between 1979 and 2009, the number of staffers in state legislatures has gone from _____ to _____.
   a. 17,000; 28,000
   b. 20,000; 35,000

   c. 28,000; 17,000
   d. 35,000; 20,000

7. In a short essay, describe the arguments for and against term limits in state legislatures. Which do you find most compelling?

5.4 Analyze the controversies over redistricting.

8. What is gerrymandering?
   a. Drawing district boundaries to benefit a party, group, or incumbent
   b. Attempting to influence redistricting through the efforts of interest groups
   c. Manipulating data gathered by the U.S. Census Bureau to influence district boundaries
   d. Adjusting district boundaries to give rural and small-town voters more representation than they deserve

9. Why is the drawing of district boundaries often controversial?

5.5 Evaluate the debate regarding the methods of direct democracy available to some states.

10. Which of the following is an element of mandatory referendum?
   a. Citizen review of new government programs
   b. A required period of judicial review for legislation affecting budget policies
   c. A waiting period during which voters must approve legislation before it takes effect
   d. A government program requiring all citizens to participate in some form of direct democracy

11. Are voters sufficiently informed to effectively use direct democracy to shape state policy? How informed do you think voters need to be in order to use direct democracy effectively?

Answers to selected questions: 2. b; 6. a; 8. a; 10. c

mypoliscilab EXERCISES

Apply what you learned in this chapter on MyPoliSciLab.

Read on **mypoliscilab.com**

eText: Chapter 5

Study and **Review** on **mypoliscilab.com**

Pre-Test
Post-Test
Chapter Exam
Flashcards

Explore on **mypoliscilab.com**

Simulation: You Are Redrawing the Districts in Your State
Timeline: Initiatives and Referendums

KEY TERMS

bicameral legislature, p. 96
unicameral legislature, p. 96
party caucus, p. 101
lobbying, p. 102
lobbyist, p. 102

trustee, p. 103
delegate, p. 104
redistricting, p. 108
gerrymandering, p. 108
malapportionment, p. 108

majority–minority district, p. 110
initiative, p. 110
referendum, p. 111

ADDITIONAL RESOURCES

FURTHER READING

SHAWN BOWLER, TODD DONOVAN, AND **CAROLINE J. TOLBERT,** EDS., *Citizens as Legislators: Direct Democracy in the United States* (Ohio State University Press, 1998).

WILLIAM M. BULGER, *While the Music Lasts: My Life in Politics* (Houghton Mifflin, 1996).

JOHN M. CAREY, RICHARD G. NIEMI, AND **LYNDA W. POWELL,** *Term Limits in the State Legislatures* (University of Michigan Press, 2000).

GARY W. COX AND **JONATHAN N. KATZ,** *Elbridge Gerry's Salamander: The Electoral Consequences of the Reapportionment Revolution* (Cambridge University Press, 2002).

RICK FARMER, ED., *Legislating Without Experience: Case Studies in State Legislative Term Limits* (Lexington Books, 2007).

TYSON KING-MEADOWS, *Devolution and Black State Legislators: Challenges and Choices in the Twenty-First Century* (State University of New York Press, 2006).

THAD KOUSSER, *Term Limits and the Dismantling of State Legislative Professionalism* (Cambridge University Press, 2005).

DAVID B. MAGLEBY, *Direct Legislation: Voting on Ballot Propositions in the United States* (Johns Hopkins University Press, 1984).

ALBERT J. NELSON, *Emerging Influentials in State Legislatures: Women, Blacks, and Hispanics* (Praeger, 1991).

BETH REINGOLD, *Representing Women: Sex, Gender, and Legislative Behavior in Arizona and California* (University of California Press, 2000).

ALAN ROSENTHAL, *Engines of Democracy: Politics and Policymaking in State Legislatures* (CQ Press 2009).

ALAN ROSENTHAL, *Heavy Lifting: The Job of the American Legislature* (CQ Press, 2004).

FRANK SMALLWOOD, *Free and Independent: The Initiation of a College Professor into State Politics* (Greene Press, 1976).

DANIEL A. SMITH AND **CAROLINE J. TOLBERT,** *Educated by Initiative: The Effects of Direct Democracy on Citizens and Political Organizations in the American States* (University of Michigan Press, 2004).

PEVERILL SQUIRE AND **GARY MONCRIEF,** *State Legislatures Today: Politics Under the Domes* (Longman, 2010).

PEVERILL SQUIRE AND **KEITH E. HAMM,** *101 Chambers: Congress, State Legislatures, and the Future of Legislative Studies* (Ohio State University Press, 2005).

SUE THOMAS AND **CLYDE WILCOX,** EDS., *Women and Elective Office* (Oxford University Press, 1998).

RALPH G. WRIGHT, *Inside the Statehouse: Lessons from the Speaker* (CQ Press 2005). See also *State Legislatures,* published ten times a year by the National Conference of State Legislatures. *Legislative Studies Quarterly* often has articles on state legislatures; it is published by the Legislative Studies Section of the American Political Science Association. *Governing,* published monthly by Congressional Quarterly, Inc., regularly covers state politics and state legislative issues. *Spectrum: The Journal of State Government* is a useful quarterly published by the Council of State Governments.

WEB SITES

www.ncsl.org NCSL provides research, technical assistance, and opportunities to see the exchange of ideas among policy makers.

www.nbcsl.org NBCSL provides educational materials, research, and training programs designed to help legislators and their staff promote the interests of African American constituents.

www.cawp.rutgers.edu CAWP is a leading source of scholarly research and current data about American women's participation in politics and government.

www.nhcsl.org NHCSL provides information to help advocate on behalf of Hispanic communities.

State Governors

Except for the president, governors are the most visible and generally most widely known elected officials in the United States. Governors set the policy agenda in their states, establish spending priorities, advocate for their states at the national and international level, and are generally the most central political figures in their states. Governors make critical policy decisions that directly affect virtually every aspect of the lives of their states' residents—and sometimes governors literally make life and death decisions.

Among the governor's powers is the authority to pardon or commute (lessen the penalty of) criminal sentences or grant a stay (temporary hold) of execution. On January 11, 2003, then Governor George Ryan of Illinois, just two days before leaving office, pardoned four death row inmates and commuted the sentences of every other death row inmate in Illinois (167 at the time) to a life sentence. Ryan, a Republican and stated supporter of the death penalty, had concluded that the death penalty process in his state was flawed and that it could not be conducted in a manner that guaranteed an innocent person would never be executed. Three years earlier, Ryan had declared a moratorium on executions so that the process could be studied.

This remarkable sequence of events was triggered by work done by a group of college journalism students taking a class at Northwestern University in Evanston, Illinois. As part of a class project in 1998, students began investigating the case surrounding the conviction of Anthony Porter. Porter had been convicted and sentenced to death for the murder of two teenagers that occurred in 1982. Porter's case had been appealed and reviewed numerous times, and at one point, he was 48 hours from being executed before a stay was granted. Largely as a result of the investigative work done by the Northwestern students and the evidence it revealed, which provoked another person to confess to the crime, all charges against Porter were dropped and he was released from prison after serving 15 years. Porter's case was not an isolated example— a total of 13 death row inmates had been exonerated based on new evidence during Ryan's tenure as governor. Ryan's life-and-death decisions—celebrated by some and reviled by others—made headlines across the country and around the world. (Unfortunately for former Governor Ryan, he later received national attention for a corruption and bribery conviction for which he was sentenced to serve six and a half years in federal prison.)

Illinois is not the only state to advocate using the powers of the governor to reevaluate use of the death penalty. In May 2010, Ohio Supreme Court Justice Paul E. Pfeifer, one of the authors of Ohio's statute reinstating the death penalty back in the early 1980s when he was a legislator, urged whoever is elected governor to assemble a panel to review the cases of all those currently on Ohio's death row. Pfeifer argued that if those currently on death row were tried for the same crimes today, most would probably not receive the death penalty.[1]

As we will see in this chapter, the importance of the governor has increased substantially in recent decades. States have taken on many new responsibilities and expanded their functions significantly in recent years, elevating governors both within their states and as national political figures. We will examine how governors come into and keep their office, a governor's power and influence in state politics, how the governorship has evolved and been modernized in recent years, how governors interact with other elected state officials, and the rewards of being governor.

Becoming and Remaining Governor

LEARNING **OBJECTIVE**

6.1 Identify the typical pathways by which people attain and retain the governorship.

Each state's constitution and laws spell out the rules of eligibility, tenure, and salary for its governor. Thirty-five states require their governors to be at least 30 years old, and 28 states require candidates to be residents of the state for at least five years immediately preceding the election. Although California, Ohio, Rhode Island, South Dakota, Vermont, Washington, and Wisconsin set the minimum age at 18, the odds against election at age 18 are staggering.[2] In theory, any qualified voter of the state who meets a state's age qualification is eligible for the office of governor; in practice, there are well-traveled career paths to the governor's office.

Most governors are white males approximately 40 to 55 years old. As of early 2010, there have been 32 female governors, nearly half of whom took office in 2000 or later.[3] Most governors were state legislators or held statewide elective office before running for governor. Of the governors in office at the start of 2010, for instance, 21 served in their state legislatures, 9 served as lieutenant governors, and 7 were state attorneys general. In addition, some governors had national governmental experience, including eight who served in the U.S. House of Representatives.[4]

One of the most common paths upward is election to the state legislature, followed by election to a statewide office such as lieutenant governor, secretary of state, or attorney general, followed by a run for governor. Vermont Governor Jim Douglas was elected to the state legislature right out of college and served as secretary of state and state treasurer before becoming governor. Mayors often run for governor; the mayors of Albuquerque, Charlotte, Phoenix, Indianapolis, Las Vegas, and Maui have all run for governor in their states in recent years. In 2010, four governors had been mayors. Although serving in office is certainly helpful for building a political base, it is not essential. Thirteen governors in 2010 had not held previous elective office, although the majority had held some appointed political position.

Two hundred years ago, most states had one- or two-year terms for their governors. Today, all states except New Hampshire and Vermont have four-year terms, and all states except Virginia allow governors to run for more than one consecutive term. Some governors, such as Jim Douglas of Vermont, William Janklow of South Dakota, Roy Romer of Colorado, John Engler of Michigan, Mario Cuomo and George Pataki of New York, Jim Hunt of North Carolina, Mike Leavitt of Utah, and Tommy Thompson of Wisconsin, have been elected to three or four terms as governors, but 35 states now have a two-term limit on governors, and Utah has a three-term limit.[5]

Governors Under Pressure

Once elected, governors enjoy high visibility in their states. Governors' salaries are certainly higher than the average earnings of U.S. workers: They earn more than $100,000 in 43 states, and salaries range from $212,179 in California to $70,000 in Maine.[6] In addition, governors receive an expense allowance; all but four are provided an executive mansion; 42 have regular access to a state plane or helicopter or both.[7] But these salaries and benefits hardly compare with those of CEOs of major corporations, even though most state governments' revenues and workforces are as large as Fortune 500 companies. Whether they seek the office for the opportunity to serve the public, make history, exercise power, or get a foothold for a run for the Senate or the presidency, nonfinancial incentives are probably dominant for most gubernatorial candidates.

Even as governors have become increasingly important in recent decades, they have also had to deal with the twin problems of rising public expectations and scarcity of resources. People want better schools, uncongested highways, fine universities (with low tuition), a good job market, access to health care, protections for civil rights, low crime, and clean air and water. However, they usually also want their taxes kept as low as possible.

Bill Richardson, the Democratic governor of New Mexico, previously served in the House of Representatives. His second term as governor ends in 2011, and because of terms limits he cannot run for a third.

■ *Do you support limiting governors to two terms, or should successful governors be allowed to continue running for office?*

Female Governors

There have been only 32 female governors in all of U.S. history.* But of the 32, nearly half took office in 2000 or later. In 2010, there were six women currently serving as governors. As women have occupied increasingly powerful positions in state legislatures and in lower-level statewide offices, such as lieutenant governor, attorney general, and secretary of state, they have become much more visible as potential candidates for the governorship. African Americans and Hispanics have not made similar gains, however. As of 2010, there was only one Hispanic governor in office, Bill Richardson of New Mexico, and there were two African Americans, Deval Patrick of Massachusetts and David Paterson of New York, who succeeded Eliot Spitzer when he resigned the governorship in early 2008.

Former Arizona Governor Janet Napolitano was named secretary of Homeland Security in 2009.

Female Governors Since 2000

Governor	State	Term of Office
Judy Martz	Montana	2001–2005
Ruth Ann Minner	Delaware	2001–2008
Jane Swift	Massachusetts	2001–2002
Jennifer Granholm	Michigan	2003–
Janet Napolitano	Arizona	2003–2009
Linda Lingle	Hawaii	2003–
Kathleen Sebelius	Kansas	2003–2009
Olene Walker	Utah	2003–2005
Kathleen Blanco	Louisiana	2004–2008
M. Jodie Rell	Connecticut	2004–
Christine Gregoire	Washington	2005–
Sarah Palin	Alaska	2007–2009
Beverly Perdue	North Carolina	2009–
Jan Brewer	Arizona	2009–

SOURCE: "History of Women Governors," Center for American Women and Politics, Eagleton Institute, Rutgers University, January 2007, www.cawp.rutgers.edu/Facts/Officeholders/govhistory.pdf; and *The Book of the States, 2009* (The Council of State Governments), p. 176.

Jennifer Granholm became Michigan's first female governor in 2003.

CRITICAL THINKING QUESTIONS

1. In early 2010, 16 percent of governors were women, the same percentage of women in the U.S. Senate and in the U.S. House of Representatives. Women were more common in state legislatures—approximately 24 percent in 2010.[†] Why might women be more frequently found in state legislatures than in these other offices?

2. Four of the current six female governors are in western or plains states. These states have generally been more likely than other states to elect women to state or national office. Why might that be so?

* The Book of the States, 2009 (The Council of State Governments, 2009), p. 176.
[†] For more information on women in elected office, see Rutgers University's Center for American Women and Politics Web site, www.cawp.rutgers.edu/.

Former New York Governor Mario Cuomo (who served from 1983 until 1995) used to say he was always running into people who wanted him to expand programs. He would look them in the eye and say, "Now what are you going to give me so that I can pay for it? Do you want to wait longer in line at the motor vehicle office to get your license renewed? Do we stop paving the road in front of your home? Do you mind if we plow the snow less often?" Typically, of course, people requesting additional spending did not want to forgo any of those things, which prompted him to say, "Well, then, I don't understand. Where do I get what I need to do what you want?" Cuomo's point was simple. Given limited resources, elected officials must make choices. They cannot do everything people would like. You must "give to get."[8]

Governors and state legislators face the challenge of administering federally mandated environmental, educational, welfare, and homeland security programs with fewer federal dollars. They have campaigned for the federal government to give more money to the states—without strings. The Republican-controlled U.S. Congress in the late 1990s responded by terminating some underfunded federally mandated programs and shifting a few other federal programs to the states. But in the 2000s, Congress continued to pass legislation that imposed new costs on the states, such as the No Child Left Behind Act of 2002, which some governors say is underfunded.[9]

Reelection

Incumbent governors are typically reelected when they run. Between 1970 and 2004, 74 percent of incumbent governors seeking reelection won.[10] In recent years, incumbents' success has been even greater: In 2006, 25 of 27 incumbents won, for a reelection rate of 93 percent.[11] In 2008, all eight incumbent governors running for reelection won. Incumbent John Corzine lost his bid for reelection in New Jersey in 2009. In 2010, five of the seven Democratic incumbents and all six Republican incumbents running won reelection. The two Democrats who lost were Chet Culver in Iowa and Ted Strickland in Ohio, with Strickland losing by only 2 percentage points. Thus, even while Republicans were winning most of the open seat contests, incumbents from both parties were very successful in holding onto their seats.

Governors' reelection chances may be helped by the insulation of most gubernatorial elections from the sometimes large party swings found in presidential elections. In 34 states, elections for governor are held only in nonpresidential or midterm election years (for example, 2010). Five other states—Kentucky, Louisiana, Mississippi, New Jersey, and Virginia—elect governors in odd-numbered years. Reformers have successfully argued that presidential and gubernatorial elections should be separated so that state elections are not swamped by the tides of national politics. Still, research shows that voting behavior in states can still be affected when national political issues are stressed during a gubernatorial race.[12] Only 11 states hold gubernatorial elections at the same time as presidential elections: governors in New Hampshire and Vermont are elected for two-year terms in all even-numbered years, and nine states elect governors to four-year terms in presidential election years. (See Figure 6–1 for the party affiliations of the governors who held office in 2011.)

Incumbency, however, is not always an advantage for reelection. Governors receive a great deal of public attention—and in Arizona, Alabama, Arkansas, Connecticut, Illinois, New Jersey, and New York, governors have left office in recent years because of personal scandals. Governors also have to make tough decisions, which can antagonize major interests and arouse public criticism. Sometimes governors refuse to run again because they are so unpopular. In 2004, for instance, 3 of 11 incumbent governors decided not to run for reelection even though they were eligible—all 3 had low public approval ratings.[13]

Republican John Kasich, shown here, defeated incumbent Ted Strickland for governor in Ohio. Kasich's victory was one of many for Republicans in 2010, though nearly every other incumbent governor running for re-election won. ■ *Why do you suppose one party can win so many open-seat contests for governor while incumbents running from either party can still hold onto their offices?*

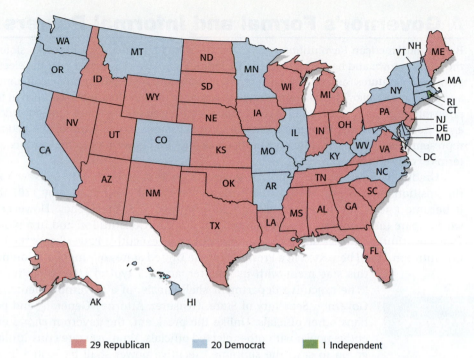

FIGURE 6–1 Party Control of the Governor's Office, 2011.
After the 2010 elections, Republicans held a majority of governor's offices.
■ *Why does it matter which party controls the governor's office?*

■ 29 Republican   ■ 20 Democrat   ■ 1 Independent

Public anger over taxes and budgets was clearly behind the 2003 California recall election. Gray Davis was widely criticized for having tripled the registration fee, or "car tax," that motorists paid on their vehicles. As future governor Arnold Schwarzenegger said repeatedly in his campaign, "I feel Californians have been punished enough. From the time they get up in the morning and flush the toilet, they're taxed. When they go get a coffee, they're taxed. When they get in their car, they're taxed. When they go to the gas station, they're taxed. When they go to lunch, they're taxed. This goes on all day long. Tax. Tax. Tax. Tax. Tax."[14]

Similarly, in New Jersey in 1993, Governor James Florio was narrowly defeated by Christine Todd Whitman, in part because of a recession, but mostly because Florio's approval ratings had been driven to historic lows after he recommended, and the legislature had enacted, a major tax increase after having promised not to raise taxes during his previous campaign.[15] That tax increase came back to haunt Florio when he ran for U.S. senator in the New Jersey Democratic primary in 2000. His opponent, Jon Corzine, ran ads stressing Florio's role as a big spender and won the primary.

Circumstances often dictate what a governor can or cannot do. The health of the state's economy is a critical factor; incumbents sometimes lose because of a depressed state economy.[16] Their electoral fortunes are also affected by whether voters approve or disapprove of the job the president is doing.[17] The good economic times in the late 1990s plainly helped most governors who ran for reelection; bad economic times hurt them in the early 2000s and again in 2010. Before the 2010 election, Democrats held 29 governorships and Republicans held 21. Following the 2010 election, Republicans emerged with control of 29 governorships, while Democrats held 20. (Rhode Island elected Lincoln Chafee, and Independent who formerly served in the U.S. Senate as a Republican.)

Promises to cut taxes have been effective campaign strategies for several candidates. Many governors in the 1990s, including Christine Todd Whitman of New Jersey and George Pataki of New York, made tax cutting a central part of their campaigns for election and reelection. However, although proposing tax increases can be politically risky, it may not be political suicide for governors.[18] Many other issues can affect governors' prospects for reelection. Governor Jim Doyle of Wisconsin made stem cell research a central issue of his campaign, an issue that has also entered the campaigns in other states.[19] Other issues that have been prominent in recent campaigns are the increasing costs of health insurance, illegal immigration, education quality and funding, and environmental protection.

A Governor's Formal and Informal Powers

LEARNING **OBJECTIVE**

6.2 Identify the formal and informal powers of governors, and assess governors' use of these powers to influence policy.

Before the American Revolution, royal governors were appointed by and responsible to the British crown and had broad powers, including extensive veto power over the elected colonial legislatures. As anti-British sentiment increased, royal governors became more and more unpopular. The position of state governor in the new Republic was born in this atmosphere of distrust. In the 1770s and 1780s, state legislatures elected state governors, a method that ensured that governors would remain under the control of the people's representatives. The early state constitutions also limited governors to few powers and terms of only one or two years.

Gradually, however, the office of governor grew in importance. In New York, the position of chief executive was sufficiently developed and effective by 1787 that it became one of the main models for the proposed U.S. presidency. However, if we compare the formal sources of authority in the U.S. Constitution and in a typical state constitution, we see significant differences. "The executive Power," says the U.S. Constitution, "shall be vested in a President of the United States of America." Compare this statement with its counterpart in a typical state constitution: "The executive department shall consist of a Governor, Lieutenant Governor, Secretary of State, Treasurer, Attorney General," and perhaps other officials. Unlike the president, the governor *shares* executive power with other elected officials. Yet most state constitutions go on to say, "the supreme executive power shall be vested in the Governor, who shall take care that the laws be faithfully executed." Thus, the public looks to the governor as the one state official responsible for executing and enforcing the laws and managing the state administrative system, although the governor's actual authority is often circumscribed.

Governors also enjoy a number of informal powers that stem from such factors as the size of their electoral victory to their job approval rating and how far away the next election is. Political scientists Thad Beyle and Margaret Ferguson have developed a method of measuring both the formal and personal powers of governors, which is reported in Table 6–1.[20] These formal and informal powers are political tools that governors may or may not use to exert real influence in their states. Governors with strong formal powers, for instance, appoint most other top executive officials rather than deal with numerous independently elected executives. Strong governors can succeed themselves for more than one or two terms and have the time to learn their job, carry out major initiatives, and convince legislators that *their* political futures turn in part on cooperation with the governor. Strong governors also have extensive budgetary powers and the ability to veto specific items in bills and budgets passed by the legislature. Governors with high approval ratings from their citizens and/or large electoral mandates also have more potential power than do their less popular counterparts.

A governor's power and influence depend not only on formal authority but also on his or her ability to persuade.[21] This ability, in turn, usually depends on a particular governor's reputation, knowledge of what should be done, and, of course, ability to communicate. Governors usually also benefit from being the leader of their party in the state and from their capacity to draw the attention of state residents through the media, major speeches, and talks around the state. Governors, in short, must have political skills if they are to provide leadership. Yet even the savviest governors need sufficient constitutional authority in order to exert real influence over a state's policies and the administration of its laws.

TABLE

6–1	Rankings of States According to the Formal Powers of the Governor

STRONG

Alaska	Massachusetts
Arkansas	Nebraska
Colorado	New York
Connecticut	Ohio
Iowa	West Virginia

MODERATELY STRONG

Arizona	New Jersey
California	New Mexico
Florida	Oregon
Illinois	Tennessee
Kansas	Utah
Maryland	Vermont
Michigan	Wisconsin
Montana	

MODERATE

Delaware	Mississippi
Georgia	Missouri
Hawaii	New Hampshire
Idaho	North Dakota
Indiana	Pennsylvania
Kentucky	South Dakota
Minnesota	Texas

WEAK

Alabama	Rhode Island
Louisiana	South Carolina
Maine	Virginia
Nevada	Washington
North Carolina	Wyoming
Oklahoma	

SOURCE: Thad Beyle and Margaret Ferguson, "Governors and the Executive Branch" in Virginia Gray and Russell L. Hanson, eds., *Politics in the American States: A Comparative Analysis*, 9th ed (2008).

Most governors have the following constitutional authority:

- To make appointments
- To prepare the state budget
- To veto legislation and to exercise an item veto over appropriations measures
- To issue executive orders
- To command the state National Guard
- To pardon or grant clemency
- To help establish the legislature's agenda

We will next take a closer look at each of these.

Appointive Power

Perhaps a governor's most important job is to recruit talented leaders and managers to head the state's departments, commissions, and agencies.[22] Through recruitment of effective people and prudent delegation of responsibilities to them, a governor can provide direction for the state government.

In most states, the governor is one executive among many, with only limited authority over elected officials, whom the governor can neither appoint nor dismiss. Moreover, if these officials are from a different political party than the governor, they are likely to oppose the governor's recommendations. Governors have greater, yet still limited, power over officials they appoint. Some governors appoint hundreds of key officials; others, such as those in Mississippi, South Carolina, and Texas, have severe restrictions on their appointive power. Moreover, in most states, governors must share their appointive power with the state senate and may remove people only when they have violated the law or failed in their legal duties. State administrators whose programs are supported by federal funds also have a measure of independence from the governor.

Along with appointive power comes a host of challenges. First, salaries for cabinet and agency administrators are modest in many states, especially in the smaller ones, and it is often hard to get candidates to leave better-paying jobs in private industry. Second, powerful politicians may demand that their friends be appointed to certain top posts, and they may threaten to be uncooperative if the governor does not go along with their "suggestions." Finally, relatively high turnover in many state positions often hampers a governor's efforts to carry out programs.

Fiscal and Budgetary Power

A governor's financial planning and budgetary powers are key weapons in getting programs passed. Purchasing, budgeting, and personnel matters are centralized under the governor. When implemented by a strong staff and backed by a strong political base, a governor's fiscal powers are extremely important.

In nearly all states, the governor has responsibility for preparing a budget and presenting it to the state legislature. This takes place every year in 29 states and every second year in 21 states.[23] The art of budget making includes assessing requests from various departments and agencies and balancing them against available resources. Governors and their staffs have to calculate the costs of existing and newly proposed programs and weigh those costs against estimated revenues for the state.

The budget process is similar in most states. In May and June, the governor's budget office, which is called different things in different states, including Office of Management and Budget or Department of Administration, sends request forms to the various executive agencies. From July to October, the agencies complete their detailed requests and send them back for consideration. Their requests are typically higher than the governor's proposed guidelines. The governor's budget chief evaluates all requests, sometimes holds internal administrative hearings, and then makes recommendations to the governor. Finally, the governor presents the recommendations to the legislature at the beginning of the new year. Governors frequently use their annual State of the State Address to present these recommendations and continue to promote them during speeches given throughout the budget process.

Although the governor and chief budget officials may appear to control the budgetary process, considerable budgeting influence remains in the hands of the executive branch agencies. Further, a governor's budget reflects to a very high degree budgetary decisions made throughout the years as well as other factors not easily controlled by governors in the short run. For instance, spending on health care is driven by long-standing eligibility policies, economic cycles that affect how many people qualify for health care, and the rising costs of health care. Spending on prisons is greatly affected by past sentencing practices, among other things. Also, some spending is mandated by the federal government, such as state "matching" dollars in support of federal grants. In summary, governors usually can only tinker with or adjust expenditures at the edges of the overall budget. For example, as much as 80 percent of California's state budget is dictated by factors beyond the governor's control.

The final budget document is presented to the legislature for adoption as an *appropriations measure.* State monies cannot be spent without legislative appropriations. Legislators can, and usually do, make a number of alterations in a governor's budget. Because of this, governors are also forced to anticipate the preferences of each legislative chamber when proposing a budget, or they risk the legislature simply ignoring them and writing their own budget from scratch. Nonetheless, a governor who uses this budget proposal power effectively has an important asset.

In 2007, states spent about 36 percent of their budgets on education, including K–12 schools and higher education institutions. Public welfare, health care, and hospital spending accounted for another 35 percent. Highway spending absorbed another 7 percent of state budgets, and spending on police and corrections took up slightly more than 4 percent. The remaining portion of state spending went to a wide variety of smaller items, such as state parks and recreation facilities, environmental programs, libraries, public health, and general aid to local governments. (Note that these figures represent state spending only; see Chapter 10 for more on state and local spending.)

To pay for these many activities, about half of a state's revenue comes from taxes (approximately 24 percent from sales taxes, 18 percent from personal income taxes, and 3.7 percent from corporate income taxes), while another 30 percent comes from the federal government. The remaining 19 percent comes from fees, bonds, and a variety of other state revenue sources. (See Chapter 10 for more on state and local revenue sources.) When state revenues do not match expenses, governors have to cut or delay programs because every state is required to balance its budget, and states cannot print money as the federal government can.

Veto Power

Among the most useful gubernatorial powers is the **veto,** the power to reject legislative bills, especially appropriations measures. Michigan Governor Jennifer Granholm vetoed more than 30 bills in her first 18 months in office, including one that would have banned late-term abortions, another that would have created a process for specialty license plates, and another that would have given suburbs more control over the Detroit Water and Sewer Board. Her veto activity led the *Detroit Free Press* to title a story on her tenure, "Granholm Stars in Her Own 'Kill Bill.'"[24]

All state constitutions give governors some veto authority, but in 43 states, governors have the **line item veto,** which permits them to veto individual items in an appropriations bill while signing the remainder of the bill into law. Thus, they can influence the flow of funds to the executive departments and thereby attempt to control their activities. In May 2006, for example, Florida Governor Jeb Bush vetoed $448.7 million from the state's $74 billion budget.[25]

In 12 states, a governor can reduce particular appropriations; this power is called the **reduction veto.** In ten states, governors can exercise what is called an **amendatory veto,** which allows the governor to return a bill to the state legislature with suggested language changes, conditions, or amendments.[26] In this last case, legislators must decide to accept the governor's recommendations or approve the bill in its original form,

veto
Rejection by a president or governor of legislation passed by a legislature.

line item veto
The right of an executive to veto parts of a bill approved by a legislature without having to veto the entire bill.

reduction veto
The power of governors in a few states to reduce a particular appropriation.

amendatory veto
The power of governors in a few states to return a bill to the legislature with suggested language changes, conditions, or amendments. Legislators then decide either to accept the governor's recommendations or to pass the bill in its original form over the veto.

which in some cases requires a majority vote and in other cases, a three-fifths or super-majority vote.

Governors in Wisconsin have enjoyed particularly powerful veto powers, which at various times have allowed them to delete individual words, phrases, letters, or numbers from a bill allowing them to completely change the bill's meaning. Because it allows governors to delete words and "stitch together" the remaining parts to form a new bill, this power has recently been referred to as the "Frankenstein" veto. However, its overuse has occasionally provoked a backlash among voters. (The *You Will Decide* box on the following page discusses the line item veto further.)

State legislatures can override a governor's veto; in most states, it takes a two-thirds majority of both legislative chambers. Some governors, such as Wisconsin's Tommy Thompson, have vetoed thousands of legislative measures. New York Governor George Pataki vetoed 1,379 provisions the legislature sent him in 1998.[27] Governors on average veto around 4 percent of the bills sent to them, but only approximately 2 percent of gubernatorial vetoes are overridden by legislatures.[28] Most governors believe the veto power should be used sparingly. Indeed, some observers think too-frequent use of the veto is a sign of gubernatorial weakness because an effective governor usually wins battles through negotiations rather than by confronting state legislators.[29]

Legislators in several states have established a *veto session*—a short session following adjournment—so that they can reconsider any measures vetoed by their governor. This is clearly an effort to assert the legislature's check-and-balance authority in relationship to the governor. Most states using veto sessions have legislatures that meet for a limited time; in full-time legislatures, a veto session would be unnecessary.

Executive Orders

One long-standing power of governors is their authority to issue **executive orders,** which have the force of law. Even though executive orders differ from statutes or formal acts passed by the legislature, they have almost the same binding effect. Depending on the state, governors get their authority to issue executive orders from implied powers as chief executive, from specific constitutional grants, or from delegations of authority by their state legislatures. Executive orders supplementing a law are both more detailed and more important than the general guidelines contained in legislation. Governors have issued executive orders during such emergencies as natural disasters and energy crises, in compliance with federal rules and regulations, and to create advisory commissions. However, governors can also use executive orders to make policy. Governor Arnold Schwarzenegger of California, for example, used executive orders in 2006 to promote the use of biofuels, to set up a system to identify high-risk sex offenders, and to promote state contracts with small businesses. State legislators are sometimes angered by sweeping executive orders. They insist that they, not the governor or the courts, should be the primary lawmakers in a state.

Governors do not always have to issue executive orders to change the interpretation of state laws, however. Even though he opposed same-sex marriages, Governor Mitt Romney of Massachusetts reminded local officials in 2004 that they had to follow the state's Supreme Judicial Court decision allowing same-sex marriage of state residents. At the same time, however, he also said he intended to use a 1913 law to prohibit the marriage of same-sex couples from other states. Such marriages would be null and void under his interpretation, he argued, thereby preventing Massachusetts from drawing same-sex couples from across the United States.[30]

Commander in Chief of the National Guard

Emergencies can enhance the authority of an executive because they call for decisive action. As commander in chief of the state's National Guard when it is not in federal service, a governor may use this force when local authorities are inadequate—in case of

executive order
A directive issued by a president or governor that has the force of law.

DECIDE Should Governors Have an Item Veto?

The item veto, which is sometimes called the line item veto, permits governors to nullify parts or items of an appropriations bill without vetoing the entire bill. The legislature may override item vetoes, usually by a supermajority vote. The item veto is available in 43 states, although the provisions vary. Some states only permit governors to veto a specific dollar amount and any language directly associated with that amount, such as "$20,000,000, to be spent by Agency X on construction of a bridge on Highway Y in Town Z." Some states give governors more expansive authority. Governors can nullify not only entire items but also parts of items, including language describing the object and purpose of the expenditure. For instance, the governor could strike out "of a bridge" from the example, or "in Town Z," or every word after "Agency X," all of which would give the governor greater flexibility in using the money appropriated to Agency X.

The main impetus behind the basic item veto was to give governors the power to curtail legislative "pork barrel" spending—spending on items targeted at individual districts, such as a new public park, a specific road expansion, or a new building at a public university. Such spending items are often bundled together into a single bill. Each item typically benefits only a small minority of state residents and is supported by only a few legislators, but when all the items are bound together, they may secure support from a majority of legislators as enough legislators get a piece of the pie. Of course, what is wasteful "pork barrel" spending to one person is an essential project to another. The criticism against such legislative practices is that the state may end up spending a great deal of money on items that help a small number of people but, from the state perspective, are not worth the costs.

What do you think? Should governors have an item veto? What are the arguments for or against it?

THINKING IT THROUGH

One argument against item vetoes is that they do not accomplish their goals. Research on the effects of item vetoes is inconclusive. They are sometimes associated with lower spending in states, but it is unclear whether the item vetoes are the cause. Most studies find that different states use them at different rates. They are most common in states where the governor faces a legislature controlled by a different political party, suggesting a partisan bias in how governors apply the item veto. They also frequently amount to a very small portion of the state's budget, suggesting that governors use them more for their symbolic value rather than to actually affect state spending.

Another argument against providing item veto authority applies to its expanded versions. Such item vetoes can give enormous, largely unchecked, positive legislative power to the governor. If the governor can nullify language within the bill, not only entire appropriation items (money amounts plus language describing the item), he or she can actually create new legislation without approval from the legislature. As discussed, Wisconsin governors have been doing this sort of "Frankenstein vetoing" for years.

Some argue, in response, that expansive item vetoes are needed to check legislatures, which are including more and more legislation in appropriations bills. Legislatures do this because appropriations bills must eventually be passed, and so they include legislation—sometimes having little to do with spending—that the governor would veto if it stood alone. Expansive item vetoes allow governors to check this effort to push through legislation on the back of the appropriation bills.

Critical Thinking Questions

1. Should all governors have item veto authority? If so, how extensive should the power be—should it permit the item veto to be used in flexible, creative ways, including the striking out of language, not only entire "items"?

2. Your answer to that question probably depends on your answer to another: What is more problematic, executive dominance or legislative dominance? Why?

---

riots, floods, and other catastrophes. The National Guard played a role in the aftermath of floods in midwestern states, riots and earthquakes in California, fires in Florida, and hurricanes throughout the southeastern states. National Guard troops from Louisiana and Mississippi—joined by troops from 40 other states—were mobilized for search and rescue operations after the devastation and flooding produced by Hurricane Katrina in the Gulf Coast in the summer of 2005.[31]

Congress provides most of the money to operate the National Guard. This fact, along with the supremacy clause of the U.S. Constitution, gives Congress and the president the power to take charge of a state's National Guard even against the wishes of a governor. In 1990, the Supreme Court ruled unanimously that Congress can authorize the president to call National Guard units to active duty and send them outside the United States despite the objections of the governors, several of whom had tried to keep President Ronald Reagan from calling their respective National Guards to training exercises in Honduras.[32] President George W. Bush deployed National Guard troops in Iraq and Afghanistan. More than 250,000 National Guard troops have seen action in these two wars—some serving tours of duty as long as 22 months.[33] States could, if they wished, provide and maintain from their own funds a defense force exempt from being drafted into the armed forces of the United States, but none has done so.

One of the issues surrounding Hurricane Katrina was whether the governor of Louisiana or the president had the authority to direct Louisiana's National Guard response to the disaster. President Bush sought control, but then Democratic Governor Kathleen Blanco resisted. In response, in 2007, Congress altered the 200-year-old Insurrection Act to allow the president to take control of the National Guard for domestic disasters.[34]

Pardon Power

In two-thirds of the states, governors have exclusive and unconditional authority to pardon violators of state law. In the other states, they share this duty with a pardoning board.[35] Except in cases of impeachment or certain specified crimes, the governor may pardon the offender, commute a sentence by reducing it, or grant a reprieve by delaying the punishment. The governor is normally assisted by pardon attorneys or pardon boards that hold hearings and determine whether there are sufficient reasons for a pardon.

Because pardons are usually politically unpopular, some governors issue them only during their final days in office. A Tennessee governor, Ray Blanton (1975–1979), caused considerable controversy and sparked a federal investigation when he pardoned or paroled several dozen convicts just before leaving office in 1979. Critics charged that some of these convicts allegedly "purchased" their releases. Blanton's misuse of his pardon powers created such outrage that his elected successor, Lamar Alexander, was sworn in early and the locks to the governor's office were quickly changed so that Blanton was not able to enter, let alone grant any additional pardons.[36] Yet most pardons are uncontroversial because governors typically administer them with appropriate care.

Similar to a governor's pardon power is the authority to grant a stay of execution in death penalty cases. This is one of the most controversial aspects of executive power in states that permit the death penalty.[37] We opened this chapter with an account of former Illinois Governor George Ryan's use of this power regarding death penalty cases in his state. No other governor has adopted a moratorium, and Texas Governor George W. Bush allowed more than 130 executions during his time in office.

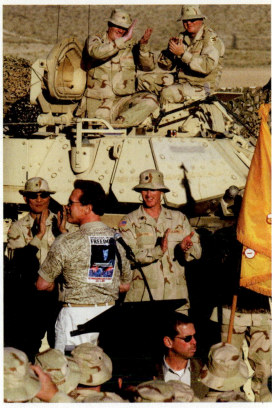

As commander in chief of the state's National Guard when it is not in federal service, a governor may use this force to handle state emergencies such as fires, floods, earthquakes, and other disasters. Here, Governor Arnold Schwarzenegger provides a morale boost for a California National Guard unit. ■ *How does control over the National Guard reflect the distribution of power in federalism?*

Policy-Making Influence

Although governors' formal powers vary widely from state to state, to change public policies, all governors face the challenge of securing the cooperation of many other people and institutions. To enact new legislation, governors may need to bargain with top legislative leaders (often of the opposite party), interest group representatives, local governments (which often lobby for or against legislation and budgets), and the state's bureaucracy (whose expertise is sometimes important in getting legislative support). In some cases, governors need to negotiate with federal agencies for a "waiver," an agreement by a federal agency to permit a state to implement a state law that would otherwise conflict with federal law. Governors must use their formal powers, political strengths, and personal skills to persuade these and other largely independent people and institutions to do what the governor needs them to do, usually by making it clear to such people that it is in their own political interest to do so.

Most governors have many tools at hand in their efforts to persuade. One is their opportunity to focus the public's attention on particular issues, problems, or policy proposals. They can attract more public attention to their views than any single legislator can, although even governors do not have many opportunities to get their message across to the public. Perhaps the most important chances they get are the annual State of the State messages, which they generally deliver to legislatures in the first months of each year. These messages usually highlight certain problems or issues, outline major policy proposals, and sketch the general shape of the executive budget. The effectiveness of such speeches depends not only on the governor's rhetorical skills but also on his or her popularity and reputation for pushing hard and persistently for his or her proposals. It is also essential that the governor's themes resonate with other state officials' views of what is feasible and needed for the times, particularly the current economy and the state's fiscal conditions. All of these speeches given by governors since 2000 are available online at http://www.stateline.org/live/resources/State+Speeches.

The governor's role as party leader may also add to his or her effectiveness in changing policy. Governors can be helpful in raising campaign contributions for state party organizations as well as for state legislators within their own party, usually by giving speeches at major fund-raisers. This kind of help is greatly appreciated and remembered by legislators, who have a much harder time raising large campaign chests because of their lower visibility and more localized networks of supporters. Most legislators also want to help make a governor of their own party successful. Not only are they likely to agree with the governor on many issues, but they may feel that their future reelection chances will be enhanced by a popular governor on their party's ticket.

However, the success of a purely partisan strategy depends in part on whether state legislatures are strongly partisan. In many states, winning legislative coalitions often include members of both political parties. This fluidity of legislative coalitions in states means that successful governors typically must maintain good relationships with many legislators, even those of the opposing party, and thus keep open the possibility of building bipartisan coalitions. Governors new to state politics often learn this lesson the hard way. After his first year in office—a year when he took a very confrontational approach to dealing with legislators—California Governor Arnold Schwarzenegger switched to a more accommodating political style after learning how poorly aggressive tactics worked in state politics:

> I have absorbed my defeat and I have learned my lesson. And the people, who always have the last word, sent a clear message—cut the warfare, cool the rhetoric, find common ground, and fix the problems together. So to my fellow Californians, I say—message received.[38]

Persuasion is time-consuming for governors, so another critical element of policy leadership is their management of time. Governors find it easy to become preoccupied with daily housekeeping tasks and public appearances. Although many governors come to office hoping to introduce new programs and reforms, they often spend most of their time raising money just to keep current programs operating. Some governors are thus viewed as mere "budget balancers" rather than as leaders or shapers of a state's future. Former Vermont Governor Madeleine Kunin recalls that she fixed problems as they happened and yet simultaneously had to define her policy vision for the future. "Finding the time, energy, and perspective to carry out a dual strategy was to be the physical and mental challenge of governing."[39]

Because many governors come to office with impressive legislative and administrative experience, they are more likely to be real executive heads of government, not mere figureheads. Some have initiated creative efforts to expand health insurance coverage, bring more high-technology businesses into their states, increase the quality and accountability of public schools, and make state and local tax systems fairer and more dependable sources of public revenues. Because states are now playing a larger role in many areas of domestic policy in the United States, the policy-making capacities of governors are clearly important to democratic governance in U.S. government as a whole.

Governors and Media Relations

Governors often attempt to shape their influence through aggressive media outreach. Many worked effectively with the media during their gubernatorial campaign and therefore understand their potential. Once in office, however, governors are thrust into a defensive role. Instead of running aggressive advertisements for their campaign, they are now under the media's magnifying glass, subject to scrutiny and investigation by reporters. They are quickly evaluated in light of their campaign promises and in comparison with previous governors.[40]

Past governors have been very aware of the media, with a handful having professional backgrounds in reporting or public relations. For example, former Governors Tom McCall of Oregon and Thomas Kean of New Jersey both had prior experience in public

The national health care reform adopted by Congress in 2010 shared many similarities with the state plan Republican Governor Mitt Romney, pictured here, signed into law in Massachusetts in 2006. Those similarities will likely be a political issue if Romney decides to run for president in 2012. ■ *What are the pros and cons of the national government using state policies as blueprints for national policies?*

relations positions—McCall as a journalist and radio announcer and Kean as a state campaign chair for President Ford and a television reporter during the Reagan campaign. Governor Kean notes the importance of communication with the media: "The most important power the governor has is the power of communicating. If that isn't done properly, you lose your power very fast."[41]

Not all governors are effective in dealing with the media, nor do they necessarily enjoy it. As Minnesota's former Governor Jesse Ventura says of the media: "The American media are suffering from very serious problems, and now I've seen them firsthand. They have the most twisted set of biases I've ever seen. As their whipping-boy-of-choice, I've been in a unique position to see what the media have become. There are a few honorable exceptions, but for the most part, they're corrupt, shameless, and irresponsible as hell."[42]

Each governor tends to have a personal style in dealing with the media. Some are very vocal, preferring to host daily radio or television talk shows, while others prefer to avoid the spotlight unless necessary. Governors sometimes request special time on television to explain and make an argument for policy changes. Others become visible by attending community functions, such as building dedications or opening ceremonies. It is especially important for governors to be publicly active as a calming influence during an emergency situation. During a disaster, such as an earthquake, hurricane, or terrorist action, governors have the ability to call out the National Guard and organize official aid groups. To visit, show concern for, and help ameliorate the suffering of involved families can do wonders for a governor's public opinion ratings. Governors must face public scrutiny, yet they can use the media to set and gain support for their agendas.[43]

On April 20, 2010, an explosion on the Deepwater Horizon drilling rig killed 11 workers and triggered a massive oil spill in the Gulf of Mexico. Officials from all levels of government responded, including Louisiana Governor Bobby Jindal, pictured here speaking to local fisherman impacted by the spill. ■ *What role should the local, state, and federal governments have in dealing with environmental disasters? Who should pay the costs of such efforts? Who should make the decisions about what to do?*

The Job of the Governor: Managing the State

LEARNING OBJECTIVE

6.3 Evaluate the effectiveness of governors as managers of the state's executive branch.

Governors and their senior staffs are also responsible for managing their state's executive branch, whether by providing strategic planning and vision, initiating policy, settling disputes among different agencies, promoting the state (attracting tourism, exports, and investment), recruiting top state administrative and judicial officials, developing the budget, pulling in federal dollars, or negotiating with the federal government and with nearby states.

Much recent federal legislation, which turns programs over to the states, specifically designates the governor as the chief planning and administrative officer. This role has given governors both more flexibility and more headaches. On one hand, governors can now dispense federal funds as a form of patronage, supporting services and programs for influential professional and local communities. On the other hand, this new intergovernmental relations role requires more time, more staff, and constant negotiations both with the "feds" and with local interest group leaders vying for money or services.

Some reformers have suggested that all state agencies should be accountable to the governor all the time, but others believe that politics should be kept out of the day-to-day operations of a state agency. For example, how much influence should a governor have over the running of the department of corrections in a state? Should public agencies respond to fluctuations in public opinion or to a governor's political mood? Which policy decisions should be made by professionals and experts, and which should be controlled by elected officials or by partisan appointees?

Modernizing State Administrations

Governors in recent years have had more managerial control over their states as a result of the use of modern management techniques: strategic planning, systems analysis, performance measurement and management, customer focus, and sophisticated information technology and budgeting systems. The Pew Center on the States Government Performance Project, mentioned in Chapter 2, provides performance grades for state governments (http://www.pewcenteronthestates.org/gpp_report_card.aspx).[44]

In urban states with competitive party systems, such as New York, Illinois, New Jersey, Pennsylvania, Washington, and California, governors have considerable formal constitutional authority to organize their administrations as they see fit. Even in more rural states, such as South Dakota, scores of agencies have been consolidated into a few comprehensive units as the result of executive orders from the governors.

A few years ago, in the wake of highly publicized scandals, the South Carolina legislature agreed to abolish 75 state boards, folding them into 17 larger executive agencies. This restructuring also gave the governor the authority to hire and fire the directors of most of these agencies.[45] In 2003, Texas enacted a plan to replace 11 health and human services agencies with four departments in order to increase efficiency and improve services.[46]

During the past several decades, various reformers have urged that the governor be made the true manager of the executive branch, by consolidating agencies into a smaller number of more tightly controlled departments, giving the governor greater power to hire and fire senior executives, modernizing state government through better information technology, relying more on private sector contractors to carry out functions previously performed by public agencies, and using performance measures to assess how well contractors and public agencies are achieving their major goals.

However, in some states, reorganization commissions have submitted reports that were filed away and forgotten. Groups that profit from the existing structure will resist change, as will officials who fear loss of jobs or prestige. Also, legislators are sometimes reluctant to approve recommendations that may make a governor too powerful.

Many critics oppose not so much the idea of reorganization as the basic principle of strengthening executive power and responsibility, which has dominated the reorganization movement. Often, they say, there is little evidence to support the adoption of these reforms, and there is a real danger that reorganizers are overlooking basic values in their concern with saving money. Intent on efficiency and economy, reformers often fail to foresee the risks in creating a powerful chief executive where no effective party or legislative opposition exists to keep a strong governor in check.

Effects of Reorganization

Although states have realized large savings through centralized purchasing and modern money management practices, it is difficult to measure the results of consolidating departments, strengthening the governor's control over the executive branch, or establishing an ombudsman office to handle citizen complaints. However, the best-governed states do seem to be those in which the administrative structure has been closely integrated under the governor.

Overall, formal reorganization is not the only way states modify and modernize their governmental structures. Often they change in stages, copying innovations from other states. Certain states, in fact, serve as exporters of innovations. So does the federal government. When the federal government created the Department of Housing and Urban Development, states responded by creating similar departments; when the federal government established the Department of Transportation, so did several of the states; and when the federal government formed special White House-level office for trade, many governors set up their own offices for trade and export responsibilities.

In recent decades, many governors have experimented with management reforms. Mario Cuomo of New York and Pete Wilson of California tried ideas from the private sector, including total quality management (TQM) and performance-based pay initiatives, although public employee labor unions resisted these reforms at the time.[47] More recently, governors have attempted to implement reforms that make state government more accountable on the basis of performance on measurable goals. These reforms typically give state administrators greater flexibility in *how* they manage programs, while they collect more data on the outcomes of public programs and hold the managers accountable for achieving results.[48] However, many agencies have a hard time getting good and timely measures of outcomes or determining precisely how much of an effect their programs have on outcomes compared with the influences of other factors. For instance, discerning the effects of a job training program on employment, distinct from the effects of the economy and demographic changes, is no simple matter.

"Although the analogy between a governor and a private sector chief executive is apt," writes political scientist Thad Beyle, "governors have a distance to go before possessing comparable power of appointment and removal."[49] Many governors do not have the flexibility in hiring and firing personnel that business executives have, and they must share control with various boards, commissions, and elected officials.

In summary, governors can be influential in leading certain reforms and introducing management improvements, but they are rarely as influential and as effective as most citizens assume is the case. All kinds of constitutional, legal, and political restraints put brakes on their attempts to bring about fundamental change. Still, in good economic times, governors are generally able to begin new programs and improve the performance of existing state operations.

Assisting the Governor: State Executive Officials

Other executive officials elected by the people in most states include the lieutenant governor, secretary of state, attorney general, and treasurer. These offices each have important duties and powers and often constitute rungs on the ladder of political ambition. Many candidates for governor first held one of these other offices in their state. (See Table 6–2 for an inventory of state executive officials.)

Lieutenant Governor

Forty-two states have a lieutenant governor, a post similar to vice president at the national level. In nearly half the states, the lieutenant governor is elected on the same ticket as the

LEARNING OBJECTIVE

6.4 Outline duties and powers of other top executive officials in state government.

TABLE

6–2 | State Executive Officials

Position	Role	Prominence	How Acquired
Lieutenant Governor	Second in command to the governor	Present in 42 states	By popular election in all states
Attorney General	Represents the state before the courts	Present in all 50 states	By appointment in 5 states By popular election in 43 states Elected by the legislature in 2 states
Secretary of State	Publishes the laws; oversees state elections	Present in 47 states	By appointment in 9 states By popular election in 35 states Elected by the legislature in 3 states
Treasurer	Guardian of the state's money	Present in 46 states	By appointment in 7 states By popular election in 35 states Elected by the legislature in 4 states

■ *What is the most common means for selecting executive officials across the states? Why do you suppose that is?*

governor, and in those states, the job is indeed like that of the vice president—the job and its influence depend very much on the discretion of the governor. In 26 states, the lieutenant governor presides over the state senate. The lieutenant governor becomes governor or acting governor in case of the death, disability, resignation, or absence of the governor from the state. Doubtless for this reason, more governors have sprung from this office than from other statewide elective offices. For example, David Paterson assumed the governorship in New York after Governor Eliot Spitzer resigned in the wake of a scandal in 2008.

In states where the governor and lieutenant governor are elected on the same ticket, the lieutenant governor is likely to be given some significant responsibilities. Still, many lieutenant governors have no statutory duties, and in some states, being lieutenant governor is actually a part-time job. Where the lieutenant governor is elected independently of the governor, he or she can sometimes be a member of the opposition party and become a thorn in the side of the chief executive. This is particularly a problem in a state such as Texas, where the state constitution gives the lieutenant governor even greater budgetary powers than the governor.[50]

Although the position of lieutenant governor has worked well in some states, the view persists that lieutenant governors are often in search of job assignments that make them look important. The staffs and cabinets currently growing up around governors put the governor's chief of staff in a position of greater influence than most lieutenant governors. Moreover, many candidates for lieutenant governor seek the post for the name recognition and statewide experience to advance their political careers. In summary, the value to the state of the often-obscure office of lieutenant governor is debatable.[51] You can learn more about the office of lieutenant governor at the National Lieutenant Governors Association Web site at http://www.nlga.us/.

Attorney General

The attorney general—the state's chief lawyer—gives advice to state officials, represents the state before the courts, and in some states, supervises local prosecutors. Some state attorneys general have authority over local prosecutors, and may prosecute cases on their own initiative, although in most states, criminal prosecution remains under the control of the local county prosecutor. Attorneys general have the authority to make sure the state's laws are implemented properly. They work in narcotics enforcement, investigate illegal activities, and often concentrate on laws that protect consumers, the environment, and public safety. They can also issue advisory opinions to state and local officials, and in many cases, review legislation.

In many states, attorneys general have taken the lead as champions of the consumer and protectors of the environment. They often have their own legislative agendas, separate from the governor's. In 1998, 46 state attorneys general settled their lawsuits against the tobacco companies and produced "a new regime of tobacco control," one that required the companies to pay more than $240 million to state governments and the National Association

Making Government More Ethical

Since the Progressive Era of the 1890s, ethics and corruption in government have been a major political issue. States have made progress throughout the years, but much work remains. Governors are entrusted by voters with the responsibility of running their states honestly and fairly. Earning that trust has been getting harder for governors as continued scandals fuel the concerns of an increasingly skeptical public. In just the last few years, sitting or former governors in South Carolina, New York, Illinois, and North Carolina have faced serious charges regarding legal and ethical violations. A group calling itself Citizens for Responsibility and Ethics in Washington has produced what it calls a report on America's Worst Governors (http://www.citizensforethics.org/worst governors). The group claims to base its evaluations on how well governors abide by their states' ethics, campaign finance, and transparency in government laws.

How can governors respond? Beverly Perdue, the current governor of North Carolina, offers one example. While her predecessor was still being investigated for possible federal corruption charges, Perdue used her power to issue executive orders to mandate stronger ethics standards for top state officials. Such officials will face longer waiting periods after leaving their posts before they can work as a lobbyist or take a job with a firm their agency regulated. She also requires anyone seeking appointment to a state commission or board to disclose conflicts of interest, previous criminal record, tax problems, or formal grievances filed against them. Perdue was quoted as saying, "The people of North Carolina should rightfully expect and deserve integrity from their public servants."*

Many governors have enacted similar reforms in recent years, hoping to restore

Beverly Purdue, governor of North Carolina.

voter confidence in the governorship regardless of who actually governs. Although efforts like this will not fully eliminate corruption and ethical lapses, they do place the question of ethics higher on a state's agenda. As Governor Perdue's comments suggest, holding our governors and other top officials to the highest ethical standards helps to ensure that our leaders will be guided by what their voters value.

CRITICAL THINKING QUESTIONS

1. What can governors do to help instill a sense of trust in state governments among their citizens?

2. Should governors focus their ethics reform efforts only on the executive branch? What complications arise if governors try to set ethical guidelines for legislators, or vice versa?

3. The framers of the U.S. Constitution were skeptical of government having too much power, but they were also skeptical of too much direct involvement by citizens. How might these considerations affect how open the operations of government should be to public scrutiny?

---

* Perdue was quoted in a news story posted by Cullen Browder, a reporter for WRAL TV in North Carolina, titled "Perdue Tightens Up State Ethics Rules," http://www.wral.com/news/local/politics/story/7360866/.

---

of Attorneys General (http://www.naag.org/) and that imposed new restrictions on the advertising and marketing of tobacco.[52] The lawsuits were largely based on claims that smoking increased the costs of state Medicaid programs. Attorneys general also waged antitrust investigations against corporations such as Microsoft. In California, following allegations of overcharging customers, Attorney General Bill Lockyer filed complaints against four major power companies.[53] New York State's former attorney general, Eliot Spitzer, became a nationally recognized figure through his investigations of Wall Street fraud, Internet fraud, computer chip price fixing, insurance fraud, environmental damages, and other "white collar" crimes, and he used that visibility to build a highly successful campaign for governor in 2006—although he resigned in the wake of his own scandal a year after taking office.[54]

Secretary of State

The secretary of state publishes the laws, supervises elections, licenses professionals, and issues certificates of incorporation. In some states, the secretary issues automobile licenses and registers corporate securities. In states without a Secretary of State these duties are filled by the Lieutenant Governor or some other official. Voters in 35 states elect secretaries of state. In nine states, governors appoint people to this position. In three states, secretaries of state are elected by the legislature. And three states do not have this position at all.

Although all secretaries of state have some duty to oversee state elections, their responsibilities differ greatly from state to state. However, nearly all are implementing the 2002 federal Help America Vote Act, which gave states funding to replace outdated voting equipment and improve the accuracy and accountability of election administration.

Nearly all also share a commitment to increasing voter education and turnout. In 1998, the National Association of Secretaries of State (http://www.nass.org/) launched the "New Millennium Project" to encourage greater participation among young citizens.

Treasurer and Auditor

The treasurer is the guardian of the state's money. Although in some states the job is largely ministerial, state treasurers generally have the responsibility of ensuring that cash is available to meet the obligations of the state and that all available funds are invested to maximize interest return. Treasurers are elected by popular vote in 35 states, elected by the legislature in 4 states, and appointed in 7 states. You can learn more from the National Association of State Treasurers at http://www.nast.net/.

The auditor in most states has two major jobs: to authorize payments from the state treasury and to make periodic audits of officials who handle state money. In Montana, the state auditor serves as insurance commissioner. Before money can be spent, the auditor must sign a *warrant* certifying that the expenditure is authorized by law and that the money is available in the treasury. This job is more accurately called the *preaudit* and is increasingly being assigned to a comptroller appointed by and responsible to the governor. Auditing *after* money has been spent, however, is a job most observers believe should be given to an officer responsible to the legislature. Even advocates of much more centralized administrations believe that the auditor should not be responsible to the governor; however, most auditors are appointed, although in 18 states, they are elected. Learn more online at the National Association of State Auditors, Comptrollers, and Treasurers at http://www.nasact.org/.

Other Officials

Such positions as superintendent of public education, agriculture commissioner, public utilities commissioner, comptroller, and insurance commissioner are less likely to be elected than treasurers or auditors. Putting positions like these on the ballot results in a longer ballot, and voters sometimes pay little attention to them. The proliferation of elected officials also makes it more difficult for governors to manage and lead state government.

As part of the trend toward integrated administration, the duties of elected state officials have generally been limited to those specified in the state constitution. Some important functions have been given to officials appointed by the governor. In many states, the budget director appointed by the governor has a more important role than the elected treasurer or secretary of state. Yet elected officers can often control patronage, attract a following, and thus develop a political base from which to attack the governor's program and administration.

Sometimes progressive and controversial initiatives in state governments come from elected officials. An attorney general in Texas helped design and pass the Texas Open Records Act, one of the broadest and most strictly enforced freedom-of-information statutes in the country. A secretary of state in Massachusetts modernized election laws, helped enact campaign finance laws, and championed conflict-of-interest reforms. A state treasurer in Colorado battled to transfer some of his state's revenue deposits from a few large Denver banks to smaller banks around the state and devised incentives for these banks to lend money to students and small businesses and to support low-income housing and family farms.

Governors Today: Challenges and Rewards

LEARNING OBJECTIVE

6.5 Evaluate the challenges and rewards for governors today.

Although the constitutional powers of governors vary from state to state, U.S. citizens evaluate and rate their governors using many of the same criteria they apply to rating presidents.[55] Lamar Alexander, former governor of Tennessee, said a governor needs to "see the state's few most urgent needs, develop strategies to address them, and persuade at least half the people that he or she is right."[56]

Today, a governor is expected to be, among other things, the state's chief policy maker, shaper of the state budget, savvy political party leader, chief recruiter of the best available advisers and administrators, and inspiring renewer of confidence in state

By the People

Who Is Governing Your School?

One of the major areas of policy responsibility for governors is public higher education. In administering the state's higher education system, virtually every governor works with one or more university board or commission. Sometimes each individual campus has a governing board, and sometimes, multiple campuses are part of a system under a single board. Sometimes the members of these boards are appointed, and sometimes, they are elected. In many states, there is a student representative that serves on the board. Find out how your university is governed and who the board members are. In particular, identify whether they have a student member, how the student member is selected, and whether student members have full voting rights.

What issues is your school's governing board currently considering, and do they reflect the priorities of the students? You could organize a forum on campus and invite one or more current board members to field questions from the audience. To prepare, collect survey data from current students regarding their views. If you do not feel your interests are being represented, write a letter to the editor of your local community paper or start a petition drive on campus.

How your school is governed and the decisions the governing board makes can have a dramatic effect on your educational opportunities. If board members come primarily from the business community, they may view the role of colleges as preparing future workers for narrowly focused jobs in industry. Board members with roots in education might place more value on a general liberal arts education rather than training for specific careers. You should seek out this information and then get involved.

CRITICAL THINKING QUESTIONS

1. What are the pros and cons of having a separate board governing higher education, instead of giving this authority to the state department of education?

2. How important is the makeup of the board governing higher education? Should board members be elected by voters or appointed by the governor? How important is student representation on such a board?

---

programs. The governor must also champion the state's interests against the encroachments of federal or local governments and be the state's chief booster to attract business and tourism. In order to be effective, governors are expected to take trips abroad to encourage foreign investment in their states and promote their local products.[57] Thirty-eight states even operate some form of overseas office, including trade mission posts in Harare and Kuala Lumpur.[58] Governors also work with their legislatures to raise revenues for such programs as welfare, education, and economic development. They act as crucial links among the states and between local and the national governments.

No one thinks governors have an easy job. However, most governors earn praise for their leadership, and most enjoy solid public approval ratings.[59] "A governor achieves his personal best by being honest and by staying in touch with the people who elected him to serve them," says Alexander.[60] Former Governor Tom Kean of New Jersey echoed similar thoughts: "I have tried to show during my political career, and especially my years as governor, that responsible government can meet people's needs and bring them together, that government can make a difference in the way we live."[61]

Ultimately, the best governors are ones who have a keen sense of history and their own circumstance. A popular former governor of Utah, the late Scott Matheson, wrote that they have been the men and women who have the right combination of "values for quality service, the courage to stick to their convictions, even when in the minority, integrity by instinct, compassion by nature, leadership by perception, and the character to admit wrong, and when necessary, to accept defeat."[62]

CHAPTER SUMMARY

6.1 Identify the typical pathways by which people attain and retain the governorship.

Governors usually have had experience in state government before they reach office, as either legislators, executives, or both. Although most governors are usually white males in their 40s or 50s, more women have become governors in recent decades. Most gubernatorial elections are insulated from national political swings, and at least three out of four governors who run again win reelection. However, most governors cannot remain in office long because of term limits.

6.2 Identify the formal and informal powers of governors, and assess governors' use of these powers to influence policy.

Governors' most important formal powers are their appointive and budgetary powers. They also have veto and pardon powers, they have the power to issue executive orders, and they are commanders in chief of the National Guard. Although differences across states in the formal powers of governors have declined in recent years, substantial differences may still be found.

To be effective, governors must use not only their formal powers but also use their informal powers to draw public attention, lead their party, build and maintain good personal relationships with many officials and institutions, and work well with the media. Governors help set the policy agenda and frame the debate on important public issues.

6.3 Evaluate the effectiveness of governors as managers of the state's executive branch.

During the past generation, reforms in management and organization have strengthened most governorships. Most governors have gained powers that enable them to achieve more of their goals—and they have modernized state government while strengthening their control over the executive branch. Nonetheless, constitutional, legal, and political restraints continue to limit governors' efforts.

CHAPTER **SELF-TEST**

6.1 Identify the typical pathways by which people attain and retain the governorship.

1. Which is one of the most common paths to the governorship?
   a. Serving in the military
   b. Working as an attorney
   c. Being elected to the state legislature
   d. Serving in charitable organizations
2. Why do 75 percent of incumbent governors who seek reelection win?

6.2 Identify the formal and informal powers of governors, and assess governors' use of these powers to influence policy.

3. What is one difference between the federal executive (president) and state executive (governor)?
   a. They are the symbolic heads of their parties.
   b. They share executive power with other officials.
   c. They can veto legislation that has been passed by the legislature.
4. In a short essay, describe three specific formal powers held by governors and compare them across states. Describe how governors can use each of these powers to accomplish their policy goals.
5. In a short essay, describe how governors use their influential position with the media to advance their policy goals, resolve personal scandals, and promote their states.

6.3 Evaluate the effectiveness of governors as managers of the state's executive branch.

6. According to political scientist Thad Beyle, what is one reason governors are not yet as effective as private-sector chief executives in their respective jobs?
   a. State governments are vastly more complex than even large private-sector companies.

6.4 Outline duties and powers of other top executive officials in state government.

In addition to a governor, the voters in most states also elect other statewide officials such as a lieutenant governor, secretary of state, attorney general, and state treasurer. Many of the officials play important political and policy roles in their states, and many current governors previously served in some other statewide elected capacity. State attorneys general have been particularly important in prosecuting fraud, winning major settlements, and other activities in recent years.

6.5 Evaluate the challenges and rewards for governors today.

The job of governor is one of the most important and -exacting in U.S. political life. A governor is expected to be the state's chief policy maker, the architect of the state budget, the chief manager of the state administration, and the political and symbolic leader of the state. Specific expectations for governors change over time, especially in response to economic conditions.

b. Many governors do not have as much flexibility in hiring and firing personnel.
   c. State legislators are more ambitious and self-centered than most employees in private companies.
   d. Many governors have little experience or training in running an organization as large and complex as a state government.
7. Some have suggested giving the governor more direct control over state agencies. Identify one reason for and one against such reform.

6.4 Outline duties and powers of other top executive officials in state government.

8. Which top state official has no statutory duties in many states?
   a. State auditor
   b. Secretary of state
   c. Attorney general
   d. Lieutenant governor
9. In a short essay, compare the duties of three top executive officials in state government. Consider the statutory responsibilities, practical influence, and political roles of each.

6.5 Evaluate the challenges and rewards for governors today.

10. Identify and describe three roles people expect their governors to fill.
11. Imagine you are the governor of your state. In a short essay, identify and describe your most important role, responsibility, and policy goal.
12. U.S. citizens evaluate and rate their governors using many of the same criteria they apply to presidents. In a paragraph, argue what those criteria should be.

Answers to selected questions: 1. c; 3. b; 6. b; 8. d

 **EXERCISES**

Apply what you learned in this chapter with these resources on MyPoliSciLab.

Read on **mypoliscilab.com**

    eText: Chapter 6

✓ **Study** and **Review** on **mypoliscilab.com**

    Pre-Test
    Post-Test
    Chapter Exam
    Flashcards

Watch on **mypoliscilab.com**

    Video: New York's 2010 Governor's Race
    Video: Wisconsin Governor Seeks to Remove 'Sexting' DA

Explore on **mypoliscilab.com**

    Comparative: Comparing Executive Branches
    Simulation: You Are a Governor

KEY **TERMS**

veto, p. 124
line item veto, p. 124

reduction veto, p. 124
amendatory veto, p. 124

executive order, p. 125

ADDITIONAL **RESOURCES**

FURTHER READING

THAD L. BEYLE, ED., *Governors and Hard Times* (CQ Press, 1992).

THOMAS M. CARSEY, *Campaign Dynamics: The Race for Governor* (University of Michigan Press, 2000).

DAN T. CARTER, *The Politics of Rage: George Wallace, the Origins of the New Conservatism, and the Transformation of American Politics,* 2d ed. (Louisiana State Press, 2000).

ROBERT S. ERIKSON ET AL., *Statehouse Democracy: Public Opinion and Policy in the American States* (Cambridge University Press, 1993).

ALVIN S. FELZENBERG, *Governor Tom Kean: From the New Jersey Statehouse to the 9–11 Commission* (Rutgers University Press, 2006).

VIRGINIA GRAY AND **RUSSELL HANSON,** EDS., *Politics in the American States: A Comparative Analysis,* 9th ed. (CQ Press, 2007).

MADELEINE M. KUNIN, *Living a Political Life* (Vintage Books, 1995).

BROOKE MASTERS, *Spoiling for a Fight: The Rise of Eliot Spitzer* (Holt, 2007).

SARAH M. MOREHOUSE, *The Governor as Party Leader* (University of Michigan Press, 1998).

ALAN ROSENTHAL, *Governors and Legislatures: Contending Powers* (CQ Press, 1990).

ETHAN G. SRIBNICK, ED., *A Legacy of Innovation: Governors and Public Policy* (Pennsylvania State University Press, 2008).

SUE THOMAS AND **CLYDE WILCOX,** *Women and Elective Office* (Oxford University Press, 1998).

TOMMY G. THOMPSON, *Power to the People: An American State at Work* (HarperCollins, 1996).

T. HARRY WILLIAMS, *Huey Long* (Vintage Books, 1981).

WILLIAM F. WINTER, *The Measure of Our Days: Writings of William F. Winter* (University Press of Mississippi, 2006). See also the quarterly *Spectrum: The Journal of State Government, Governing, State Policy Reports,* and *State Government News.* See also the valuable University of Nebraska Press series on state politics in the individual states, each of which has a chapter on governors.

The National Governors' Association publishes a variety of surveys, reports, and studies, including the weekly *Governors' Bulletin* and the *Proceedings of the National Governors' Association* annual meetings. These and related documents can be purchased by writing to the National Governors' Association, 444 N. Capitol Street NW, Washington, D.C., 20001.

WEB SITES

http://www.stateline.org/ Stateline.org provides news and information on policy and politics in the 50 states.

The following are Web sites for professional associations dedicated to the various top statewide executive branch officials:

www.nga.org/ National Governors Association.

www.nlga.us/ National Lieutenant Governors Association.

www.naag.org/ National Association of Attorneys General.

www.nass.org/ National Association of Secretaries of State.

www.nasact.org/ National Association of State Auditors, Comptrollers, and Treasurers.

Massey Energy Gets $50 Million Verdict Overturned Again

By ——— ——————— November 13, 2009 00:01 EST

Nov. 13 (Bloomberg) — Massey Energy Co., the fifth-largest U.S. ——————— for a second time in getting a $50 million jury verdict ——— U.S. Supreme Court said West Virginia's highest court ——— ——— justice should have recused himself.

——————— of West Virginia again reve——— ———————————————————————————terday. In Novem———

Judges and Justice in the States

State courts play a major role in how citizens and their government come into contact with each other. Most of the nation's judicial business is conducted by its nearly 30,000 state and municipal judges. Put into perspective, federal courts confront approximately 2 million annual cases, whereas state courts see more than 100 million.[1] State judges preside over most criminal trials, settle most lawsuits between individuals, and administer most estates. They play a vital role in determining who gets what, where, when, and how. Thus, they are crucial in making public policy.

Although federal judges are appointed for life, most state court judges must be elected to either attain or retain their positions. Thus, in many respects, state courts face pressures more similar to other elected officials than do federal judges. This comes with potential advantages and disadvantages that will be discussed in this chapter. However, recent events surrounding campaign contributions to state supreme court candidates have raised some concerns about selecting state judges this way.

One example occurred in West Virginia. In 1998, the Harman Mining Company filed a lawsuit against A.T. Massey Coal Company regarding a contract dispute. In 2002, a state court found in favor of Harman and ordered Massey to pay $50 million in damages. The ruling was appealed to the West Virginia Supreme Court. While the case was pending, Massey's CEO created a nonprofit organization that he used to funnel more than $3 million of his own money to a candidate named Brent Benjamin, who was running for a seat on the state supreme court. Benjamin won the race. *Harman* v. *Massey* finally came before the court in 2007, and the Harman president petitioned for now Justice Benjamin to **recuse** himself from the case—that is, to withdraw from participating in making a ruling to avoid any actual or perceived partiality or bias. Benjamin refused, and in 2008, the court ruled in favor of Massey (thereby overturning the lower court's damage award of $50 million to Harman) by a vote of 3 to 2 with Benjamin voting in the majority. This decision was appealed to the U.S. Supreme Court, which ruled (5 to 4) on June 9, 2009, in *Caperton* v. *A.T. Massey Coal Co.*, that Benjamin should have recused himself. The case was sent back to the West Virginia Supreme Court. Benjamin was replaced on the case by a retired judge, and three other justices who heard the original case were no longer on the court. Massey again won, this time 4-1.[2]

This case pits the principles of freedom for groups and individuals to participate in the electoral process against the desire for an impartial judiciary. How states manage this tension will be a major issue surrounding judicial politics in the coming years.

This tension has been magnified recently because state courts have become more prominent in the political life of their state, and state judges have become embroiled in controversial issues. As the public has pressed for tougher action against criminals, the number of criminal cases processed by the courts has risen, and political debates have developed over standards for sentencing and imprisonment. In civil court, a revolution in tort law—law relating to compensation for injuries to person, reputation, or property—has flooded state courts as more people sue more often about more disputes. This has triggered a backlash so that many states have instituted legislative tort reforms that make it more difficult to bring lawsuits or that limit damage payments. Finally, with the rise of a **new judicial federalism** in many states, judicial interpretations of state constitutions have resulted in controversial rulings in such areas as the right to privacy, public school financing, and equal protection of the law.[3] Thus, what state courts do, how judges make decisions, and how judges are selected have become important political questions.

recuse
To withdraw from participating in making a ruling to avoid any actual or perceived partiality or bias.

new judicial federalism
The practice of some state courts using the bill of rights in their state constitutions to provide more protection for some rights than is provided by the Supreme Court's interpretation of the Bill of Rights in the U.S. Constitution.

The Structure of State Courts

Each state has its own court system, so it is difficult to generalize about them. For convenience, we categorize and discuss state courts as (1) minor courts of limited jurisdiction, (2) trial courts of general jurisdiction, and (3) appellate courts (see Figure 7–1).

Minor Courts

In most states, minor courts handle **misdemeanors**—relatively minor violations of state and local laws—as well as traffic cases and civil suits involving small amounts of money. In some places, they also hold preliminary hearings and set bail for more serious charges. Decisions of the minor courts may be appealed and, in most instances, tried *de novo*—that is, tried all over again without reference to what happened in the minor courts. In most places, these courts are financed and administered by a local government. In cities, these minor courts are known as *municipal courts* and are often divided into traffic courts, family courts, small claims courts, and police courts. Paid *magistrates* trained in the law preside over most of them.

The *justice of the peace* system is being phased out but survives in some states (Arizona, Arkansas, Delaware, Louisiana, Montana, Texas, and Wyoming) and in rural areas; in New York, the justices are called *town justices*. Justices of the peace are elected for short terms, usually two to six years. They need not be trained in the law, and their authority is limited to performing marriages, notarizing papers, handling traffic violations, and hearing misdemeanors, usually those incurring fines less than $200. They also hear minor civil disputes.

Courts handling minor crimes are often so crowded that cases are processed quickly with little individual attention. Although many critics of the legal system contend that judges are too lenient and criminals are back on the streets too quickly, others charge that poor and ignorant defendants often spend days in jail waiting for their cases to go to trial. A new and apparently effective reform is the establishment of *court-watching groups.* In some cities, these groups are sponsored by organizations concerned with seeing that the courts treat fairly those charged with crimes. In other cities, they are supported by those concerned that judges are too easy on defendants. Court watchers make prosecutors, public defenders, and judges more sensitive to the views of the general public.

Trial Courts of General Jurisdiction

Trial courts of **original jurisdiction,** where cases first appear, are called county courts, circuit courts, superior courts, district courts, and common pleas courts. They administer common, criminal, equity, and statutory law. In most states, **felonies** are tried in trial

misdemeanor
A minor crime; the penalty is a fine or imprisonment for a short time, usually less than a year, in a local jail.

original jurisdiction
The authority of a court to hear a case "in the first instance."

felony
A serious crime, the penalty for which can range from imprisonment in a penitentiary for more than a year to death.

> **CALIFORNIA SUPREME COURT**
> Highest state court; seven justices

> **COURTS OF APPEAL**
> Intermediate court; reviews decisions of superior courts; divided into six districts

> **SUPERIOR COURTS**
> One in each county; 58 in the state.
> Each court may have many departments.
> Decide questions of fact and law.

SMALL CLAIMS	CRIMINAL	CIVIL	JUVENILE
Claims of $2,500 or less.	Felonies: crimes punishable by imprisonment in state facilities.	Disputes where the claim is over $2,500 and cases involving wills, land titles, divorce, child custody, etc.	Correction of offenders under age 18. Protection of abused and neglected minors.

FIGURE 7–1 The California State Courts.

■ *How does the state court system compare to the federal court system?*

SOURCE: Guide to California Courts, www.courtinfo.ca.gov/reference/guide.

courts; felonies are serious crimes, and the penalty can range from imprisonment in a penitentiary for more than a year to death. Some states maintain separate courts for criminal and civil matters. States generally also have special *probate courts* to administer estates and handle matters related to wills. These courts are all *courts of record* in which trials take place, witnesses testify, and juries render verdicts, although most cases are heard and decided by a judge. *Appellate courts* may review decisions of trial courts; however, most decisions of trial judges are not reviewed and are final. These courts do more than apply the law; they also participate in the never-ending process of shaping the law and public policy.[4]

Appellate Courts

In a few states with relatively smaller caseloads—Delaware, Montana, New Hampshire, Nevada, North Dakota, Rhode Island, West Virginia, and Vermont—trial court decisions are appealed directly to the state supreme court. (In North Dakota, the supreme court can assign cases to a court of appeals composed of three judges chosen from among the trial judges.) Most states, however, have intermediate appeals courts that fit into the system in much the same way that the U.S. Courts of Appeals fit into the federal structure.

Family court judges deal with the legal issues of minors—children under the age of 18. ■ *What issues might a court-watching group be keeping an eye on in a juvenile court case?*

All states have a *court of last resort,* usually called the supreme court. In Maine and Massachusetts, the court of last resort is called the supreme judicial court; in Maryland and New York, it is the court of appeals; in West Virginia, it is the supreme court of appeals. And if that is not confusing enough, in New York, the trial courts are called supreme courts. Texas and Oklahoma have two courts of last resort—a supreme court that handles civil matters and a court of criminal appeals. Unless a federal question is involved, state supreme courts are the highest tribunal to which a case may be appealed.

All state judges of all state courts take an oath to uphold the supremacy of the U.S. Constitution, and all state courts have the power of **judicial review.** That is, they may refuse to enforce, and may restrain state and local officials from enforcing, state laws, regulations, or actions if they believe these conflict with the state constitution or the U.S. Constitution. State judges may also declare actions of federal officials or federal laws or regulations to be in conflict with the U.S. Constitution, subject to final review by the U.S. Supreme Court.

State supreme courts have led the way in making judicial decisions available on the Internet. All have Web sites, and nearly all provide access to written opinions and decisions, along with other information, and 10 percent make oral arguments available.[5] The Web site of the National Center for State Courts (www.ncsc.org) provides links to state court Web sites.

State Courts and State Politics

U.S. judges are prominent actors on the political scene, at both the national and state levels. But state courts differ from federal courts in several important ways. State judges are more likely to decide cases involving their legislative and executive branches than the U.S. Supreme Court is to engage in congressional and presidential matters.[6] In addition, state judges are not constrained by the doctrine of federalism when dealing with local units of government. Furthermore, in nine states, the state supreme court can give advisory opinions at the request of the governor or state legislature. An **advisory opinion** is an opinion unrelated to a particular case that gives a court's view about a constitutional or legal issue. An advisory opinion is often requested when there is a question about the constitutionality of a bill or proposal under consideration by the governor and/or legislature.

judicial review
The power of a court to refuse to enforce a law or a government regulation that in the opinion of the judges conflicts with the U.S. Constitution or, in a state court, the state constitution.

advisory opinion
An opinion unrelated to a particular case that gives a court's view about a constitutional or legal issue.

State judges are likely to be part of the state's legal culture, and state judges can claim to be representatives of the people. Most have been educated in the state's law schools.[7] In addition, most state judges serve for limited terms and stand for election. "As elected representatives, like legislators, they feel less hesitant to offer their policy views than do appointed judges."[8] However, they also can be held accountable by voters for their actions.

How Judges Are Chosen

LEARNING **OBJECTIVE**

7.2 Evaluate the different methods of selecting judges.

Judges are selected in four different ways (see Figure 7–2): appointment by the governor, election by the legislature, popular election, or a modified appointment plan known as the Missouri Plan, in which a special commission provides a short list of nominees from which the governor selects one to appoint as judge.

Appointment by the Governor and Election by the Legislature

In Delaware, Hawaii, Maine, New Jersey, New York, and Vermont, judges are appointed by the governor and confirmed by the state senate. In Delaware and Massachusetts, governors select appointees from names submitted by judicial nominating commissions. Election by the legislature is the constitutional practice in South Carolina and Virginia. Even in states that elect judges, a majority "are in fact initially appointed by the governor to fill midterm vacancies, usually occasioned by the retirement or death of sitting judges…and these appointed judges are overwhelmingly favored in their first electoral bids following appointment."[9]

In addition to this formal process of nomination and selection, several informal processes play a role in identifying good candidates for judgeships. Lawyers interested in becoming judges may make their interest known either directly or indirectly to party officials. Leaders of the local bar associations may promote favored members, and various members of the bar may seek out candidates and recruit them. Political leaders and interest groups also participate. Following such suggestions, the candidates go through the formal appointment process.[10]

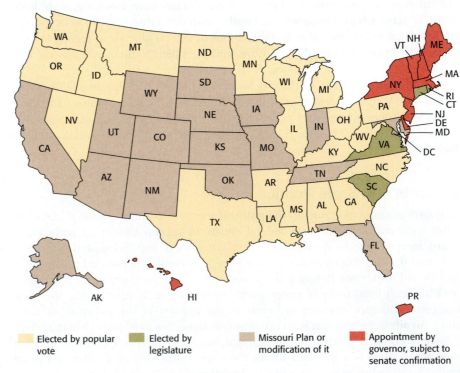

FIGURE 7–2 Method for Selection of Judges of the Court of Last Resort.

■ *Which participants or interests would favor each of these methods of selection, and why?*

SOURCE: *The Book of the States, 2005* (The Council of State Governments, 2005), pp. 318–321.

Elected by popular vote

Elected by legislature

Missouri Plan or modification of it

Appointment by governor, subject to senate confirmation

For the People

GOVERNMENT'S GREATEST ENDEAVORS

Public Funding of Judicial Campaigns

As judicial election campaigns have become more hotly contested and, thus, more controversial, a number of reformers have advocated providing public funding for judicial candidates so that they do not need to raise funds from individuals, companies, or other groups with pending or potential cases coming up in the court. North Carolina has responded with an innovative program of public funding for state supreme court and court of appeals candidates. The program, which first went into effect for the 2004 election cycle, requires potential candidates to first raise a sufficient amount of money from North Carolina registered voters as a way to demonstrate their viability as candidates. Once they qualify, candidates receive a fixed amount of money to run their campaigns. Candidates who

accept the funds must abide by spending limits and are barred from accepting any funds from political parties or political action committees (PACs).

One of the most important features of the North Carolina program is the "rescue funds" provision. Because the public funding program is voluntary, potential candidates might be concerned that an opponent might choose not to participate and then greatly outspend those candidates who do participate and must abide by spending limits. To combat this, the North Carolina system provides that candidates who opt into the program will be eligible for additional funds above the spending limit if they find themselves facing an opponent who did not accept public funding and is spending much larger amounts. In 2004 and 2008, 23 of

29 possible candidates participated, and several of those who did not participate chose not to because they were unchallenged. The North Carolina program is being touted as a model for how to help insulate judicial elections from undue influence from campaign contributors. The program has survived challenges that it unduly limits free speech because it is voluntary.

CRITICAL THINKING QUESTIONS

1. What are the pros and cons of public funding for judicial elections? Can states afford to spend public money on campaigns? Can they afford not to?

2. What constitutional issues regarding the First Amendment are raised by public election funding programs?

Popular Election

More than 85 percent of all state and local judges face elections, resulting in a greater number of elections for judges than for state legislators and executive officials. Appellate court judges in eight states face partisan elections, 13 states hold nonpartisan elections, and another 19 states have retention elections for state judges.[11] Nonpartisan judicial elections do not necessarily mean that political parties do not participate. In at least half of the states with nonpartisan judicial elections, parties actively campaign on behalf of candidates. Some states try to isolate judicial elections from partisan politics by holding them separately from other elections.

In 1986, California amended its constitution to forbid political parties from endorsing candidates for judicial office. However, federal courts declared the proposition unconstitutional, and California political parties are once again endorsing judicial candidates. The prevailing view, as Justice Thurgood Marshall observed, was that "the prospect that voters might be persuaded by party endorsements is not a *corruption* of the democratic political process; it *is* the democratic political process."[12]

Until recently, there was little interest in judicial elections, and voter turnout tended to be low. But judicial elections are becoming increasingly spirited. Interest groups focus attention on judges whose decisions they find objectionable. In some states, the death penalty is the issue. In Texas and California, efforts to limit liability lawsuits and damage awards have led to campaign clashes over judicial candidates, with trial lawyers, consumers, and union groups on one side and business interests on the other. In Idaho, one candidate for the supreme court campaigned on a platform stating that the theory of evolution could not be true—and won. An Illinois judge was unseated because of his decisions in abortion cases. Now more than ever, judges have to act like politicians and "feel they are under increasing pressure to be accountable to public opinion."[13]

As judicial elections become more hotly contested, spending in the campaigns has escalated. Between 2000 and 2009, candidate fund raising more than doubled compared with the previous decade, rising from $83.3 million during the 1990s to more than $206 million in the 2000s. Nineteen states set all-time high records for fund raising by high court candidates during the 2000s, and candidates raised more than $45 million collectively in three of the last five election cycles. Nearly half of the money raised during the decade was spent on

In states with elected judges, campaigns can become very competitive. ■ *What are the advantages and disadvantages of electing judges?*

TV advertising. Parties and interest groups are responsible for 40 percent of all TV advertising spending. A survey conducted in 2001 found that more than 90 percent of elected judges nationwide said they feel pressure to raise money in election years—a figure that jumps to 97 percent of elected high court judges.[14] In many states that elect judges, it is increasingly clear that judicial candidates depend on a small number of law firms, businesses, or special-interest groups, such as the U.S. Chamber of Commerce and the Business Roundtable, for their campaign funds.[15]

Much of the rising cost of judicial campaigns stems from the increased reliance on televised campaign advertising. As recently as a decade ago, most candidates even for state supreme courts did not run TV ads during their campaigns. Those who did generally ran very tame biographical spots focused on their own qualifications and experience. However, as the contests have heated up, so has the advertising. Candidates now routinely face attack ads that are every bit as aggressive as those targeting candidates for other offices. Some examples from 2008 can be found online at http://judicialcampaignoversight. org/2008ads/2008ads1.html.

In response to concerns about the campaigns in judicial elections, most states adopted provisions similar to the American Bar Association's code of judicial conduct that bar judicial candidates from telling the electorate anything about their views on legal and political matters. Some states went even further: the Minnesota Supreme Court, for instance, prohibited judicial candidates from soliciting campaign contributions, declaring their party affiliation, or publicly voicing their positions on controversial issues. However, the U.S. Supreme Court struck down Minnesota's ban on judicial candidates' announcing their positions on controversial legal and political matters as a violation of the First Amendment guarantee of free speech.[16] State and federal courts in Alabama, Georgia, Michigan, Ohio, and other states have also handed down decisions perceived by some as "a roadblock for efforts to curb the increasingly raucous nature of judicial politics."[17] Striking down these limits has contributed greatly to making judicial campaigns look much more like their hotly contested counterparts for legislative and executive offices.

In response to the growing cost of state judicial elections, the American Bar Association, the American Judicature Society, and other organizations are promoting the public financing of state judicial campaigns and elections.[18] Three states—Wisconsin, North Carolina, and New Mexico—provide public financing for some judicial elections. Wisconsin has had publicly financed elections for state supreme court justices since the 1970s; candidates are eligible for $97,000 in state money if they agree to a $215,000 spending limit. The system is paid for through a $1 check-off contribution on income tax returns and has been historically underfinanced. In 2004, North Carolina's Judicial Campaign Reform Act went into effect. Under the Act, all appellate-level judicial races are nonpartisan, and candidates who agree to fund-raising and spending limits receive public financing in the general election.

Minority Representation   The one-person, one-vote rule that applies to legislative elections does not apply to judicial elections.[19] States may create judicial districts so that one judge "represents" many more voters than another judge. Although there is no requirement that states elect judges, if they choose to do so, the federal Voting Rights Act of 1965 applies to these judicial elections.[20]

Because the Voting Rights Act of 1965 forbids any practice or procedure that dilutes the voting power of minorities, it raises a question about the constitutionality of at-large judicial elections. When judges are elected at large for a city or a state, African American and Hispanic candidates sometimes find it difficult to get elected. African American and Hispanic voters tend to be concentrated in the inner cities or in certain geographical areas; thus, their impact is diluted in citywide or statewide elections. For example, in a state in which the population consists of 20 percent African American voters, 20 percent Hispanic voters, and 60 percent white voters, with five judges to be elected on a statewide basis, few if any African American judges or Hispanic judges will be elected. Some Hispanics and African Americans argue that the solution is to divide such a state into five districts, with one judge elected in each district, and draw district lines in such a way that African Americans and Hispanics make up a majority of voters in as many districts as possible, giving them a chance to elect at least one of their own.

Of the People

Women and Minorities on State Supreme Courts

Although state judges were once overwhelmingly white males, that has changed in recent years. A 2008 study found that nearly 12 percent of all state judges were racial or ethnic minorities, and slightly more than half of those minority judges were African American. States with the highest percentages of minority judges include California, Hawaii, Louisiana, Maryland, New Mexico, New York, North Carolina, and Texas. States with the lowest percentages include Alaska, Idaho, Kentucky, Maine, Montana, New Hampshire, North Dakota, South Dakota, Vermont, and Wyoming. Women have become more prominent in state courts as well. In early 2010, the National Association of Women Judges (www.nawj.org) reported that 26 percent of all state judges were women.

CRITICAL THINKING QUESTIONS

1. How might having more women and minorities on the bench affect the decisions of state supreme courts?

2. Should a state change the way it selects judges in order to increase the number of women and minorities on the bench? Why or why not?

Chief Justice Wallace B. Jefferson of Texas was the first African American state supreme court justice in Texas when he was appointed in 2001 by Governor Rick Perry. He was named chief justice in 2004, making him the first African American to hold that post in Texas as well.

SOURCE: Barbara L. Graham, "State Judicial Diversity," *The Book of the States, 2009* (The Council of State Governments, 2009); and The National Association of Women Judges, www.nawj.org.

Merit Selection: The Missouri Plan

Many lawyers and political scientists have argued in favor of a screening process before judges are appointed or elected to ensure that only candidates of merit will be considered. Merit systems are used in 16 states.

One of the oldest merit plans is the Missouri Plan.[21] As used in most states, the **Missouri Plan** provides that when a judicial vacancy occurs, a special *nominating commission* (usually composed of three lawyers elected by the bar, three citizens appointed by the governor, and the chief justice) nominates three candidates.[22] The governor selects one, who then serves as a judge for at least a year. At the next general election, the voters are asked if the appointee should be retained in office. If a majority of the voters agree, the judge serves a new full term (typically 6 to 12 years); if not, another person is selected by the same procedure. At the end of his or her term, an elected judge may ask to have his or her name placed on the ballot, and the voters are again asked whether they want to retain that judge in office.[23] These uncontested elections, in which judges run against their own record, are called **retention elections,** and some require a supermajority vote.

Until recently, retention elections generated little interest and low voter turnout.[24] In the 6,306 judicial retention elections held between 1964 and 2006, fewer than 60 judges were removed by voters, although a few decided not to run when they realized they might fail to be retained.[25] Recently, some state supreme court justices have been vigorously challenged in retention elections, especially when their decisions differed appreciably from the mainstream of public opinion and aroused the hostility of significant special interests. Frequently, the charge was that the judge was "soft on crime." Interest groups have learned that it is relatively easy to target incumbents, and because of constraints on the way judicial candidates are expected to campaign, it is "difficult for targeted judges to defend themselves."[26] One Pennsylvania Supreme Court justice lost a retention race in 2005, and another nearly lost, after a huge voter backlash to a pay raise adopted by the state legislature that increased the salaries of state officials, including judges.

Most voters know little about judges, and what information they have comes from interested parties and persons, especially those who dislike what the judges have done.

Missouri Plan

A system for selecting judges that combines features of the appointive and elective methods. The governor selects judges from lists presented by panels of lawyers and laypersons, and at the end of their term, the judges may run against their own record in retention elections.

retention elections

Elections where judges run uncontested for reelection and voters simply vote for or against keeping them in office.

145

To provide a more balanced picture, a few states—Alaska, Utah, Colorado, Arizona, and Tennessee—have tried to supply more neutral information about judicial performance. In Colorado, an *evaluation committee* in each judicial district—jointly appointed by the chief justice, governor, president of the senate, and speaker of the house—disseminates information through newspaper supplements, including a final recommendation of "retain" or "do not retain."[27] In Alaska, a judicial council composed of three lawyers, three nonlawyers, and the chief justice provides evaluations that are widely publicized.[28] In Utah, the Judicial Council—consisting of the chief justice, another justice, an appellate court judge, five district court judges, two juvenile court judges, three other lower court judges, a state bar representative, and the state court administrator—certifies incumbents, and this certification, or lack of it, is indicated on the ballot.

Even though contested retention elections are the exception, sitting judges are aware that if they make decisions that offend organized interest groups, they may face opposition the next time their names are placed on the ballot. Whether these pressures threaten the independence of the courts, or are necessary to ensure judicial accountability within our political system in which judges play such an important role, remains a matter of political debate.[29]

Judicial Conduct

Although federal judges hold office during "good behavior"—essentially for life—only Rhode Island's judges have life appointments. In Massachusetts and New Hampshire, judges serve to age 70. In all the other states, they serve for fixed terms ranging from 3 to 15 years.[30] Thirty-seven states and the District of Columbia mandate the retirement of judges at a certain age, usually 70.[31]

The states, rather than the national government, have taken the lead in establishing procedures to judge judges. Each of the 50 states has a board, commission, or court to handle allegations of judicial misconduct. Despite the objections of many judges, these commissions are most often composed of both nonlawyers and lawyers. They investigate complaints and hold hearings for judges who have been charged with improper performance of their duties or unethical or unfair conduct. Establishment of these commis-sions appears to have helped restore public confidence in the state judicial systems.[32] In addition, nonpartisan groups such as the Constitution Project and the Brennan Center for Justice act as watchdog groups because they monitor the operation of and advocate for judicial independence.

The Criminal Justice System

LEARNING **OBJECTIVE**

7.3 Describe the roles of the participants in the criminal justice system.

Justice is handled in the United States by a series of institutions only loosely connected to each other. In addition to judges, there are juries, prosecutors, defense counsels, public defenders, victims, prison officials, and defendants.

The Jury

Although most of us will never be judges or serve as professionals in the administration of justice, all adult citizens have an opportunity—even an obligation—to be jurors. Trial by jury in civil disputes is used less often these days; people make settlements before a trial, elect to have their cases decided by a judge alone, or refer their cases to a mediator or arbitrator. Furthermore, only a small fraction of criminal cases are actually disposed of by a trial before a jury. Still, jury trials, or their possibility, remain a key feature of our justice system.

We have moved from a system in which jury service was restricted to white male property owners to one in which it is the responsibility of *all* adult citizens. But because jury service may be time-consuming and burdensome, many busy people do their best to avoid serving, and today, more time and energy are spent trying to persuade (or coerce) people to serve than in excluding them.

In the past, judges were often willing to excuse doctors, nurses, teachers, executives, and other highly skilled people who pleaded that their services were essential outside the jury room. As a result, juries were often selected from panels consisting in large part of

DECIDE Should State Judges Be Selected Through Appointment or Popular Election?

After a campaign dubbed eerily similar to one in John Grisham's novel *The Appeal,* sitting Judge Louis Butler lost his bid for a ten-year term to the Wisconsin Supreme Court on April 1, 2008. The state's first and only African American supreme court justice and a former public defender, Butler was appointed to the state's highest court by Governor Doyle in 2004. He was defeated in a close race by Michael Gableman, a circuit county court judge and former prosecutor. Court watchers believe that the election of Gableman will shift the balance of the court from a 4-to-3 court that leaned liberal to a 4-to-3 court leaning conservative. Turnout for the election was approximately 20 percent.

The campaign dismayed nearly everyone in the state. For the second year in a row, third-party groups dominated the race. Although the race was technically nonpartisan, conservative groups, including the state's largest business lobby, an antitax group, and a group advocating traditional families, lined up behind Gableman. The state's largest teachers' union and other liberal organizations backed Butler.

Television ads by these third-party groups were roundly criticized as misleading and undermining the reputation of the court. A controversial ad by Gableman implied that as a public defender, Butler had relied on a technicality to release from prison a convicted child molester who then assaulted another child. Like Butler, the man was black, and the ad ended with a picture of the convicted rapist alongside Butler. In fact, the man was released from prison because he had completed his sentence, not because of Butler's work as a public defender. A watchdog group for judicial elections, the Wisconsin Judicial Campaign Integrity Committee, called the ad "a disgraceful attack" that was "highly offensive and deliberately misleading." Gableman's campaign defended the ad, claiming it was a comparison ad highlighting his career as a prosecutor and Butler's as a public defender.*

What do you think? Should state judges be selected through election? What are the arguments for or against it?

THINKING IT THROUGH

Advocates of an appointive system point to Wisconsin's recent campaign as emblematic of the problems with judicial elections. Contested elections too often generate biased advertisements with incomplete and inaccurate information. Interest groups jump into the fray, hoping to influence the outcome, and their voices drown out those of the candidates. On the bench, judges are supposed to be dispassionate and impartial, making a decision based on the evidence presented. But in a contested campaign, they are pulled into an ideological fray that threatens the independence of the judiciary.

The many uncontested elections are not much better. They are sleepy affairs offering the public no real choice, and incumbent judges are routinely returned to office. In either case, advocates of the appointive method contend that voters are generally uninformed about candidates and not competent to assess legal learning and judicial abilities.

Those who favor judicial elections counter that judges should be directly accountable to the people. When appointed, they may lose touch with the general currents of opinion of the electorate. Moreover, the appointive process gives governors too much power over judges, and merit systems such as the Missouri Plan give too much influence to the bar association, a group with its own interests to protect. Even if judicial elections do not result in the defeat of many sitting judges, elections foster accountability because judges do not want to be defeated and will try to maintain popular support.

Critical Thinking Questions

1. Is judicial accountability an important goal? Or should we put more emphasis on judicial independence? Defend your answer.

2. Which method of selecting judges, appointments or elections, better meets the goals of both accountability and independence? Why?

State of Wisconsin CASE # 1984CF000250

A third party ad falsely linking Judge Butler with a convicted rapist, both of whom are African American, was widely criticized.

*Scott Bauer, "Monitoring Group Slams Gableman Ad Featuring Convicted Rapist," *Associated Press,* March 17, 2008.

older people, those who were unemployed or employed in relatively low-paying jobs, single people, and others who were unable to be excused. Most states have reacted to these problems by making it more difficult to be excused. In addition, many states have adopted a "one-day, one-trial" policy, which makes jury service less frequent and less onerous. Because jury trials take more time than bench trials (trials before judges) and cost more, some states use juries of fewer than the standard 12 people for some criminal trials. A few states also permit verdicts by less than a unanimous vote. The U.S. Supreme Court has approved these practices, provided the juries consist of at least six people.[33] However, when deliberating whether to impose the death penalty, a jury must make a unanimous decision.

The Prosecutor

The prosecutor is largely a U.S. invention, one of the few government positions we did not inherit from England. The 2,344 chief prosecutors in the United States (often called *county attorneys* or *district attorneys*) are usually county officials; most are locally elected and subject to little supervision by state authorities. However, in Connecticut, they are appointed by judges, and in New Jersey, by the governor with the consent of the state senate. There are also about 24,000 assistant prosecutors.[34] A prosecutor has "more control over life, liberty, and reputation than any other person in America."[35]

When presented with a case by the police, the prosecutor must decide first whether to file formal charges. He or she may (1) divert the matter out of the criminal justice system and turn it over to a social welfare agency; (2) dismiss the charges; (3) take the matter before a grand jury, which almost always follows the prosecutor's recommendation; or (4) in most jurisdictions, file an **information affidavit,** which serves the same function as a grand jury **indictment.**

A prosecutor who decides not to charge a person accused of some notorious crime is often subject to political pressure and public criticism. But for routine crimes, the prosecutor is politically in a better position to dismiss a charge than the police are. Police are supposed to enforce every law all the time. Of course, it is impossible for them to do so, and they must exercise discretion.[36] But officers who fail to arrest a person alleged to have committed a crime could well be charged with failing in their duty. The prosecutor, however, has more leeway. In fact, the prosecutor is less likely to be criticized for dropping a case because of insufficient evidence than for filing a charge and failing to get a conviction.

information affidavit
Certification by a public prosecutor that there is evidence to justify bringing named individuals to trial.

indictment
A formal written statement from a grand jury charging an individual with an offense; also called a *true bill.*

All citizens have an obligation to serve on juries, and lawyers develop skills in selecting people they think may be sympathetic to their clients. ■ *How does this jury compare to the population at large in terms of race, age, and gender?*

Defense Counsel, Public Defenders, and Others

Many defendants cannot afford the legal counsel to which they are constitutionally entitled. The **assigned counsel system** is the oldest system to provide such defendants with an attorney, and it continues to be used, especially in rural areas. Judges appoint attorneys to represent defendants who cannot afford them. Most such attorneys are paid by the court that appoints them, but sometimes they are expected to do the work **pro bono**—for the public good. Seldom are they given funds to do any investigatory work on behalf of their clients. Some less scrupulous lawyers make their living as assigned counsel; because it is often to their financial advantage to do so, they are quick to plead their clients guilty. They are known contemptuously as members of the "cop-out bar."[37]

Dissatisfaction with the assigned counsel system led to the creation of the **public defender system,** first started in Los Angeles in 1914 and now used in most big cities. Under this system, the government provides a staff of lawyers whose full-time job is to defend individuals who cannot pay. This system provides experienced counsel and relieves the bar of an onerous duty. Critics—including some defendants—protest that because public defenders are paid employees of the state, they are not likely to work as diligently on behalf of their clients as if they were specifically assigned to those clients. But most observers consider the public defender system superior to the assigned counsel system. Steps are being taken to increase the pay of public defenders, protect their independence, and see that they win the confidence of the defendants they represent.

Victims and Defendants

When we talk about our criminal justice system, we sometimes forget the two most important parties in any criminal case—the victim of the crime and the person accused of it.

The rights of victims or potential victims are not of the same order as the rights of the accused; the rights of the accused are constitutional rights spelled out in amendments, but nowhere in the Constitution is there any mention of the rights of victims or the public. The framers of the Constitution apparently were much more worried about protecting citizens against the government than about protecting citizens from each other.[38]

In general terms, defendants are likely to be "younger, predominantly male, disproportionately black, less educated, seldom fully employed, and typically unmarried. By the time the sorting process has ended, those sent to prison will consist of an even higher proportion of young, illiterate, black males."[39] Victims, too, tend to be young, black or another minority, and uneducated. A substantial number never report crimes to police and prosecutors—either because of lack of knowledge of what to do or fear of doing it, or, as in the case of rape victims, because they believe they have little chance of proving their attackers guilty. Our system puts the responsibility for prosecuting criminals on the government. In most instances, victims have no role other than as witnesses.

As a result, in recent decades, a victims' rights movement has emerged. The movement originated with liberals (chiefly feminists concerned about the difficulty of winning prosecutions for rape and about the harsh treatment of female witnesses), but it has gained the support of conservatives who consider the judicial system unfair to victims. In the 1984 Victims of Crime Act, Congress authorized federal funds, distributed by the Office of Crime Victims in the Department of Justice, to support state programs compensating victims and providing funds to some victims of federal crimes as well.

Thirty-five states have amended their constitutions to provide for a "victims' bill of rights,"[40] which makes it easier for victims to recover stolen property held in police custody, among other things. Many states also give victims a chance to be heard when prosecutors file formal charges, when judges set bail and impose sentences, and when parole boards consider releasing prisoners. These victims' bills of rights are not without constitutional problems. The introduction of *victim impact statements* by prosecutors seeking the death penalty has been controversial, for instance. The U.S. Supreme Court, after first holding to the contrary, has upheld the right of prosecutors to make victim impact statements to a jury in murder trials citing the personal qualities of the victim and has allowed the jury to consider evidence relating to the murder victim's personal characteristics and the emotional impact of the crime on the victim's family.[41]

A disproportionate number of prisoners tend to be young, poorly educated black males.
■ *What are some of the factors that cause this pattern? How do you think states should respond?*

assigned counsel system
An arrangement whereby attorneys are provided for people accused of crimes who are unable to hire their own attorneys. The judge assigns a member of the bar to provide counsel to a particular defendant.

pro bono
To serve the public good; a term used to describe work that lawyers (or other professionals) do for which they receive no fees.

public defender system
An arrangement whereby public officials are hired to provide legal assistance to people accused of crimes who are unable to hire their own attorneys.

Plea Bargaining

Only a handful of those accused of committing a crime actually stand trial, and only 5 to 10 percent of those convicted are declared guilty as the result of a formal trial before either a judge or a jury. Most people who go to prison, or who have to pay a criminal fine, do so because they plead guilty.[42] In a common practice called a *plea bargain*, the prosecution offers to reduce the seriousness of the charge and sentence if the defendant will enter a plea of guilty to a lesser crime.

Critics say plea bargaining forces defendants to give up their rights; moreover, they often do not get off much more leniently by pleading guilty to lesser offenses than if they had stood trial on the original charge.[43] Defenders of plea bargaining contend that it works, producing "a result approximating closely, but informally and more swiftly, the results which ought to ensue from a trial, while avoiding most of the undesirable aspects of that ordeal."[44] Many experts and investigators who have looked into the matter have endorsed plea bargaining.

Plea bargaining offers something to all involved. Prosecutors are able to dispose of cases quickly, avoid long and drawn-out trials, eliminate the risk of losing, and build up better conviction records. The accused avoid the danger of being sentenced for more serious charges. Defense attorneys avoid "the dilemma of either incurring the expense of going to trial with a losing case or appearing to provide no service whatsoever to their clients."[45] By being able to handle more clients, they can also make more money. Judges are able to dispose of cases on their dockets more rapidly. In fact, if every case were tried, it would overwhelm the judicial system.

Once the bargain between the prosecutor and the defendant's attorney has been accepted, the matter is taken before a judge, who questions the defendant: "Are you pleading guilty because you are guilty? Are you aware of the maximum sentence for the crime to which you are entering a guilty plea? Were you coerced into pleading guilty or offered anything in return for it? Are you satisfied with the representation afforded by your attorney?" Following appropriate responses, the plea is accepted.[46] As long as defendants know what they are doing and enter into the bargain intelligently, they waive their constitutional rights to trial by pleading guilty and may not back out of the arrangement. Prosecutors must also live up to their side of the bargain.[47]

Sentencing

Due process—the principle of upholding the rights of all those involved, including the prisoner—must be observed in sentencing, which takes place in open court. The prisoner must be present and represented by counsel. In many places, social workers are assigned to help the judge determine the proper sentence. The judge also receives recommendations from the prosecution (and in some jurisdictions from the victim as well), hears the arguments of the defense, and then sets the sentence within the limits prescribed by the state.

The judge sets the sentence, but concerns about sentencing permeate the judicial system. Early in our national history, retribution, deterrence, and protection of society were the primary purposes of sentencing. Then rehabilitation became the major goal, and many people thought it was a more humane approach. The indefinite sentence became popular, motivated by the idea that each prisoner should be considered an individual suffering from an "illness." Each should be diagnosed, a course of treatment should be prescribed, and if and when such experts as psychologists and social workers could certify a "cure," the prisoner should be released.

Most political leaders and many scholars have become disillusioned about our ability to bring about "cures."[48] Others are disillusioned about the deterrent effect of imprisonment. A comprehensive study of rehabilitative efforts inside prisons, although rejecting the conclusion that "nothing works," nonetheless stated, "We do not know of any program or method of rehabilitation that could be guaranteed to reduce the criminal activity of released offenders."[49]

due process

The principle of upholding the rights of all those involved when making a judgment or ruling, including those of the accused or convicted.

By the People

Family Court Watch

As more and more of the country's pressing public issues are dealt with through the court system, there is increasing attention on monitoring court behavior by "court watch" groups. One such group is the National Family Court Watch Project. This group monitors family courts across the country, focusing particular attention on how women's rights and conditions are affected by these courts. They seek to ensure that women receive fair treatment on child custody, property, visitation, and child support disputes. The group was founded by a mother in Michigan in 2004, and it recruits volunteers to observe family court proceedings and record how women are affected.

Court proceedings are public events. Yet most citizens remain ignorant of how the courts conduct their business. You can get involved. Find the time and place your local courts meet to conduct their business. You could join the efforts of a group like the Family Court Watch Project, or you could observe traffic courts or general criminal courts. Spend a few hours attending a court hearing. Observe how the judge, the lawyers, and the various other people involved in the cases behave. Go online and see if you can find any court watch groups in your area. Research their goals and consider joining one.

CRITICAL THINKING QUESTIONS

1. Courts face the competing pressures of providing for justice for each case yet also processing many cases as quickly as possible. Which groups seem most at risk from a system that must process so many cases? What alternatives to the current system might states consider?

2. How important is it that citizen groups observe the proceedings of state and local courts? How should we balance the need for court proceedings to be public with the need for individuals involved in such cases to have their privacy protected?

Moreover, judges may enjoy considerable discretion in sentencing, and they frequently give different sentences to defendants convicted of the same crime.[50] To reduce such disparities in sentencing, several reforms have been suggested, including establishing more precise legislative standards, creating advisory sentencing councils, and adopting the British practice of allowing appellate courts to modify sentences.

Disillusionment with rehabilitation and disparate sentencing by judges, combined with growing concerns about crime and mounting criticism about alleged judicial leniency, have fueled legislative action for mandatory minimum sentencing requirements and for narrowing judicial discretion.[51] State after state has adopted mandatory prison terms—also known as *determinate sentencing*—for more and more crimes. About half the states have passed so-called three-strikes-and-you're-out laws, which prescribe a mandatory life sentence after three felony convictions.[52]

The Death Penalty

Four years after ruling that death penalty statutes in most states violated the U.S. Constitution, the U.S. Supreme Court in 1976 upheld death penalty statutes in Georgia, Texas, and Florida, holding that the states' revised laws met standards of due process. Today, 35 states allow capital punishment; in the other 15 states, the most severe punishment is a life sentence with no possibility of parole.

Even though most states allow capital punishment, its use varies widely. Since 1976, for example, Texas has executed 457 individuals, and 341 are currently on death row.[53] New Hampshire and Kansas, however, have executed none and have a combined total of 11 inmates currently on death row. Although Illinois still has a statute allowing capital punishment, it has had no executions since 2000, when then-governor Ryan imposed a moratorium on executions (see Chapter 6 opener). The peak in the number of annual executions occurred in 1998, when a total of 98 individuals were executed. Since then, there was a steady decline down to 37 executions in 2008, but it rose again to 52 in 2009.

In December 2007, New Jersey became the first state since 1976 to eliminate the death penalty through an act of the legislature. At the time, there were eight people on death row, but the state had not executed anyone since 1963. In 2008, legislation to abolish the death penalty was introduced in Maryland, Connecticut, Nebraska, Virginia, and Alabama, but it did not pass in any of those states.

LEARNING **OBJECTIVE**

7.4 Assess the controversy over the increased use of imprisonment.

Prisons

More people are imprisoned in the United States than in any other country. As of 2008, including juvenile facilities, the United States has more than 2.4 million people behind bars, more than 1.5 million in state and federal prisons, 785,556 in local jails, and nearly 100,000 in juvenile facilities[54] (see Figure 7–3). *Prisons* are for committed criminals serving long sentences. *Jails* are for short-term stays for people awaiting trial and those with sentences of a year or less. "The American inmate population has grown so large that it is difficult to fathom: imagine the combined population of Atlanta, St. Louis, Pittsburgh, Des Moines, and Miami behind bars."[55]

In addition to those in prison or jails, in 2008, more than 5 million adult men and women are on probation or parole. *Probationers* are offenders the courts have placed in community supervision rather than in prison; more than 4.2 million adults were serving probation. *Parolees* are people released after serving a prison term who are under supervision and subject to being returned to prison for rule violations or other offenses; more than 825,000 adults were parolees.[56]

The prison population in the United States has skyrocketed since the 1970s. State and federal prison populations actually declined during the 1960s, but public demands for tougher sentences caused them to climb after 1969. Since 1980, the number of people in prison has more than tripled (see Figure 7–4), although the rate of increase slowed considerably after 1999.

The increase in the prison population has resulted in serious overcrowding. In some states, conditions were so bad that in the 1990s federal judges issued orders calling for either immediate improvement or the release of people being held in conditions that violate the Eighth Amendment prohibition against cruel and unusual punishment. Most states responded to judicial intervention by spending millions to build new prisons and renovate old ones. It costs more than $60,000 to build each cell, and an average of more than $23,000 a year must be spent for each prisoner.[57]

privatization

Contracting public services to private organizations.

recidivist

A repeat offender.

Some cities and counties have even resorted to **privatization,** turning over the responsibility for operating jails to private firms on a contractual basis. Texas has the largest number of inmates in private facilities, and New Mexico has the largest proportion of its inmate population in private prisons (44 percent).[58] Correctional officers strongly oppose privatization and have become a powerful interest group making major contributions to gubernatorial elections.

The high cost of corrections is leading some states to rethink the wisdom of mandatory sentencing. Because half the people in prison and half the trials held are about victimless crimes such as using marijuana, *decriminalization* could substantially reduce the load on the courts and rates of incarceration. Six states, for example, have already repealed statutes on public drunkenness and now consider alcoholism a disease rather than a crime.

States are also considering alternatives for nonviolent offenders such as halfway houses, mental health and drug treatment centers, intensive probation, work release programs, and other community corrections facilities. In 2007, at least six states passed laws designed to shift many more offenders into community-based supervision programs and away from prisons.[59] For example, Nevada expanded eligibility for home confinement, first pioneered in New Mexico in 1983, whereby prisoners serve their time at home while being observed by a variety of monitoring devices.[60] The problem is that these alternative solutions are subject to political attack as being "soft on criminals." Even so, the cost of continued imprisonment is so great that it is prompting state legislatures to convene task forces and to charge corrections departments with researching innovative sentencing options.

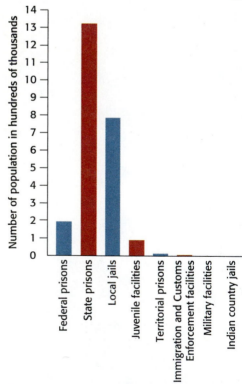

FIGURE 7–3 **Total Incarcerated Population at Year-end 2008.**

■ *Does the total number of prisoners or their distribution among facilities surprise you?*

SOURCE: U.S. Department of Justice, Bureau of Justice Statistics, "Prisoners in 2008," December 2009.

Finally, states are exploring ways to reduce **recidivism.** Research suggests that "50 percent of offenders will return to prison within three years of release."[61] Reentry programs offer offenders services, such as employment and training programs and substance abuse and mental health treatment, to better prepare them for life outside prison. States have begun to realize that prison growth is not simply a consequence of the crime rate or the state's population. Rather, it is related to state policies regarding criminal justice, including sentencing, the use of community supervision for nonviolent offenders, and failure to reduce parole violations and recidivism.

Judicial Reform

Crime is a national issue, confronting everyone. The public's attention has been focused on terrorist attacks, drive-by shootings, random killings—especially in schools—and other forms of violence. Yet courts are already overwhelmed by a huge volume of cases. As the American Bar Association observed, "Justice in the United States takes too long, costs too much, and is virtually inaccessible and unaffordable for too many Americans....Our courts are grossly overburdened...and woefully underfunded....The justice system is no longer a 'court of last resort'...but is becoming an emergency room for every social trauma."[62]

We are, many charge, a "litigious society." Dockets are crowded, relief is costly, and delays are common.[63] These problems have led to numerous efforts to improve the administration of justice, in areas including the ways in which judges are selected, the quality of the judicial pool, the way courts operate, and alternative means of dispute resolution and criminal sentencing.

Some reform efforts centered on trying to increase the quality of judges propose increasing their salaries. In most states, judges earn considerably less than most practicing attorneys of the same age and experience. They are unable to earn anything beyond their salaries, and they must be cautious about investments in order to avoid conflicts of interest. Reformers argue that judges should be paid adequately so that they have the financial independence to concentrate on their work and so that successful lawyers will be willing to serve on the bench.

Effective courts also require professional administration. A court can be very large; for example, the court in Hennepin County, Minnesota, has more than 500 employees and 78 judicial officers. Presiding judges are not always given the time or training they need to administer such a system. Training these head judges, reducing their caseloads, and providing additional compensation are some of the recent changes adopted by some states.[64] Advocates of judicial reform also argue that rule-making powers should be given to the state supreme court or its chief justice.

Another way to improve the operation of the courts is to develop alternative methods of resolving disputes. *Alternative dispute resolution* (ADR) procedures serve as alternatives to formal trials. They include mediation, arbitration, conciliation, private judging, and advisory settlement conferences. From time to time, Congress has made grants to encourage states and localities to develop alternative dispute resolution mechanisms, especially for domestic relations issues. ADRs can be part of the established court system or separate from it in neighborhood justice centers or arbitration and mediation forums. Half the states operate arbitration programs as part of their court system.

Despite the disparaging nickname "rent-a-judge," an old practice of hiring private decision makers has been revived. Retired judges and lawyers are paid by the parties involved in the dispute, who agree in advance to abide by the outcome. In some states, appeals courts can review these decisions. Some worry that these alternative practices are drawing the best lawyers into the private system, perhaps resulting in a private system for the rich and a public one for the poor.

Some people have proposed that traffic violations, automobile injury cases, and so-called victimless crimes be handled by some procedure other than a court trial. New York has led the way in removing from the courts minor traffic offenses that do not include serious moving violations; other states are following its lead. Adopting no-fault insurance programs could reduce the large number of cases stemming from automobile accidents.

There is widespread agreement that our justice system, on both the civil and the criminal side, is in recurring crisis. There is less agreement on what to do about it. The problems are complex, the issues are enmeshed in partisan, ideological, and issue politics, and each suggested reform has costs and benefits. Change and reform are likely to come slowly, and perhaps this is as it should be, for our justice system has been created throughout the centuries, built on the accumulated wisdom of the past. How best to administer justice is a question likely to remain on our political agenda.

LEARNING **OBJECTIVE**

7.5 Evaluate the proposals and goals of the judicial reform movement.

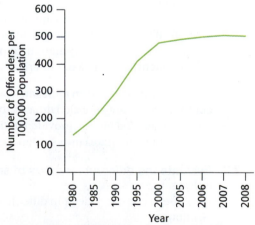

FIGURE 7–4 Incarceration Rates in Federal and State Jurisdictions.

■ *What are some of the impacts, on both the prison system and society, of having a high rate of incarceration?*

SOURCE: U.S. Department of Justice, Bureau of Justice Statistics, http://bjs.ojp.usdoj.gov/content/glance/tables/incrttab.cfm.

CHAPTER **SUMMARY**

7.1 Outline the structure of a state court system.

Each state has its own court system. Although the systems vary, they generally include minor courts of limited jurisdiction, trial courts of general jurisdiction, and appellate courts. Each state has a court of last resort, usually called the supreme court. Unless a federal question is involved, state supreme courts are the highest tribunal to which a case may be appealed.

7.2 Evaluate the different methods of selecting judges.

In six states, judges are appointed by the governor and confirmed by the state senate. In a few states, judges are elected by the state legislature. In about half of the states, judges are chosen through a popular election. In the remaining states, judges are chosen through a merit system modeled along the lines of the modified appointment plan known as the Missouri Plan. Most legal reformers and political scientists favor a merit selection system, such as the Missouri Plan, over judicial elections.

7.3 Describe the roles of the participants in the criminal justice system.

Judges, together with jurors, prosecutors, defense counsel, public defenders, and corrections officials, make up a loosely interrelated justice system. Many observers believe that this system is not properly dispensing justice to individual defendants or protecting the public from career criminals. In recent years, more attention has been paid to the rights of victims at both the national and state levels, including amendments to state constitutions giving victims and their families the right to participate in the trial and providing for compensation to victims and their families.

7.4 Assess the controversy over the increased use of imprisonment.

With more than 2 million people in our prisons, the United States has more prisoners than any other country. Imprisonment has been justified as retribution, deterrence, protection of society, and rehabilitation. Disillusionment with rehabilitation and the disparate sentencing by judges has led to the enactment of mandatory minimum sentencing requirements, including three-strikes-and-you're-out legislation. Because of the high cost of imprisonment, states are now considering alternative approaches, including decriminalization, community corrections facilities, and reentry programs.

7.5 Evaluate the proposals and goals of the judicial reform movement.

Judicial reforms are aimed at reducing the crowded dockets and delay that plague courts. Reforms focus on increasing the quality of judges through measures such as higher salaries. Reforms also include improvements in the administration of the court as well as developing alternative methods of resolving disputes.

CHAPTER **SELF-TEST**

7.1 Outline the structure of a state court system.
1. Matching the following terms and definitions.

a. tort law	i. statement charging an individual with an offense
b. misdemeanor	ii. provides attorneys for those who cannot afford their own
c. public defender system	iii. relating to injuries to person, reputation, or property
d. indictment	iv. a minor crime

2. If a state does not have an appellate court system, trial court decisions are appealed directly to _____.
3. Using the general outline provided in this chapter, describe how the state court system works.

7.2 Evaluate the different methods of selecting judges.
4. How does a retention election differ from a normal election?
5. Describe which selection method for state judges comes closest to the way U.S. Supreme Court justices are selected.
6. Most state and local judges are elected in some manner. List and explain three benefits and three potential drawbacks of this method of selection.

7.3 Describe the roles of the participants in the criminal justice system.
7. Draw a diagram relating the jury, prosecutor, defense counsel, victim, defendant, and judge to the U.S. justice system. Show how the system works, and detail the specific roles of each actor in the process.
8. Explain how a plea bargain works.
9. Describe both sides of the controversy surrounding mandatory minimum sentencing.

7.4 Assess the controversy over the increased use of imprisonment.
10. Define recidivism. Explain how it relates to the high rates of incarceration in the United States.
11. Write a brief essay exploring some of the possible causes of the high U.S. incarceration rates. What does it say about U.S. society that so many of its citizens are in jail?

7.5 Evaluate the proposals and goals of the judicial reform movement.
12. Write a brief persuasive essay for *one* of the reforms listed in the chapter, detailing and addressing the arguments that could be raised against it.
13. Explain why most judges are unable to earn anything beyond their salaries and must be cautious about investments they make. To help your explanation, use examples (either real or fictitious).

Answers to selected questions: 1. a. iii; b. iv; c. ii; d. i

mypoliscilab EXERCISES

Apply what you learned in this chapter on MyPoliSciLab.

Read on **mypoliscilab.com**

    eText: Chapter 7

✓ **Study** and **Review** on **mypoliscilab.com**

    Pre-Test
    Post-Test
    Chapter Exam
    Flashcards

Watch on **mypoliscilab.com**

    Video: Abuse at Facility for the Mentally Disabled
    Video: Pot Possession Now Like Speeding Ticket

Explore on **mypoliscilab.com**

    Comparative: Comparing Judicial Systems

KEY TERMS

recuse, p. 139
new judicial federalism, p. 139
misdemeanor, p. 140
original jurisdiction, p. 140
felony, p. 140
judicial review, p. 141

advisory opinion, p. 141
Missouri Plan, p. 145
retention elections, p. 145
information affidavit, p. 148
indictment, p. 148
assigned counsel system, p. 149

pro bono, p. 149
public defender system, p. 149
due process, p. 150
privatization, p. 152
recidivist, p. 152

ADDITIONAL RESOURCES

FURTHER READING

STEPHEN J. ADLER, *The Jury: Trial and Error in the American Courtroom* (Times Books, 1994).

LAURENCE BAUM, *American Courts: Process and Policy,* 6th ed. (Houghton Mifflin, 2008).

GREG BERMAN AND **JOHN FEINBLATT,** *Good Courts: The Case for Problem-Solving Justice* (New Press, 2005).

MATTHEW BOSWORTH, *Courts as Catalysts: State Supreme Courts and Public School Finance Equity* (State University of New York Press, 2001).

DAVID COLE, *No Equal Justice: Race and Class in the American Criminal Justice System* (New Press, 1999).

SUSAN P. FINO, *The Role of State Supreme Courts in the New Judicial Federalism* (Greenwood Press, 1987).

JULIA FIONDA, *Public Prosecutors and Discretion* (Oxford University Press, 1995).

JOHN B. GATES AND **CHARLES A. JOHNSON,** *The American Courts: A Critical Assessment* (CQ Press, 1991).

MARIE GOTTSCHALK, *The Prison and the Gallows: The Politics of Mass Incarceration in America* (Cambridge University Press, 2006).

JOSEPH R. GRODIN, *In Pursuit of Justice: Reflections of a State Supreme Court Justice* (University of California Press, 1989).

RANDOLPH JONAKAIT, *The American Jury System* (Yale University Press, 2003).

LAURA LANGER, *Judicial Review in State Supreme Courts: A Comparative Study* (State University of New York Press, 2002).

ANN CHIH LIN, *Reform in the Making: The Implementation of Social Policy in Prison* (Princeton University Press, 2000).

CHARLES LOPEMAN, *The Activist Advocate: Policy Making in State Supreme Courts* (Praeger, 1999).

DAVID W. NEUBAUER, *America's Courts and Criminal Justice System,* 8th ed. (Wadsworth, 2004).

DAVID M. O'BRIEN, ED., *Judges on Judging: Views from the Bench* (CQ Press, 2004).

MICHAEL SOLIMINE AND **JAMES WALKER,** *Respecting State Courts: The Inevitability of Judicial Federalism* (Greenwood Press, 2000).

MATTHEW J. STREB, ED., *Running for Judge: The Rising Political, Financial, and Legal Stakes of Judicial Elections* (New York University Press, 2007).

G. ALAN TARR AND **MARY CORNELIA ALDIS PORTER,** *State Supreme Courts in State and Nation* (Yale University Press, 1988).

PAUL B. WICE, *Court Reform and Judicial Leadership* (Praeger, 1995). See also *Judicature: The Journal of the American Judicature Society,* published bimonthly, and its Web site at www.ajs.org.

WEB SITES

www.ncsc.org The National Center for State Courts provides research information and comparative data to support improvement in judicial administration in state courts.

www.nawj.org The National Association of Women Judges advocates for equal justice and access to the courts for women and minorities.

www.brennancenter.org/ The Brennan Center for Justice, a public policy and law institute, is a source for judicial scholarship and advocacy.

Local Governments and Metropolitics

Local governments provide most of the public services ordinary citizens consume on a daily basis. From elementary and secondary schools to traffic lights to electricity and water, we rely on local governments to help us meet our daily needs. One of the major functions provided by local governments are city and county jails. In 2010, National Public Radio (NPR) ran a three-part series on local jails, the system of providing bail for petty offenses, and the powerful bail bondsman lobby that has emerged in recent years.[1]

The NPR story reports that 20 years ago, most defendants accused of petty crimes were released on their own recognizance—meaning they were simply trusted to come to court when required. Today, most defendants are required to post bail or be held in county jails until they can post bail or until their case is resolved. Posting bail requires either making a full cash deposit with the court that is returned to the defendant if they come to court as required, or by paying a bail bondsman a fee—typically 10 percent of the bail level—to post the funds. So, a person arrested and given a bail of $1,000 can either provide the entire amount to the court as a security deposit, which he will get back if he comes to court as required, or he can pay a bondsman $100 (or sometimes more) in a nonrefundable fee and then the bondsman posts the $1,000 deposit. In theory, the bondsman now has the incentive to make sure the defendant comes to court so as not to lose the $1,000 deposit.

In practice, it often does not work that way. NPR found that in Lubbock, Texas, for example, the court routinely only requires a bondsman to pay 5 percent of the total bail amount as a penalty if the defendant does not appear in court. So if the bondsman charges a fee of 10 percent or more, the bondsman makes a profit whether the defendant shows up or not. It turns out that this situation is quite common across the country.

Another consequence of the increasing reliance on bail is a dramatic increase in the number of people housed in city and county jails for extended periods as they await trial because they cannot afford the bail or even the bondsman's 10 percent fee. NPR documented cases that cost county taxpayers thousands of dollars to house defendants accused of stealing a handful of blankets or a single television.

A number of counties have explored alternatives generally called pretrial release programs. Such programs release defendants rather than jail them but provide some sort of monitoring (often including GPS-enabled ankle bracelets) instead of releasing folks on their own recognizance. Broward County, Florida, had a very successful program up and running that cost approximately $7 per day to monitor a defendant, compared with the $116 per day it cost to house them in jail. The program allowed the county to avoid building a new jail at a cost of approximately $20 million as well. However, NPR reports that the same county commissioners that created the program voted two years later to dramatically cut its operations after a local bondsman hired a lobbyist and began making substantial campaign contributions. Pretrial release programs are very unpopular with bondsmen because it substantially reduces their customer base.

This example illustrates two important features to consider when studying local governments. First, local governments make very important decisions that affect citizens in their communities to a great degree. Second, concentrated interests in local communities can have a tremendous impact on local policy making. In the coming pages, we will examine the politics of state and local government and the ways in which these decisions are made.

The Nature of State and Local Relations

LEARNING **OBJECTIVE**

8.1 Characterize local government in the United States and the basic relationship between state and local governments.

Local governments vary in structure, size, power, and relationship to one another. Local governments in the United States employ approximately 11.9 million people in more than 89,000 different jurisdictions (see Table 8–1).[2] They are not mentioned in the U.S. Constitution, but in a *constitutional* sense, they all rely on power given to them by the state. That is, most state constitutions create a **unitary system** in which power is vested in the state government, and local units exist only as agents of the state and exercise only those powers expressly given to them by their respective state governments.[3]

Because local governments are typically created by the state and usually have no constitutional authority in their own right, there are fewer obstacles to state interference in local matters than there are to national interference in state matters. State officers participate in local government to a much greater extent than federal officers do in state politics. When doubts arise about the authority of local governments, courts generally decide against them.

Initially, state legislatures had almost unlimited authority over their local governments and ran them pretty much at will. They granted, amended, and repealed city charters; established counties; determined city and county structure; set debt limits; and passed laws for the local units.

But by the end of the nineteenth century, voters had amended or adopted state constitutions that curtailed the power of state legislatures over state local governments. Constitutional provisions determined the structure, and in some cases even the processes, of local governments. **Constitutional home rule** granted constitutional independence to some local units, primarily larger cities, giving them constitutional authority over their form of government and a wide range of other matters. With this protection, state legislatures could no longer determine the structure and powers of these local units.

The extent of state control over local units today varies from state to state and also among the different kinds of local government within each state. At one extreme, local officials merely have to file reports with specified state officials. At the other, state officials have the authority to appoint and remove some local officials, thus exerting considerable control over local affairs. When local governments prove ineffective, state officials may offer them financial assistance with certain strings attached or may even take over responsibilities previously handled locally. The state of Pennsylvania, for instance, took control of Philadelphia's 200,000-pupil school system in 2002 after years of poor achievement and budget problems. Among other things, the state decided to privatize 45 of the city's worst-performing elementary and middle schools, the largest experiment yet in the privatization of public schools.[4] With the passage of the federal No Child Left Behind law in 2002, the federal government extended state involvement in local schools by requiring

unitary system

A constitutional arrangement in which power is concentrated in a central government.

constitutional home rule

State constitutional authorization for local governments to conduct their own affairs.

TABLE

8–1 Governments in the United States

Type of Government	Number of Governments				
	1967	1977	1987	1997	2007
U.S. government	1	1	1	1	1
State governments	50	50	50	50	50
Local governments	81,248	79,862	83,186	87,453	89,476
County	3,049	3,042	3,042	3,043	3,033
Municipal	18,048	18,862	19,200	19,372	19,492
Township	17,105	16,822	16,691	16,629	16,519
School district	21,782	15,174	14,721	13,726	13,051
Special district	21,264	25,962	29,532	34,683	37,381
Total	**81,299**	**79,913**	**83,237**	**87,504**	**89,527**

■ *The total number of governments has increased since 1967, but which types of governments increased in number, and which decreased?*

SOURCE: For 1967–1997: U.S. Census Bureau, *Statistical Abstract of the United States: 2008*, www.census.gov/compendia/statab. For 2007: U.S. Census Bureau, "2007 Census of Governments," www.census.gov/govs/www/cog2007.html.

states not only to measure schools' progress in meeting standards in reading/language arts, mathematics, and science but also to take corrective action against schools that consistently failed to meet minimal expectations.

Defining Local Government Structures

Before we proceed into the specifics about each level of local government, we will first introduce the big picture. In the United States, a **county** is a local level of government below the state. Counties are used in 48 of the 50 states, and there are on average 62 counties per state. Sub-county governments include **municipalities** and **townships,** which are generally organized around population centers. Because the classification of population centers is a matter of state law, the definition of a city or town varies widely from state to state.

A large city that is a significant economic, political, and cultural center for the region is called a **metropolis.** This metropolis and its adjacent zone of influence, typically one or more closely neighboring cities, is considered a **metropolitan area.** Areas of high population density are considered urban; residential areas—typically within commuting distance of a city—are referred to as suburbs; and rural areas have low population density. (See Figure 8–1.)

Why is there such complexity to local government in this country? The basic pattern was imported from England, as were many of our governmental forms. Over time, new governments were created to take on new jobs when existing units proved either too small or unequal to the task. The past three generations have seen millions of citizens moving from the cities to the suburbs, and then beyond the suburbs to places that were rural only a generation ago. The need to establish and maintain new schools, water and sewage services, law enforcement agencies, roads, and bridges, and the need to meet the many other demands of a sprawling population that have contributed to increasing governmental complexity.

Although our system of local governments is sometimes costly and inefficient, it performs many essential functions and provides opportunities for political officials and citizens to respond, sometimes in innovative ways, to public problems or political views that state and federal governments overlook. Communities have enacted ideas such as

county
The largest local level of government below the state, currently used in 48 states.

municipality
A local level of government within counties that are usually organized around population centers.

township
A local level of government below the county used primarily in 20 northeastern states.

metropolis
A large city or municipality that serves as an economic and cultural center for a region.

metropolitan area
The larger area surrounding a metropolis that is heavily influenced by the metropolis, generally consisting of suburbs and other smaller cities.

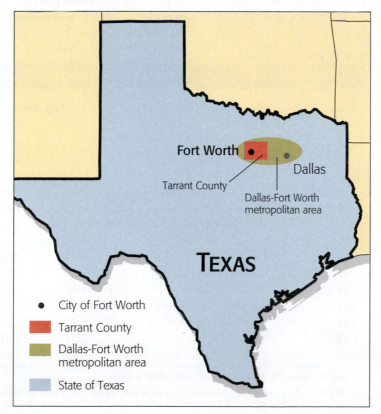

- City of Fort Worth
- Tarrant County
- Dallas-Fort Worth metropolitan area
- State of Texas

FIGURE 8–1 Local Government in Fort Worth, Texas.

■ *Based on the figure, what are five types of government operating in Fort Worth, Texas?*

"living wage" laws (companies doing business with the city must provide their workers enough income for a decent standard of living), public financing programs for election campaigns, and market-based approaches to education reform (such as charter schools and vouchers).[5] National surveys of citizens' views reveal the responsiveness of local governments, which usually come out ahead of both the federal and state governments when people are asked which they trust to perform well in carrying out their responsibilities.[6]

Counties

LEARNING **OBJECTIVE**

8.2 Assess the role of county government.

Counties are the largest jurisdictions within a state and are among the oldest and most stable local governments in terms of their boundaries not changing. Urban and suburban counties have many of the same governmental structures as their rural counterparts, but they are more intertwined with their urban centers. Some suburban counties are better known than any of the cities or municipalities within them—for example, Westchester County, New York; Montgomery County, Maryland; Marin and Orange Counties, California; and Bucks County, Pennsylvania. Some cities, such as Boston, Denver, Baltimore, Philadelphia, San Francisco, and Honolulu, are simultaneously cities and counties; New York City consists of five counties or boroughs—New York (Manhattan), Kings (Brooklyn), Queens, the Bronx, and Richmond (Staten Island). In Louisiana, counties are called *parishes,* whereas in Alaska, they are called *boroughs.* Connecticut and Rhode Island have geographic units called counties, but their counties do not have functioning governments.

There are 3,033 county governments throughout the United States, and they vary in size, population, and functions. Loving County, Texas, for example, had 45 inhabitants in 2009; Los Angeles County, California, had an estimated 9.9 million.[7] Table 8–2 lists the 15 largest counties. Although they represent only 0.5 percent of the 3,033 counties in the United States, more than 48 million people live in them—or 16 percent of the total U.S. population. In fact, more than half the people in the United States live in the most populous 5 percent of all counties.

Counties were originally organized on the idea that the county seat—the town or city where the county government is based—would be no more than a day's journey for anyone within the county's borders. Farm families could pile into their wagons and head for the county seat, and while farmers were attending to business, their families could

TABLE

8–2	The 15 Largest U.S. Counties by Population (2009)	
Rank	**Geographic Area**	**Pop. Estimate July 1, 2009**
1	Los Angeles County, CA	9,848,011
2	Cook County, IL	5,287,037
3	Harris County, TX	4,070,989
4	Maricopa County, AZ	4,023,132
5	San Diego County, CA	3,053,793
6	Orange County, CA	3,026,786
7	Kings County, NY	2,567,098
8	Miami-Dade County, FL	2,500,625
9	Dallas County, TX	2,451,730
10	Queens County, NY	2,306,712
11	Riverside County, CA	2,125,440
12	San Bernardino County, CA	2,017,673
13	Wayne County, MI	1,925,848
14	King County, WA	1,916,441
15	Clark County, NV	1,902,834

■ *Why is the county a useful jurisdiction within a state?*

SOURCE: U.S. Census Bureau, *2009 Population Estimates,* census.gov. Based on Table 7: Resident Population Estimates for the 100 Largest U.S. Counties.

shop and pick up the local gossip. Then they could all get home in time to do the evening chores. Today, of course, we can drive across a whole state or several states in a day.

The traditional functions of counties include law enforcement, highway construction and maintenance, tax collection and property assessment, recording of legal papers, and administration of welfare programs. Until recently, counties were convenient subdivisions that largely carried out policies established elsewhere. During the past generation, however, although counties in a few states have given up some of their responsibilities, in most others, especially in the South, they have taken over from the states such urban functions as transportation, water and sewer operation, and land use planning.[8] Elsewhere, cities are contracting with counties to provide such joint services as employee training, law enforcement, and corrections, and in some instances, cities and counties are merging some governmental functions such as local public education—something we explore further later in this chapter. County governments are least active in the New England states, where the county is often little more than a judicial and law enforcement district; county officials may do some road building but not much else.

County Government

Most counties have limited legislative power. The typical county has a central governing body, variously titled but most frequently called the *county commission* or *board of supervisors.* Most boards have three to seven members, although in very large counties, boards sometimes have several dozen members. They administer state laws, levy taxes, appropriate money, issue bonds, sign contracts on behalf of the county, and handle whatever jobs the state laws and constitution assign to them (see Figure 8–2).

Traditionally, many county boards were composed of the supervisors of townships or other township officials. Now, most of the boards in larger counties are elected from districts. The smaller boards are usually, though not always, elected in at-large elections. (At-large elections are countywide contests, not elections in which each board member is chosen from a different district; usually, the several top vote getters all win seats in at-large elections.) At-large elections make it more difficult for minorities to be elected to office, especially when they are concentrated in a few areas.

The county board shares its powers with a number of other officials, most commonly the sheriff, the county prosecutor or district attorney, the county clerk, the coroner, and the auditor, who are generally elected rather than appointed. Sometimes county treasurers, health officers, and surveyors are also found on the ballot.

Most counties still vest both legislative authority (the power to enact local ordinances and adopt budgets) and executive powers (the administration of policies and the hiring and firing of county employees) in the county commission or board of supervisors. However, an increasing number of counties—more than 40 percent now—assign executive responsibilities to a single individual, and Arkansas, Kentucky, and Tennessee mandate that their counties have a single elected top executive.[9] Some appoint a chief administrative officer who serves at the pleasure of the county commissioners, but the trend is toward an independently elected *county executive.* One recent estimate indicates that more than 700 counties now have elected executives who are responsible for most administrative functions (see Figure 8–3).[10]

County Performance

How well do counties perform? Most adequately perform their traditional duties of assessing property; keeping records; maintaining roads; and administering elections, local courts, and jails.[11] Some struggle with these functions, whereas others have expanded their responsibilities to include child welfare, consumer protection, economic development, water quality, public safety, and employment/training.

Differences in the relative wealth and growth rates of counties likely contribute to differences in performance. Counties rely heavily on their own revenue sources. In 2002, they received only 3 percent of their revenues from the federal government and 33 percent from their states.[12] This means they must rely on their own revenue base to attract

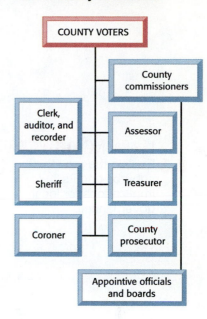

FIGURE 8–2 The Commission Form of County Government.

FIGURE 8–3 The Council with Elected Executive Form of County Government.

professional staff, provide adequate services, and have up-to-date facilities and information systems. This revenue base may be quite weak in many rural and older urban areas.

Yet the trend is toward expanded functions and improved capacity to perform these functions. Their jurisdictional boundaries give counties great potential to solve complex problems difficult to address at the city level or decentralized to local levels of government by the states. The growing professionalization of county workforces and the trend to elect or appoint professional county executives are improving efficiency.

Towns and Suburbs

LEARNING **OBJECTIVE**

8.3 Explain the growth of suburbs and its implications for local governance.

Towns, also called townships, are the basic unit of government smaller than a county in 20 northeastern and midwestern states. The number of towns in the United States has declined as growing municipalities have absorbed them (see Table 8–1). In most states that have them, towns are governed by elected officials typically including a supervisor, town board, and clerk. In New England, citizens do not only vote for members of the town board and other officers; in at least 1,000 towns, they also participate in annual town meetings. The New England town meeting is our most complete example of *direct democracy;* voters participate directly in making rules, passing new laws, levying taxes, and appropriating money. Maine has 209 towns that use a pure town meeting system of democracy,[13] and, according to the Massachusetts Constitution, towns of 6,000 residents or less must adopt a town meeting form of government.[14]

A group of active citizens that provides political and policy-making leadership usually dominates town meetings. Officers elected there perform most of the actual day-to-day governing of the town. Some large towns have adopted a modified *representative* town meeting, electing 50 to 200 town residents to represent their neighborhoods. Yet the open town meeting, at least in small towns in New England, still provides a vital way for people to participate in the policy making of their communities.

During the last half-century, the areas around cities have been the fastest-growing places in the United States (see Figure 8–4). At least 50 percent of U.S. citizens now live in suburban communities. Suburbs have grown up at the expense of cities for a variety of reasons: inexpensive land, lower taxes, cleaner air, more open space for recreational purposes, less crime, and better highways. Resistance to mandatory busing to achieve integrated schools in the 1960s and 1970s contributed to so-called white flight.[15] But it was just as much a matter of class as of race, with middle- and upper-middle-income-level

The New England town meeting, like this one in Sandwich, New Hampshire, has long been a celebrated U.S. institution. ■ *How are town meetings examples of direct democracy?*

Percentage of Americans Living in Suburbs and Central Cities at Each Census

■ Suburbs ■ Central cities

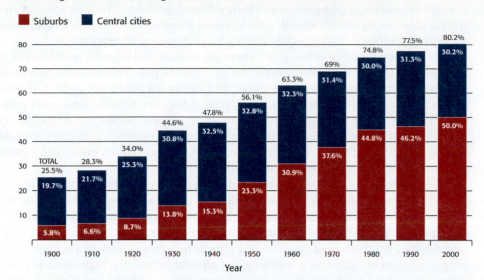

FIGURE 8–4 **Moving to the Suburbs.**

SOURCE: U.S. Census Bureau, *Population Estimates,* factfinder.census.gov.

whites, Asians, and African Americans moving to the suburbs to escape urban crime and to seek more attractive environments in terms of class, religion, race, and lifestyle.[16]

Suburbs have also grown because industries have moved from the central cities in search of cheaper land, lower taxes, and less restrictive building and health codes. Other businesses, including shopping centers, followed the people and the industries. This exodus was accelerated by federal policies promoting interstate highways and mortgages insured by the Federal Housing Administration. Most of the new jobs created in the United States continue to be located in the suburbs or newer cities on the fringes of the central cities. For example, although the St. Louis metropolitan area was fairly compact in 1950, by the end of the twentieth century, it had expanded into 11 counties in both Missouri and Illinois, and high-density areas are now found many miles from the central city (see Figure 8–5). Many of these newer areas are disconnected from other urbanized localities.

The form of suburban government employed by states varies widely. Suburbs have grown in formerly rural townships and in previously unincorporated areas of counties. Smaller municipalities located near larger central cities have also been swallowed up by the growth of suburbs and absorbed by the larger metropolitan area composed of the

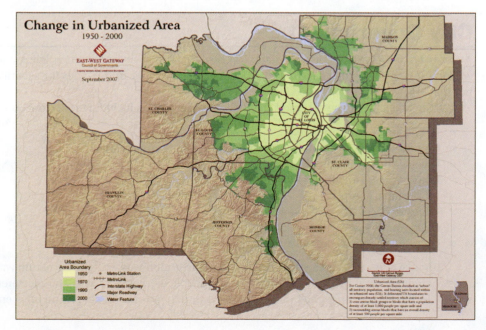

FIGURE 8–5 **Map of St. Louis.** This map shows the expansion of urban areas around St. Louis, Missouri, between 1950 and 2000. Areas are considered urban when their population density exceeds 1,000 people per square mile.

■ *What are some of the factors that account for the urban sprawl seen around St. Louis?*

SOURCE: East-West Gateway Council of Governments—St. Louis, Missouri, http://www.ewgateway.org/pdffiles/maplibrary/ChangeUA3.pdf.

central city and all its suburban areas. The existing governments of these areas have had to adapt to new, larger populations and their different demands. The metropolitan areas around larger cities usually stretch across several counties and often into other states, presenting significant challenges in planning for land use and transportation.

The major tasks of suburban government are often bound together with those of the metropolis.[17] Larger cities usually maintain an elaborate police department with detective bureaus, crime detection laboratories, and communications networks, but police jurisdiction stops at the city line even though crime does not. Suburbs have fewer police, seldom trained in criminology, so they call on urban police expertise. Intercity highways, which have local access roads, also tie cities and suburbs together. In matters of health, there are often wide differences in services between city and suburb, even though germs, pollutants, and smog do not notice city signposts.

Some larger suburban town governments have begun to resemble city governments, both in the professionalization of elected officials and bureaucracy and in the services that residents of the towns expect to receive. Older suburbs are now experiencing some of the problems long associated with urban disinvestment and population decline. Some suburbs, too, are challenged by sprawling growth that creates crowded schools, traffic congestion, loss of open space, and a lack of affordable housing. Many people believe there is a need for collaborative city–suburb strategies to address sprawl and the structural challenges facing older suburbs and inner cities.

Eminent Domain

Since the founding of the United States, governments have had the power to take private land for public purposes, even without the consent of the landowner. This power, called **eminent domain,** comes from English common law. State and local governments have mostly used eminent domain in cases of clear public need—for instance, the construction of a road or bridge—and tempered it by recognizing a right to just compensation for the landowner, usually paying the market rate for the land.

Eminent domain has recently generated some controversy when the Supreme Court ruled that New London, Connecticut's plan to redevelop an older residential neighborhood and turn it over to a private development company to build commercial and residential properties was permissible under the Fifth Amendment's eminent domain provision.[18] This decision generated a lot of criticism in the media, and most states quickly enacted laws revoking or restricting their local governments' powers to use eminent domain for economic development.[19]

City Government

LEARNING **OBJECTIVE**

8.4 Outline the different ways of structuring city government, and describe the functions of mayors.

A city is not merely different real estate; it is also people—men and women living and working together. Aristotle asserted that people came together in the cities for security, but they stayed there for the good life.

Different people define the "good life" differently, yet it often includes these attractions:

- Employment opportunities
- Cultural centers, museums, performing arts centers, and theaters
- Diverse educational institutions
- Entertainment and nightlife
- Professional sports teams
- Wide variety of stores and specialty shops
- Good restaurants
- Diversity of people, architecture, and lifestyles

Although a few cities existed when the U.S. Constitution was written, the nation was overwhelmingly rural in 1787, and seven of ten people worked on farms and clustered mainly in the villages and small towns scattered throughout the 13 states and adjacent

eminent domain

The power a government has to take private land to use for a public purpose.

YOU WILL

DECIDE
Does Economic Development Justify Eminent Domain?

One issue raised in the Supreme Court decision of *Kelo* v. *City of New London* (2005) was the question of whether a government may transfer ownership of property from one private owner to another by exercising its power of eminent domain in support of economic development goals.* The city of New London in Connecticut has long suffered from a declining population and high levels of unemployment. When a pharmaceutical corporation began building a large research facility in the city, New London officials decided it would be an excellent opportunity to revitalize the largely run-down area near the corporation's facility by promoting the construction of a hotel, a conference center, a new state park, new residences, and office space. The city set up a private agency to create and implement an ambitious development plan for the area, including acquiring the land needed to put the plan into effect. The development corporation bought many of the parcels of land needed for the plan, but a few landowners refused to sell their land, and the development

corporation, under the city's authority, then exercised the power of eminent domain.

The landowners sued, and the case eventually came before the U.S. Supreme Court, which had to decide whether this use of eminent domain qualified as a "public use" in the federal constitution's "taking clause," which states that private property shall not "be taken for public use, without just compensation."† Most of the landowners suing the city lived on the properties, and no claims were made by the city that these particular properties were blighted or in poor condition. One owner had lived on the property (indeed in the particular house) since her birth in 1918.

What do you think? Should local governments be able to use eminent domain to seize private property for the use of economic development? What are some of the arguments for or against it?

THINKING IT THROUGH

In an opinion written by Justice John Paul Stevens, the Court determined that the taking of these properties was constitutional, even though the properties would in the end be owned, developed, and used by private parties. The reason was that the city's goal was a *public* purpose, to promote economic growth and development, a traditional function of government. Even though some private persons may benefit from the use of eminent domain and the subsequent transfer of property, those facts did not mean the taking of property primarily served private purposes.

Justice Sandra Day O'Connor wrote a dissent arguing that the Court's decision opened the possibility that governments could take property simply because they decided other owners would make more productive use of it. She argued:

> nearly any lawful use of real private property can be said to generate some incidental benefit to the public. Thus, if predicted...positive side effects are enough to render transfer from one private party to another constitutional, then the words 'for public use' do not realistically exclude *any* takings, and thus do not exert any constraint on the eminent domain power.

Further, she wrote, "Nothing is to prevent the State [or City] from replacing any Motel 6 with a Ritz-Carlton, any home with a shopping mall, or any farm with a factory."

Although the case raised many complex questions about the federal constitution, the decision quickly pushed the issue onto the agendas of city councils and state legislatures, which were pressured by the public's (largely negative) reaction to *Kelo* to alter guidelines regarding what local governments may do regarding the taking of land and property in service of economic development goals.**

Critical Thinking Questions

1. Is it ever justifiable for a city or state government to use its eminent domain authority to transfer property from one group of property owners to another to promote economic development in a distressed city or town? Why or why not?

2. If you think this use of eminent domain is justifiable under some circumstances but not others, or only after certain procedures are followed, what should those circumstances or procedures be?

---

*545 U.S. 469 (2005).

†The "takings clause" is found at the end of the Fifth Amendment to the U.S. Constitution and was incorporated into the Fourteenth Amendment to apply to states and localities. The Supreme Court has typically deferred to state and local governments' decisions about what constitutes a "public use."

**For state legislative responses to *Kelo*, see the Web site of the National Conference of State Legislatures, http://www.ncsl.org/?Tabid=17604.

---

territories. These were the indispensable workshops of democracy, the places where democratic skills were developed and political issues were debated.

The United States is now a nation of about 19,492 municipalities, more than 9,000 of which have fewer than 1,000 residents, and only 58 have 300,000 residents or more.[20] Although some small cities or incorporated villages have only a few hundred people, the largest have millions. Three U.S. supercities and their suburbs (New York, Los Angeles, and Chicago) each have populations larger than the total population of the Republic in the 1780s.

A **charter** is to a city what a constitution is to a national or state government. It outlines the structure of the government, defines the authority of the various officials, and provides for their selection. Different structures are not neutral in their impact; they encourage

charter
A city "constitution" that outlines the structure of city government, defines the authority of the various officials, and provides for their selection.

FIGURE 8-6 The Mayor–Council Form of City Government.

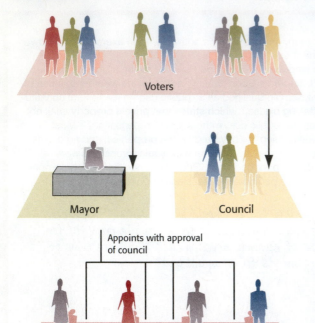

Voters

Mayor

Council

Appoints with approval of council

Department heads

different kinds of participation and responsiveness. Decisions about who gets what, where, and how are shaped by a city's structural arrangements.

The Mayor–Council Charter

The **mayor–council charter** is the oldest type (see Figure 8–6). Under this type of charter, the city council is usually a single chamber. The size of the council varies from as few as 2 members to as many as 50, although 7 is the median size in cities with more than 5,000 people. Most small cities and municipalities use this type of charter. It is also still the most common type in the largest cities, and in medium-sized cities in the East and Midwest.

Many methods are used to select council members: nonpartisan and partisan elections, elections by large and small wards (specific districts in the municipality), or elections from the city at large when the city is not divided into separate geographic districts. Large cities that elect members affiliated with political parties generally choose them by small districts or wards rather than at-large. This arrangement tends to support strong party organizations. Nonpartisan at-large elections make party influence difficult. The larger the election districts, the more likely citywide considerations will affect the selection of council members and the greater the influence of citywide institutions such as local newspapers.

The difference between at-large citywide elections and elections based on small, single-member districts within a city can be significant for racial and ethnic representation on the city council. The at-large system tends to produce councils made up of the city's elite and middle classes. Smaller districts give minorities and the less advantaged a somewhat better chance for representation, especially where neighborhoods have high concentrations of one minority or income group.[21]

The Voting Rights Act of 1965 forbids states and cities with a history of discrimination against minority voters from adopting the at-large system for electing council members if the effect would be to dilute the voting strength of these minorities. In fact, no local government in the 11 former Confederate states can make a change in its voting system without the approval of the U.S. attorney general. But what of cities or counties that have long had at-large elections? Can they be forced to give them up because at-large elections virtually ensure that minorities will never be elected? In a 1980 case, the Supreme Court found that the Constitution forbids only practices adopted or maintained *with the intent to discriminate;* the Court permitted Mobile, Alabama, to keep its seven-decades-old system of choosing city commissioners in at-large elections, even though no black person had ever been elected to the three-person commission, because there was no direct evidence that the system was established with a discriminatory intent.[22] However, Congress rejected this interpretation when it enacted the extension of the Voting Rights Act in 1982. In the revised Act, voters can challenge a voting scheme, such as at-large elections, by demonstrating that the voting arrangements, based on all the evidence presented, were racially discriminatory in their effects regardless of intent.[23]

Weak and Strong Mayor Councils

The powers of the mayor–council form of government vary from charter to charter and even more widely from city to city and mayor to mayor. There are, however, two basic variations of the mayor–council form: the weak mayor council and the strong mayor council.

In cities with the **weak mayor–council form,** mayors are often chosen from members of the elected city council rather than elected directly by the people. The mayor's appointive powers are usually restricted, and the city council as a whole generally possesses both legislative and executive authority. The mayor must usually obtain the council's consent for all major decisions. Often weak mayor–council cities permit direct election by the voters of a number of department heads, such as police chief or controller. In weak mayor–council cities, there is no single administrative head for the city, and power is fragmented. The weak mayor–council plan was designed for an earlier era, when

mayor–council charter
The oldest and most common form of city government, consisting of either a weak mayor and a city council or a strong mayor elected by voters and council.

weak mayor–council form
A form of local government in which the members of the city council select the mayor, who then shares power with other elected or appointed boards and commissions.

cities were smaller and government was simpler. It is ill-suited to large cities, where political and administrative leadership is vital.

Under the **strong mayor–council form,** the mayor is elected directly by the people and given fairly broad appointment powers. The mayor, often with the help of his or her staff, prepares and administers the budget, enjoys almost total administrative authority, and has the power to appoint and dismiss department heads. This system obviously calls for a mayor to be both a good political leader and an effective administrator—qualities not always found in the same person.

Many people believe the strong mayor–council system is the best form of government for large cities because it gives the cities strong political leaders and makes responsive administration possible. Further, by centering authority in the hands of a few individuals, it makes less likely the growth of "invisible government" by people who have power but are not publicly accountable for its use.

The Council–Manager Charter

Reformers in the early 1900s acclaimed the **council–manager plan** (also known as the *city-manager plan*), in which the city council hires a professional administrator to manage city affairs. It was indeed a significant governmental innovation. In 1908, the small city of Staunton, Virginia, appointed a general manager to oversee the city's work. Little note was taken of the step, but the council–manager plan soon became the darling of both reformers and the business elite. They liked the idea that the council would serve as a sort of "board of directors" in the business sense of setting broad policies, while a professional executive would see that these policies were carried out with business-like efficiency (see Figure 8–7).

Under the council–manager charter, the council is usually elected in nonpartisan primaries and elections, either on a citywide basis or by election districts much larger than the wards in mayor–council cities. The council appoints a city manager and supervises the manager's activities. The council still makes the laws and approves the budget, and although it is not supposed to interfere in administration, the council often supervises city government through the manager. The mayor is expected to preside over the council and represent the city on ceremonial occasions, but many mayors in fact do a good deal more than this. The mayor in council–manager cities can sometimes be a strong policy and political leader as well as a dominant influence in exercising political power.[24] This has been the case in cities as different as Cambridge, Massachusetts; San Antonio, Texas; and Colorado Springs, Colorado.

The city manager advises the council on policy and supervises the administration of city business. Because council–manager cities try to attract the best available people, few of their charters require the councils to select managers from among local citizens, nor do they prescribe detailed qualifications. Although council–manager charters seem to call for a nonpolitical city manager who does not make policy but merely carries out policies adopted by the council, and for council members who refrain from interfering with the administration of city affairs, real politics is not so simple. Managers often influence policy, if only informally, and council members get involved in administrative affairs. Indeed, it is often difficult to distinguish clearly between making and applying policy.

Today, more than 3,100 cities located in virtually every state operate under a council–manager charter. In fact, it has become the most popular form of local government in medium-sized cities of more than 10,000 citizens. It is especially popular in California, where approximately 98 percent of the cities use it, as well as in other western and Sun Belt cities. Some of the larger cities operating under a city manager are Dallas, San Antonio, San Jose, Kansas City, Cincinnati, Fresno, Colorado Springs, and Fort Worth.

strong mayor–council form
A form of local government in which the voters directly elect the city council and the mayor, who enjoys nearly total administrative authority and appoints the department heads.

council–manager plan
A form of local government in which the city council hires a professional administrator to manage city affairs; also known as the *city-manager plan*.

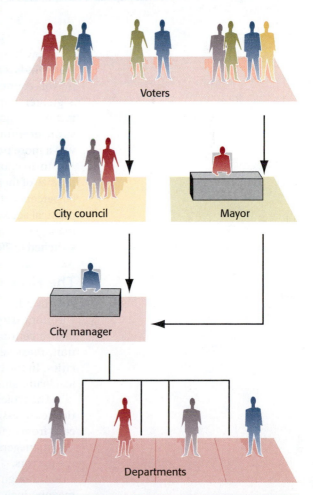

FIGURE 8–7 The Council–Manager Form of City Government.

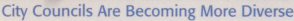
City Councils Are Becoming More Diverse

City councils are becoming more racially and ethnically diverse; the number of people of color serving nearly doubled in the last two decades, in all categories of cities (small, medium, and large), from 7 percent to 13 percent.

During the last decade, Hispanic council membership has increased the most in medium cities, with populations of 70,000 to 199,999—jumping from 0 to 6 percent—and in large cities, with populations of more than 200,000, growing there from 1 percent to 11 percent. During the same time, the percentage of Asian Americans declined from 3 percent to 1 percent.

The representation of women on city councils increased as well. It grew from 21 percent to 25 percent in small cities, from 25 percent to 36 percent in medium-sized cities, and from 33 percent to 36 percent in large cities.

CRITICAL THINKING QUESTIONS

1. What explains the predominance of whites on city councils, as seen in this table?

2. Do you think the representation of women in city councils will continue to increase, stay at present levels, or decline? Why?

Percentage of Council Members

Year	White	African American	Hispanic	Asian	Native American	Other
1979	92	5	1	—	—	—
1989	86	10	1	3	—	1
2001	87	8	3	1	1	1

Percentages may not add to 100 percent because of rounding.

SOURCE: National League of Cities, *Research Brief on America's Cities: The Faces of America's City Councils* (September 2003), available at www.nlc.org. Used by permission.

How has the city-manager plan worked? The literature is mixed, but one empirical study finds no significant difference in the relative efficiency of council–manager versus mayor–council forms of government.[25] Another study found that strategic planning had a greater impact on development policy in council–manager cities compared with mayor–council cities.[26] The study also found that population and median income are stronger influences on developmental policy in mayor–council cities, whereas poverty was a more powerful force on development policy in council-manager systems.

In an effort to become more responsive, some council–manager cities have expanded the size of their councils and abandoned at-large elections for district elections. More than 60 percent of the city-manager cities now also directly elect their mayors to provide greater political accountability and leadership.[27] Some cities have recently moved from a council–manager form of government to a strong mayor–council form, such as San Diego, which switched in 2006.[28]

The Role of the Mayor

Two hundred years ago, the notion of a strong mayor providing vigorous leadership was nonexistent. The need for strong mayoral leadership developed in the late nineteenth century as a means to deal with the social revolution brought on by urbanization, massive waves of immigration, and mounting economic problems of growing cities. In the larger cities, the office of mayor gradually became a key position for political leadership.

The typical mayor is a college graduate, a business or legal professional, and an experienced grassroots politician between 40 and 50 years old. Mayors in the largest cities earn from $90,000 to $216,000 and in middle-sized cities, between $40,000 and $80,000. City managers, chief city administrators, and top appointees sometimes make more than the mayors.

Although most mayors are male, several of the nation's largest cities have had female mayors, including Baltimore, Atlanta, Chicago, Pittsburgh, Houston, Dallas, San Diego, San Antonio, and Portland. As of July 2009, 17.6 percent of municipal governments in the

United States with a population of 30,000 or more were headed by women.[29] Many worked their way up through service on school boards and city councils and in the League of Women Voters. Many African Americans also serve as mayors, especially in larger cities. The first African Americans elected to be mayors in big cities were Carl Stokes of Cleveland and Richard Hatcher of Gary, Indiana, both elected in 1967. Of the 100 largest cities with elected mayors, 39 have had black mayors as of 2007, including six of the ten largest cities in the United States: New York (David Dinkins), Los Angeles (Tom Bradley), Chicago (Harold Washington), Houston (Lee Brown), Philadelphia (Wilson Goode, John Street, and Michael Nutter), and Dallas (Ron Kirk).[30] The National Conference of Black Mayors claims to represent more than 650 black mayors across the United States.[31]

The main job of the mayor is administrative in the broadest sense of the term. Mayors supervise the line agencies—police, fire, public safety, traffic, health, and sanitation—as well as a host of special agencies such as the board of elections, the city planning agency, and commissions that regulate particular occupations and professions. Big-city mayors usually have staffs that carry out typical executive office functions such as human resources, management, budgeting, scheduling, and public relations. In this respect, mayors face the same tasks as corporate executives: coordinating a variety of activities, assigning responsibilities, checking that projects are carried out, finding the ablest people to take charge, and allocating money through control of the budget.

Usually mayors work with the private sector to promote economic opportunities. They try to secure additional jobs, increase the tax base, make the city more attractive to certain kinds of businesses, and coordinate public service expansion with private sector requirements. The private sector undertakes economic development because its success depends on having an educated labor base with appropriate skills, a constant consumer population, stable communities, and increasing property values.

Sometimes a mayor must depend on the party organization to ensure support in the council, as in Chicago, where the huge city council consists of 50 members. Other mayors may have to deal with smaller councils, but they are likely to be weak unless they have enough political support to win cooperation.

Although partisan politics is waning as a feature of city government, mayors as party leaders still often dominate the party's city organizations. Mayors help recruit candidates for office, deal with revolts and opposition within their parties, and represent their parties in Washington or the state capitals. As chief legislators, mayors draw up proposed legislation and also make many specific policies. As chief fund-raisers, mayors bargain for more money for their cities before state and national legislatures. Mayors often climb the political ladder to run for governor and senator. For example, there were ten current or former mayors running for governor in 2010, and six of them won—in California, Colorado, Connecticut, Tennessee, Rhode Island, and Maine. Seven current or former mayors ran for seats in the U.S. House of Representatives, and five of them won. Current U.S. Senators George Voinovich, Richard Lugar, and Jake Garn had been mayors of Cleveland, Indianapolis, and Salt Lake City, respectively.

Only three presidents had served as mayors—Andrew Johnson, Calvin Coolidge, and Grover Cleveland—and only Cleveland had been mayor of a major city (Buffalo). The most recent former mayor to run for president was Hubert Humphrey in 1968; he lost that election to Richard Nixon, but he had begun his long and otherwise successful political career as mayor of Minneapolis. Former Mayor Rudolph Giuliani of New York City ran for the Republican presidential nomination in 2008 but dropped out quickly after a series of poor finishes in state primaries.

Mayors are expected to help revitalize the economy and attract investors, sports teams, tourists, and conventions. Many mayors,

Michael Bloomberg of New York City seriously considered running as a third-party candidate for U.S. president in the 2008 elections, and the national media closely followed his vacillation and final decision not to run. His name has also been brought up as a potential candidate in 2012. ■ *What would make a mayor a strong presidential candidate?*

such as those in New York, San Francisco, Seattle, Atlanta, Chicago, and Miami, have their own "foreign policies." That is, they play host to foreign dignitaries and business delegations and travel abroad seeking foreign investments as they sing the praises of local exportable goods.[32] It takes courage and missionary zeal to overcome the pessimism and decay that beset most inner cities. But several mayors—including Rudolph Giuliani in New York City and both Richard J. Daley and his son Richard M. Daley in Chicago—succeeded in reducing crime, increasing economic opportunities, and revitalizing downtown businesses and residential areas.

In recent decades, mayors, like presidents and governors, have grown in power and importance. Most cities have altered their charters to give their mayors power to appoint and remove heads of departments, investigate departmental activities, send legislative messages to the city councils, prepare budgets, and veto council ordinances. In other words, mayors have been given a share in policy making, and city administration has been centralized under the mayor's direction.

Central City Politics

LEARNING **OBJECTIVE**

8.5 Describe the challenges facing central cities and metro areas.

Today, most people live in *metropolitan areas,* which include large cities and their suburbs, rather than in the small towns so beloved and often idealized. The U.S. Census Bureau, which counts 363 metropolitan areas, defines a Metropolitan Statistical Area (also called a metro area) as at least one "core" urban area of at least 50,000 people and any adjacent outlying counties "that have a high degree of social and economic integration (as measured by commuting to work) with the urban core."[33]

Approximately 84 percent of U.S. citizens (252 million people) live in metropolitan areas, and 27 percent live in cities of populations greater than 100,000.[34] Between 2000 and 2007, the five fastest-growing large metropolitan areas (of those with a population of more than 1 million) were in the South and the West: Las Vegas, Nevada; Raleigh, North Carolina; Phoenix, Arizona; Austin, Texas; and Riverside, California. All increased their populations by more than 25 percent in only seven years.[35]

In the nineteenth century, masses of new immigrants arrived in the cities from Europe. In the twentieth century, migrants came from rural areas, especially from the South. More recently, this country experienced waves of newcomers from Cuba, Korea, Vietnam, the Philippines, Nicaragua, Haiti, Mexico, and other Latin American countries. Many newcomers settle first in the inner cities—usually in the poorest and most decayed sections—which inevitably puts great stress on the schools and sometimes on community safety as well. Overcrowding and substandard housing in these areas increase health and fire hazards.

Central cities have historically faced a number of problems. They have more "high-cost citizens" (truly needy, handicapped, and senior citizens), and most aging cities have been losing population. They have also lost businesses because land, rents, utilities, operating costs, and taxes are often less expensive in the outer suburbs. Businesses move out of the city to lower their operating costs, and their departure means that cities have smaller tax bases.

The shrinking tax base has made it difficult for cities to raise sufficient revenue from sources such as the property tax. However, the demand for services has not decreased. Many suburban dwellers commute into cities and use city services during the workday but do not pay income taxes in the city. Most of the states have not permitted their cities to raise funds in any meaningful way with a local income tax, which means that cities cannot use the most direct method to make up the lost revenue.[36]

In an effort to recapture part of the tax base that escapes to the suburbs in the evenings, some cities have imposed local payroll or other types of *commuter taxes* to obtain revenue from people who work in the central cities and make frequent use of city facilities yet live in the suburbs. Some city officials say the payroll or commuter tax is an effective way to shift some of the burden to those who benefit from the city but live beyond its borders. But others say it is unlikely to provide significant long-term revenue growth, and they think it encourages even more businesses to leave the city.

For the People

Local Government Discretion

The state government in Arizona passed a series of new laws on immigration in the spring of 2010. Among them is a provision requiring individuals to carry immigration documents with them, allowing local police greater latitude on stopping people suspected of being in the country illegally. Another provision effectively requires local officials to ask someone for proof of legal residence if the police have any suspicion that the person might not be in the country legally.

The catch to these new provisions: Like many state laws, they rely in part on local county sheriffs for enforcement. Clarence W. Dupnik is the sheriff of Pima County, where Tucson is located, and which shares a 123-mile border with Mexico. He has openly stated that he will not enforce the law as he considers it likely to encourage racial profiling, and he feels that enforcing immigration rules is a burden better suited for the federal government. He published an editorial to this effect in *The Wall Street Journal*.*

In contrast, Sheriff Joe Arpaio, his counterpart in Maricopa County, which includes Phoenix, strongly supports the law. In fact, the self-proclaimed "America's Toughest

Sheriff" has engaged in his own crusade to crack down on illegal immigrants for several years before this law was passed.†

Both sheriffs have held their jobs for decades, and both are responding to what they think is right for the citizens of their counties. This is local government in action—responding to citizens and deviating from state policy where they see fit. Depending on your own views regarding legal and illegal immigration, you might applaud the efforts of one of these sheriffs and deplore the efforts of the other, but there is no question that they are exercising what

they feel is the local discretion they have to enforce or not enforce state laws.

CRITICAL THINKING QUESTIONS

1. Should local law enforcement officials have the discretion to enforce some state laws vigorously and others not at all? What are the consequences of your answer?

2. Should dealing with illegal immigrants be primarily a national, state, or local policy problem? Where should policies be set? Which level should pay for them? Who should be charged with implementing those policies?

Sheriff Dupnik has stated he will not enforce the new law.

Sheriff Arpaio supports the new law.

*http://online.wsj.com/article/SB10001424052748704342604575222420517514084.html.
†See this National Public Radio story from 2008 at http://www.npr.org/templates/story/story.php?storyId=88002493.

The incidence of child poverty is another problem central cities face. Child poverty is statistically associated with many other problems, such as poor health, infant mortality, stunted growth, low achievement and behavioral problems at school, and future unemployment as a young adult.[37] Poverty is more common among children than adults; in 2008, 19 percent of all children in the United States were estimated to be living in poor households, compared with 12 percent of people between the ages of 18 to 64 and 10 percent of people the age of 65 and older.[38] Child poverty rates are also higher in cities than in suburban or nonmetropolitan areas, but they differ enormously across large cities; Atlanta and Cleveland have some of the highest child poverty rates, nearly *half* of all children in the city, whereas in Seattle and Virginia Beach, fewer than one in eight children were in poor households.[39]

The picture of central cities as being composed exclusively of homeless youth gangs and unemployed masses, however, is misleading. Recently, many of the once-declining central cities have shown signs of rejuvenation and gentrification. **Gentrification** in an area refers to relatively wealthier people buying property in poorer areas of a city and moving there, which results in revitalization of the area and increased property values but is often accompanied by displacing the poor. Cities such as Atlanta, Kansas City, and Newark, which were losing population a decade or two ago, are now gaining new residents. Gentrification and "yuppie" development have attracted some suburbanites to come back to central cities. The reasons for the rebound of many central cities vary from city to city, yet the sustained economic boom

gentrification
A process where relatively wealthier people buy property in poorer areas of a city and relocate there, which results in revitalization of the area and increased property values but is often accompanied by displacing the poor.

Urban renewal has brought new life to the Inner Harbor in Baltimore, Maryland.
■ *How might investment in development and renewal projects pay off for cities in the long run?*

in the 1990s increased local tax revenues, which were then invested heavily in local infrastructure to make cities more appealing. The boom and investment in cities also helped create more jobs.[40]

The Rise of "Edge Cities"

In recent decades, cities have been built on the edges of metropolitan areas. Writer Joel Garreau calls these "edge cities" and suggests that virtually every expanding U.S. city grows in the fashion of Los Angeles, with multiple urban cores.[41] Thus, we have Tysons Corner, Virginia, outside Washington, D.C.; the Perimeter Center at the northern tip of Atlanta's Beltway; the Galleria area west of downtown Houston; and the Schaumburg area northwest of Chicago.

Edge cities have 5 million or more square feet of office space, 600,000 or more square feet of retail space, and more jobs than bedrooms. More often than not, they were empty spaces or farmland only 30 years ago. New freeways appeared first, then a shopping mall or two, and then industrial parks.

Some of the problems of the inner city have caught up with edge cities, just as they have with suburbs: traffic congestion, parking problems, crime, pollution, and urban blight. Political problems have cropped up as well. Most edge cities are in unincorporated areas of counties—that is, they are not part of any city, town, or other municipality—and are subject in varying degrees to be controlled by county governments. Edge cities are sometimes run by "shadow governments"—private owners who set the fees for policing, transportation, and various other services that are normally financed by taxes. There is not much room for government by the people in a community that is essentially a business.

Greeley, Colorado, approximately 50 miles north of Denver, is the core city of what was one of the fastest-growing metro areas in the nation. The area's population grew by 35 percent between 2000 and 2007. However, after the downturn in the housing market in 2007 and 2008, Greeley briefly led the nation in the rate of foreclosures and many recently built homes remain unsold.

Metropolitics Today: Meeting the Challenges of Growth and Development

Until recently, nearly everybody wanted to see his or her city grow. The local newspaper, television stations, radio stations, Chamber of Commerce, union leaders, business community, developers, teachers, and proud citizens worked together to attract new industries. Such industries would bring, they hoped, new jobs, more amenities, increased land values, and more opportunities for young people. The consensus was that a city with a growing population was a healthy one; one with a decreasing population was a sick one.

Local politicians found it risky to oppose economic development and economic growth; those who did feared they would not be reelected. However, beginning about two decades ago, an *antigrowth* movement developed in many cities. There had always been restraints in the wealthy suburbs outside the central cities; in fact, many suburbs were created to escape the growth taking place in central cities. These suburbs adopted building and zoning codes and land use regulations to make it difficult, if not impossible, for industries to be located there and to keep people out who could not afford large houses on large lots. New suburbs were carefully planned to ensure that they would not become too crowded. These zoning regulations were attacked in the courts as strategies to keep the poor and minorities out, but the U.S. Supreme Court ruled in 1977 that as long as zoning rules were racially neutral on their face, they did not violate the Constitution.[42]

LEARNING **OBJECTIVE**

8.6 Evaluate strategies for meeting the various challenges of governance in metropolitan regions.

Strategies to Govern Metropolitan Regions

Divided executive authority, fragmented legislative power, splintered and noncompetitive political parties, the absence of strong central governments, and the necessity to bargain with national, state, and local officials—all these factors suggest that metro regions are challenges to coherent governance. In some places, fragmentation is especially daunting. The St. Louis metropolitan area, for instance, includes the city of St. Louis, 15 surrounding counties, 274 smaller cities, 107 townships, 136 school districts, and 411 special districts in two states.[43]

At the turn of the twentieth century, reformers were afraid of domination by political bosses. But in the modern metropolis, political machines do not run the central city. Urban bureaucracies may wield a lot of power, but they do not offer metropolitan leadership. Special interests seldom actually control the metropolis, nor does a business elite. Who, then, governs the metropolis? It is typically a "nobody's in charge" arrangement.

Growing fragmentation of government in large metropolitan areas has brought about a variety of reform movements and structural innovations aimed at improving efficiency, effectiveness, and performance. Political scientists and public administration specialists have never been bashful about proposing remedies. Here are the better-known ideas, all of which have been tried somewhere, yet none of which has been adopted nationwide.

Annexation   Annexation is when one (typically large) city absorbs neighboring areas into it. Supporters argue that the resulting larger single government reduces duplication and facilitates solving problems that used to cross municipal borders. In the South, West, and Southwest, large central cities have absorbed adjacent territories. Oklahoma City, for example, added nearly 600 square miles. Houston, Phoenix, San Antonio, El Paso, Colorado Springs, and Kansas City, Missouri, also expanded their boundaries. The now-extended cities serve almost as regional governments.[44]

But annexation has not proved helpful to cities in the Northeast and Midwest because these cities are ringed by entrenched suburban communities that seldom want to be annexed, and state laws make it difficult for the central city to do so against the wishes of the suburbs. Even in such places as the Houston metropolitan area, the annexation option is plagued by legal obstacles and political jealousies.

The Port Authority, jointly headed by the governors of New York and New Jersey, manages much of the transportation infrastructure in the New York City area. Here, Port Authority police officers monitor one of the entrances to the Holland Tunnel.
■ *What are the benefits and challenges in having these services run by a public authority?*

Agreements to Furnish Services The most common solution to the problems of overlapping and duplicating jurisdictions is for the units of government to contract for services. This reform is applauded by many economists, who say it comes close to providing a market that operates according to laws of supply and demand. Most of these agreements call for a few cities to share a single activity. For example, a city may provide hospital services to its neighbors or contract with the county for law enforcement. Especially popular in the Los Angeles area, the contract system is being used with increasing success in many parts of the country. Of course, to be successful, both governments in the contract must agree to its terms.

Public Authorities Public authorities such as the Port Authority in the New York City area and the Tennessee Valley Authority in the South were established to undertake specialized functions in their regions. They have a legal mandate granted by the state (or states) to raise money, hire experts, and take over some city services, such as transportation, water, and housing. The Port Authority of New York and New Jersey built the Twin Towers of the World Trade Center, which were destroyed by the 2001 terrorist attacks. It now shares responsibility with Silverstein Properties for redeveloping the area and for overseeing the operation and security of the bridges and tunnels connecting New York and New Jersey.

Why public authorities? In part because state legislatures sometimes prefer to place important functions outside the reach of mayors and political machines and in part because such authorities have financial flexibility (for example, they may be able to incur debt outside the limits imposed on the city by the state). But most important, many problems are simply too big or cover too wide a geographical area to be handled properly by a city or a group of cities.

Public authorities pose a special problem for mayors. Not only do they remove many of the vital functions of metropolitan government from the mayors' direct control, but even worse, public authorities and special districts constantly come into conflict with local agencies dealing with the same problems in the city.

But if public authorities are a problem for mayors, they are also a temptation. By sponsoring these independent agencies, mayors can sometimes cut down on their administrative load. They can tap other sources of funds and keep city tax rates lower than they would otherwise be. If things go wrong, mayors can say they did not have authority over a certain function and hence cannot be held responsible.

Special Districts Special districts are units of government typically established to provide one or more specific services, such as sewage disposal, fire protection, water supply, or pollution control for a local or regional area. They are often created to enable an existing unit of government to evade tax and debt limits and to spread the tax burden over a wider area than individual municipalities or counties. Many smaller special districts are formed in suburban areas to obtain urban services without having to create a city government or be annexed by one.

Special districts usually have governing boards appointed by officials of other governments or elected by the general public. Special districts are useful for dealing with urgent problems that overlap boundaries of existing government units. Many urban and regional problems defy city and county boundaries, and special districts offer economies of scale that make sense. But critics charge that the rapid increase in the number of special districts during the last 30 years has prevented comprehensive planning. They also lament that few citizens know who runs these special districts, and even fewer know how these officials make decisions.

Regional Coordinating and Planning Councils Nearly all metro regions have some kind of *council of government* (COG). COGs began in the 1950s and were encouraged by the national government. Congress, in fact, mandated that certain federal grants be reviewed by regional planning groups. In essence, these councils bring locally elected officials together. They devote most of their time and resources to physical planning; rarely do they tackle problems of race, poverty, and financial inequities in metro regions. Councils are set up, moreover, in such a way as to give suburbs a veto over virtually any project that would threaten their autonomy. In a few regions, the councils assume operating responsibilities over such regional activities as garbage collection, transportation, and water supply. Critics say these councils rarely provide for creative area-wide governance, yet they serve as an important common ground for elected officials to talk about mutual problems, and they help solve problems in many of the regions.

City–County Consolidations   One traditional means of overcoming the fragmentation of metro regions is to merge the city with the county. This is a pet reform of business elites, the League of Women Voters, and Chambers of Commerce, who view it as a rational, efficient way to simplify administration, cut costs for taxpayers, and eliminate duplication.

More than 30 city–county mergers have taken place. In addition, one city occasionally joins with another, as Sacramento and North Sacramento did in the 1960s. Such mergers can usually be brought about only by a referendum approved by the citizens of the region. Most of the successful ones have taken place in smaller urban areas. Indianapolis, Jacksonville, and Nashville are some of the larger consolidations. The experience of Indianapolis is typical of these consolidations, most of which are in the South and West. In 1970, Indianapolis combined with Marion County to create UNIGOV. This merger required special permission from the legislature. UNIGOV provides many services, but the school systems remain separate, as do the police and sheriff departments. One successful regional merger was the 2000 consolidation of the city of Louisville and Jefferson County, Kentucky.[45]

Many proposed mergers have been rejected by county voters. But it is no longer unusual to find counties running what used to be city jails, zoos, libraries, and similar services. Formal and informal agreements abound as cities and counties remedy overlap and fragmentation by shifting responsibilities for providing specific services among themselves. "City–county functional consolidation in areas such as emergency medical services and natural-disaster planning is growing throughout the United States.... Increasing cooperation is likely to occur in the future as cities and counties struggle to provide more services to a tax-resistant public."[46]

Federated Government   A federated government attempts to take political realities into account by building on existing governments but assigning some crucial functions to an area-wide metro government.[47] One of the few attempts—and there have been only a few—to create a federated government is the Twin Cities Metropolitan Council for the Minneapolis–St. Paul region. This regional organization, established by the legislature in 1967, consists of a 17-member council. Sixteen members are appointed by the governor to represent equal-population districts, while the remaining member is a full-time executive who serves at the pleasure of the governor.

Today, the Metropolitan Council, in essence a new layer of government superimposed on top of existing units, serves as a metropolitan planning, policy-making, and policy-coordinating agency. It reviews applications for federal funds from the region, guides regional planning and development, and opposes local actions that would endanger the overall welfare of the region. It also has taxing authority for the region. The Twin Cities model appears a ready candidate for transfer elsewhere, yet this has happened only in Portland, Oregon.

Portland adopted a bold new charter for the Portland Metropolitan Services District in 1992, which was amended by votes in 2000 and again in 2002.[48] It is a directly elected regional government serving three counties and 24 cities. Its nonpartisan commission members and elected executive officer have an impressive budget and more than 1,200 employees. They oversee waste collection, a zoo, recycling, waste disposal, transportation planning, and regional air and water quality programs, and they constructed Portland's new Convention Center. They have also created a greenbelt around the metro area that preserves extensive open areas.

By the People
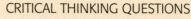

MAKING A DIFFERENCE

Community School Boards

The Wake County public school system in North Carolina, which includes the city of Raleigh and the surrounding area, had served for decades as a model of promoting socioeconomic diversity in its schools, in part through a comprehensive system of zoning and busing. However, the program came under increasing criticism from residents in the outlying areas of the county. Several unhappy citizens formed a group they called the Wake Schools Community Alliance (WSCA) and

campaigned to get their candidates onto the school board. As one of the founders said, "If you want to change the policy, you have to change the policy makers."*

The WSCA was successful in electing all four of its candidates to open seats on the Wake County school board in October of 2009. By May of 2010, the new school board had officially ended the system's diversity program in favor of a "neighborhood schools" format that critics argue will effectively segre-

gate schools into white wealthy suburban schools and poor black city schools.

Regardless of your views on school zoning and student assignment, the WSCA demonstrated that a small group of motivated citizens can make a huge difference in local politics. Are school board elections in your community partisan or nonpartisan? Are there groups organized to support school board candidates in your community besides political parties? If so, what are their guiding principles? Go to the next public school board meeting, and hear what is on the agenda. Talk to the board members, and express your views. Consider organizing a group to attend and to participate in the board's next meeting. Political officials respond to those who participate, so get involved.

CRITICAL THINKING QUESTIONS

1. How much power should elected school board members have to set school policy compared with the power of appointed officials such as superintendents and school principals?

2. Does the WSCA example represent a triumph of local political participation and democracy, or is it an example of those with greater resources shaping policy to fit their needs at the expense of those with fewer resources?

Students try to influence the Wake County school board decision.

* http://www.newsobserver.com/2009/09/30/118498/wake-diversity-policy-could-be.html.

Community Self-Help Countless people are coming together in their own neighborhoods to tackle common problems or to form neighborhood cooperatives. Some of these self-help groups simply handle baby-sitting arrangements or organize charity events or golf tournaments; others undertake neighborhood crime watches or Little League field construction. Local nonprofit groups in New York have built award-winning apartment complexes amid burned-out inner-city tenements. Other groups have mobilized to bring about storefront revitalization, street improvement, and area beautification programs by initiating farmers' markets, miniparks, and gardens.[49] The contemporary self-help movement is rooted in a past that has long been marked by volunteerism and local associations. In former times, the whole community often rallied when a neighbor's barn burned down; volunteer fire departments emerged out of this tradition.

Many local groups seeking help from city hall or from county officialdom give up after running into a maze of building codes, zoning rules, and countless regulations that inhibit innovation in local government. The alternative to despair is to do it yourself. And this is exactly what is happening at the grassroots level right now. The more successful experiments are watched carefully by the professionals at city hall, and some of the innovations are copied by those in office.

Sometimes progress or justice comes about because some activists take issues to court. Such was the case in bringing in alternative housing for lower-income residents in Mount Laurel, New Jersey. And it was also the case in addressing the fatal effects of toxic dumping by businesses in Woburn, Massachusetts.[50]

The Future of Metropolitan Reorganization

In most metropolitan regions, to combine city and suburbs would be to shift political power to the suburbs. In most northern centers, this would give suburban Republicans more control of city affairs. In other cases, it would enable Democrats to threaten the one-party Republican systems in the suburbs. Under these circumstances, neither Democratic leaders in the central cities nor Republicans in the suburbs show much enthusiasm for metropolitan schemes. African Americans and Hispanics often oppose area consolidation or similar reform proposals that would invariably dilute their political power, often severely.

Some people believe that solutions to metropolitan problems are beyond the capacity of the metropolis itself. They favor a strengthened role for the national government, with special emphasis on ensuring "equity" or on relating services directly to needs. Some advocate reviving federal revenue sharing. Others believe that the job must be done by the states, which hold the fundamental constitutional power. Still others put forward bold proposals to establish regional planning and governance arrangements that would embrace "citistate" areas that include two or more metropolitan clusters, like Baltimore and Washington, D.C.[51]

Today's aging central cities unquestionably face problems: congestion, smog, tension, loss of community, drugs, unsafe streets, neglected children, and visual pollution. They live with racial and ethnic tensions, not only white–black rivalry but rivalry among Latinos, Koreans, and a host of other racial and ethnic groups. Gangs, poverty, broken families, drive-by shootings, and drug-related crimes make life miserable for many who live in the inner cities. Yet is this new? Writers and critics since Thomas Jefferson have projected an unflattering image of the city as a cold, impersonal, and often brutal environment in which crime flourishes and people lose their dignity.

Supporters contend, however, that the big city is not only a place of smog and sprawl; it is the center of innovation, excitement, and vitality. In the last couple of decades, many major cities, including Boston, New York, and Washington, have promoted the redevelopment of run-down areas. In this view, the city offers social diversity and puts less community pressure on the individual to conform. The large

Great public projects at the local level sometimes require great persistence. Frank Lloyd Wright first designed the Monona Terrace Community and Convention Center, to be built on Lake Monona in Madison, Wisconsin, in 1938. However, political controversies, war, and Wright's death in 1959 delayed final approval and funding for the project until 1992, when voters narrowly approved construction, financed by local hotel room taxes and bonds.

community is a meeting place for talent from all around the nation and the world: dancers, musicians, writers, scholars, actors, and business leaders. On the other hand, some critics have charged that redevelopment is *gentrification,* displacing the original lower-income inhabitants with new wealthier residents. The displaced poor then concentrate even more in other blighted neighborhoods.

Some observers dismiss the notion of an "urban crisis." They contend that most city dwellers live more comfortably than ever before, with more and better housing, schools, and transportation. By any conceivable measure of material welfare, the present generation of urban dwellers is better off than other large groups of people anywhere at any time. Most cities, especially in the West and South, are thriving, and many older cities such as Boston, Pittsburgh, and Indianapolis are generally viewed as revived and vital, not decaying.

Throughout history, cities have been threatened by political, social, and environmental catastrophes. Urban decay, in one form or another, has always been with us.[52] Cities thrive because over time they respond to crises and because they are an economic necessity. The economy, transportation systems, past investments, and cultural contributions all make cities inevitable. How well cities survive, and with what mix of people, will depend on the tides of the national economy, the way our regions are organized, the way our social and economic policies are designed, the vision and leadership individual cities muster to build their future, and the degree to which our national leaders promote policies that can help our central cities.[53]

CHAPTER **SUMMARY**

8.1 Characterize local government in the United States and the basic relationship between state and local governments.

Local government is big, costly, and overlapping. Local governments in the United States have a variety of jurisdictions and structures, and they perform many essential functions. Because constitutional power is vested in the states, most counties, cities, towns, and special districts are agents of the state, although some local governments are granted constitutional home rule, which gives them greater independence.

8.2 Assess the role of county government.

Counties are extremely diverse in their functions, power, and size. They also vary in their structures, which have changed in recent decades. The most common government form at the county level is a board of county commissioners, although larger urban counties are moving to council–administrator or council-elected executive plans.

8.3 Explain the growth of suburbs and its implications for local governance.

Suburbs have been the fastest-growing population areas in the United States for several decades. There is no typical suburb. Although many suburbs are homogeneous, the suburban United States is highly heterogeneous. Suburbs are confronting the same problems as the urban areas they surround. Big cities and their suburbs are now referred to as metropolitan areas and are growing most rapidly in the South and West.

8.4 Outline the different ways of structuring city government, and describe the functions of mayors.

The most common government forms at the city level are the mayor–council and council–manager (city-manager) plans. Mayor–council governments generally have a strong mayor elected by voters, although some plans have a weak mayor elected by the council. Council–manager plans appoint a professional administrator. Mayors of major cities play many roles, including administering large city bureaucracies, working with the private sector and even foreign governments to spur economic development, and influencing policy making in the city.

8.5 Describe the challenges facing central cities and metro areas.

Inequalities between many central cities and their middle and outer rings of affluent suburbs are increasing. Central cities often struggle with economic hardship, racism, drugs, and crime. Fragmentation and dispersal of political authority in the metropolitan areas often make it difficult to treat their problems.

8.6 Evaluate strategies for meeting the various challenges of governance in metropolitan regions.

A variety of strategies have been used in an effort to solve these problems—annexation, agreements to furnish services, public authorities, special districts, regional coordinating and planning councils, city–county consolidations, federated government, and community self-help programs. Nearly all the strategies for meeting the challenges of growth and economic development involve shifts in political power.

CHAPTER **SELF-TEST**

8.1 Characterize local government in the United States and the basic relationship between state and local governments.

1. Why are there usually fewer obstacles to state interference in local matters than there are to federal interference in state matters?
   a. Local governments have less authority than state legislatures.
   b. Local governments are typically created by state legislatures.
   c. State constitutions often have to be approved every two years.
   d. State governments are often more permissive than local governments to outside influences.
2. What are two or three reasons why a state government may intervene in a local government's jurisdiction?

8.2 Assess the role of county government.

3. Which of the following is *not* a traditional function of counties?
   a. Tax collection
   b. Gathering of census data
   c. Administration of welfare programs
   d. Highway construction and maintenance
4. In a short essay, describe the role of counties in government. Consider their original role, how it has changed over time, and why.

8.3 Explain the growth of suburbs and its implications for local governance.

5. Which of the below is the most significant reason why suburbs have grown?
   a. People wanted to live in smaller communities where they would have more direct control over local government.
   b. The growing middle class grew to dislike the environment of cities.
   c. Traditional cities were unable to meet the growing technological needs of the population.
   d. People wanted to escape deteriorating inner cities.
6. Approximately what percentage of the U.S. population lives in suburban areas?
   a. 10 percent
   b. 25 percent
   c. 50 percent
   d. 80 percent
7. In a short essay, describe suburban governments. Consider their specific responsibilities and how they differ from urban governments.

8.4 Outline the different ways of structuring city government, and describe the functions of mayors.

8. Match the features of city charters on the left with the appropriate type of charter on the right.

   a. The mayor prepares and administers the budget.
   b. The mayor has broad appointment powers.
   c. There is no single administrative head for the city.
   d. Mayors are often chosen from members of an elected city council.
   e. The city council is elected in nonpartisan primaries and elections.
   f. The city council hires a professional administrator to manage city affairs.

   1. Strong mayor–council
   2. Weak mayor–council
   3. Council–manager

9. In a short essay, identify and describe the roles of a mayor in local politics, foreign policy, and economics. Consider the actions of famous mayors such as Rudolph Giuliani, Richard J. Daley, and Harold Washington.

8.5 Describe the challenges facing central cities and metro areas.

10. What percentage of U.S. children was estimated to be living in poverty in 2008?
    a. 5 percent
    b. 12 percent
    c. 19 percent
    d. 24 percent
11. Identify a cause of the current financial problems of many cities.

8.6 Evaluate strategies for meeting the various challenges of governance in metropolitan regions.

12. Which strategy includes residents coming together to form neighborhood cooperatives?
    a. Special districts
    b. Community self-help

c. City–county consolidations
d. Regional coordinating and planning councils

13. In a short essay, describe three strategies to govern metro regions. Consider how they are alike and how they are different. Which do you think would be most effective for the metro area closest to you?

Answers to selected questions: 1. b; 3. b; 5. d; 6. c; 8: a. 1, b. 1, c. 3, d. 2, e. 3, f. 3; 10. c; 12. b

---

mypoliscilab EXERCISES

Apply what you learned in this chapter with these resources on MyPoliSciLab.

Read on **mypoliscilab.com**

eText: Chapter 8

Study and **Review** on **mypoliscilab.com**

Pre-Test
Post-Test
Chapter Exam
Flashcards

Watch on **mypoliscilab.com**

Video: Battling City Corruption

Explore on **mypoliscilab.com**

Simulation: You Are the Mayor and Need to Get a Town Budget Passed

---

KEY TERMS

unitary system, p. 158
constitutional home rule, p. 158
county, p. 159
municipality, p. 159
township, p. 159

metropolis, p. 159
metropolitan area, p. 159
eminent domain, p. 164
charter, p. 165
mayor–council charter, p. 166

weak mayor–council form, p. 166
strong mayor–council form, p. 167
council–manager plan, p. 167
gentrification, p. 171

ADDITIONAL RESOURCES

FURTHER READING

KENNETH D. ACKERMAN, *Boss Tweed: The Rise and Fall of the Corrupt Pol Who Conceived the Soul of Modern New York* (Carroll & Graf, 2005).

GERALD BENJAMIN AND RICHARD P. NATHAN, *Regionalism and Realism: A Study of Governments in the New York Metropolitan Area* (Brookings Institution Press, 2001).

FRANK M. BRYAN, *Real Democracy: The New England Town Meeting and How It Works* (Cambridge University Press, 2004).

ADAM COHEN AND ELIZABETH TAYLOR, *American Pharaoh: Mayor Richard J. Daley—His Battle for Chicago and the Nation* (Little, Brown, 2000).

PETER DREIER, JOHN MOLLENKOPF, AND TODD SWANSTROM, *Place Matters: Metropolitics for the Twenty-First Century* (University Press of Kansas, 2001).

JEFFREY R. HENIG AND WILBER C. RICH, EDS., *Mayors in the Middle: Politics, Race, and Mayoral Control of Urban Schools* (Princeton University Press, 2003).

DENNIS R. JUDD AND TODD SWANSTROM, *City Politics: Private Power and Public Policy,* 7th ed. (Longman, 2007).

SUZANNE M. LELAND AND KURT THURMAIER, EDS., *Case Studies of City–County Consolidation* (Sharpe, 2004).

HENRY J. PRATT, *Churches and Urban Government in Detroit and New York,* 1895–1994 (Wayne State University Press, 2004).

DICK SIMPSON, *Inside Urban Politics: Voices from America's Cities and Suburbs* (Longman, 2004).

RAPHAEL J. SONENSHEIN, *The City at Stake: Secession, Reform, and the Battle for Los Angeles* (Princeton University Press, 2006).

HEATHER ANN THOMPSON, *Whose Detroit? Politics, Labor, and Race in a Modern American City* (Cornell University Press, 2002).

J. PHILLIP THOMPSON, *Double Trouble: Black Mayors, Black Communities, and the Call for a Deep Democracy* (Oxford University Press, 2006).

ROGER VOGEL AND JOHN J. HARRIGAN, *Political Change in the Metropolis,* 8th ed.

(Longman, 2007). See also *Governing: The Magazine of States and Localities,* published monthly by Congressional Quarterly; *The National Civic Review,* published by the National Civic League; *The Municipal Yearbook,* published annually by the International City Management Association; and the Web site of the U.S. Conference of Mayors at www.usmayors.org.

WEB SITES

www.naco.org/ The National Association of Counties conducts research, reports on policy initiatives, operates a variety of programs, and represents the interests of county governments in Washington D.C.

www.natat.org/ The National Association of Towns and Townships lobbies in Washington D.C. for policies and programs that help small communities, towns, and suburbs acquire their fair share of federal funding and serve their residents.

www.nlc.org/ The National League of Cities, the oldest national organization representing municipal governments throughout the United States, seeks to strengthen and promote cities as centers of opportunity, leadership, and governance.

www.usmayors.org/ The United States Conference of Mayors is the official nonpartisan organization of cities with populations of 30,000 or more. It lobbies the federal government and provides a forum for the exchange of ideas.

www.icma.org The International City/County Management Association's mission is to create excellence in local governance by developing and fostering professional local government management worldwide

Making State and Local Policy

At least since the 1983 Nation at Risk Report,[1] which documented a range of short-comings in public education in the United States, state and local governments have been searching for innovative ways to reform education policy. One plan being explored is to provide cash incentives to students for good performance. Roland Fryer Jr., an economist at Harvard University, conducted a major experiment recently to explore whether such incentives would work.[2] Public schools in four different cities—Chicago, Dallas, Washington, D.C., and New York City—participated in the study. Some were randomly assigned to receive no form of payment, whereas others were selected for a variety of payment programs. Some were paid primarily for outcomes, mostly in the form of test scores and grades. Others were paid primarily for behaviors—reading, attending school, participating in class discussions, etc. Although the results were mixed, fairly strong support emerged in favor of providing students with cash benefits for performing tasks that are completely under their control, like reading and attendance. Less success was found for programs focused strictly on grades. Fryer speculates this is because students do not feel they have complete control over grades, and they do not always know which efforts translate into better grades.

Not everyone supports what Fryer is attempting. Psychologists like Edward Deci of the University of Rochester note a number of studies that suggest providing money as an incentive often devalues or diminishes the action itself. Paying someone to perform a task can turn it from something a person intrinsically enjoys into something done for money. Turning learning into work may diminish a student's love of learning or reduce the likelihood of it ever developing in the first place. Fryer and his supporters respond that millions of kids are not learning now for love or any other reason, and if cash incentives work, that it is worth trying. What do you think? Does paying students to perform well teach them to value education, or does it teach them to learn for pay rather than for personal growth? Although Fryer's initial findings look promising, do you think the effect would last over time, particularly if the payments were reduced or eliminated later on? These are the kinds of policy innovations states and localities must consider as they seek to provide the best policies they can for the lowest cost.

Of course, state and local officials constantly wrestle with a wide range of policy decisions and controversies beyond public education. What is the best way to attract business and increase the number of jobs yet encourage environmental quality? How should the state deal with the soaring costs of providing Medicaid? What can be done about traffic congestion? And what role should state and local authorities play regarding terrorism threats?

Mayors, governors, state legislators, county commissioners, judges, union officials, developers, Chambers of Commerce, political party leaders, and citizens strive to develop public policy compromises to such dilemmas. These deliberations receive little media attention compared with decisions made in Washington, D.C., yet the effect of these choices on our day-to-day lives is often equally or perhaps even more important.

This chapter examines some of the policy areas that consume much of the attention and budgets of state and local governments. State and local governments spend most of their budgets on education, welfare and health-related matters, highway and transportation systems, and safety and law enforcement. We will discuss them as well as the issues of planning and regulation.

CHAPTER OUTLINE & CHAPTER LEARNING OBJECTIVES

Public Education

LEARNING **OBJECTIVE**

9.1 Outline local, state, and federal government roles in elementary and secondary education.

In ancient Greece, Plato and Aristotle saw education as a vital task of government. Thomas Jefferson, too, was convinced that an educated citizenry was essential to democratic government. But only in the twentieth century did it become generally accepted that government should provide tax-supported education for everyone. Today, free public education for grades 1 through 12 is an established practice in the United States and specifically provided for in many state constitutions. Approximately one-quarter of all state and local government expenditures are for kindergarten–high school (K–12) education.[3]

State and local governments have the primary responsibility for education and provide most of the money to pay for it (see Figure 9–1). Since 1979, overall state funding for education has surpassed local government funding, with the exception of a few states in which revenues for education continue to come primarily from local government. The state role in financing education has increased during the last generation as a result, at least in part, of pressure from state courts to equalize expenditures on education across local school districts. Across the states, spending per student varies widely. The national average in 2006–2007 was $9,683 but ranged from a high of more than $16,163 in New Jersey to a low of $5,706 in Utah.[4]

Administration of Public Education

Unlike most other democracies, which typically administer and fund education at the national level, the basic unit responsible for public elementary and secondary education in the United States is the local school district, and there are slightly less than 14,000 of these.[5] In nearly all districts, voters elect a board of education that sets the school tax rate, appoints a superintendent of schools and other personnel, hires teachers, and runs the schools from kindergarten through grade 12. Each state has a state superintendent of public instruction or commissioner of education. In about a third of the states, this official is popularly elected; in nearly all states, he or she shares authority with a state board of education.

Although actual operation of the public schools is the responsibility of the local community, state officers have important supervisory powers and distribute financial assistance to the communities. State money is distributed according to many formulas, but the trend is toward giving more money to poorer communities to equalize education spending. Many policies are established at the state level, and it is up to local authorities to enforce them. They must ensure that new school buildings meet the minimum specifications set by the state. In some states, officials have the authority to set the course of study in schools—that is, to determine what must be taught and what may not be taught. In several states, especially in the South and Southwest, state authorities determine which textbooks will be used as well, and there is an increasing push in many states to adopt common standards for performance for students.[6]

The Role of the Federal Government in Public Schools

After the former Soviet Union's successful 1957 launch of *Sputnik*, the first satellite put into orbit, Congress responded by providing funding to strengthen mathematics and science education. In 1965, Congress adopted the Elementary and Secondary Education Act, the major federal law dealing with education. The federal government's share in financing local education rose from approximately 2 percent in 1940 to approximately 9.2 percent by 2007.

Through the Department of Education, which was created in 1979, and other agencies, the federal government makes grants to the states for facilities, equipment, scholarships, loans, research, model programs, and general aid at the elementary, secondary, and higher education levels. But federal control over how the money may be spent comes with these federal dollars. Today, federal regulations cover school lunch programs, employment practices, admissions, record keeping, care of experimental animals, and many other matters. Indeed, local school authorities regularly complain that there are more regulations than dollars. With the passage of No Child Left Behind in 2002, and the more recent grant competition developed by the

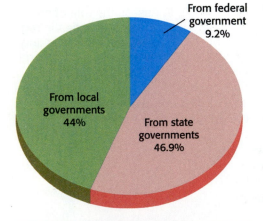

FIGURE 9–1 Spending on Public Elementary and Secondary Schools.

■ *What are some of the implications of the vast majority of public education spending coming from state and local governments rather than the federal government?*

SOURCE: *Digest of Education Statistics, 2007,* Table 162.

Obama administration called "Race to the Top," the role of the federal government in shaping what schools do has continued to increase.

Educational Controversies

What shall be taught, and who shall teach it, are hotly contested matters. Schools are favorite targets for groups eager to have children taught the "right" things. Of course, little agreement exists on what the "right" things are. Religious groups want family values and morality emphasized, and some want constraints imposed on the teaching of evolution. Others want the schools to teach facts only, without regard for values, especially in areas such as sex education. Labor leaders want students to get the right impression about labor and its role in society. Business leaders are eager for children to see the free enterprise system in a favorable light and want high school graduates who will be well-prepared for increasingly technical jobs. Minorities and women's groups want textbooks to present issues from the perspective they consider correct. Professional educators and civil libertarians try to isolate schools from the pressures of all outside groups—or at least the ones with which they disagree. They say decisions regarding what textbooks should be assigned, what books should be placed in school libraries, and how curricula should be designed are best left to professionals.

There have been many attempts to keep public education relatively free of partisan political influences. For example, local school boards are usually nonpartisan and are often elected when no other partisan races are on the ballot. This separation is strongly supported by parent–teacher associations, the National Education Association, the American Federation of Teachers, and other educational groups. However, education is of such concern to so many people, and there are so many different ideas about how schools should be run, that it can never be fully separated from politics.

Public School Integration   During the 1970s and 1980s, battles were fought in many cities over how to overcome racial segregation in the public schools. In many places, people lived in segregated neighborhoods, which meant that eliminating overt segregation at neighborhood-centered schools would not produce racially diverse schools. One method, which became controversial, was to bus students from one neighborhood to another to achieve racial balance in the schools and overcome the effects of past segregation.

A woman observes a hearing of the Texas State Board of Education, which determines what goes into the textbooks for students in Texas. The decision has far reaching ramifications because what Texas wants ends up in textbooks used all over the country. The Board made a number of controversial changes to their social studies curriculum in 2010 which numerous historians argued were motivated by promoting a conservative ideology rather than accurately reflecting history. ■ *Who should decide what is taught in public schools?*

Of the People

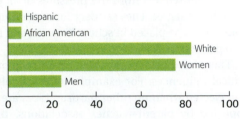

Teachers in the Classroom

Lessons on diversity often start in the classroom. Yet, while the changing face of America has impacted the makeup of students in the classroom, it has had little affect on the teachers, the majority of whom are white and female. According to the most current statistics from the U.S. Census Bureau, the percentage of women in the classroom has actually increased somewhat during the past 20 years in elementary, junior high, and senior high schools.

The large percentage of women in the classroom dates back to the first public schools but also reflects the lack of interest among men in teaching. Salaries for teaching are lower than for comparable jobs requiring a college degree elsewhere in the U.S. economy, in part because public schools are often a target for local budget cuts and in part because women are generally underpaid regardless of their profession.

Minorities have made slightly more progress in becoming public school teachers,

in part because colleges and universities are working harder to recruit minorities to the profession and because public schools are under greater pressure to increase teacher diversity. Although the percentage of minority teachers has risen only slightly during the past two decades, the trend appears to be toward greater representation, especially in junior and senior high schools. When students see the changing face of teaching, they may be more likely to embrace the changing face of diversity in the U.S. economy generally.

Although the U.S. Census Bureau has not followed the percentage of female and minority teachers in private schools as closely, its 2000 figures suggest no difference between the percentage of female teachers in public and private schools but a significantly lower percentage of minority teachers in private schools.

CRITICAL THINKING QUESTIONS

1. What differences might it make in the classroom to have more minority teachers?

2. In what ways may education have to change in order to attract more men to teach in public schools?

Demographic Characteristics of Full-Time Public School Teachers, 2007–2008

Bar chart showing: Hispanic (small), African American (small), White (~80), Women (~75), Men (~20); x-axis 0 to 100.

SOURCE: National Center for Education Statistics, U.S. Department of Education, "Characteristics of Public, Private, and Bureau of Indian Education Elementary and Secondary School Teachers in the United States: Results from the 2007–08 Schools and Staffing Survey," Table 2 and Table 3, http://nces.ed.gov/pubs2009/2009324/tables.asp.

However, as more middle-class families—many of them white—moved from the cities to the suburbs, busing became an ineffective tool to achieve integration because the courts declined in most cases to require states to integrate cities and suburbs. Racial segregation is still the pattern for the inner-city schools of most large cities in parts of the North, South, and West of the country. Indeed, during the last 15 years, substantial slippage toward segregation has occurred in most of the states that had experienced solid desegregation.[7] In 2009, for the first time, the majority of students in public schools in the South were nonwhite.[8] At the same time, white flight away from the public schools has caused the percentage of students in private schools in the South to double.[9]

Standards and Testing   In 1990, only 14 states had standards for their core curriculum, but now nearly every state has adopted standards for subjects such as mathematics, reading, and science. Some have also adopted "high-stakes testing," tests children must pass to go on to the next grade level or graduate from high school. Advocates of standards and testing argue that such devices are necessary to raise the quality of education provided and to ensure accountability.

Opponents argue, however, that testing is unlikely to produce positive changes in education. Some critics contend that it is unfair and misleading to use standardized tests to measure learning. Minority students and students in districts in impoverished areas may not do well on these tests, and expecting them to do so without addressing inequities in educational resources is counterproductive and unfair. Other critics worry that the use of such tests will force teachers to "teach to the test." Sensitive to the fact that their students will be compared with students in other classes, teachers will devote extensive time to subjects covered on the test, ignore other vibrant topics, and overemphasize test-taking strategies. Not surprisingly, several companies have developed entire sets of textbooks and other curricular materials designed explicitly around the state tests. Finally, some people worry that states will adopt standards that are not very demanding. These critics point out that although states are celebrating gains in state tests, results from a nationwide test given to a sample of students every year show little to no educational improvement.[10]

After much debate and encouragement from George W. Bush, Congress adopted one of the most controversial educational reforms in decades, the No Child Left Behind Act of 2002. A reauthorization of the Elementary and Secondary Education Act, the law requires that, in order to receive federal funds, states must design state standards and annually test children in grades three through eight to determine whether schools are making adequate progress in achieving the standards. Schools that do not make sufficient progress can be identified as "failing" schools, and parents have the right to move their children to another school.

Although the general goals of the No Child Left Behind Act have been embraced, policy makers and educators still struggle with how best to fund and implement the standardized testing. They dislike having their local schools labeled as "in need of improvement" or "failing," and local authorities complain that state and national standards often measure factors beyond the control of a particular school and its staff. "It's really not fair to judge a school whose kids come without having ever read a book, and compare it to a school where kids go to the library and have libraries in their home," says Lynn Stockleg, a middle school teacher in Tulsa, Oklahoma. "It's rather discouraging when you're one of those schools. You know you're working very, very hard and yet your scores are consistently low."[11]

State and local officials have also discovered that complying with the No Child Left Behind Act is far more expensive than originally estimated. One study suggests that fully implementing the requirements of the Act could cost more than $140 billion, yet the federal government has appropriated only a fraction of that amount.[12] State and local officials are seeking more federal funding and more flexibility in implementing the goals of the Act. An independent, bipartisan commission studying the implementation of the Act acknowledged the need for some flexibility but also recommended new requirements because "dramatic improvements" were still needed.[13]

Vouchers   Some reformers contend that we will not see real progress in public education until we inject competition into the system by permitting parents to shop for schools the way they shop for goods and services in the economy. One way to do this is to provide parents with a set amount of money—in the form of **vouchers**—they could use to pay for part or all of their children's education in a public or private school of their choice.[14]

Voucher programs have been tried since the mid-1980s in New York, Indianapolis, San Antonio, and Milwaukee. Advocates say vouchers could help the neediest students escape failed schools and get valuable academic preparation at private or religious schools.

Opponents criticize the voucher system, even for public schools, for the negative impact it may have on school reform. Their main contention is that vouchers will badly injure financially struggling public schools by diverting much-needed money. Opponents also argue vouchers would promote "skimming," meaning higher-achieving students would opt out of public schools, leaving behind students who struggle academically and have discipline problems. In rural areas, where few private schools exist, some people fear that vouchers may encourage parents to keep the money under the guise of providing "private" home schooling.

The debate over vouchers has also raised questions about the separation of church and state. Some proponents have argued that voucher programs should include religious schools. More than 80 percent of the students receiving vouchers in places such as Milwaukee and San Antonio attend religious schools, most of them Catholic. Opponents of vouchers for religious schools argue that such an arrangement violates the constitutional separation of church and state. They fear also that in some parts of the country, vouchers would be used for schools that largely exclude racial minorities.

vouchers
Money provided by the government to parents for payment of their children's tuition in a public or private school of their choice.

Secretary of Education Arne Duncan participates in a "Let's Read, Let's Move" event at Columbia Heights Youth Club. Secretary Duncan has led the Obama administration's Race to the Top program, which awards federal money to school systems that adopt reforms the administration hopes will improve public education. ■ *What role should the federal government play in setting education policy?*

In 2002, a divided U.S. Supreme Court ruled that poor children could be granted public money (vouchers) to attend religious schools without violating the separation of church and state provisions in the Bill of Rights. Chief Justice William Rehnquist wrote that his majority opinion was "not an endorsement of religious schooling" but merely a means "to assist poor children in failed schools."[15] Other state courts, however, have ruled that voucher plans violate provisions in state constitutions. In 2004, Colorado's supreme court ruled that the state's voucher program violated the state constitution's requirement for local control of schools. Plaintiffs also charged that the voucher program violated the constitution's provisions regarding the separation of church and state, but the court did not decide that issue.[16] Voters have defeated proposals for school vouchers in several states, including Oregon, Washington, Michigan, California, and Utah. The political movement pushing vouchers has lost some of its steam because of these defeats, the intense opposition of the teachers' unions, and court rulings that said poor families do not have the right to demand vouchers from state and local governments to allow their children to attend better schools.

Charter Schools   Another educational reform that provides a publicly funded alternative to standard public schools is the **charter school.** Some states now grant charters to individuals or groups to start schools and receive public funds if they can meet standards specified by law. In exchange for meeting specified learning standards, these schools are exempt from adhering to many of the procedural requirements that must be followed by traditional public schools. Unlike vouchers, which provide funds to the parents, charter schools are under the direct authority of local school boards. There are more than 3,600 charter schools, with more than a million students. Charter schools are the fastest-growing form of choice in K–12 education, and they received a big boost from the federally enacted No Child Left Behind Act, which holds out conversion to charter schools as a possible solution for ineffective traditional public schools.

charter school
A publicly funded alternative to standard public schools in some states, initiated when individuals or groups receive charters; charter schools must meet state standards.

Like privatization in other government services, charter schools are intended to interject the competition of the marketplace into elementary and secondary education. Proponents believe that reducing state and local regulation of charter schools will enable them to improve teacher quality and adopt innovative educational programs. Charter schools generally have more flexibility to hire and fire teachers and are not subject to the collective bargaining arrangements that prevail in many public school systems. Some of their teachers may not have as extensive training as certified teachers in traditional public schools, yet proponents maintain that classroom performance is more important than the undergraduate major of the teacher.

Some charter schools have been very successful. Two "Teach for America" alumni launched a series of charter schools under the name Knowledge Is Power Programs or KIPP. With elementary schools in Houston, New York City, North Carolina, and elsewhere, they have demonstrated effective results. The key to their success is a strict and strong initial commitment by parents and pupils to a philosophy of hard work, longer hours of class time and homework, and no shortcuts. That, coupled with carefully recruited, dedicated teachers, has proved successful.[17]

Another success story is California's first charter school, the Vaughn Street Elementary School, now called the Vaughn Next Century Learning Center. Most of the children at this school speak English as a second language and live in dangerous neighborhoods. In 1993, when the charter school was established, Vaughn Street's pupils' test scores were some of the lowest in the state. Under Principal Yvonne Chan's leadership, test scores have steadily risen, and the school is considered an educational model. Chan attributes these improvements to the greater autonomy of a charter school that allowed her to develop smaller classes, accountability for teachers, and numerous community partnerships.[18]

Some educational activists oppose charter schools. Teachers' unions fear they may lose their collective bargaining position with school boards if charter schools multiply. Other opponents contend that in school systems already strapped for money, it does not make sense to divert funds from struggling schools to such untested experiments. Critics also raise questions about what will be taught in

The 2010 award-winning documentary film, *Waiting for Superman,* explores the state of public education in America. It investigates the practices of successful charter schools to create a model for how America can turn its failing public schools around. ■ *To what degree do you think teachers' compensation should depend on the performance of their students?*

charter schools, the level of teacher competence, and whether religious schools should qualify for public funds as charter schools.

The debate over charter schools is complicated by the fact that they vary widely in quality across the country. A nationwide study of schools conducted by the National Center for Education Statistics within the federal Department of Education found that fourth graders who attended traditional public schools did better in reading and mathematics than their counterparts at charter schools.[19] This led critics of the charter movement to say there is no credible evidence that deregulating public education leads to higher student achievement. Supporters contend that most charter schools enroll students with academic and family problems who are poorly served by traditional public schools. Plainly, there are some excellent and some below-average charter schools. Opponents and supporters agree that good-quality schools must be constructed—one at a time.

Higher Education

Public higher education has generally been provided by states. States support many kinds of universities and colleges, including land-grant universities such as Michigan State University, which were created by the Morrill Act of 1862. In addition, since the end of World War II, there has been a major expansion in the number and size of public *community colleges,* which typically receive funds from local as well as state governments and which allow students to attend the first two years of college or receive a technical education in their own communities.

LEARNING **OBJECTIVE**
9.2 Assess the concerns about state funding of higher education.

Administration of Higher Education

State colleges and universities are governed by boards appointed by the governor in some states and elected by the voters in others. These boards are designed to give public institutions of higher education some independence from state politics, even though many public universities rely heavily on their state legislatures and governors for funding.

With approximately 80 percent of the more than 15 million college students now attending publicly supported institutions, the control and support of higher education have become significant political issues. States have created boards with varying degrees of control over operations and budgets. In addition, governors have tried to impose controls on universities and colleges that many university administrators insist are inappropriate. Yet institutions of higher education have greater independence from political oversight than other tax-supported institutions. Publicly funded colleges and universities usually can control teaching loads, internal procedures, areas of teaching emphasis, hiring and promotion, and the allocation of funds among internal units.

Funding Higher Education

In the twenty-first century, we face questions of access and funding for our colleges and universities. Access to colleges and universities for all students who wish to go has long been the declared goal in many states, but is it desirable? Should students be required to pay higher tuition to cover the cost of their education, or should federal and state governments provide more student aid? What should states do about the underrepresentation of minorities in our colleges and universities? And should illegal immigrants be allowed to attend state colleges at in-state tuition rates?

Tuition at state universities has increased during the last few decades, often at two or three times the rate of inflation. Professors' salaries have not kept pace with tuition increases and have grown only slightly more than the rate of inflation. Although many people agree we need an infusion of new money to update college laboratories, improve libraries, and recruit and keep first-rate college professors, there is little consensus about who should pay for these efforts. The federal government is the chief supplier of student financial aid, and many states are now making major efforts to expand their programs of student aid. Many states, such as Georgia, California, Washington, and Alaska, are investing in programs aimed at keeping top students in their states at state-run as well as independent colleges.

In Illinois, where the state's share of the University of Illinois operating costs has decreased from 38.8 percent to 16.4 percent in the last two decades, staff has been eliminated, faculty have faced salary freezes and unpaid furloughs, student aid has been cut, and classes have been canceled. Parents and teachers protested the cuts to education, but the broke state government has few other options.

Most institutions of higher education—both independent and state-run—receive some kind of government subsidy, through a variety of devices so that students do not pay the full cost of their education. The federal government and most states provide need-based financial assistance in the form of loans and grants, and students with the greatest financial need at the higher-cost institutions are eligible for the most aid. Thus, higher education has what is in effect a limited voucher system; students receive funds and can choose the kind of college or university that best serves their needs. Because of financial aid, we have avoided a *two-track system*—one set of colleges and universities for the poor and another for the rich. Along with students from higher-income families, low-income students can be found in most high-cost independent colleges and universities.

Although states spend 8 to 15 percent of their budgets on higher education, funding for public universities must compete with the rising costs of other state services, notably Medicaid, transportation, elementary and secondary education, and the criminal justice system. In most states, the legislature has an easier time controlling appropriations for higher education on a yearly basis than spending on these other functions. As a result, state funding of public colleges and universities is unstable, rising when state revenues are growing but declining sharply during economic downturns.[20]

With shrinking state budgets in 2009 and 2010, many states' higher education systems have seen dramatic cuts to their budgets. The Center on Budget and Policy Priorities reported in May of 2010 that 41 states had made significant cuts to their higher education budgets.[21] Many states are therefore experimenting with new ways to fund higher education. Some, including New Mexico and West Virginia, have turned to lottery money to fund scholarships for students. Vermont is using lottery revenue to replace some of the state's higher education appropriation from general funds.[22] Colorado adopted a program that gives each undergraduate a voucher to cover some of the costs of attending state public institutions and also gave those institutions more control over setting tuition.[23] As state funds for higher education have declined in many states, public colleges and universities have been allowed to raise tuition levels. Gradually, the burden of paying for college is being shifted from the state to students and their parents, a change that may further reduce access to public higher education for low- and moderate-income families.[24]

Social Services

LEARNING OBJECTIVE

9.3 Describe the role of the state in public assistance programs, and assess the challenges facing state social service programs.

What role should state and local governments play in making sure all citizens have their basic housing, health, and nutritional needs met? How important are these social services compared with government's obligation to provide police and fire protection, education, parks and recreation, and other services? For much of our history, human service needs were left to private charities that ran orphanages, old-age homes, hospitals, and other institutions. Philosophically, this reliance on private charity fit well with U.S. notions of limited government and self-reliance. That view changed dramatically during the Great Depression of the 1930s, when poverty, unemployment, and homelessness affected such large numbers of people that the government could no longer act as if these were private matters. Then in the mid-1960s, with President Lyndon Johnson's Great Society agenda, the nation embarked on a second major wave of social service programs, which Johnson called the War on Poverty. Today, we continue to debate whether such programs accomplish their goals and whether alternatives would prove more successful.

DECIDE

Should the Federal Government Encourage Increased State Funding of Higher Education?

As discussed in the chapter, the cost of higher education is rising. Financing higher education is a shared responsibility of students and parents, institutions of higher education, the federal government, and state governments. Yet, state spending on higher education is unstable; it tends to rise when state revenues are growing and decline during economic downturns. Arguing that states need to consistently bear their part of the burden, a proposed measure would require a state to increase spending on higher education each year by an amount equivalent to its average increase during the previous five years. If a state does not maintain this level of increased spending, it would not receive new federal matching funds through the Leveraging Educational Assistance Partnership program, a program that rewards states for supporting low-income students.

What do you think? Should the federal government employ this approach to encourage increased state funding of higher education? What are some of the arguments for or against this?

THINKING IT THROUGH

Supporters of this approach charge that the increased cost of higher education has been borne by students and their parents, institutions of higher education, and the federal government. The cyclical nature of state spending on higher education creates problems for institutions of higher education as well as enrolled students who often must pay higher tuition and fees, even though they too are facing financial challenges. Also, supporters note, during periods of economic growth, state spending increases slowly, and it often takes several years to return to its prerecession level. States need to do their part, supporters declare. "We're pleased that Congress, for the first time, is looking to states and tasking states with some responsibility," said Daniel J. Hurley, director of state relations and policy analysis for the American Association of State Colleges and Universities.*

Critics argue that in the long run this requirement would reduce rather than increase state funding for higher education. The National Association of State Budget Officers estimated that between 2008 and 2012, the provision would lead states to spend about 10 percent less than they would otherwise. Critics assume that in order to protect themselves from funding obligations in the future, states would limit increases in appropriations to the smallest amount possible, and they would be discouraged from appropriating large spending increases during periods of economic growth. Opponents also complain that such a provision would constitute unjustified meddling by the federal government into state affairs. The federal government does not provide sufficient funding for higher education to justify this kind of mandate, they observe. "It would set a dangerous precedent for federal intrusion into state policy and appropriations authority," charged RaeAnn Kelsch, Republican legislator from North Dakota and chair of the National Conference of State Legislatures (NCSL) education standing committee.

Critical Thinking Questions

1. Who should pay most of the cost of higher education—students, their parents, the federal government, or state governments?

2. Does the federal government have to cover a larger share of the cost of higher education in order to justify a mandate that state governments maintain a certain level of funding for education over time?

*Sara Hebel, "Disputed Plan Would Let Congress Weigh In on State Budgets for Colleges," *Chronicle of Higher Education,* February 29, 2008, p. 25

Public Assistance

Pressure to reform the welfare system increased among both Democrats and Republicans in the last decades of the twentieth century. The number of U.S. families on welfare—programs that provide assistance to poor families with children—increased from approximately 600,000 households in 1950 to more than 5 million in the early 1990s, growing 13 times as fast as the general population.[25] Why such growth? Some said this increase occurred because those who were eligible for assistance were finally receiving it. Others charged that "government handouts" robbed recipients of the self-confidence they need to go to work and succeed; in this sense, dependence on welfare is viewed as a curse.

In 1996, fundamental changes were made in welfare policy, including the roles of the federal and state governments. Landmark legislation called **Temporary Assistance for Needy Families (TANF)** replaced the 60-year-old program known as Aid to Families with Dependent Children (AFDC).[26] Under AFDC, states provided monthly cash payments to poor families, largely to single mothers to help them take care of their children. States set different benefit levels, which varied enormously, and states determined whether a smaller or larger proportion of poor families were eligible. The federal government picked

Temporary Assistance for Needy Families (TANF)

A federal welfare reform law that replaced Aid to Families with Dependent Children, the 60-year-old assistance program for poor families with children. This 1996 law strengthened work requirements for recipients, limited the time that families can receive benefits, and gave states flexibility to develop service programs supporting work, marriage, and self-sufficiency.

up most of the costs of AFDC because it matched state spending at rates ranging from one federal dollar for every state dollar spent (in wealthy states such as Connecticut) to about three federal dollars for every state dollar (in low-income states such as Mississippi).

Most of the administrative burdens, however, fell on state and local governments. Every state had a department of human services or welfare that either administered welfare programs directly or, in 13 states, supervised county officials who administered these programs. Administration of AFDC was strictly regulated by federal rules, which were designed to minimize errors and fraud and to ensure that families got the benefits they were entitled to receive given their financial circumstances.

TANF differs from AFDC in several ways. First, it imposes new restrictions on families receiving cash assistance. Welfare is no longer an entitlement for families in financial need. Under most circumstances, adults in the family must work soon after they begin getting benefits, and families may no longer receive benefits indefinitely—most can receive cash assistance for only five years in an adult's lifetime.

Second, TANF expanded the goals of welfare policy. Instead of trying to make it possible for women to care for children rather than work, the program now aims to help parents, most of whom are women, find jobs. Teen parents receiving cash benefits are discouraged from setting up their own households and are required to attend school and live at home with their parents. In addition, states are encouraged to adopt programs that promote marriage and reduce out-of-wedlock births.

Third, states were given greater flexibility in designing and administering welfare policies. States now receive block grants from the federal government and may use these grants to support a wide variety of programs; they need not spend most of their welfare dollars on monthly cash payments to families, as they did under AFDC. Rather, states may spend the grant dollars on services, such as child care for working families, transportation assistance, help in getting and keeping jobs, or programs that promote sexual abstinence among unmarried teens. States are also freed from many of the federal rules they followed when administering AFDC. For instance, they no longer need to use public bureaucracies to administer welfare but may instead use private agencies, even including for-profit corporations and religious institutions.

In exchange for this flexibility, each state must report to the federal government what proportion of its welfare cases (that is, families with able-bodied adults receiving cash assistance) are either working at jobs or engaged in some other work-related activity (such as job search). Each state also files a plan with the secretary of health and human services every two years that describes its TANF program, such as how the state will ensure that recipients engage in work activities within two years of receiving benefits, and the state's goals in preventing and reducing out-of-wedlock pregnancies. Money is distributed to states based on the highest amount of federal funding they received in the years just before TANF was passed. To continue receiving federal funds, states must spend at least 75 percent of the amount they spent in 1994 to ensure that states continue to pay their fair share. Grants to states may also be cut if the states fail to engage enough of their adult cases in work activities. Additional federal funds are available to states as incentives for high performance and as loans if states experience financial hardship.

After TANF was enacted, many states used their flexibility to make major changes in their welfare programs. Some states adopted policies that imposed even stronger restrictions on cash benefits than did the federal law. For example, most states require families with able-bodied adults to participate immediately in work-related activities, not only after two years as required by federal law. Also, 20 states provide no additional benefits to families in which children were born while the family was receiving welfare; 8 states have stricter time limits than the federal law on how long families may receive cash assistance in their lifetimes; and 20 states withdraw all benefits to a family not complying with work requirements even after only one violation.[27]

However, many states have also adopted policies and administrative practices that provide assistance to family heads who seek employment. Nearly all states, with federal help, have greatly increased their spending on child care for low-income working families. Nearly all states also allow families to keep a larger share of the income they receive from jobs than was the case under AFDC. Most states have also increased their provision of employment services to welfare families and those who recently left welfare, including programs that help parents to prepare themselves for jobs, find jobs, train for better jobs, and pay for some of the expenses that go along with work, such as transportation and clothing. Some states have experimented with **workfare** programs designed to help welfare recipients who do not have preschool-aged children develop the self-confidence, skills, and habits necessary for regular employment; many states have developed **responsibility contracts,** requiring recipients to sign a written agreement specifying their responsibilities and outlining a plan for them to obtain work and achieve self-sufficiency.[28]

Partly as a result of the 1996 welfare reform, the number of families receiving welfare has dropped by 63 percent since the law was enacted—from 4.4 million families in August 1996 to 1.7 million families in December 2007.[29] Much evidence also suggests that welfare reform has greatly increased employment rates among low-income single mothers with children, the most common heads of families on welfare. It is widely accepted that welfare reforms have contributed to changes in the sources of income among poor families with children; public cash assistance has declined substantially, while earnings from jobs have grown.

Not all these developments were caused by federal and state welfare reforms. They were doubtless helped by the booming economy of the late 1990s, which created many new jobs.[30] As economic growth slowed after 2000, the employment rate of single mothers declined, and the number of single mothers who neither work nor receive welfare increased. A much larger proportion of the families living in poverty are now *not* receiving welfare benefits. Also, the reforms did not seem to help the hardest cases— typically people with little education, limited skills, and no work experience. Although poverty rates fell in the 1990s, they have since risen, especially among children.[31] One critic who worked in the Clinton administration when federal welfare reform was passed, Georgetown University's Peter Edelman, says: "The main lesson of the 1996 law is that having a job and earning a livable income are two different things."[32]

In early 2006, TANF was reauthorized by Congress, which adopted even more stringent work requirements for people on cash assistance. But it is clear that states are now the prime laboratories for making and implementing social policy.[33] The federal government originally became active in welfare programs because states had been unwilling or unable to tackle these problems on their own. Yet, now the states will determine whether the needs of poor people will be given a higher or lower priority, and how poor families will be treated in bad as well as good economic times.

States, along with the federal government, also provide unemployment benefits distributed to those who are out of work through no fault of their own. Benefit amounts and eligibility requirements vary across the states, though one estimate reports that average benefits are about 36 percent of a worker's former salary.[34] Unemployment benefits are paid for by taxes the federal and state governments levy on employers, which are placed in a state trust fund. If states are not able to cover all of their obligations they can borrow from the federal trust fund, but states must repay those loans. As of April 2010, states had already borrowed nearly $40 billion to help pay for their unemployment programs.[35] Individuals are generally eligible for benefits for 26 weeks, but there are programs available that can extend those benefits up to another 26 weeks if eligibility requirements are met.

Public Health

Prevention and control of disease are major state and local responsibilities. Thousands of local governments—counties, cities, townships, and special health districts—have some kind of public health program. Every state has an agency, usually called a department of health, which administers the state program and supervises local health officials. At the national level, agencies like the U.S. Public Health Service and the Centers for Disease

workfare
A welfare strategy adopted by some states that gives able-bodied adults who do not have preschool-aged children the opportunity to learn job skills that can lead to employment.

responsibility contract
A welfare strategy adopted by some states in which recipients sign a written agreement specifying their responsibilities and outlining a plan for obtaining work and achieving self-sufficiency.

Control and Prevention (CDC) conduct research, assist state and local authorities, and administer federal grants to encourage local agencies to expand their programs.

Every state also administers various federally funded medical benefit programs for the needy and uninsured, such as Medicaid. When it was adopted in 1965, Medicaid was designed as a program to enable states to fund health care for people who were poor and received public assistance. Since then, eligibility has been expanded to include low-income children, pregnant women, families, the disabled, and the elderly.[36] Today, only a minority of Medicaid recipients is on welfare, and two of three live in families with an adult in the workforce. More than half the recipients have family income above the poverty level.[37]

Not to be confused with Medicare—the federal health care program for people over the age of 65—Medicaid now serves more than 55 million people, or 13 percent of the population.[38] States feel some pressure to expand Medicaid to deal with the increasing number of people who are uninsured and to improve the quality of health care provided to poor and low-income people. But these pressures, along with the rising cost of prescription drugs, long-term health care, and other health services, add up to a Medicaid program whose expenditures grow much faster than the rest of the average state budget.

State officials acknowledge that soaring Medicaid spending threatens other policy goals, such as reducing public school class size, increasing public transportation infrastructure, and funding innovative environmental programs. Some have reached into the funds received in settling their suits with tobacco companies, or tapped public employee pension funds, or drained their rainy day reserves in order to meet the requirement in state constitutions that they balance their budgets.[39] Governors around the country pressed President George W. Bush and Congress to increase the federal share of Medicaid's costs, to no avail.

In early 2006, Congress passed the Deficit Reduction Act, which includes many new options for states trying to reduce the growth of Medicaid spending. The Act allows states to develop different benefit packages for different types of Medicaid recipients. For example, Kentucky created four benefit plans designed to address the health needs of particular groups, such as those with mental disabilities who need long-term services, and assigns participants to the plan that best meets their health care needs. The Act also allows states to require some recipients to pay for part of their health care. Idaho now requires beneficiaries to pay a monthly premium of $15 and copayments for using the emergency room. Other states have adopted wellness programs, such as smoking-cessation or weight-loss programs, in the hope that healthier lifestyles will lead to lower health care costs. Citizens who participate in these programs can receive additional health care benefits or bonus points to use for additional wellness activities.[40]

Citizens wait to see a nurse or doctor at a public health clinic. Once all of the federal health care reforms are implemented, every citizen should have health insurance, which should greatly reduce the reliance on free clinics and the expense of emergency room treatments. ■ *Do you think all persons should be required to have health insurance?*

In addition to changes to the Medicaid program, states are experimenting with reforms of the health care system generally. They have tried to expand access to private insurance through small business incentives and tax credits. Some have tried to reform the private insurance marketplace by requiring employers to offer their employees health insurance or pay the state a fee for those who are uninsured. Another reform effort focuses on the "connector model," a quasi-governmental authority or agency that aims to pool—or connect—individuals so that they can buy insurance together at a lower rate.[41] In 2006, Massachusetts reformed its health care system in order to provide insurance coverage to virtually all of its residents.[42] Hawaii has, since 1974, required all employers to provide health care benefits to any employee who works 20 hours a week or more. Although it is hard to make causal claims, Hawaii also has among the lowest insurance premiums for its citizens as well one of the healthiest state populations.[43]

Hoping to increase access to health care for children, in 1997, Congress adopted the State Children's Health Insurance Program, commonly called SCHIP. In this program, the federal government provides matching funds to states to help cover the costs of providing health care to children under the age of 19 who live in families with incomes up to two times the federal poverty line. States can choose to set their own eligibility levels below this level, but they need to receive authorization from the federal government to set it higher, as that would extend coverage to additional children. In 2009, Congress passed and President Obama signed an extension that added more than $30 billion to the program in order to extend coverage to another 4 million children.

In 2010, the U.S. Congress passed and President Obama signed into law a number of reforms to the nation's health care system. Key provisions of that legislation include barring insurance companies from dropping people from coverage when they get sick, allowing younger adults to stay covered under their parent's health insurance plans until age 26, and making it harder for insurance companies to deny coverage to individuals with pre-existing conditions. The plan also creates new insurance exchanges by the year 2014 and requires virtually every person to obtain some form of health insurance coverage or pay a tax or fee if they do not.

A number of states have challenged these reforms in federal court. Earlier in 2010, Virginia passed a law prohibiting any individual from being required to purchase health insurance. Florida, along with seventeen other states, filed a similar lawsuit in federal court challenging the constitutionality of the federal mandate, arguing that it usurps the authority of states to regulate health insurance, thereby infringing on state sovereignty. A number of state legislatures have also taken actions designed to nullify parts of the federal health care reform.

Critics of the various legal challenges pursued by the states counter that the federal government clearly has the authority to tax citizens and regulate health care under the Commerce and Necessary and Proper clauses of the Constitution. They also note that virtually all of the state public officials leading these efforts are Republicans and assert that their motivations are based on partisan politics rather than Constitutional arguments. Most Constitutional scholars think these challenges to the federal law will end up before the U.S. Supreme Court, which they expect to reject the claims of the states.

Law Enforcement

Many state and local government powers stem from their **police powers,** the inherent power of states to use physical force if necessary to protect the health, safety, and welfare of their citizens. This power is among those *not* delegated to the federal government by the Constitution and is instead reserved to the states. On this basis, mayors and governors impose curfews, as they have in some urban riots. Most law enforcement takes place at the local level, but states also have a significant role.

The State Police

In 1835, the famous Texas Rangers were organized as a small border patrol. In 1865, Massachusetts appointed a few state constables to suppress gambling, a job the local police had proved unable or, more probably, unwilling to do. But not until 1905, with the organization of the Pennsylvania State Constabulary, did a state police system come into being. State police became a part of our law enforcement system for a variety of reasons. The growth of urban and metropolitan areas, the coming of the automobile (and the resulting demand for greater protection on the highways and the creation of a mobile force for catching fleeing criminals), and the need for a trained force to maintain order during strikes, fires, floods, and other emergencies all promoted the creation of state police.

The jurisdiction of the state police is generally concentrated on those areas outside of the normal jurisdictions of city police and county sheriffs. That includes enforcing travel laws on state and interstate highways, providing security at the state capitol, and often supporting training and support services for local jurisdictions.

Local and Other Police Forces

At the local level, nearly every municipality maintains its own police force; the county has a sheriff and deputies, and some townships have their own police officers. In fact, there

LEARNING OBJECTIVE

9.4 Trace the growth of states' responsibilities for law enforcement.

police powers
Inherent powers of state governments to pass laws to protect public health, safety, and welfare; the national government has no directly granted police powers but accomplishes the same goals through other delegated powers.

By the People

Neighborhood Watch Groups

On March 14, 1964, a woman named Kitty Genovese was raped and murdered in Queens, New York. In the newspaper coverage that followed, it was reported that numerous bystanders witnessed the attack but did nothing to help her. Although these accounts of witness behavior are likely inaccurate,* they are credited with creating the impetus for some of the first neighborhood watch programs designed to get citizens involved in reducing and preventing crimes. In 1972, the National Sheriffs Association began a concerted effort to encourage neighborhood watch programs across the country. USA Freedom Corps, Citizen Corps, and the U.S. Justice Department joined with the National Sheriffs Association in 2002 to launch USAonWatch in an effort to revitalize neighborhood watch programs in the wake of the September 11, 2001, terrorist attacks.

Most neighborhood watch programs focus on having volunteers in a position to observe and report to the police suspected criminal behavior; volunteers are strongly encouraged not to intervene. USAonWatch provides training information and a number of other resources for interested groups and individuals through its Web site at www.usaonwatch.org. Another organization called the National Neighborhood Watch Institute offers signs and other materials for neighborhood watch groups to purchase (www.nnwi.org).

Find out if there are neighborhood watch programs in your community or neighborhood. Many colleges and universities also operate similar volunteer programs, often focused on walking with individuals to and from student centers, libraries, and dorms during late-night hours. Find out if your school has such a program. Consider getting one organized through your student government, campus security, or other organization. As noted above, such programs are not about confronting criminals and escalating a negative situation. Rather, the goal is to prevent such events in the first place by the presence of more people or to be able to quickly call in professional police and security officers.

CRITICAL THINKING QUESTIONS

1. Should citizens actively participate in policing their own neighborhoods, or should the work be left to professional police officers? What are the pros and cons of neighborhood watch programs?

2. Should neighborhood watch participants be required to take training and receive certification? What sort of liability do neighborhood watch participants face if something bad does happen while they are on patrol?

* Jim Rasenberger, "Nightmare on Austin Street," *American Heritage Magazine*, October 2006,

---

are almost 18,000 separate state and local law enforcement agencies in the United States, employing more than 700,000 officers.[44] Local police concentrate on law enforcement and criminal investigation within their local cities, whereas in many counties, sheriffs provide law enforcement outside of incorporated cities. State police, county sheriffs, and local police are all charged with enforcing state and most federal laws. Some cities and counties have further local ordinances that local police enforce as well. In many respects, the police system individuals encounter has more to do with *where* they have committed some act and less to do with *what* they actually did.

State and local governments spend more than $125 billion a year on police protection and correctional or prison institutions.[45] Local governments pay for nearly 70 percent of all police protection costs, including such routine activities as controlling traffic and patrolling neighborhoods but also maintaining court security and preventing juvenile crime. From 1987 to 2003, the number of full-time employees working in local police departments increased by 27 percent, or approximately 135,000 people. The percentage of police officers that were female increased from 7.6 percent to 11.3 percent during the same period.[46] With crime an ever-important issue to many voters, crime control is always on the minds of elected officials.

State police are not the only law enforcement agencies maintained by state governments. There are liquor law enforcement officials, fish and game wardens, fire wardens, detective bureaus, and special motor vehicle police. This dispersion of functions has been criticized, yet each department insists it needs its own law enforcement agency to handle its special problems.

Federal—State Action

The federal government has gradually moved into law enforcement, although local governments still bear the main cost of local law enforcement. Today, for example, it is a federal offense to transport kidnapped individuals or stolen goods across state lines. Taking firearms, explosives, or even information across state lines for illegal purposes is also a federal offense. Federal law enforcement agencies include the Federal Bureau of

Investigation (FBI); the Bureau of Alcohol, Tobacco, Firearms, and Explosives (ATF); and the Drug Enforcement Administration (DEA).

Both violent crime rates and property crime rates have been declining since the early 1990s.[47] Despite these positive trends, politicians in both parties continue to press for government to do more about crime. Some advocate stricter laws regulating guns, whereas others favor more police on the streets or more prisons. Because politicians fear appearing "soft on crime," taking action on crime is almost always a high priority at all levels of government.

Since the September 11, 2001 terrorist attacks on New York City and the Pentagon, every state has designated a homeland security coordinator. These state officials work with the federal Department of Homeland Security to conduct preparedness and training efforts aimed at preventing and dealing with future terrorist attacks. In 2002, the federal government approved funds to train and equip first responders and to prevent bioterrorism.[48] In 2008, federal grants-in-aid to the states for homeland security totaled $1.69 billion.[49]

Although there is a clear need for new and expanded homeland security efforts, few states have the resources to support them. Many local and state officials have complained that most new federal funds are being redirected toward new homeland security concerns such as bioterrorism preparedness, while traditional and basic public safety systems are ignored. This has added to budget shortfalls in most states and has led state and local officials to insist on more federal funds and greater flexibility in how states and localities decide what their priorities are.[50]

Planning the Urban Community

Are our cities good places in which to live and work? Are crime, pollution, garbage, crowded shopping areas, dented fenders, slums and blighted areas, inadequate parks, challenging traffic patterns, and shattered nerves the inevitable costs of urban life?

LEARNING **OBJECTIVE**

9.5 Outline states' tools and priorities for urban planning.

For at least the first century of the United States' existence, its cities were allowed to grow unchecked. Industrialists were permitted to erect factories wherever they wished. Developers were allowed to construct towering buildings that prevented sunlight from reaching the streets below. Commuters, bicyclists, and pedestrians ended up with transportation systems that rarely met their needs. With increased industrialization and urbanization, political pressures emerged in the late 1800s and early 1900s to reform the city.

Zoning Laws

The most common method of ensuring orderly growth is *zoning*—creating specific areas and limiting property usage in each area. A community may be divided into designated areas for single-family, two-family, or multifamily dwellings; for commercial purposes; and for light or heavy industry. Regulations restrict the height of buildings or require that buildings be located a certain distance apart or a certain distance from the boundaries of the lot.

Zoning regulations help the city or county government coordinate services with land use. Zoning laws also help stabilize property values by preventing, for example, garbage dumps from being located next to residential areas. Day-to-day enforcement is usually the responsibility of a building inspector who ensures that a projected construction project is consistent with building, zoning, fire, and sanitary regulations before granting a building permit. A zoning ordinance, however, is no better than its enforcement. In most cases, a zoning or planning commission or the city council can amend ordinances and make exceptions to regulations, and these officials are often under tremendous pressure to grant exceptions. But if they go too far in permitting special cases, the whole purpose of zoning is defeated.

Zoning is only one kind of community planning. Until recently, city planners were primarily concerned with streets and buildings. Today, most are also concerned with the quality of life. Consequently, planning covers a broad range of activities, including methods to avoid air pollution, improve water quality, and provide for better parks. Planners collect all the information they can about a city and then prepare long-range plans. Can smaller-scale communities be devised within urban centers? Can downtown areas be revitalized, and if so, how? Where should main highways or mass-transit facilities be constructed to meet future needs? Will the water supply be adequate for the population 10, 20, or 50 years

Urban gardens, like this one in Seattle, allow residents to maximize the use of urban spaces, provide for a greener urban environment, and promote greater neighborhood self-sufficiency. ■ *Should local governments do more to encourage these kinds of actions?*

from now? Are hospitals and parks accessible to all? Does the design of public buildings encourage crime or energy waste?

Controlling Growth

Critics of urban and state planning are skeptical whether governors, mayors, or state and local legislators can prevent what they sometimes call the "Los Angelization" of the United States, by which they mean sprawling urban growth without much planning for transportation, environmental protection, or management of water and other resources. Unregulated market forces can cause severe harm to residents, and "politics as usual" does not ensure sensible growth patterns or protect the air, water, and beauty of most states and communities.

Seattle and San Francisco residents voted to limit the height and bulk of downtown buildings in an effort to protect these cities from excessive growth. Maryland and many other states have passed "smart growth" laws aimed at preserving large blocks of contiguous land and ensuring that the necessary roads, sewers, and schools are in place before development proceeds. This legislation is implemented in two ways. The state gives priority funding to development in areas designated by counties as having the proper infrastructure and meeting other guidelines; state funds are also allocated to local governments and private land trusts to purchase the development rights to land "rich in agricultural, forestry, natural, and cultural resources."[51]

A few urban planners recommend looking at European cities such as Paris, where choice neighborhoods in the heart of the city combine elegant six- and seven-story apartment buildings above neighborhood retail stores. A close look at European cities often finds a great number of interior gardens within apartments and meticulously groomed neighborhood parks. A U.S. group called Community Greens helps residents create and share parks in cities across the country.[52] Real estate analyst Christopher Leinberger observed that "walkable urbanism," neighborhoods in which residents can walk to shops, schools, and parks, are now much in demand by a growing segment of the U.S. population.[53]

Obviously, planning and sensible growth depend on public support. They also depend on market forces. No plan will be effective, however, unless it reflects the interests and values of major groups within the community. Planning is clearly a political activity. Different groups view the ends and means of planning differently, and agreements on tough policy options are often hard to reach. Moreover, one of the barriers to successful planning is the general fear of government power. Effective planning therefore requires imaginative collaboration among planners, community leaders, and the popularly elected officials who must bear the responsibility for implementing the plans.[54]

Transportation

Before the automobile, long-distance commercial travel was conducted mainly by canal and railroad. Local roads were built and repaired under the direction of city, township, and county officials. Able-bodied male citizens were required either to put in a certain number of days working on the public roads or to pay taxes for that purpose. By the 1890s, bicycle clubs began to urge the building of hard-surfaced roads, but it was not until the early 1900s and the growing popularity of the automobile that road building became a major industry. This function was gradually transferred from local governments to state governments and the federal government, but counties and townships still have important building and maintenance functions.

Although much of the money comes from the federal government, state and local governments build the highways, public buildings, airports, parks, and recreational facilities. States do the planning, estimate the costs, and arrange for the construction work, even when they receive federal assistance. In order to receive support, however, states

The I-35W bridge spanning the Mississippi River collapsed in Minneapolis during rush hour in the summer of 2007. Paying for the maintenance of transportation infrastructure has become an increasing burden for states. When the federal government passed an economic stimulus package to combat the 2008–2009 recession, funds for transportation repairs were included. ■ *Once roads and bridges are built, who should pay for their maintenance?*

must submit their plans to, and have their work inspected by, the U.S. Department of Transportation (DOT). All federally funded highways must meet DOT standards governing the engineering of the roadbed, employment conditions for construction workers, and weight and load conditions for trucks.

The federal government has supported state highway construction since 1916, and through legislation passed since then, federal aid has increased. Under the Federal Highway Act of 1956, states planned and built the National System of Interstate and Defense Highways. The Eisenhower Interstate System consists of more than 46,000 miles of superhighways linking nearly all cities with a population of 50,000 or more. The federal government paid 90 percent of the cost of this system, with most of the money coming from taxes on gasoline, tires, and trucks that are placed in a trust fund designated for that purpose.

In 2005, Congress passed a $244 billion, five-year authorization of the federal highway, public transportation, and safety programs. After Interstate 35W bridge collapsed in Minneapolis in August 2007, concerns have been raised about the safety of the nation's transportation infrastructure. In January 2008, the National Surface Transportation Policy and Revenue Study Commission concluded the nation needed to spend $225 billion a year for 50 years to maintain and upgrade surface transportation. Because the current 18.4 cents per gallon federal gas tax has not been increased since 1993 and because the highway transportation fund is expected to face a significant shortfall in fiscal year 2009, the commission recommended an increase in the gas tax to pay for these repairs.[55]

Traffic has become a major problem in recent years—especially in cities such as Boston, Denver, Los Angeles, Seattle, San Francisco, Washington, D.C., and New York. The population is growing and more people own cars, but drivers are also driving more each year. As a result, traffic and congestion have become pressing issues for state governments.[56] Building public transportation systems, increasing road space, or establishing staggered work hours should help; however, transportation policy makers have not found solutions to be simple. Advocates of public transportation point out that even though public transportation is more energy efficient than driving, the federal government provides much less aid to states and localities for mass transit than it does for highways.[57] Adding roads or lanes often leads more people to drive and may ultimately result in new traffic patterns that are no better than the old ones. Staggering work hours is difficult because businesses work most effectively through collaboration, so it is most efficient for workers to be on the job at the same time each day. But with higher gas prices and growing concern over climate change, citizens, businesses, and state and local governments are starting to pursue alternatives to reduce miles driven, and this in turn could reduce traffic congestion.

For the People
GOVERNMENT'S GREATEST ENDEAVORS

Creating Government Efficiency

States spent much of 2009 and 2010 looking for ways to cut their budgets. Much of that involved cuts to programs, but many other efforts were made to reduce operating costs and streamline government operations. "The budget crisis is so severe that it's now possible to do some things that everyone knew were smart but couldn't get done because of political considerations," said John Thomasian, the director of the Center for Best Practices at the National Governors Association.*

A story appearing in *USA Today* described several efforts by states.† For example, Iowa established a centralized purchasing and information technology operation that eliminated 13 separate boards and is projected to save the state $127 million per year. Missouri ended a paid holiday for state workers for the

Friday after Thanksgiving, saving $1.2 million a year. Michigan combined ten finance authorities into one as part of a sustained effort that has eliminated more than 300 boards in recent years at a projected savings of more than $3 billion per year. Indiana combined the administration of two large pension funds, producing an estimated savings of $10 million in the first year. Although these kinds of programs alone are not enough to close the budget gaps that states faced at this time, they demonstrate innovative efforts to make state governments operate more efficiently so that they can do more work with less tax money.

Of course, as states eliminate duplication and consolidate operations to achieve greater efficiency, they are also concentrating power and authority into the hands of fewer and fewer top officials. Decisions can be made

easier and fewer employees are needed, but mistakes can be compounded. Engineers often design back-up systems and built-in redundancies so that when a primary system fails, a secondary system takes over and minimizes the impact of the first failure.

CRITICAL THINKING QUESTIONS

1. What are the pros and cons of streamlining government programs and operations? In which areas does it make sense to consolidate operations, and in which ones might it be more important to have duplication?

2. How important is efficiency as a goal for government operations? How should we try to measure efficiency in government operations?

---

*The Center for Best Practices Web site is located at http://www.nga.org/portal/site/nga/menuitem.50aeae5ff70b817ae8ebb856a11010a0/.
†"States Streamline, Reorganize Amid Fiscal Crisis" *USA Today*, March 15, 2010, http://www.usatoday.com/news/nation/2010-03-14-state-budget-cuts_N.htm?POE=click-refer.

Economic Development

Another central priority for governors and mayors, as well as other state and local officials, is providing jobs for their citizens. Governors commonly spend a significant amount of time encouraging companies to relocate within their borders, courting corporate officials, going on trade missions to other countries to promote their states' products, and negotiating favorable tax and other incentives with new businesses. This interest is not new. What is new is the international scope of activities.[58] For example, while in Cuba to sign a deal to export $11 million of his state's wheat, Nebraska Governor Dave Heineman explained that "expanding trade relationships is good for Nebraska and altogether good for America."[59]

States compete with one another because economic development is the key to increasing the tax base that funds government services. But states face a dilemma because satisfying the demands of new businesses can be expensive, and tax incentives can reduce the tax return the new companies will generate. Competition among states has intensified to the point that localities are worried about keeping the jobs they have, not only persuading new companies to move to their area. New York City has offered billions of dollars in incentives to influence several companies not to leave. Critics of these "bidding wars" believe that states should spend tax money on rebuilding infrastructure and strengthening education rather than offering public funds to selected large private companies.

Regulation

LEARNING OBJECTIVE

9.6 Assess the role of states and communities in regulating and in enforcing compliance with federal and state regulations.

States and local communities adopt health and safety regulations on the assumption that the benefits to the general public will outweigh the costs to the individuals and groups being regulated. Thus, laws requiring drivers' licenses, compelling motorists to stop at red lights, mandating seat-belt use, and imposing severe penalties on people caught driving under the influence of alcohol or drugs are intended to protect the safety and freedom of innocent pedestrians and occupants of other motor vehicles. We accept most such laws as both necessary and legitimate.

Environmental Regulation

State and local governments have long been concerned about managing land use and protecting the environment. In such heavily polluted places as Pittsburgh, smoke abatement ordinances were enacted as early as 1860, but aggressive action on air pollution did not come until after World War II.[60]

In the 1950s and 1960s, the federal government's role in environmental regulation was limited to providing state and local governments with grants for research and assistance in developing and implementing their own environmental standards. In the late 1960s and early 1970s, pressure on the federal government to develop and implement national environmental standards increased, particularly with the recognition that air and water pollution does not acknowledge state boundaries. Important legislation dealing with specific environmental problems was adopted in the 1970s, including the Clean Air Act of 1970, the Clean Water Act of 1972, the Safe Drinking Water Act of 1974, the Toxic Substances Control Act of 1976, and the Superfund Act (federal Comprehensive Environmental Response, Compensation, and Liability Act) of 1980. Most of these Acts have been amended one or more times since their initial adoption. In the 1970s, President Nixon created the Environmental Protection Agency (EPA) and gave it primary responsibility for environmental protection programs.

The basic model of environmental regulation has been for the federal government to set national standards for water and air quality. State and local governments are typically put in charge of both implementing standards and monitoring compliance. Yet, because federal environmental grants to states have not increased since the early 1990s, states have come to take on a greater role in expanding legislation and research for environmental programs and to absorb an increasingly large share of the costs. They now pay approximately 80 percent of the costs of federal environmental programs.[61]

One area in which states are increasingly responsible for environmental policy is waste management. Although the Superfund Act cleans up the most contaminated toxic dump sites, state and local policies have been established to cover toxic sites that do not qualify as Superfund sites but still warrant cleanup action.[62] Not unexpectedly, states whose economies are growing have regulated waste management more aggressively than economically hard-pressed states that fear driving industries away with regulations and constraints. But concerns about nuclear waste, acid rain, and hazardous wastes have sparked extensive efforts at regulation within states, as well as court battles with nearby states over the export of unwanted byproducts of energy development.

Another area in which states have become very active is energy use and sustainability. A recent press release by the National Governors Association declares that states are generating new advances in clean energy policy.[63] Many states have been using alternative renewable energy both to cut down on energy costs and to rejuvenate dwindling rural economies. Large-scale wind-energy projects, for example, have been started in New York, Pennsylvania, Colorado, Iowa, Kansas, Texas, and Washington, among other states. As fossil fuel costs became increasingly unpredictable, states started to diversify their approach by investing in biomass, wind, hydroelectric, solar, and geothermal projects. Some states have even implemented innovative tax incentives and "net metering" programs (a practice allowing customers who have solar panels or other personal energy-generating capital to sell their energy back to the overall grid) in order to encourage more individual responsibility. Although none of these tactics has yet become widely accepted, nor is renewable energy expected to soon replace traditional energy sources, they are evidence of active state and local environmental efforts.

Although the EPA has responsibility for the development of national standards, states sometimes take the lead in adopting more demanding standards of environmental protection and pushing the EPA for action. For example, California adopted a law in 2006 "requiring a 25 percent reduction in the state's carbon dioxide emissions by 2020."[64] Although California has the authority to develop its own air quality standards, it has to receive a waiver from the EPA to do so. In late 2007, the EPA denied the state's request for a waiver and blocked California from implementing rules designed to reduce greenhouse gas emissions from cars and trucks. In response, California has sued the EPA, hoping

Cities and states often provide their residents with greater health and safety protections than those mandated by the federal government. Many states have passed measures banning smoking in public areas, and some mandate helmet use with bicycles or motorcycles. Often, actions tested at the state level can lead to federal policies. ■ *What are some other examples of states functioning as "laboratories for democracy?"*

to prevent the agency from blocking the rules that it developed and that other states hope to follow. In a press release announcing the lawsuit, Governor Schwarzenegger declared, "It is unconscionable that the federal government is keeping California and 19 other states from adopting these standards. They are ignoring the will of millions of people who want their government to take action in the fight against global warming."[65] In June of 2009, the EPA announced it would grant California's waiver after all.[66]

Working Conditions

Despite expanded federal regulation, state and local governments still have much to say about working conditions.

- *Health and safety legislation:* States require proper heating, lighting, ventilation, fire escapes, and sanitary facilities in work areas. Machinery must be equipped with safety guards. Some standards have also been established to reduce occupation-related diseases. Health, building, and labor inspectors tour industrial plants to ensure compliance with the laws.
- *Workers' compensation:* Today, all states have workers' compensation programs based on the belief that employees should not have to bear the cost of accidents or illnesses incurred because of their jobs. The costs of accidents and occupational diseases are borne by employers and passed on to consumers in the form of higher prices. In the past, employees had to prove that their employers were at fault if they suffered an accident on the job. Today, if people are injured or contract a disease in the ordinary course of employment, they are entitled to compensation set by a prearranged schedule. Workers' compensation is a controversial issue, with employers arguing that employee claims of workplace stress are excessive and will make U.S. firms uncompetitive.
- *Child labor:* All states forbid child labor, yet state laws vary widely in their coverage and in their definition of child labor. Many states set the minimum age for employment at 14. Higher age requirements are normal for employment in hazardous occupations and during school hours. Many of these regulations have been superseded by stricter federal laws.
- *Consumer protection:* The consumer protection movement, which became prominent in the 1960s and 1970s, says consumers should be provided with adequate

safety information and should have their complaints heard. Most states have offices to hear consumer complaints, including lawyers working in the offices of the state attorney general. State governments often establish professional standards and handle complaints about legal and medical services or insurance practices.

Recent state activity to protect consumers has focused on fraud, especially mailed "guaranteed prize schemes," to which millions of people respond. When the prize is not exactly what was promised or the method for selecting winners proves deceptive, people often complain to their state governments. Other areas in which state governments have been active in attempting to protect consumers include charitable solicitations by telephone, long-distance phone service promotions, credit card offers and promotions, and irregularities and fraud in corporations.

The Importance of State and Local Policy

All 50 state governments and more than 86,000 local governments are on the front lines of trying to solve community and regional social problems. They must often work closely with one another and the national government, and this is a frequent source of frustration.[67]

Divided government in Washington, when it occurs, has meant that neither political party could have its way with domestic policy. Presidents Bill Clinton and George W. Bush had different priorities, and the generally divided U.S. Senate has taken a cautious approach on such issues as environmental regulation. Health care reform barely passed a Congress with Democratic majorities in both the House and Senate.

State officials continue to be frustrated with national legislation such as the No Child Left Behind Act and homeland security legislation in recent years that mandates extensive federal requirements into core areas of state and local policy responsibilities yet provides inadequate federal funds to assist in the achievement of these goals.

Innovative governors and state legislators have sponsored important changes in welfare reform, educational testing, transportation, urban planning, and insurance regulation. But the challenges facing state and local officials continue to unfold.

CHAPTER **SUMMARY**

9.1 Outline local, state, and federal government roles in elementary and secondary education.

The federal government's share in financing K–12 education has increased over time but is still low. The influence of the federal government has increased considerably, however, particularly because of the requirements of the No Child Left Behind Act of 2001, a reauthorization of the Elementary and Secondary Education Act. This Act emerged from a reform movement pushing for changes to increase the quality of education, but controversy has developed over the impact of the federal regulations.

9.2 Assess the concerns about state funding of higher education.

State funding of higher education is unstable, rising during periods of economic growth and falling during periods of economic decline. Some public colleges and universities can often raise tuition to make up for lost state revenues, but these tuition increases mean that the burden of paying for higher education shifts to students and their parents.

9.3 Describe the role of the state in public assistance programs, and assess the challenges facing state social service programs.

The national welfare overhaul legislation in 1996 imposed new work requirements and time limits on families receiving cash assistance. It also gave states much greater flexibility in designing and administering programs that serve low-income families with children. The new law established block grants of federal money that must be matched by state funds and focused assistance more on providing employment services, child care, and other forms of noncash services and supports.

States have long sought to eradicate disease and foster practices conducive to a healthy population. The challenges for states today include managing the administration and rising costs of Medicaid and other health care systems.

9.4 Trace the growth of states' responsibilities for law enforcement.

The growth of urban and metropolitan areas and the need for a trained force to maintain order during emergencies led to the creation of the state police.

Additional enforcement agencies have emerged as states have regulated such activities as the sale and use of alcohol, fishing, and hunting. After the September 11 terrorist attacks, state law enforcement agencies took on the additional responsibility of trying to provide for homeland security.

9.5 Outline states' tools and priorities for urban planning.

States attempt to ensure orderly growth through zoning laws and community planning. Transportation is also a major area of state and local government activity. Although the federal government provides financial assistance for the construction of roads, highways, and urban mass transit, the responsibility of planning, building, and maintaining these transportation systems lies with the states. States openly compete with one another in the area of economic development by offering tax incentives, waiving environmental regulations, and giving other enticements to businesses to locate or stay within their boundaries.

9.6 Assess the role of states and communities in regulating and in enforcing compliance with federal and state regulations.

Generally, the federal government sets regulation standards, and states implement them and monitor compliance. Recently, states have taken a more active role in setting environmental regulations regarding waste management, energy use, sustainability, and climate change. State and local governments also set regulations for working conditions that provide protection to employees.

CHAPTER **SELF-TEST**

9.1 Outline local, state, and federal government roles in elementary and secondary education.

1. Do you think the federal government should ensure that the amount spent on education per student does not vary from state to state? Explain your position and respond to one or two likely arguments from those who disagree.
2. Imagine that you are a state commissioner of education in a state that ranks in the bottom 10 percent for educational attainment by students. Write two to three paragraphs explaining how you will resolve the problems in your state's educational system. Anticipate and respond to arguments from those who disagree with your plan.

9.2 Assess the concerns about state funding of higher education.

3. What percentage of a typical state's budget is spent on higher education?
   a. 1 to 7 percent
   b. 8 to 15 percent
   c. 16 to 20 percent
   d. 21 to 25 percent
4. In a short paragraph, explain why you feel that state governments should do more (or less) to fund the higher education of students within their states.

9.3 Describe the role of the state in public assistance programs, and assess the challenges facing state social service programs.

5. Write one or two paragraphs outlining the major differences between AFDC and TANF.
6. Write a paragraph explaining why welfare reform and health care coverage have headed in opposite directions in the last 15 years as far as coverage is concerned.

9.4 Trace the growth of states' responsibilities for law enforcement.

7. Why has there been such a great expansion of people employed in law enforcement in the last 50 years?
8. In one or two paragraphs, tell why it is or is not necessary for different agencies within a state to have their own law enforcement groups. Explain how you would deal with the problems associated with this specialization.

9.5 Outline states' tools and priorities for urban planning.

9. How have cities in the United States tried to prevent uncontrolled growth? List as many means as you can think of. Write a few sentences about which methods you think would be most effective and why.
10. In a paragraph, explain the major points in the evolution of transportation as explained in the chapter.
11. What competing challenges do states face in the pursuit of economic development? What do you think they should do about their dilemma?

9.6 Assess the role of states and communities in regulating and in enforcing compliance with federal and state regulations.

12. In a paragraph, highlight the major points in the development of environmental regulation since the beginning of the twentieth century.
13. In one or two paragraphs, argue whether the growth of federal regulation over the states should continue, and explain why or why not.

Answers to selected questions: 3. b

mypoliscilab EXERCISES
Where participation leads to action!

Apply what you learned in this chapter with these resources on MyPoliSciLab.

📖 **Read** on **mypoliscilab.com**

    eText: Chapter 9

👁 **Watch** on **mypoliscilab.com**

    Video: Suspected Salmonella Outbreak at Texas Plant

✓ **Study** and **Review** on **mypoliscilab.com**

    Pre-Test
    Post-Test
    Chapter Exam
    Flashcards

KEY TERMS

vouchers, p. 187
charter school, p. 188
Temporary Assistance for Needy Families (TANF), p. 191
workfare, p. 193
responsibility contract, p. 193
police powers, p. 195

ADDITIONAL RESOURCES

FURTHER READING

REBECCA BLANK AND RON HASKINS, EDS., *The New World of Welfare* (Brookings Institution Press, 2001).

JASON DEPARLE, *American Dream: Three Women, Ten Kids, and a Nation's Drive to End Welfare* (Viking Penguin, 2004).

R. KENNETH GODWIN AND FRANK KEMERER, *School Choice and Tradeoffs: Liberty, Equity, and Diversity* (University of Texas Press, 2002).

VIRGINIA GRAY AND RUSSELL HANSON, *Politics in the American States: A Comparative Analysis,* 8th ed. (CQ Press, 2003).

JOHN J. HARRIGAN AND DAVID NICE, *Politics and Policy in States and Communities,* 9th ed. (Longman, 2005).

DAVID HURSH, *High-Stakes Testing and the Decline of Teaching and Learning* (Rowman & Littlefield, 2008).

CATHY MARIE JOHNSON, GEORGIA DUERST-LAHTI, AND NOELLE NORTON, *Creating Gender: The Sexual Politics of Welfare Policy* (Lynne Rienner, 2007).

NORMAN R. LUTTBEG, *The Grassroots of Democracy: A Comparative Study of Competition and Its Impact in American Cities in the 1990s* (Lexington Books, 1999).

DAVID C. NICE, *Policy Innovation in State Government* (Iowa State University Press, 1994).

MICHAEL A. PAGANO AND ANN O. M. BOWMAN, *Cityscape and Capital: The Politics of Urban Development* (Johns Hopkins University Press, 1997).

DAREL PAUL, *Rescaling International Political Economy: Subnational States and the Regulation of the Global Political Economy* (Routledge, 2005).

PAUL E. PETERSON AND MARTIN R. WEST, EDS., *No Child Left Behind? The Politics and Practice of School Accountability* (Brookings Institution Press, 2003).

BARRY G. RABE, *Statehouse and Greenhouse: The Emerging Politics of American Climate Change Policy* (Brookings Institution Press, 2004).

DENISE SCHEBERLE, *Federalism and Environmental Policy,* 2d ed. (Georgetown University Press, 2004).

MARK SCHNEIDER, PAUL TESKE, AND MELISSA MARSCHALL, *Choosing Schools: Consumer Choice and the Quality of American Schools* (Princeton University Press, 2002).

SANDRA VERGARI, ED., *The Charter School Landscape* (University of Pittsburgh Press, 2002).

JOHN F. WITTE, *The Market Approach to Education: An Analysis of America's First Voucher Program* (Princeton University Press, 1999). See also *Governing: The Magazine of States and Localities,* published monthly by Congressional Quarterly; and the series of excellent books on state government public policy making published by the University of Nebraska Press.

WEB SITES

www.sheriffs.org The National Sheriffs Association is a professional association dedicated to serving the Office of Sheriff and its affiliates through education, training, and information resources.

http://www.grandlodgefop.org/ The Fraternal Order of Police focuses on improving the working conditions of law enforcement officers and the safety of those we serve through education, legislation, information, community involvement, and employee representation.

www.cdc.gov The Centers for Disease Control and Prevention conducts research and disseminates information about health and health related issues facing citizens in the Unites States and throughout the world.

CHAPTER 10

Staffing and Financing State and Local Governments

P assing laws is not easy, but the hardest work sometimes begins after a bill becomes law, as every policy needs qualified people to implement it and funds to pay for it. The states faced significant budgetary shortfalls in 2009 and 2010 resulting from the recession that began in 2008. That produced short-term pressures on states to cut programs, furlough state employees, and raise some taxes and fees. However, the long-term consequences may be even more important.

A report in *The New York Times* in the spring of 2010 described how many states were creating long-term debt problems for themselves as they tried to navigate this budget-tightening period, through such practices as unbalancing budgets, masking debt with account gimmicks, and ignoring the massive number of public workers that will be owed their pensions when they retire.[1] For example, New Hampshire tried to use $110 million from its medical malpractice insurance pool to balance its budget. Colorado has tried to use money from its workers' compensation program for the same purpose. Illinois is trying to defer payments because it is $9 billion behind in paying its bills to vendors. Connecticut is trying to issue new accounting rules, and California forced companies to pay 70 percent of their 2010 corporate income taxes by June. In addition, states face a range of other long-term commitments, with the real ticking time bomb, according to economists Joshua Rauh and Robert Novy-Marx, being future pension obligations states owe. They estimate that states' future pension obligations currently sit at approximately $5.17 trillion, but that states have currently set aside less than $2 trillion to cover those obligations. That leaves a $3.23 trillion hole for states to fill.

The fear is that these practices may create a credit crisis for states similar to what many businesses faced in 2008–2009 and what the country of Greece faced in 2010. States, like businesses, often borrow money to pay for some expenses. For example, states can borrow money for rebuilding roads now and then pay it back over time. This commonly occurs by selling bonds that states promise to repay to investors with some interest. Some economists, such as Kenneth Rogoff and Carmen Reinhart, worry that if states are unable to meet their current and future debt obligations, investors will simply stop purchasing state bonds—essentially creating a credit freeze for states. They write, "When an accident is waiting to happen, it eventually does."

These are major challenges for states. The recent recession has drawn greater attention to these problems. However, the immediate need to balance current budgets (hopefully before the next election) with as little pain as possible works against taking serious steps toward heading off this potential long-term debt crisis that looms ahead for states.

This chapter examines the personnel and fiscal issues faced by state and local governments. It will also discuss the role of state and local employees and the different ways in which they are selected and retained in office, and the reasons governments rely on private agencies instead of their own workforce to perform some functions. The chapter also examines how state and local governments raise the money to pay for their workers and the many services they provide, and it reviews the challenges states and localities face now and in the future as needs increase and funding gets tighter.

Staffing State and Local Governments

Unlike the federal workforce, which actually has relatively few employees who work directly with citizens, nearly all state and local employees have contact with the public. More than 7.8 million work in elementary, secondary, or higher education; nearly 1 million

LEARNING OBJECTIVE

10.1 Describe the hiring process for public employees, and assess attempts at reform and privatization.

207

are police officers and firefighters; and another 800,000 work in state, county, and city hospitals. In addition, 730,000 work as prison guards and corrections officers, and nearly 200,000 work in parks and recreation.[2]

Also unlike the federal government, state and local governments have a large and growing workforce. As of 2008, state and local governments employed about 14.8 million full-time and 4.9 million part-time workers—approximately seven times the number who worked in the federal government.[3] According to the U.S. Bureau of Labor Statistics, state and local governments will continue to grow. By 2016, more than 20.7 million American adults will work in the nation's approximately 89,000 state and local governments. During the same period, the federal government is expected to stay approximately the same size.[4]

Public Employees

More than one-third of the cost of state and local government is employees' salaries. How are these people chosen? A few are elected. A larger number, including many top administrators, are appointed by elected officials. By far the greatest number, however, are typically hired through some kind of **merit system** in which selection and promotion depend on demonstrated performance (merit) rather than political patronage. Although in many jurisdictions it still helps to know the right people and belong to the right party, patronage is not nearly as prevalent as it once was.

Throughout much of the nineteenth century, governments at all levels were dominated by political patronage, a political **spoils system** in which employment was a reward for partisan loyalty and active political support in campaigns and elections. In 1883, Congress passed the Pendleton Civil Service Reform Act, which began to move the federal government from the spoils system to the merit system. Although the Act did not directly affect state and local governments, many of the states began to institute the merit system. In 1939, Democratic Senator Carl Hatch of Arizona pushed through Congress the first Hatch Act, which further promoted the merit principle and limited the political activities of federal, state, and local employees whose salaries were supported with federal funds. Subsequently, state and local governments enacted "little Hatch Acts" that enforced merit principles and restricted the political activities of their employees. Merit testing is now used in most states for hiring or promoting employees. Moreover, under a 1976 Supreme Court decision, states cannot dismiss civil servants for political reasons.[5]

Merit systems are generally administered by an office of state personnel, which prepares and administers examinations, provides lists of job openings, establishes job classifications, and determines salary schedules. It also serves as a board of appeal for employees who are discharged. State personnel offices are concerned with training the already employed, bargaining with labor unions, administering affirmative action programs, and filling top-level executive positions.

However, merit systems increasingly came under attack, particularly in the 1990s. Critics complained that state personnel systems were overly centralized and regulated. State personnel offices used procedures, job descriptions, and tests that often failed to fit the needs of diverse state agencies. Job descriptions were detailed and hard to change, and agency managers were thus prevented from adapting their workforces to changing needs. Procedures for filling jobs involved several levels of bureaucracy, and vacancies took a long time to fill.

Critics also complained that hiring and firing rules deprived responsible officials of authority over their subordinates. They argued that there was so much emphasis on insulating public employees from political coercion that employees enjoyed too much job security. Administrators could not get rid of incompetents. Sometimes, it took months and several elaborate hearings to dismiss public employees unwilling or unable to do their jobs. Also, public managers could not use salaries to reward and retain the best employees because most of the older merit systems permitted only a narrow pay range for any one job. In summary, although merit systems were supposed to emphasize ability and minimize political favoritism, they came to be viewed by many as clumsy, complicated, and unresponsive to the needs of public managers and agencies—and as obstacles to efforts by state and local governments to attract the most skilled people to public sector jobs and reward good performance.

merit system
A system of public employment in which selection and promotion depend on demonstrated performance rather than on political patronage.

spoils system
A system of public employment based on rewarding party loyalists and friends.

The Diverse State and Local Workforce

Like the federal government, state and local governments have become more diverse during the past two decades and will become even more diverse as they add new jobs. Excluding schoolteachers, who are overwhelmingly white and female, the U.S. Census Bureau reports that the state and local workforce is also becoming an employer of choice for minorities. The increasing percentage of Hispanics is largely due to population growth in states such as California, Florida, and Texas, where Hispanic workers are moving into state and local government jobs at high rates.*

Although the percentages of women and minority workers have increased during the past two decades, both groups remain underpaid relative to males and whites. In 2005, males made an average of $44,090 a year, compared with $36,417 for females,

$35,265 for African Americans, and $38,904 for Hispanics. Among high-paid professional jobs, men made approximately $7,000 a year more than women did, in part because men concentrated in the higher-paying professions such as law, finance, and health administration, whereas women tended to concentrate in historically underpaid professions in human services such as child welfare. However, higher rates of pay for men compared to women were also found in all other major occupational categories, such as officials and administrators, technicians, and administrative support workers.

CRITICAL THINKING QUESTIONS

1. Why do you think African Americans make up a larger share of state and local government employees than their percentage in the U.S. population (about 13 percent)?

2. Why do you think Hispanics constitute a smaller share of state and local government employees than their percentage in the U.S. population (approximately 15 percent)?[†]

Percentage of State and Local Government Workers Who Have the Following Characteristics, 1983 and 2007		
	1983	2007
Male	60%	55%
Female	40	45
White, Non-Hispanic	76	70
African American	17	18
Asian	n/a	3
Hispanic	5	1

*For 2005 data, see U.S. Equal Employment Opportunity Commission, *Job Patterns for Minorities and Women in State and Local Government* (EEO-4), "2007 Employment Summary by Job Category," http://www.eeoc.gov/eeoc/statistics/employment/jobpat-eeo4/2007/us.html. For earlier data, see U.S. Census Bureau, *Statistical Abstract of the United States: 2008* (U.S. Government Printing Office, 2008), Table 450.

[†]Population figures from U.S. Census Bureau, *Statistical Abstract of the United States: 2008* (U.S. Government Printing Office, 2008), Table 18, www.census.gov/compendia/statab/tables/08s0018.xls.

Reforming Personnel Systems

Criticisms against some aspects of merit systems became more acute as new management philosophies spread among governors and other top state and local government executives. Driven by books such as David Osborne and Ted Gaebler's *Reinventing Government,* by national commissions calling for reform, and by the growing number of governors and public executives with business training or experience, movements grew in many states to reform personnel systems and give public managers greater control over their workforces.[6] In part, the idea was to increase government managers' flexibility in determining how to achieve the goals of government programs, while making managers and their agencies more accountable for achieving measurable results, such as improvements in environmental quality, reductions in the time citizens need to register a vehicle, or increased "customer" satisfaction when using a state park.

Many state governments have in fact deregulated aspects of their personnel systems, especially since the early 1990s.[7] For instance, most states decentralized control over tests and the selection of candidates by reducing the power of state personnel offices and increasing the authority of agencies and managers. Many states also reduced the number of specific job levels and increased the pay ranges that people in particular positions or grades may receive at the discretion of managers. Managers could thus reward high-performing workers. In some states, many of the safeguards in traditional merit systems were eliminated and public managers were given the authority to fire employees who failed to perform well—and the procedures for terminating such employees were simplified.[8]

Georgia and Florida went particularly far in giving managers greater control over employees. In the 1990s, Georgia introduced a merit pay plan, in which employees' salaries were tied to managers' assessments of their performance.[9] The state gave greater control over personnel to operating agencies (as opposed to a single statewide personnel

Sharing Best Practices for Budget Reform

The National Governors Association has developed its Center for Best Practices* to facilitate the communication of effective and innovative developments in state government to governors and their staffs. In early 2010, the center issued a report called "The Big Reset," in which it described ways for governors to push the reset button on how their states operated with an eye toward greater efficiency at a lower cost.†

The report offers a number of suggestions for cost savings based on the best practices from across the states. It recommends that states find ways to move nonviolent offenders out of prisons and into some other form of supervised arrangement. In K–12 education, it advocates greater consolidation of school districts and greater use of online materials. The report suggests substantial reductions in pensions and other benefits offered to state employees in order to reduce future spending obligations. In higher education, the report advocates a shift in funding away from enrollments and toward degree completions, noting that only about half of students who begin a four-year college program ever graduate. It suggests pulling resources away from programs that serve very few students, reducing the number of credit hours required for some degrees, allowing high school students to take courses for college credit, and moving more educational content online.

This report represents a concerted effort by thoughtful professionals to help governors manage their states more effectively and with fewer resources. Of course, each of these proposals might save money, but some may be more "costly" than others.

CRITICAL THINKING QUESTIONS

1. What are both the short-term and long-term trade-offs for adopting the various reforms for higher education posed in the report, "The Big Reset"?

2. One of the stronger predictors of a state's economic health is the size of its college-educated workforce. What can states do to increase the number of students who begin and graduate from college?

*Located online at http://www.nga.org/center/.
† The report is online at http://www.nga.org/Files/pdf/1002STATEGOVTAFTERGREATRECESSION.PDF.

---

office) so that each agency could tailor its recruitment, selection, and promotion processes to its own needs. Finally, the state required that all newly hired or promoted persons serve "at will," that is, at the discretion of the managers. Employees could be fired for any reason, so long as it was not illegal under federal or state laws such as antidiscrimination statutes. Florida adopted similar reforms.[10]

Although most states did not make changes as extensive as those in Florida and Georgia, more than half the states (such as Arizona, Colorado, Delaware, Idaho, Iowa, Nebraska, South Carolina, Texas, and Vermont) have moved more public employees into at-will positions.[11] It is still unclear what effects the reforms have had. Terminations of employees are easier. Top executives, including governors, probably have more leverage over public employees than before the reforms went into effect.[12] However, whether this greater top-down control has produced more innovation, responsiveness, productivity, or resourcefulness is unknown. Some employee surveys have found declines in employee morale after reforms as well as reports that favoritism in hiring, promotion, and reviews has grown.[13]

The answer probably depends on who gets elected. Some governors—along with their appointees—may use their growing power over public bureaucracies to recruit and promote highly skilled individuals and encourage them to formulate flexible, creative approaches to solving state problems. Other governors and state executives, however, may use their power simply to cut costs, put in their own political supporters, or enforce particular ideological viewpoints in state bureaucracies.[14] Indeed, the most drastic personnel reforms have been pushed by conservative, pro-business governors in states where public employee unions are weak, and the reforms are often accompanied by hostility toward public employees.[15] It is possible that the spread of at-will jobs in some state governments could produce a new form of "spoils" system, if and when governors use their control over state jobs to replace some state employees with ideological allies and intimidate the rest into obedience.

Privatization of Public Services

Rather than relying on their own employees, many state and local governments have "contracted out" public services to private sector organizations, including for-profit corporations as well as nonprofit agencies. This practice, called **outsourcing,** can sometimes have advantages. Private organizations can bring a lot of expertise to public projects. Government agencies, for instance, often contract with information technology consultants to set up new computing systems. Contracting can also give governments flexibility. It allows governments

outsourcing
Contracting of government services to private firms.

to pay only for the completion of a specific project and not be responsible for maintaining a workforce between projects—or a workforce whose skills are not appropriate for later projects. In addition, when governments award contracts competitively—that is, when many private firms seek contracts by submitting bids—there are incentives for suppliers to improve the quality of their services and reduce their costs.

Another reason state governments outsource or "privatize" certain services is that many elected officials distrust their states' own public bureaucracies. In the last two decades, for instance, many state and local governments have privatized major parts of their welfare services. This shift was made possible by federal welfare reforms that gave states the authority to use private organizations to determine eligibility for welfare benefits and to provide services to low-income families.[16] Yet the decision in many states to use this authority was often driven by the belief of legislators and governors that state welfare bureaucracies were unlikely to put welfare reforms into effect.

In Wisconsin, for example, the state's legislature and governor enacted a 1995 welfare reform program called "Wisconsin Works" (also called "W-2") that required Milwaukee to contract with private agencies to implement the new program.[17] The major motivation for turning over the program to private agencies was frustration with the city's welfare bureaucracy; conservative lawmakers in particular believed that public agencies would not implement reforms designed to reduce welfare caseloads and replace cash assistance with a work program. Although Milwaukee's reliance on private agencies has encountered some setbacks and scandals throughout the years, privatization remains in effect. The state uses a fairly sophisticated set of performance measures to control the private contractors.[18] Payments to the private agencies—now mostly nonprofit corporations—are based in part on their record of placing W-2 clients into jobs, getting people into jobs they keep for at least 180 days, finding jobs with good wages, providing job skills training, and moving people with disabilities into programs appropriate for them.[19]

Other states have also privatized major parts of the social service systems. Florida and Arizona have contracted out the administration of all aspects of their welfare-to-work programs.[20] Texas was even more ambitious in its effort to outsource the management of human service programs. It created centralized toll-free call centers where any citizen seeking public assistance could reach private employees with instant computer access to eligibility information about all these programs, as well as the caller's own financial information. These operators could tell each caller whether he or she qualified for a variety of programs, including food stamps, Medicaid, cash assistance, and health insurance for their children. However, five years after the state legislature authorized this vast privatization initiative, the system is reported to be plagued with errors and lost information.[21]

Although these problems in Texas may eventually be resolved, these and other stories about outsourcing show that privatization of social services is often hard to put into practice, as it often demands that public officials exercise quite sophisticated management skills in developing appropriate contracts, finding and evaluating competing contractors, and closely monitoring the quality of services provided by the private agencies. For instance, successful privatization requires the contract between the government and the private company to define that service to the satisfaction of both parties. This task may be feasible in service areas such as garbage collection and snow removal, which can easily be defined and specified in a contract, making them attractive for privatization.[22] However, private contracts may be much more difficult to word when state and local governments want to outsource the wide range of services provided by local police or health departments.

Delegation of emergency and police powers to profit-making corporations also raises many other fundamental questions, particularly those touching on liability and protection of individual rights. A growing number of states, for instance, have outsourced some of their corrections facilities. But stories of prisoner abuse by private contractors have led some state officials to slow or even reverse this movement. Outsourcing also raises fears that private contractors will hire transient or even overseas help at lower pay, undermining merit systems and public employee morale and angering some citizens. Nonetheless, despite all the issues raised by privatization, it is likely to continue or even grow, as cities and states pressed for cash look for ways to cut back on their permanent workforces and rely increasingly on private contractors to provide basic services.

DECIDE Should Governments Contract with Faith-Based Organizations?

The expansion of government contracting with private organizations has produced many controversies in recent years, but perhaps the most divisive has surrounded the use of religious or "faith-based" organizations to provide publicly funded services. This is not a new issue, but it took on a new urgency in the wake of President George W. Bush's "Faith-Based and Community Initiative," which promoted greater governmental use of faith-based and community organizations as service providers. Faith-based organizations usually include churches, synagogues, and mosques; nonprofit organizations affiliated with a religious institution; and agencies that clearly incorporate religion in the ways they conduct their operations.

The U.S. Constitution does not allow for public funds to be directly used to support "exclusively religious" activities, such as worship, religious instruction, or proselytizing. Government should also offer and award grants in a neutral manner, favoring neither religion nor nonreligion in choosing contractors. Finally, governments need to ensure that people eligible for the services can exercise real choice between several alternative service providers, including a variety of faith-based and secular organizations.

What do you think? Should government allow or even encourage faith-based organizations to play a larger role in delivering publicly funded social services? What are some arguments for or against this?

THINKING IT THROUGH

Governments must be neutral between faith-based and secular programs, but they are not prohibited from taking steps that would encourage the involvement of faith-based service organizations. They can distribute their contracting notices more widely; they can reduce the size of individual contracts and simplify the process, thereby opening the competition to smaller faith-based and community organizations; and they can even offer training and assistance programs to less experienced organizations in order to expand the pool of service agencies able to compete for government contracts. In fact, a 2005 survey found that more than half of the states engaged in activities designed to affect government partnerships with faith-based social service providers.*

But should governments be doing this? Those who want state and local governments to open contracting processes to faith-based organizations argue that many U.S. citizens are deeply religious, and that service agencies comfortable with religion and religious concerns are more likely to connect with citizens who need help. They sometimes also argue that, despite their lack of professional training, staff in many small faith-based organizations may be more personally committed to their work and compassionate in dealing with clients. Supporters also claim that churches and other congregations are rooted in the community and can therefore help troubled clients find other people and local organizations able to help them connect back into the community.

Those who argue against such efforts dispute many of these claims. In fact, there is not much evidence on either side about the special capacities of faith-based agencies. Opponents argue that it is very difficult to create voucher systems that offer a wide array of faith-based and secular choices, except perhaps in our largest cities, and that it is hard if not impossible for most state and local governments to monitor whether all clients, regardless of their religion, are treated fairly by faith-based programs. Some opponents of contracting with faith-based organizations actually come from religious communities; they argue that getting public money compromises their independent role in society and undermines their charitable mission, which is to serve all people in need, not only those who qualify for public programs.

For more information, see the Pew Forum on Religion and Public Life, pewforum.org.

Critical Thinking Questions

1. Can you think of other possible advantages or disadvantages in using more faith-based organizations to deliver government services?

2. Do you think the advantages are likely to outweigh the disadvantages, or vice versa? If you feel the balance depends on the circumstances, what circumstances are likely to be most important?

*Mark Ragan and David J. Wright, *The Policy Environment for Faith-Based Social Services in the United States: What Has Changed Since 2002?* (Roundtable on Religion and Social Welfare Policy, 2005), p. i, www.religionandsocialpolicy.org/docs/policy/State_Scan_2005_report.pdf.

Paying for State and Local Government

LEARNING **OBJECTIVE**

10.2 Outline sources of revenue for state and local governments and associated issues and constraints.

John Shannon, an authority in the field of public finance, has written that three R's shocked state and local governments from the late 1970s to the early 1990s. The first "R" was the *revolt* of the taxpayers, which started with California's Proposition 13 (which capped property taxes) and quickly became a national phenomenon. The second "R" was the *recession* of the late 1980s and early 1990s, which placed demands on state and local governments to care for the unemployed and needy. And the third "R" was the *reduction* in federal grants, which meant state and local governments were on their own.[23] States had to search for ways to make ends meet and live within their revenue projections.

State revenues grew vigorously from 1993 through mid-2001. However, the recession of 2001–2002 had a substantial impact on state budget revenues. The recession was not severe, yet revenues dropped consistently through mid-2002, and growth remained sluggish until 2004. Meanwhile, the federal government tightened many grants. Although federal grants to the states grew from $286 billion in 2000 to nearly $449 billion in 2007, more than half of the increase was due to increased spending for health care under the Medicaid program for low-income citizens. In 2007, Medicaid alone made up 43 percent of all federal grants to state and local governments.[24]

Although state revenues increased consistently from 2004 through 2007, another drop in revenues was evident by early 2008.[25] Those declines became extreme in 2009 and do not look to be rebounding any time soon (see Figure 10–1).[26] As we have mentioned in other chapters, Medicaid and other health care programs are taking up more and more resources. Transportation and other infrastructure needs have become acute, as highways become more and more congested and aging bridges collapse. And the costs of pension benefits for an aging state and local government workforce are growing rapidly and will continue to do so well into the future.[27] Given the federal government's large deficits and financial struggles, there is also little hope that it will give states more aid, and federal spending on programs that affect the states will likely be cut. In summary, the volatility of state revenues in recent years, combined with the near-continuous growth in demand for resources, creates great challenges for state revenue systems.

Where the Money Comes From

State and local governments get most of their money from taxes. In 2007, they raised 18.8 percent of general revenues from sales taxes, 12.4 percent from personal income taxes, and 16.4 percent from property taxes (see Figure 10–2). Another 20 percent came from federal grants-in-aid, such as federal support for Medicaid, transportation, and welfare-to-work programs. Other revenues came from charges to users of government services—such as tuition from students in public universities and colleges—and from a wide variety of other sources, such as earnings from interest or property sales.[28]

The U.S. Constitution does not dictate where state and local governments are to find revenue; they are free to extract whatever taxes they wish from whomever they wish, as long as their taxing practices meet a few constitutional stipulations and do not conflict with

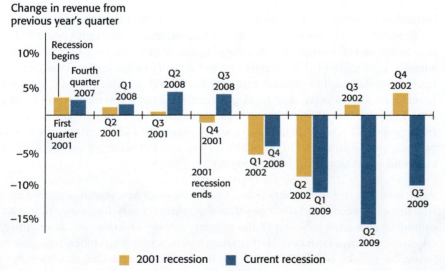

Change in revenue from previous year's quarter

■ 2001 recession   ■ Current recession

FIGURE 10–1 **2001 Recession Compared to Current Recession.**

States experienced large revenue decreases in the months following the 2001 recession. This recession has already surpassed those declines, and revenue figures are expected to continue to take a hit. ■ *What are the major differences between the recession in 2001 and the one today?*

SOURCE: "How the Recession Might Change the States," The Pew Center on the States, *State of the States*, February 2010, http://www.pewcenteronthe states.org/uploadedFiles/State_of_the_States_2010.pdf.

FIGURE 10–2 **Percentage of General Revenues Received by State and Local Governments from Major Sources, 2007.**

■ *Based on the major sources of state and local government revenue, why is it that revenue can be so volatile from one year to the next?*

SOURCE: U.S. Census Bureau, *State and Local Government Finances: 2006–07.*

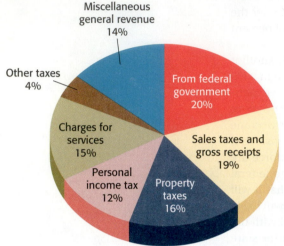

Miscellaneous general revenue 14%

Other taxes 4%

From federal government 20%

Charges for services 15%

Sales taxes and gross receipts 19%

Personal income tax 12%

Property taxes 16%

federal laws. The Constitution has been interpreted to prohibit states from taking the following actions:

1. Taxing exports or imports or levying tonnage duties without the consent of Congress
2. Using taxing powers to interfere with federal operations
3. Discriminating against interstate commerce, unduly burdening it, or taxing it directly
4. Using taxing powers to deprive people of equal protection of the law
5. Depriving individuals of their property without due process

Constitutional lawyers and judges spend much of their time applying these principles to concrete situations. Out of hundreds of disputes, courts have decided that states may collect sales taxes from interstate sales and income taxes from people and corporations within the states, even if the income was earned from interstate business. However, states may not tax the privilege of engaging in interstate commerce or the profits made through interstate transactions that cannot be apportioned to a single state.

State constitutions can and do restrict state legislatures' taxing powers. Certain kinds of property, such as that used for educational, charitable, or religious purposes, are exempt from taxation. State constitutions frequently list the kinds and amounts of taxes that may be collected and from which sources.[29]

Within these constitutional and legal constraints, state and local governments still have considerable flexibility in designing and altering their tax systems. In making these decisions, they may take into account several criteria. A good tax, for instance, may be one that is easy to administer fairly; one that does not burden individuals and corporations with a lot of extra paperwork and activities; one that does not demand enormous and intrusive governmental agencies to ensure compliance; and one that does not allow some people to avoid paying their taxes much more easily than others. A good tax should also distribute financial burdens fairly; that is, it should be at least roughly related to people's or corporations' ability to pay. Governments may also want taxes that are stable or predictable; great uncertainty about future revenues can make it difficult to make basic decisions about budgets and programs. A good tax would also provide what governments need to pay for public programs and be adaptable to changing fiscal needs. We could formulate many other tests as well, but keep these basic criteria in mind as we review the different ways in which state and local governments raise revenues.

The Property Tax

In 1890, economist Edwin Seligman called the property tax "the worst tax known in the civilized world." The tax is not easy to administer, and it sometimes bears little relationship to taxpayers' income or other measures of their ability to pay.[30] In public opinion surveys, a plurality of U.S. citizens has consistently called it the "worst" or "least fair" tax.[31] Nonetheless, the **general property tax** is still a major revenue source for local governments; 23.6 percent of local government general revenues came from property taxes in 2007.[32] New Hampshire earns more than 60 percent of state and local tax revenue from property taxes, making it the most dependent of all the states on this source of revenue. At the other end of the scale, Hawaii and Delaware get less than 15 percent of state and local taxes from the property tax.[33]

general property tax

A tax levied by local and some state governments on real property or personal, tangible property, the major portion of which is on the estimated value of one's home and land.

Administration of the Property Tax   A hundred years ago, wealth primarily consisted of *real property*—land and buildings—that was relatively easy for assessors to value. Their estimate was a good indicator of the property owner's ability to pay taxes. Today, wealth takes many forms—both *tangible* (furniture, jewels, washing machines, rugs, paintings) and *intangible* (stocks, bonds, money in the bank), and it is possible to concentrate a large amount of wealth in the contents of a small rented apartment. The nature of real property has also changed. It no longer consists mainly of barns, houses, and land but rather of large industrial plants, huge retail stores, and office buildings whose value is hard to measure. In addition, property ownership is less likely these days to reflect the ability to pay taxes. An elderly couple with a large house valued at $450,000 may be living on Social Security payments and a small allowance provided by their children. But they must pay higher property taxes than a young couple with two healthy incomes who live in a rented apartment.

Although many communities stipulate that the general property tax be imposed on all property, this is not what actually happens. Significant amounts of real property are exempted from property taxes because they are owned by tax-exempt groups, such as churches, charitable organizations, and colleges. Local governments also often waive the tax as an economic development inducement or for other reasons. As a result, two taxpayers may own similar property, but one is assessed at a higher rate. Intangible personal property is also seldom taxed.

The general property tax is hard to adjust to changing circumstances. It is typically administered by an assessor, whose **assessment** may or may not reflect the real market value of the property. In some states, the assessment is legally required to be a percentage of market value—say, 25 percent. The property tax rate is usually a set amount per $1,000 of assessed valuation or a similar measure. Modern advances in computer record keeping and the use of sophisticated geographic information services have made it easier to keep assessments current. Local and state governments can do very little to change the assessment, but they can raise or lower the tax rates.

A property tax bill typically includes fees or taxes charged by three, four, or more government units, such as the city, county, school board, water utility, and other special districts. The lump-sum payment aspect of the property tax is one reason for its widespread unpopularity and has prompted some places to permit taxpayers to pay their taxes in installments, often collected when homeowners make their monthly mortgage payments to banks, which in turn pay the local government when the property taxes are due.

Property Taxes and Public Education   Local reliance on the property tax to support public schools has generated increasing controversy in recent years. The amount of money available to finance education varies tremendously from area to area; rich suburban areas with a high property valuation per pupil can spend much more than poor areas such as the central cities. Reformers have urged the states to take over the financing of public education or at least to assume a greater share of the burden, in order to reduce differences from community to community or to provide enough support to offer an adequate education in all communities. Most states distribute funds to local districts in an attempt to ensure more equitable expenditures, although differences in district expenditures remain large in many states.

assessment
The valuation a government places on property for the purposes of taxation.

Those wanting to reduce differences in expenditures across public school districts have often turned to the courts. As noted in our "For the People" feature in Chapter 3, several state courts have ruled that wide differences between school districts in per-pupil expenditures are inconsistent with the equal protection clause of the Fourteenth Amendment.[34] The California Supreme Court, for example, saw such differences as violating the state constitution.[35] However, in 1973, the U.S. Supreme Court held that there is no federal constitutional requirement that the amount spent per pupil in each school district be the same.[36]

This decision temporarily slowed the push toward equalization of school expenditures, but the controversy remains. School funding cases have been brought in 45 of 50 states, some focusing on a right to an "adequate" education. Adequacy lawsuits usually ask state courts to enforce provisions in state constitutions requiring state governments to guarantee a "sound basic education."[37] The suits claim "all schools must receive the resources [usually some minimum financing per pupil] necessary to provide

Third-grade students at Green Bay Elementary School in North Chicago, Illinois, which has the highest poverty level in its district. ■ *Why do some people argue that funding for public schools shouldn't come primarily from local property taxes?*

students with the opportunity for a meaningful education that enables them to meet challenging new standards."[38] Adequacy suits have been successful in recent years. By early 2010, courts in 28 states had handed down rulings requiring states to remedy either the equity or the adequacy of their education systems; 20 of those rulings were based on adequacy claims.[39]

The Property Tax Revolt   Hostility to the property tax spawned the tax revolts of the last three decades of the twentieth century. The watershed event in the politics of tax cutting was the 1978 passage of California's Proposition 13, which limits increases in property taxes to a maximum of 2 percent each year. Throughout the 1970s, California property taxes had risen dramatically, spurring voters to write this initiative to cut them. Its passage led to similar property tax limitations in other states, but local governments still get nearly three-fourths of their tax revenue from the property tax.[40] In states such as California that have the most stringent limits on the growth of property taxes, the effect has been to shift more of the spending to the state level, where revenues are usually provided by income and sales taxes. Because states usually attach conditions to their aid, local governments then lose control over local programs, such as education. Because the property tax is more stable than most other taxes, when it is limited as a revenue source, the whole state and local tax system becomes more volatile, prone to big declines during recessions and large increases in times of economic growth.

Passage of Proposition 13 made tax reduction an important issue nationwide. It triggered taxing and spending limits in more than a dozen states and helped launch movements for constitutional amendments setting federal spending limits, requiring a balanced federal budget, and **indexing** income tax brackets (automatically adjusting income tax rates to rise with inflation so that, in effect, they remain constant). Tax reduction was not limited to ballot initiatives but spread to state legislatures, most of which reduced income, sales, or property taxes.

Tax cuts are only one way of attempting to curb government spending. States and localities have also adopted various limits that restrict future spending to current levels, hold annual increases to a fixed percentage, or tie them to increases in personal income or inflation.[41] New Jersey was the first state to enact spending limits that applied to both state and local governments. In 1976, it limited growth in state expenditures to the annual percentage increase in per capita personal income and restricted localities to increases of no more than 5 percent without voter approval. As of December 2008, 30 states operated with some sort of tax or expenditure limit.[42]

Property Tax Reform   Despite its weaknesses, the general property tax remains an important source of revenue for local government. Supporters say it is practical and suitable because real property is the chief beneficiary of many local services, such as fire protection. It is also a stable, predictable source of funding, especially important for local governments, because many of their functions—such as police and fire protection, record keeping, and provision of prisons, jails, schools, and libraries—are fairly constant from year to year. This stability can be critical during and after recessions. For instance, state funding of K–12 education dropped substantially during and after the economic slowdown of 2001–2002 because of sharp drops in income and sales taxes. However, local funding of education—most of which came from property taxes—continued to grow in most states between 2002 and 2010, mitigating some of the effects of state cuts.[43]

Communities may correct some of the bad features of the general property tax by improving assessment and administration methods. One reform effort is the *circuit-breaker exemption* (sometimes called a *negative income tax*) by which most states and certain cities give a form of tax relief to lower-income families and the elderly. The idea is to protect family income from property tax overload in the same way an electrical circuit breaker protects a family home from an electrical current overload: "When the property tax burden of an individual exceeds a predetermined percentage of personal income, the circuit breaker goes into effect to relieve the excess financial pressure."[44] The circuit-breaker property tax exemption seems most popular in the Great Lakes and Plains states and least popular in the Southeast, where property tax burdens are low.

indexing
Providing automatic increases to compensate for inflation.

Other Taxes

Although the property tax is the main source of *local* revenue, state and some local governments raise revenues through a wide range of other taxes. Many have been used for several decades, but they have become a larger part of total state and local tax collections since the property tax revolts of the 1970s and 1980s discussed earlier. States and localities seek to diversify their taxes to "spread the pain" of taxes as much as possible (refer back to Figure 10–1).

Sales Taxes   Born during the Great Depression, the **sales tax** is the most important source of revenue for states, which collected more than $352 billion in 2007.[45] The national average for percentage of tax revenues that come from the sales tax is 33 percent, but states like Washington (62 percent), Tennessee (61 percent), Florida and South Dakota (56 percent), and Texas (50 percent) are all well above the national average.[46] Nearly all states impose some kind of general sales tax, normally on retail sales.

Local sales taxes were uncommon until after World War II, but now 35 states allow counties and cities to impose sales taxes. Sales taxes are unpopular with local merchants, who fear they drive business away. In most cases, this is a minor issue that arises only along state borders where consumers can easily drive into another state with a lower sales tax to make purchases.

Sales taxes are easy to administer and produce large amounts of revenue. Many consumers consider them relatively painless because paying a small amount every day means not having to pay a large tax bill all at one time. But labor groups and low-income consumers remain opposed to sales taxes, favoring wider use of the income tax instead. They argue that people with small incomes spend a larger percentage of their budgets on food and clothing than the wealthy do, so sales taxes on these items fall most heavily on those least able to pay. That is why many states exempt necessities—primarily food and medicine—from the sales tax.

Although nearly all states tax some services, none has a broad-based tax on services.[47] It is politically difficult to establish such taxes, as each service industry fights its tax in state

sales tax
A general tax on sales transactions, sometimes exempting food and medicine.

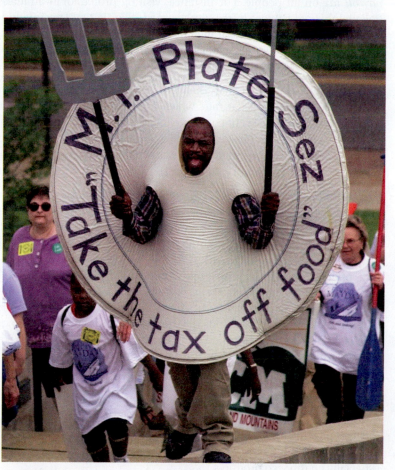

Tennessee legislators considered adopting an income tax in 2001 and 2002 to deal with their state's fiscal crisis. Adding a small personal income tax made sense to many legislators because the state relied very heavily on its sales tax, which was already one of the highest in the nation. However, protests in the summers of both years strengthened opposition to the proposed tax, and Tennessee still does not tax personal income. Some protestors, such as this one, sought relief from the state's very broad sales tax. ■ *What are the trade-offs for a state in relying on a sales tax versus an income tax for its primary source of revenue?*

legislatures and governors' offices. "Expanding the tax base to consumer services is good tax policy," said one economist, "but the service providers rarely see it that way."[48] That may change in the future, however, as the states face greater pressures to find new revenues, and as the U.S. economy continues to shift away from producing goods and toward the provision of an ever-wider array of services. Among the kinds of services currently taxed are cable television, landscaping, income tax preparation, pest control, laundry and dry cleaning, and photocopying.

State and local officials listen with concern to talk about the federal government's imposing a **value-added tax (VAT)** like that used in many western European countries. This tax is imposed on the value added to a product at *each stage* of production and distribution. Should the federal government impose such a tax, state and local officials fear that their ability to use the sales tax will be reduced.

Individual Income Taxes

The state individual, or personal, income tax has been one of the fastest-growing revenue sources for most states in recent decades. Along with the sales tax, it is one of the two largest revenue sources for state government. The individual income tax accounts for approximately 34 percent of all state tax collections, with Oregon (individual income taxes account for 72 percent of its revenues), New York (56 percent), Massachusetts (54 percent), and Virginia (53 percent) well above the national average. By contrast, seven mostly western states—Arizona, Florida, Nevada, South Dakota, Texas, Washington, and Wyoming—do not collect individual income taxes.[49]

Individual income taxes, usually based on federal taxable income, are generally mildly **progressive taxes;** that is, the rate goes up with income. They do not rise as sharply as the federal income tax, however, and seldom are more than 8 percent of taxable income. In the 1990s, many states reduced their highest individual income tax rates.

States generally do not allow local governments to levy income taxes. However, some cities—following the lead of Philadelphia and Toledo—now collect a *wage tax*, and most cities in Ohio as well as cities, towns, and school districts in Pennsylvania levy a similar *payroll tax* on all people. For instance, visiting professional athletes who compete in Philadelphia are subject to the city's earned-income tax. The Toledo tax also applies to corporate profits. A municipal income tax enables hard-pressed cities to collect money from citizens who use city facilities but live in the suburbs. Similar taxes are collected by New York City, Detroit, and Louisville.

Corporate Income and Other Business Taxes

Most states also impose a corporate income tax, usually at a flat rate, which accounts for approximately 6 percent of state taxes.[50] Many states have cut corporate income tax rates or granted generous exemptions as a way to try to attract businesses to their state. States also collect a variety of other kinds of taxes on business activity, including taxes on business assets, corporate franchise taxes, licensing taxes and fees, and taxes imposed when new businesses are formed.

Excise Taxes

Nearly all states tax gasoline, alcohol, and cigarettes; these taxes on specific items are known as **excise taxes.** Because many cities also tax these items, the combined local, state, and federal levies often double the cost of these items for the consumer. Gasoline taxes are sometimes combined with the funds collected for automobile and driver's licenses and are earmarked for highway construction and maintenance. Liquor taxes often consist of both license fees to manufacture or sell alcoholic beverages and levies on their sale or consumption; they are often used for general government spending.

Some states own liquor stores, whose profits go to the state treasury. High taxation of liquor is justified on the grounds that it reduces the amount consumed, falls on an item that is not a necessity of life, and eases the task of law enforcement. Some states, such as North Carolina, set aside part of their alcohol taxes for mental health programs and the rehabilitation of alcoholics. If the tax is raised too high, however, liquor purchases tend to be diverted into illegal channels, and tax revenues fall off.

The rationale for taxing cigarettes is similar. High tobacco taxes in states such as Alaska, New Jersey, and Hawaii, which do not grow tobacco, and low tobacco taxes in tobacco-growing states such as Virginia, North Carolina, and South Carolina, have led to interstate smuggling. Some states levy a general sales tax on top of the excise tax, especially on tobacco products.

value-added tax (VAT)
A tax on the increased value of a product at each stage of production and distribution rather than just at the point of sale.

progressive tax
A tax graduated so that people with higher incomes pay a larger fraction of their income than people with lower incomes.

excise tax
A consumer tax on a specific kind of merchandise, such as tobacco.

Severance Taxes In several states, **severance taxes** have been a key source of revenue. These are taxes on the privilege of "severing" or removing from the land such natural resources as coal, oil, timber, and gas. In the nation as a whole, severance taxes account for only slightly more than 1 percent of all state taxes. But a few states rely heavily on them. Severance taxes are the main tax source in Alaska, where they make up 50 percent of tax collections, and Wyoming (46 percent); New Mexico, North Dakota, and Oklahoma also get more than 10 percent of their tax revenue from the severance tax.[51] Although 35 states have some type of severance tax, significant revenues from it are not available to most because they do not produce large amounts of natural resources. Tax revenues from severance taxes go up and down with the price of oil, gas, and coal.

The state and local taxes described here do not begin to exhaust the kinds of taxes collected by state and local governments. Admission taxes, stock transfer taxes, inheritance taxes, pari-mutuel taxes, and taxes on utilities and insurance are also common.

Other Sources of Revenue

In addition to taxation, states derive revenue from fees and special service charges. At least 10 percent of the money collected by state and local governments comes from inspecting buildings, recording titles, operating courts, licensing professions, disposing of garbage, and other services. Parking meters have become an important revenue source for some cities. Municipal governments frequently operate water supply and local transit systems. City-operated liquor stores are administered by, and turn a profit in, certain cities in Alaska, Minnesota, North Carolina, and South Dakota. Some states and cities run other business enterprises, such as cable television services, from which they make money (and sometimes lose it, too). North Dakota, for example, operates a state-owned bank. Municipally owned gas and power companies often contribute to city treasuries. In some cases, utility profits are large enough to make other city taxes unnecessary.

Legalized Gambling Recent years have seen a dramatic increase in legalized gambling in the United States. For many years, only Nevada permitted legalized casino gambling, but in 2007, 14 states permitted commercial casinos, 28 had casinos operated by Native American tribes, and 45 permitted racetrack betting.[52] Only Hawaii and Utah do not permit some form of legalized gambling. The spread of casinos was in part a consequence of Native American tribes asserting their right to self-rule on reservations and establishing casinos in states such as California, Michigan, Connecticut, and South Dakota. In addition, gambling companies asserted that prohibitions against land-based casinos did not apply to floating ones, and they promoted gambling on riverboats and dockside casinos.

In 2006, state and local governments received revenues of $5.7 billion from taxes on the operations of casinos and pari-mutuel betting (mostly betting on horse and dog races), up from $3 billion in 1998. Yet states varied greatly in their reliance on this revenue source. In 2007, Nevada and West Virginia received 13.6 and 9.2 percent of their general revenues from gambling, and 20 other states received 2 percent or more of their revenues from these sources.[53]

Lotteries The District of Columbia, Puerto Rico, and 42 states operate lotteries as a special form of state-sponsored and state-administered gambling that raises money for public purposes.[54] In fact, the Continental Congress ran a lottery to help finance the Revolutionary War. Indeed, all 13 original states used lotteries as a form of voluntary taxation in the 1780s. Lotteries also helped establish some of the nation's earliest colleges, notably Princeton, Harvard, and Yale. In 1964, New Hampshire was the first state to revive the practice in modern times to help balance its budget.

In recent decades, state lotteries have increased in popularity, in part because they increase revenues without raising taxes. Although state-run lotteries provide only 3 percent of what states collect in taxes, they provide essential revenues that would have to be replaced by other sources, all of which are less politically popular.[55] States pay out between 50 and 70 percent of their gross receipts from lotteries in prizes and approximately 6 percent to cover administration costs. The remaining revenues are used for public purposes.

As gasoline prices rose to more than $4 per gallon in 2008, some state governments cut their gasoline taxes temporarily to give drivers short-run relief. ■ *Can the regressive nature of excise taxes be justified based on the items taxed being "nonessential" and the fact that the revenue brought in is much needed in the states?*

severance tax
A tax on the privilege of "severing" such natural resources as coal, oil, timber, and gas from the land.

States are often ambivalent about legalizing gambling. They get substantial revenues from taxes on gambling, but many voters view the activity as harmful or even sinful. States sometimes express their ambivalence by permitting gambling only in certain places, such as Indian reservations, cruise ships, or riverboats. This cruise ship, docked in South Carolina, travels into international waters before allowing passengers to gamble. ■ *How might the gambling policies in a state be affected by the gambling policies of neighboring states?*

State lotteries generated net profits in excess of $17.7 billion in 2007, up from $8.3 billion in 1993.[56] Many were adopted as a result of a statewide referendum, and states use the revenues for a variety of purposes. About half of the states earmark most or all of their proceeds for education; a significant number of others commit their proceeds to the state general fund. Some states, such as Kansas and Oregon, designate lottery profits for economic development; Minnesota commits part to the environment; Pennsylvania and West Virginia designate senior citizens' programs.

Lottery revenues are not spread evenly across the states. In 2007, approximately 38 percent of all lottery revenues were collected by California, Florida, Michigan, New York, and Texas. In fact, nearly 80 percent of lottery revenue was collected in 15 states—the remaining 27 states with lotteries collected the remaining 20 percent.[57]

Proponents of lotteries identify a popular cause such as education, the environment, or senior citizens as the beneficiaries of lottery profits in hopes of getting popular support for passage of the lottery. Opposition often comes from church groups, which contend that state lotteries are immoral because they are a form of legalized gambling. Proponents counter that churches often raise funds through raffles, bingo, and other games of chance. Opponents also argue that lotteries are a bad investment because they yield a poor rate of return. Proponents respond that tickets are purchased more for their entertainment value than as an investment.

Grants Grants between governments, usually from higher to lower levels of government, are essential and influential sources of revenue for state and local governments. Federal grants to state governments made up 30 percent of state general revenues in 2007, down slightly from recent years, but up from 26 percent in 1992.[58] The federal government once allocated large sums to cities, but its assistance was only 4 percent of local revenues in 2007. Local governments rely heavily on grants from states, however, which gave them $450 billion in assistance in 2007, or 34 percent of their total revenues.[59]

Most of the growth in federal grants as sources of revenues for state governments has come from Medicaid, a federal program that provides health coverage for low-income individuals. Medicaid accounted for 44 percent of federal grants in 2008, much more than its 30 percent share in 1990.[60] Other major areas of federal assistance include income support (21 percent in 2008), education and training (13 percent), and transportation (11 percent). Overall, federal assistance in the areas of health, social services, and income support is substantial, usually providing most of the funding for these programs at the state level. Outside these areas, however, states receive relatively little federal assistance and fund most functions with their own taxes.

State officials return revenues collected from certain taxes to local governments, often without specifying the purposes for which the money should be used. Local governments receive state and federal grants in a wide range of areas, including education, transportation, corrections, law enforcement, housing, welfare, community development, and health care. Education is particularly dependent on state aid, which grew from 46 percent of total revenues supporting schools in 1992 to a peak of 50 percent in 2001—after which state aid dropped to 48 percent of total education revenues in 2007.[61]

Local governments often see state and federal grants as enhancing the services they provide. Local governments usually need only spend a modest amount of their own revenues on a particular function to qualify for much larger sums of grant money from state or federal governments in support of the same function. But grant money may not

Secretary of Labor Hilda Solis talks with former employees of New United Motor Manufacturing, Inc. (NUMMI) at the company's Remployment Center, where the federal government is providing $19 million in grants to retrain workers. The auto manufacturing company, which closed in 2010, will reopen as production center for Tesla electric cars. ■ *What role should governments play to help businesses and workers adapt to a changing economy?*

be available for some pressing local priorities, or the strings attached to the money may permit state and federal governments to set local priorities. In such cases, are local governments wise to pursue the grants, or should they put their money into their most pressing priorities? Local governments also worry about becoming dependent on grant money now if state or federal money should dry up in the future.

Borrowing Money

State and local governments collect large sums of money to pay for current operating expenses—garbage collection, police protection, and social services. To fund long-term projects for expensive efforts such as building schools, constructing roads, and clearing slums—so-called *capital expenditures*—cities and states often have to borrow money. Because these improvements have long lives and add to the wealth of the community, it is reasonable to pay for them over time. For this purpose, governments issue bonds. Bonds are financial instruments issued by state and local governments and bought by investors. In exchange for a cash payment at the time the bond is issued, the issuing government promises the investor that it will repay the loan with interest over time, usually throughout a long period, such as 20–40 years.

During the early years of the nineteenth century, states and cities subsidized railroad and canal builders. The money for these and other public improvements came from bonds issued by the cities or states and purchased by investors. But the governments often failed to make the payments to investors, and public debts to investors piled up and remained long after the improvements had lost their value. Eventually, governments often defaulted on their obligations to repay. Aroused by the government officials' abuse of their authority, voters insisted on constitutional amendments restricting legislative discretion to borrow money. The power to borrow money for the long term now routinely requires voter approval.

Increasingly important during the last few decades are special-purpose governments or special districts: airport authorities, bridge and highway authorities, water and wastewater districts, public transit authorities, and community college districts. Their creation has led government to turn to *revenue bonds* to help finance their operations. The repayments and dividends due to investors come from tolls and fees charged by the facility. In most cases, revenue bonds do not require voter approval, making it much easier to issue this kind of debt and also to spend more on services such as public transportation.[62]

Harrisburg, Pennsylvania sold municipal bonds to help finance city construction projects, but with rising costs and shrinking tax revenue the city has $68 million in debt payments this year that it cannot pay. Its debt was downgraded to five levels below investment grade by Moody's Investors Service, and the city is considering declaring bankruptcy. ■ *What are the potential risks and benefits of selling bonds to pay for major construction projects?*

State and local bonds are attractive to investors because the interest they earn is exempt from federal income tax. State and local governments can borrow money at a lower interest rate than private businesses can, and although credit ratings differ sharply according to economic health, the credit of most cities and states is good. In 2007, for instance, more than 60 percent of the bond ratings for the 85 largest cities were at the two highest possible levels (AAA or AA, which are ratings assigned by Moody's Investors Service).[63] More recent budgetary and economic pressures have likely lowered those ratings somewhat, but thus far, cities continue to be able to find buyers for their bonds fairly easily. Cities with lower ratings also sell bonds, but they need to offer buyers a higher rate of interest; thus, it is more expensive for such cities to borrow money. Most local governments face limits on the general level of debt they can incur, but the sale of bonds is often not covered by such limits. That makes selling bonds an attractive alternative for local governments. However, as discussed in the opener, states need to be careful about maintaining their financial health in order for investors to continue buying their bonds.

State and Local Government Spending

LEARNING OBJECTIVE

10.3 Identify the major expenditures of state and local governments.

State and local governments certainly collect a lot of money through taxes, federal grants, and other sources. Where does the money go? State and local governments spent $2.26 trillion in 2007. More than half of that total went to two functions: health and education. (See Figure 10–3.) Most of the spending on health was disbursed through the Medicaid program, a joint federal–state program that provides medical assistance to low-income families. Three other spending categories were also large, between 7 and 9 percent each: public safety expenditures, which included police, fire protection, and corrections; environment/ housing, which encompassed parks and recreation facilities, housing, waste management, and natural resource management; and transportation, which mostly consisted of expenditures on roads and highways. Education spending—including spending on elementary and secondary schools, higher education, and other education programs—varied from 30 to 40 percent of the total spending in different states.

The ways in which state and local governments spend their money have varied over time. Although the percent of state and local expenditures that went to elementary and secondary schools (K–12) is the same today as it was in 1996,[64] other spending priorities have changed. Spending on health grew from 19.8 percent of all state and local expenditures in 1996 to 21.2 percent in 2007, whereas spending on cash assistance dropped from 2.3 percent of the government spending in 1996 to less than 1.0 percent in 2007. Spending on higher education also increased, from 8.5 percent in 1996 to 9.0 percent in 2007.

These patterns of spending and trends point to some of the difficulties state and local governments face in controlling costs. Health programs and elementary and secondary education absorb 45 percent of all state and local spending, yet expenditures for these functions are not easy to cut. Medicaid, for example, is a matching program, in which the federal government provides at least $1 (and sometime up to $3) for every dollar the state spends. As a result, state cuts in Medicaid can produce much larger cuts on total health care spending in a state, including revenues for politically powerful industries, such as hospitals and nursing homes.[65] Elementary and secondary education spending is also hard to control, though for different reasons. It is a mandatory function in nearly all state constitutions, and its primary constituency, parents, is large and includes many middle-class citizens who vote and have intense feelings about the quality of the educational institutions their children attend.

As a result, state and local budget cutting or control must generally focus on the remaining 55 percent. But that too is an increasingly difficult task. Cash assistance payments have been reduced dramatically since the mid-1990s, but now that they represent such a tiny part of the budget, few savings are likely to be found there in the future. Compounding the challenge is the fact that in recent years, prices for the goods and services that state and local governments tend to spend money on, such as transportation, fuel for heating and cooling buildings, road construction materials, health benefits for current and retired employees, and elementary and secondary education, have been increasing faster than general prices overall.[66]

FIGURE 10–3 State and Local Spending, 2006–2007.

■ *Based on the distribution of spending, why do you suppose state and local governments find it so difficult to cut their budgets?*

NOTE: This figure lists vendor payments in health care.

SOURCE: U.S. Census Bureau, *State and Local Government Finances: 2006–07.*

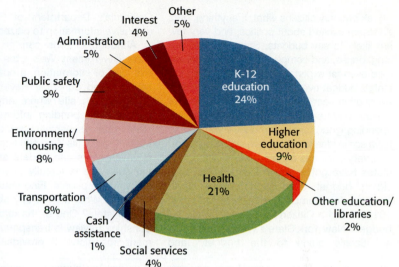

Assessing State and Local Performance

States and localities are where and how most government services are delivered. They are often responsible for delivering on the promises the federal government makes, whether in health care, education, homeland security, economic development, or social services. As the federal government remains focused on war and other national security issues, its budget deficit remains high, and Social Security and Medicare spending grows, states can expect even greater pressure to fill the gaps created by dwindling federal spending for discretionary programs.

In many ways, states have been more responsive than the federal government in recent years to public demands concerning health care coverage, stem cell research, environmental protection, education, and many other issues. However, there are grounds for concern about states' capacities to fund and administer the programs they enact. First, many people worry that state revenue systems do not function well in the new economy. For instance, these systems are better at collecting taxes on goods than on services, on tangible property (such as buildings and land) than on intangible property (such as patents and information), and on businesses whose operations occur in specific locations than on those that are partly virtual and global. In the new economy, however, services, intangible property, and business activities without clear geographic locations are increasingly common. If these trends mean that an increasing number of economic activities such as Internet sales are hard or even impossible to tax, state and local governments may either lose revenues or be forced to raise rates on the activities they can still tax, possibly increasing differences in tax burdens across different businesses and activities and exacerbating inequities. A number of states have responded with efforts to increase the collection of sales taxes on purchases

LEARNING **OBJECTIVE**

10.4 Assess the challenges facing state revenue and management systems.

By the People

MAKING A DIFFERENCE

Monitoring State Spending

Ask ordinary citizens what, if anything, gets them excited about politics, and very few are likely to say budgets. State budgets are long, dense, and complex documents that are hard even for experts to follow. Yet setting the state's budget every year (or, for some states, every other year) is one of the most important actions a state takes. Remember, states are spending (your) taxpayer money—you should have some idea what they are spending it on.

Every state has a state budget office, and states have gotten much better about providing budget information online. North Carolina, for example, provides a Budgeting 101 link and a Citizens Guide to the state's budget.* New York State's Web site also has a citizen's guide to the budget,† and

California's Department of Finance offers extensive information to citizens online.††

Although citizens can go to individual state government Web sites and hunt for this kind of information, a nonprofit organization called Sunshine Review has established a Web site where anyone can get budget and spending information for any state (http://sunshinereview.org/index.php/ Main_Page). This Web site is a wiki Web site in which users can update any element of the site—this is literally government oversight by the people. Find your state on this Web site. What does it say about spending in your state? One of the main missions of Sunshine Review is transparency in government operations. It provides a chart that

reports how easy it is to search state government Web sites for spending information (http://sunshinereview.org/index.php/States_ with_spending_online). How open is your state?

CRITICAL THINKING QUESTIONS

1. How easy should it be for citizens to track state spending? Should companies that receive state contracts have some privacy regarding their business dealings with the state?

2. What are the pros and cons of using the Internet and a wiki system like Sunshine Review to keep citizens informed about state spending?

---

* The respective links are http://www.osbm.state.nc.us/ncosbm/budget/budgeting101.shtm and http://www.osbm.state.nc.us/new_content/ Citizen_Guide_to_Budget.pdf.

† Located at http://www.budget.state.ny.us/citizen/index.html.

†† Located at http://www.dof.ca.gov/.

---

made by consumers using online retailers like Amazon.com, Overstock.com, and Blue Nile, but the U.S. Supreme Court ruled in 1992 that retailers cannot be forced to collect sales taxes for sales that cross state lines unless they have a physical presence in the state in which the customer resides.[67]

Second, states vary greatly in their fiscal capacities—the economic resources they may tax—and these differences lead to large differences in the extent to which they can meet demands for public programs. For example, states vary in average personal

The new global economy in which services rather than goods are of value, and businesses have online rather than local offices, presents a challenge to state and local governments trying to institute a fair taxing system. ■ *Should states be allowed to collect sales taxes on purchases made online by consumers in their state?*

incomes. In 2008, per capita personal incomes in Mississippi, Utah, and West Virginia were all less than $31,000, whereas in Connecticut, New Jersey, and Massachusetts, they were more than $50,000.[68] Because higher incomes are associated with higher consumption and property values, these income differences affect how easy it is for states to raise revenues not only through income taxes but also through sales and property taxes. States also vary in the natural resources, such as oil, that can be extracted from their lands, differences that in turn affect their abilities to obtain severance taxes.

We can measure state fiscal capacity in many ways, but however we do so, differences are large and also affect state spending on functions such as health care, social services, transportation, and environmental protection.[69] States therefore differ substantially in what they can do for their residents, and many people view these differences as creating inequities in our governmental system. The federal government may attempt to reduce differences by giving larger federal grants-in-aid to low-fiscal-capacity states. However, although some programs, such as Medicaid, provide more generous financial support to relatively poor states, the federal grant system as a whole does not reduce differences in state governments' revenues.[70]

Third, state and local governments also vary greatly in their administrative capabilities. Recall in Chapter 2 where we discussed a 2008 report in *Governing* magazine that rated the performance of states' governments. In that report, only five states won an A or A– grade for their financial management, and only four got an A or A– for managing their employees effectively.[71] What do these differences in state administrative capacity mean? Bad management can mean delays in completing important projects, whereas strong state management capacities can be critically important in implementing challenging new programs.[72]

Although differences remain large, states have improved their management capabilities. As one experienced observer noted in 2008:

> It has been uneven and sometimes halting, but states have been steadily improving their management capacity in most key areas over the past decade or longer. More governors are paying attention to the quality of management, and more are setting measurements of performance, pressuring top managers to meet them, and then reporting the results. Party and ideology seem to have little to do with it; in fact, the language of management reform increasingly seems to unify chief executives when ideology does not.[73]

CHAPTER **SUMMARY**

10.1 Describe the hiring process for public employees, and assess attempts at reform and privatization.

Public employees are largely hired through merit systems. Merit systems have come under attack in recent years, and many states have reformed their personnel systems to give managers greater flexibility and power over employees. The effects of these changes are not yet known, but they may have different effects depending on state leadership.

States have increased their reliance on private sector organizations to deliver many services by "contracting out" or outsourcing. Arguments made in favor of privatization include lower cost and better services, management flexibility, and the unwillingness or inability of state bureaucracies to implement certain programs, such as welfare reform. Privatization, however, is not easy to do. It often requires precisely worded contracts, useful performance measures, and extensive oversight to avoid severe problems of accountability.

10.2 Outline sources of revenue for state and local governments and associated issues and constraints.

State and local governments get most of their money from taxes, although they also raise considerable revenues from federal grants-in-aid and a diverse array of charges and fees. The national Constitution imposes some constraints on state tax policies, but it also gives state and local governments a lot of flexibility.

The general property tax, despite its unpopularity, remains a major revenue source for public schools. It contributes to inequalities in school funding across communities, but it provides schools and other local functions with a stable, predictable source of revenues. State governments depend heavily on sales taxes, income taxes, excise taxes, and severance taxes. They have recently diversified their revenue sources by turning to such devices as lotteries and other forms of legalized gambling. States also rely increasingly on federal grants-in-aid. However, these grants are concentrated in the health and income support areas, and they do not provide much support for most governmental functions. Intergovernmental grants from states to cities and school districts have increased in importance as local governments have had to deal with rising costs and expectations but limited revenues.

10.3 Identify the major expenditures of state and local governments.

State and local governments spend most of their money on only two functions: health and education. In the last decade, spending on health programs has increased, whereas spending on welfare has declined as a percentage of state and local budgets. Three other spending categories were also large: public safety expenditures, management of housing/environment, and transportation.

10.4 Assess the challenges facing state revenue and management systems.

State revenue and management systems face many challenges in the future, including the problems of raising revenues in a rapidly changing economy and reducing large differences across states in their revenue and management capacities.

CHAPTER **SELF-TEST**

10.1 Describe the hiring process for public employees, and assess attempts at reform and privatization.

1. In one or two paragraphs, explain why state and local governments employ a workforce as large as 20 million people.

2. In a short essay, evaluate the move to merit pay and flexibility in state agencies. Discuss the reasons for the shift and why you feel it has been a positive or a negative change.

3. In a short essay, describe the benefits and problems associated with privatizing government services. Argue for or against further privatization, and discuss whether problems would be reduced if some services were returned to government employees. Why or why not?

10.2 Outline sources of revenue for state and local governments and associated issues and constraints.

4. In a paragraph, discuss and critique the criteria for an effective tax. Add any additional criteria you believe would be useful.

5. Describe the original rationale for property taxes and why that rationale is no longer as tenable as it once was.

6. Imagine that you are a governor and must determine how to finance your state government's operations. Identify which taxes and other revenue sources you will use and which you will not. Defend your choices.

10.3 Identify the major expenditures of state and local governments.

7. Examine Figure 10–3. Write one or two paragraphs explaining where state and local governments spend most of their money, and give your opinion of this distribution. Explain whether you think it should change, how, and why.

8. Assess the idea of tax incentives to attract businesses to a certain locale. In a few sentences, discuss the positive and negative consequences of doing so.

10.4 Assess the challenges facing state revenue and management systems.

9. In a paragraph, explain why some feel that state revenue systems do not function well in the new economy, and show how states may adjust to the new economy.

10. Which challenge do you believe is the most pressing for state governments? In an essay, outline the challenge, its importance, and possible responses to it.

---

mypoliscilab EXERCISES

Where participation leads to action!

Apply what you learned in this chapter on MyPoliSciLab.

📖 **Read** on **mypoliscilab.com**

eText: Chapter 10

✔ **Study** and **Review** on **mypoliscilab.com**

Pre-Test
Post-Test
Chapter Exam
Flashcards

👁 **Watch** on **mypoliscilab.com**

Video: California Teacher Layoffs
Video: California Budget Crisis

✳ **Explore** on **mypoliscilab.com**

Simulation: You Are the Director of Economic Development for Los Angeles

KEY **TERMS**

merit system, p. 208
spoils system, p. 208
outsourcing, p. 210
general property tax, p. 214

assessment, p. 215
indexing, p. 216
sales tax, p. 217
value-added tax (VAT), p. 218

progressive tax, p. 218
excise tax, p. 218
severance tax, p. 219

ADDITIONAL **RESOURCES**

FURTHER READING

GLENN BEAMER, *Creative Politics: Taxes and Public Good in a Federal System* (University of Michigan Press, 1999).

JAMES S. BOWMAN AND **JONATHAN P. WEST,** EDS., *American Public Service: Radical Reform and the Merit System* (CRC Press, 2007).

DAVID BRUNORI, *State Tax Policy: A Political Perspective,* 2d ed. (Urban Institute Press, 2006).

RONALD C. FISHER, *Intergovernmental Fiscal Relations* (Kluwer, 1997).

KATHRYN A. FOSTER, *The Political Economy of Special-Purpose Government* (Georgetown University Press, 1997).

STEVEN D. GOLD, ED., *The Fiscal Crisis of the States: Lessons for the Future* (Georgetown University Press, 1995).

CHARLES T. GOODSELL, *The Case for Bureaucracy,* 4th ed. (Chatham House, 2003).

J. EDWARD KELLOUGH AND **LLOYD G. NIGRO,** *Civil Service Reform in the States* (State University of New York Press, 2006).

ISAAC MARTIN, *The Permanent Tax Revolt: How the Property Tax Transformed American Politics* (Stanford University Press, 2008).

DAVID ALAN NIBERT, *Hitting the Lottery Jackpot: State Governments and the Taxing of Dreams* (Monthly Review Press, 2000).

JOHN E. PETERSEN AND **DENNIS R. STRACHOTA,** EDS., *Local Government Finance: Concepts and Practices* (Government Finance Officers Association, 1991).

HENRY J. RAIMONDO, *Economics of State and Local Government* (Praeger, 1992).

HARVEY S. ROSEN AND **TED GAYER,** *Public Finance,* 8th ed. (McGraw-Hill, 2007).

E. S. SAVAS, *Privatization in the City: Successes, Failures, Lessons* (CQ Press, 2005).

PETER SCHRAG, *California: America's High-Stakes Experiment* (University of California Press, 2008).

RONALD SNELL, *New Realities in State Finance* (National Conference of State Legislatures, 2004).

WEB SITES

www.rockinst.org The Nelson A. Rockefeller Institute of Government seeks to assists states in a non-partisan way as they make fiscal and budgetary policy, along with initiatives in several other areas of state policy making.

www.nast.net National Association of State Treasurers is a professional association of state financial officers that seeks to promote education and the exchange of ideas, build professional relationships, develop standards of excellence and influence public policy for the benefit of the citizens of the states.

www.statelocalgov.net State and Local Government on the Net provides a directory of official websites for state, city, and county governments in the United States.

www.nasbo.org National Association of State Budget Officers is a professional organization that focuses on research, policy development, education, training, and technical assistance for state budget officers.

GLOSSARY

advisory opinion An opinion unrelated to a particular case that gives a court's view about a constitutional or legal issue.

amendatory veto The power of governors in a few states to return a bill to legislature with suggested language changes, conditions, or amendments. Legislators then decide either to accept the governor's recommendations or to pass the bill in its original form over the veto.

assessment The valuation a government places on property for the purposes of taxation.

assigned counsel system An arrangement whereby attorneys are provided for people accused of crimes who are unable to hire their own attorneys. The judge assigns a member of the bar to provide counsel to a particular defendant.

bicameral legislature A two-house legislature.

candidate expenditure limits Limits on how much money a candidate may spend in support of a campaign for elective office.

centralists People who favor national action over action at the state and local levels.

charter A city "constitution" that outlines the structure of city government, defines the authority of the various officials, and provides for their selection.

charter school A publicly funded alternative to standard public schools in some states, initiated when individuals or groups receive charters; charter schools must meet state standards.

closed primary A primary election in which only persons registered in the party holding the primary may vote.

commerce clause The clause in the Constitution (Article 1, Section 8, Clause 1) that gives Congress the power to regulate all business activities that cross state lines or affect more than one state or other nations.

concurrent powers Powers that the Constitution gives to both the national and state governments, such as the power to levy taxes.

confederation A constitutional arrangement in which sovereign nations or states, by compact, create a central government but carefully limit its power and do not give it direct authority over individuals.

Constitutional home rule State constitutional authorization for local governments to conduct their own affairs.

constitutional initiative petition A device that permits voters to place specific amendments to a state constitution on the ballot by petition.

contribution limits Limits on how much a single contributor may give to a candidate in an election or period of time.

council-manager plan A form of local government in which the city council hires a professional administrator to manage city affairs; also known as the city-manager plan.

county The largest local level of government below the state, currently used in 48 states.

crossover voting Voting by a member of one party for a candidate of another party.

decentralists People who favor state or local action rather than national action.

delegate An official who is expected to represent the views of his or her constituents even when personally holding different views; one interpretation of the role of the legislator.

delegated (express) powers Powers given explicitly to national government and listed in the Constitution.

devolution revolution The effort to slow the growth of the national government by returning many functions to the states.

disclosure laws A requirement that candidates specify where the money came from to finance their campaign.

due process Established rules and regulations that restrain government officials.

eminent domain The power of a government to take private property for public use; the U.S. Constitution gives national and state governments this power and requires them to provide just compensation for property so taken.

excise tax A consumer tax on a specific kind of merchandise, such as tobacco.

executive order A directive issued by a president or governor that has the force of law.

extradition The legal process whereby an alleged criminal offender is surrendered by the officials of one state to officials of the state in which the crime is alleged to have been committed.

federal mandate A requirement the national government imposes as a condition for receiving federal funds.

federalism A constitutional arrangement in which power is distributed between a central government and subdivisional governments, called states in the United States. The national and the subdivisional governments both exercise direct authority over individuals.

full faith and credit clause The clause in the Constitution (Article IV, Section 1) requiring each state to recognize the civil judgments rendered by the courts of the other states and to accept their public records and acts as valid.

general election Elections in which voters elect officeholders.

general property tax A tax levied by local and some state governments on real property or personal, tangible property, the major portion of which is on the estimated value of one's home and land.

Gentrification A process where relatively wealthier people buy property in poorer areas of a city and relocate there, which results in revitalization of the area and increased property values but is often accompanied by displacing the poor.

gerrymandering The drawing of legislative district boundaries to benefit a party, group, or incumbent.

implied powers Powers inferred from the express powers that allow Congress to carry out its functions.

indexing Providing automatic increases to compensate for inflation.

indictment A formal written statement from a grand jury charging an individual with an offense; also called a *true bill*.

information affidavit Certification by a public prosecutor that there is evidence to justify bringing named individuals to trial.

inherent powers The powers of the national government in foreign affairs that the Supreme Court has declared do not depend on constitutional grants but rather grow out of the very existence of the national government.

initiative A procedure whereby a certain number of voters may, by petition, propose a law or constitutional amendment and have it submitted to the voters.

interstate compact An agreement among two or more states. Congress must approve most such agreements.

judicial interpretation A method by which judges modify the force of a constitutional provision by reinterpreting its meaning.

judicial review The power of a court to refuse to enforce a law or a government regulation in the opinion of the judges conflicts with the U.S. Constitution or, in a state court, the state constitution.

line item veto Presidential power to strike, or remove, specific items from a spending bill without vetoing the entire package; declared unconstitutional by Supreme Court.

lobbying Engaging in activities aimed at influencing public officials, especially legislators, and the policies they enact.

lobbyist A person who is employed by and acts for an organized interest group or corporation to try to influence policy decisions and positions in the executive and legislative branches.

majority-minority district A legislative district created to include a majority of minority voters; ruled constitutional as long as race is not the main factor in redistricting.

malapportionment Having legislative districts with unequal populations.

Mayor-council charter The oldest and most common form of city government, consisting of either a weak mayor and a city council or a strong mayor elected by voters and council.

merit system A system of public employment in which selection and promotion depend on demonstrated performance rather than political patronage.

Metropolis A large city or municipality that serves as an economic and cultural center for a region.

Metropolitan area The larger area surrounding a metropolis that is heavily influenced by the metropolis, generally consisting of suburbs and other smaller cities.

misdemeanor A minor crime; the penalty is a fine or imprisonment for a short time, usually less than a year, in a local jail.

Missouri Plan A system for selecting judges that combines features of the appointive and elective methods. The governor selects judges from list presented by panels of lawyers and laypersons, and at the end of their term. the judges may run against their own record in retention elections.

municipality A local level of government within counties that are usually organized around population centers.

national supremacy A constitutional doctrine that whenever conflict occurs between the constitutionally authorized actions of the national government and those of a state or local government, the actions of the national government prevail.

necessary and proper clause The clause in the Constitution (Article 1, Section 8, Clause 3) setting forth the implied powers of Congress. It states that Congress, in addition to its express powers, has the right to make all laws necessary and proper to carry out all powers the Constitution vests in the national government.

new judicial federalism The practice of some state courts using the bill of rights in their state constitutions to provide more protection for some rights than is provided by the Supreme Court's interpretation of the Bill of Rights in the U.S. Constitution.

office block ballot A ballot on which all candidate are listed under the office for which they are running.

one-party state A state in which one party wins all or nearly all of the offices and the other party receives only a small proportion of the popular vote.

open primary A primary election in which any voter, regardless of party, may vote.

original jurisdiction The authority of a court to hear a case "in the first instance."

outsourcing Contracting of government services to private firms.

party caucus A meeting of the members of a party in a legislative chamber to select party leaders and to develop party policy. Called a *conference* by the Republicans.

party column ballot A type of ballot that encourages party-line voting by listing all of a party's candidates in a column under the party name.

pluralism A theory of government holds that open, multiple, and competing groups can check the asserted power by any one group.

police powers Inherent powers of state governments to pass laws to protect public health, safety, and welfare; the national government has no directly granted police powers but accomplishes the same goals through other delegated powers.

power elite A group composed of community, business, and other leaders who determine public policy or block changes in policy without themselves necessarily holding office.

preemption The right of a national law or regulation to preclude enforcement of a state or local law or regulation.

primary elections Elections in which voter choose party nominees.

privatization Contracting public services to private organizations.

pro bono To serve the public good; a tern used to describe work that lawyers (or other professionals) do for which they receive no fees.

progressive tax A tax graduated so that people with higher incomes pay a larger fraction of their income than people with lower incomes.

public defender system An arrangement whereby public officials are hired to provide legal assistance to people accused of crimes who are unable to hire their own attorneys.

public financing laws Laws authorizing grants of government funds to qualifying candidates for elective office, to be used in their campaigns.

reapportionment The assigning by Congress of congressional seats after each census. State legislatures reapportion state legislative districts.

recall elections A procedure for submitting to popular vote the removal of officials from office before the end of their term.

recidivist A repeat offender.

recuse To withdraw from participating in making a ruling to avoid any actual or perceived partiality or bias.

redistributive policy A policy that provides to one group of society while taking away benefits from another through policy solution such as tax increases to pay for job training.

redistricting The redrawing of congressional and other legislative district lines following the census, to accommodate population shifts and keep districts as equal as possible in population.

reduction veto The power of governors in a few states to reduce a particular appropriation.

referendum A procedure for submitting to popular vote measures passed by the legislature or proposed amendments to a state constitution.

reserve powers All powers not specifically delegated to the national government by the Constitution. The reserve power can be found in the Tenth Amendment to the Constitution.

responsibility contract A welfare strategy adopted by some states in which recipients sign a written agreement specifying their responsibilities and outlining a plan for obtaining work and achieving self-sufficiency.

retention elections Elections where judges run uncontested for reelection and voters simply vote for or again them in office.

revision commission A state commission that recommends changes in the state constitution for action by legislature and vote by the voters.

sales tax A general tax on sales transactions, sometimes exempting such items as food and drugs.

severance tax A tax on the privilege of "severing" such natural resources as coal, oil, timber, and gas from the land.

split ticket A vote for some of one party's candidates and some of another party's.

social stratification Divisions in a community among socioeconomic groups or classes.

spoils system A system of public employment based on rewarding party loyalists and friends.

states' rights Powers expressly or implicitly reserved to the states.

straight ticket A vote for all of one party's candidates.

strong mayor-council form A form of local government in which the voters directly elect the city council and the mayor, who enjoys nearly total administrative authority and appoints the department heads.

Temporary Assistance for Needy Families (TANF) A federal welfare reform law that replaced Aid to Families with Dependent Children, the 60-year-old assistance program for poor families with children. This 1996 law strengthened work requirements for recipients, limited the time that families can receive benefits, and gave states flexibility to develop service programs supporting work, marriage, and self-sufficiency.

township A local level of government below the county used primarily in 20 northeastern states.

trustee An official who is expected to vote independently based on his or her judgment of the circumstances; one interpretation of the role of the legislator.

two-party state A state in which the two major parties alternate in winning majorities.

unicameral legislature A one-house legislature.

unitary system A constitutional arrangement that concentrates power in a central government.

value-added tax (VAT) A tax on the increased value of a product at each stage of production and distribution rather than just at the point of sale.

veto A formal decision to reject a bill passed by Congress.

voter turnout The proportion of the voting-age public that votes.

vouchers Money provided by the government to parents for payment of their children's tuition in a public or private school of their choice.

weak mayor-council form A form of local government in which the members of the city council select the mayor, who then shares power with other elected or appointed boards and commissions.

workfare A welfare strategy adopted by some states that gives able-bodied adults who do not have preschool-aged children the opportunity to learn job skills that can lead to employment.

NOTES

Chapter 1

1. For further historical background, see Samuel J. Beer, *To Make a Nation: The Rediscovery of American Federalism* (Harvard University Press, 1993).
2. See "Eyes on the Road: States Crack Down on Texting While Driving," *State Health Notes*, 29, 523 (September 15, 2008), available at ncsl.org/default.aspx?tabid=14662.
3. William H. Stewart, *Concepts of Federalism* (Center for the Study of Federalism/University Press of America, 1984); see also Preston King, *Federalism and Federation*, 2d ed. (Cass, 2001).
4. Morton Grodzins, "The Federal System," in *Goals for Americans: The Report of the President's Commission on National Goals* (Columbia University Press, 1960).
5. Thomas R. Dye, *American Federalism: Competition Among Governments* (Lexington Books, 1990), pp. 13–17.
6. Michael D. Reagan and John G. Sanzone, *The New Federalism* (Oxford University Press, 1981), p. 175.
7. William H. Riker, *The Development of American Federalism* (Academic Press, 1987), pp. 14–15. Riker contends not only that federalism does not guarantee freedom but also that the framers of our federal system, as well as those of other nations, were animated not by considerations of safeguarding freedom but by practical considerations of preserving unity.
8. U.S. Census Bureau, *Statistical Abstract of the United States* (Government Printing Office, 2007), p. 487.
9. Charles Evans Hughes, "War Powers Under the Constitution," *ABA Reports*, 62 (1917), p. 238.
10. *Gibbons* v. *Ogden*, 22 U.S. 1 (1824).
11. *Reno* v. *Condon*, 528 U.S. 141 (2000).
12. *Champion* v. *Ames*, 188 U.S. 321 (1907).
13. *Caminetti* v. *United States*, 242 U.S. 470 (1917).
14. *Federal Radio Commission* v. *Nelson Brothers*, 289 U.S. 266 (1933).
15. See Jesse Choper, *Judicial Review and the National Political Process* (University of Chicago Press, 1980); and John T. Noonan Jr., *Narrowing the Nation's Power: The Supreme Court Sides with the States* (University of California Press, 2002).
16. See Michael S. Greve, *Real Federalism: Why It Matters, How It Could Happen* (American Enterprise Institute, 1999).
17. *Printz* v. *United States*, 521 U.S. 898 (1997); see also *New York* v. *United States*, 505 U.S. 144 (1992).
18. See *Franchise Tax Board of California* v. *Hyatt*, 538 U.S. 488 (2003).
19. *California* v. *Superior Courts of California*, 482 U.S. 400 (1987).
20. David C. Nice, "State Participation in Interstate Compacts," *Publius*, 17 (Spring 1987), p. 70; see also *Interstate Compacts and Agencies*, Council of State Governments (Author, 1995), for a list of compacts by subject and by state with brief descriptions.
21. *McCulloch* v. *Maryland*, 4 Wheaton 316 (1819).
22. Joseph F. Zimmerman, "Federal Preemption Under Reagan's New Federalism," *Publius*, 21 (Winter 1991), pp. 7–28.
23. Oliver Wendell Holmes Jr., *Collected Legal Papers* (Harcourt, 1920), pp. 295–296.
24. See, for example, *United States* v. *Lopez*, 514 U.S. 549 (1995).
25. *Seminole Tribe of Florida* v. *Florida*, 517 U.S. 44 (1996).
26. *Alden* v. *Maine*, 527 U.S. 706 (1999); *Kimel* v. *Florida Board of Regents*, 528 U.S. 62 (2000); *Vermont Agency of Natural Resources* v. *United States ex rel. Stevens*, 529 U.S. 765 (2000).
27. George Will, "A Revival of Federalism?" *Newsweek* (May 29, 2000), p. 78.
28. *United States* v. *Morrison*, 529 U.S. 598 (2000).
29. The term "devolution revolution" was coined by Richard P. Nathan in testimony before the Senate Finance Committee, quoted in Daniel Patrick Moynihan, "The Devolution Revolution," *New York Times* (August 6, 1995), p. B15.
30. John E. Chubb, "The Political Economy of Federalism," *American Political Science Review*, 79 (December 1985), p. 1005.
31. Donald F. Kettl, *The Regulation of American Federalism* (Johns Hopkins University Press, 1987), pp. 154–155.
32. See Paul J. Posner, *The Politics of Unfunded Mandates: Whither Federalism?* (Georgetown University Press, 1998).
33. *Restoring Confidence and Competence*, Advisory Commission on Intergovernmental Relations (Author, 1981), p. 30.
34. Aaron Wildavsky, "Bare Bones: Putting Flesh on the Skeleton of American Federalism," in *The Future of Federalism in the 1980s* (Advisory Commission on Intergovernmental Relations, 1981), p. 79.
35. Peterson, *Price of Federalism*, p. 182.
36. Dye, *American Federalism*, p. 199.
37. John J. DiLulio Jr. and Donald F. Kettl, *Fine Print: The Contract with America, Devolution, and the Administrative Realities of American Federalism* (Brookings Institution Press, 1995), p. 60.
38. John Kincaid, "Devolution in the United States," in Nicolaidis and Howse, eds., *The Federal Vision* (Oxford, 2002), p. 144.

Chapter 2

1. Data are for end of year, 2008. Taken from the *Bureau of Justice Statistics Summary of the Total Correctional Population*, http://bjs.ojp.usdoj.gov/index.cfm?ty=tp&tid=11.
2. John Holahan et al., "Which Way for Federalism and Health Policy?" *Health Affairs*, Web Exclusive (July 2003), pp. W3, 317–319, content.healthaffairs.org/cgi/reprint/hlthaff.w3.317v1.pdf.
3. Calculated from 2005 data in U.S. Bureau of Transportation Statistics, *National Transportation Statistics*, Appendix A–Modal Profiles, Highway Profile, www.bts.gov/publications/national_transportation_statistics/html/table_highway_profile.html.
4. U.S. Census Bureau, *Statistical Abstract of the United States: 2010* (U.S. Government Printing Office, 2010), Table 269, http://www.census.gov/compendia/statab/2010/tables/10s0269.pdf.
5. All spending data taken from the U.S. Census Bureau, *Statistical Abstract of the United States: 2010* (U.S. Government Printing Office, 2008), Tables 418, 457, and 651, http://www.census.gov/compendia/statab/.
6. Suho Bae and Robert Ward, "Long-Term Trends in State and Local Revenues and Expenditures," *Rockefeller Institute Fiscal Brief* (May 2008), www.rockinst.org.
7. U.S. Census Bureau, *Statistical Abstract of the United States: 2010* (U.S. Government Printing Office, 2010), Table 449, http://www.census.gov/compendia/statab/2010/tables/10s0449.pdf.
8. U.S. Census Bureau, *Statistical Abstract of the United States: 2010* (U.S. Government Printing Office, 2010), Table 450, http://www.census.gov/compendia/statab/2010/tables/10s0450.pdf.
9. Robert S. Lynd and Helen M. Lynd, *Middletown* (Harcourt, 1929). See also their analysis of Muncie ten years later in *Middletown in Transition* (Harcourt, 1937).
10. Floyd Hunter, *Community Power Structure* (University of North Carolina Press, 1953). For a reassessment and rebuttal of Hunter's findings, see M. Kent Jennings, *Community Influentials: The Elites of Atlanta* (Free Press, 1964).
11. Clarence N. Stone, *Regime Politics: Governing Atlanta 1946–1988* (University Press of Kansas, 1989).
12. Robert A. Dahl, *Who Governs? Democracy and Power in an American City* (Yale University Press, 1961).
13. See Peter Bachrach and Morton S. Baratz, "Two Faces of Power" *American Political Science Review* 56, no. 4 (1962): 947–952 and (1962 APSR); and Clarence N. Stone, "Systemic Power in Community Decision Making: A Restatement of Stratification Theory" *American Political Science Review* 74, no. 4 (1980): 978–990.
14. Rufus P. Browning, Dale Rogers Marshall, and David H. Tabb, *Protest Is Not Enough: The Struggle of Blacks and Hispanics for Equality in Urban Politics* (University of California Press, 1984).
15. See the interesting study of San Jose, California, by Phillip J. Troustine and Terry Christensen, *Movers and Shakers: The Study of Community Power* (St. Martin's Press, 1982). See also Clarence N. Stone, *Regime Politics: Governing Atlanta, 1946–1988* (University Press of Kansas, 1989).
16. See, for example, Peter Bachrach and Morton S. Baratz, *Power and Poverty: Theory and Practice* (Oxford University Press, 1970); Matthew A. Crenson, *The Un-politics of Air Pollution: A Study of Non-Decisionmaking in the Cities* (Johns Hopkins University Press, 1971); and John Gaventa, *Power and Powerlessness: Quiescence and Rebellion in an Appalachian Valley* (University of Illinois Press, 1980).
17. Bryan D. Jones and Lynn W. Bachelor, *The Sustaining Hand: Community Leadership and Corporate Power*, 2d ed. (University Press of Kansas, 1993), p. 254. See also Stone, *Regime Politics*.

18. Daniel J. Elazar, *American Federalism: A View from the States*, 3rd ed (Harper and Row, 1984).
19. Tobacco-Free Kids, November 2009, http://www.tobaccofreekids.org/research/factsheets/pdf/0097.pdf.
20. Orzechowski and Walker, *The Tax Burden on Tobacco: Historical Compilation* 2004 (Author, 2005).
21. Stone, *Regime Politics*, p. 232.
22. For a detailed analysis of how W. R. Grace and Beatrice Foods had to rely on law firms to fight legal actions surrounding their operations in Woburn, Massachusetts, see Jonathan Harr, *A Civil Action* (Vintage Books, 1996). See also Alan Rosenthal, *The Third House: Lobbyists and Lobbying in the States*, 2d ed. (CQ Press, 2001).
23. See Clive S. Thomas and Ronald J. Hrebenar, "Interest Groups in the States," in Virginia Gray, Russell L. Hanson, and Herbert Jacob, eds., *Politics in the American States* (CQ Press, 1999), pp. 122–158.
24. For a list of state lobbying laws, see National Council of Nonprofit Associations, *State Lobbying Laws*, www.ncna.org/_uploads/documents/live//Lobby_Regulations_Chart.xls.
25. For a general discussion of ethics reform and enforcement efforts, see *Spectrum: The Journal of State Government* (Winter 1993).
26. On various efforts to improve ethical practices and professionalism in the state legislatures and the limits of these efforts, see Alan Rosenthal, *Drawing the Line: Legislative Ethics in the States* (University of Nebraska Press, 1996).
27. For information on state lobbying laws, see the database maintained by Center for Ethics in Government of the National Conference of State Legislatures, www.ncsl.org/programs/ethics/database.htm.
28. Diane D. Blair, *Arkansas Politics and Government* (University of Nebraska Press, 1988), p. 118.
29. Richard L. Cole and John Kincaid, "Public Opinion on U.S. Federal and Intergovernmental Issues in 2006: Continuity and Change," *Publius* 36, no. 3 (Summer 2006), pp. 453–454.
30. http://www.gallup.com/poll/122915/trust-state-government-sinks-new-low.aspx.
31. http://pewresearch.org/pubs/1569/trust-in-government-distrust-discontent-anger-partisan-rancor.
32. Peter Slevin "Obama Administration to Buy Illinois Prison for Guantanamo Detainees" *The Washington Post*, December 16, 2009.
33. Paul Peterson, *City Limits* (University of Chicago Press, 1981), p. 124. See also the useful discussion of the challenge of covering state legislative politics in Browne and VerBurg, *Michigan Politics and Government*, pp. 242–245.
34. M. Jae Moon, "The Evolution of E-Government Among Municipalities: Rhetoric or Reality?" *Public Administration Review* 62, no. 4 (July/August 2002), pp. 424–433.
35. Ibid., p. 18–20.
36. Joseph F. Zimmerman, *The New England Town Meeting: Democracy in Action* (Praeger, 1999).
37. Victor S. DeSantis and David Hill, "Citizen Participation in Local Politics: Evidence from New England Town Meetings," *State and Local Government Review* (Fall 2004), pp. 166–173.
38. See, for example, Daniel Kemmis, *The Good City and the Good Life* (Houghton Mifflin, 1995); and David L. Kirp, John P Dwyer, and Larry A. Rosenthal, *Our Town: Race, Housing, and the Soul of Suburbia* (Rutgers University Press, 1997).
39. Eugene F. Rivers III, "High-Octane Faith," in E. J. Dionne Jr., ed., *Community Works: The Revival of Civil Society in America* (Brookings Institution Press, 1998), p. 61.
40. Karen Rowley, *GulfGov Reports: Response, Recovery, and the Role of the Nonprofit Community in the Two Years Since Katrina and Rita* (Rockefeller Institute of Government and Public Affairs Research Council of Louisiana, 2007), p. v.
41. For the efforts of a big-city mayor and his team of advisers, see Buzz Bissinger, *A Prayer for the City* (Random House, 1997). See also the example of Milwaukee's mayor, John O. Norquist, *Wealth of Cities* (Addison-Wesley, 1998).
42. Iris J. Lav and Phillip Oliff, *Federal Grants to States and Localities Cut Deeply in Fiscal Year 2009 Federal Budget* (Center on Budget and Policy Priorities, February 4, 2008).
43. Donald J. Boyd, "What Will Happen to State Government Finances in a Recession?" *Rockefeller Institute Fiscal Report* (Rockefeller Institute of Government, January 30, 2008), p. 17.
44. The Pew Center on the States, *One in 100: Behind Bars in America 2008* (Pew Charitable Trusts, 2008), p. 14.
45. Nelson A. Rockefeller, *The Future of Federalism* (Harvard University Press, 1962), p. 9.

Chapter 3

1. Gerald Benjamin, "The Functions of State Constitutions in a Federal System," paper presented at the American Political Science Association Round Table (Washington, D.C., 1984).
2. John Adams, quoted in Judith S. Kaye, "Federalism's Other Tier," *Constitution* 3 (Winter 1991), p. 50.
3. Christopher W. Hammons, "State Constitutional Reform: Is It Necessary?" *Albany Law Review* 64 (2001), pp. 1328–1334.
4. *The Book of the States, 2009* (Council of State Governments, 2009), Table 1.1, p. 12.
5. Steve Geissinger, "Changing the Constitution Is a Powerful Government-Reform Tool Avoided by Officials," *Alameda (Calif.) Times-Star*, November 9, 2003, p. C1.
6. South Dakota Constitution, Article XI, Section 8.
7. Alabama Constitution, Amendment 383 (1901).
8. Donald S. Lutz, "Toward a Theory of Constitutional Amendment," in Sanford Levinson, ed., *Responding to Imperfection: The Theory and Practice of Constitutional Amendment* (Princeton University Press, 1995), pp. 237–274.
9. *The Book of the States, 2009*, Table 1.1, p. 12; and John Kincaid, "State Constitutions in the Federal System," *Annals of the American Academy of Political and Social Science* 496 (March 1988), p. 14.
10. *The Book of the States, 2009*, Table 1.1, p. 12.
11. *Indiana* v. *Gerschoffer*, 763 N.E.2d 960 (2002).
12. *Anchorage Police Department Employees Association* v. *Anchorage*, 24 P.3d 547 (2001).
13. *American Academy of Pediatrics* v. *Lungren*, 490 P.2d 797 (1997).
14. Kaye, "Federalism's Other Tier," p. 54.
15. See, for example, Matthew Bosworth, *Courts as Catalysts: State Supreme Courts and Public School Finances Equity* (State University of New York Press, 2001); and Charles Lopeman, *The Activist Advocate: Policy Making in State Supreme Courts* (Praeger, 1999).
16. *Michigan* v. *Long*, 463 U.S. 1032 (1983); "Our Judicial Federalism," *Intergovernmental Perspective* 15 (Summer 1989), pp. 8–15; and William M. Wiecek, "Some Protection of Personal Liberty: Remembering the Future," and Kermit L. Hall, "Mostly Anchor and Little Sail: The Evolution of American State Constitutions," in Paul Finkelman and Stephen E. Gottlieb, eds., *Toward a Usable Past: Liberty Under State Constitutions* (University of Georgia Press, 1991), pp. 371–417.
17. Deborah Baker, "Canvassing Board Certifies Amendment Election," *Santa Fe New Mexican*, October 14, 2003, p. A1.
18. *The Book of the States, 2007*, p. 4.
19. *The Book of the States, 2009*, p. 3.
20. Fred Keeley, "California Dreamin': An On-Time Budget," *Sacramento Bee*, July 17, 2005.
21. *The Book of the States, 2005*, p. 17.
22. *The Book of the States, 2009*, pp. 3–4.
23. Tip H. Allen, Jr., "The Enduring Traditions of the State Constitutions," in Dale Krane and Stephen D. Shaffer, eds., *Mississippi Government and Politics: Modernizers Versus Traditionalists* (University of Nebraska Press, 1992), pp. xx–xxv.
24. *The Book of the States, 2002* (Council of State Governments, 2002), p. 14.
25. David B. Magleby, "Direct Legislation in the American States," in David Butler and Austin Ranney, eds., *Referendums Around the World: The Growing Use of Direct Democracy* (AEI Press, 1994), p. 225.
26. California Commission on Campaign Financing, *Democracy by Initiative: A Summary of the Report and Recommendations of the California Commission on Campaign Financing* (Center for Responsive Government, 1992), p. 25.
27. *Amador Valley Joint Union High School District* v. *State Board of Equalization*, 22 Cal. 3d 208 (1978), quoted in Eugene C. Lee, "The Revision of California's Constitution," *CPS Brief: A Publication of the California Policy Seminar* 3 (April 1991), p. 1.
28. *The Book of the States, 2007*, p. 3; see also Magleby, "Direct Legislation," p. 251.
29. *The Book of the States, 2009*, p. 3.
30. G. Alan Tarr, *Understanding State Constitutions* (Princeton University Press, 2000), p. 158; and Thomas Gais and Gerald Benjamin, "Public Discontent and the Decline of Deliberation: A Dilemma in State Constitutional Reform," *Temple Law Review* 68, No. 3 (1995), pp. 1292–1300.
31. Ibid., pp. 160–161.
32. Gerald Benjamin and Thomas Gais, "Constitutional Conventionphobia," in Burton C. Agata and Eric Lane, eds. *State Constitutions: Competing Perspectives* (Hofstra Law and Policy Symposium, 1996), Vol. 1, p. 69; Tarr, *Understanding State Constitutions*, p. 25; and *The Book of the States, 2005*, p. 17.
33. Caleb Nelson, "A Re-Evaluation of Scholarly Explanations for the Rise of the Elective Judiciary in Antebellum America," *American Journal of Legal History* 37, No. 2 (1993), p. 221.
34. Elder Witt, "State Supreme Courts: Tilting the Balance Toward Change," *Governing* (August 1988), p. 33.
35. G. Alan Tarr, keynote address, Conference on State Constitutional Reform, May 4, 2000, www.camlaw.rugers.edu/statecon/keynote.html.
36. Lee, "Revision of California's Constitution," p. 7; see also Lutz, "Toward a Theory of Constitutional Amendment," pp. 355–370.
37. "State of Rhode Island General Assembly," www.rilin.state.ri.us/studteaguide/RhodeIsland History/chapt9.html.
38. Re Jan Ruggiero, Director of Elections, Elections Division, Office of the Secretary of State, Providence, RI, www.state.ri.us.
39. Common Cause of Rhode Island, "Separation of Powers," www.commoncauseri.org/news.

40. State of Hawaii Statewide Election Summary Report, November 4, 2008, http://hawaii.gov .elections/results/2008/general/files/ histatewide.pdf.

41. Beryl E. Pettus and Randall W. Bland, *Texas Government Today* (Dorsey Press, 1979), pp. 34–36; see also Janice C. May, "Texas Constitutional Revision and Laments," *National Civic Review* (February 1977), pp. 64–69.

42. B. Drummond Ayres, Jr., "Alabama Governor Set for Tough Race," *New York Times*, February 27, 2002, p. A16.

43. Albert E. McKinley, "Two New Southern Constitutions," *Political Science Quarterly* 18 (September 1903), pp. 480–511.

44. For more information, go to the Web site of the Alabama Citizens for Constitutional Reform, www.constitutionalreform.org.

45. Associated Press, "Constitution Work May Come in 2003," *Montgomery (Ala.) Advertiser*, December 11, 2002, www. montgomeryadvertiser.com.

46. Editorial, "Constitutional Count, House Sending Clear Message: People Can't Be Trusted," *Birmingham (Ala.) News*, March 21, 2002, p. A20.

47. Manuel Roig-Franzia, "Vote Opens Old Racial Wounds; School Segregation Remains a State Law as Amendment Is Defeated," *The Washington Post*, November 28, 2004, p. A1.

48. See, for instance, the Web site of Alabama Citizens for Constitutional Reform, www.constitutionalreform.org.

49. *The Book of the States, 2005*, pp. 3–9.

Chapter 4

1. *Crawford* v. *Marion County Election Board*, 553 U.S. 181 (2008).

2. U.S. Constitution, Article I, Section 4.

3. U.S. Constitution, Article II, Section 2.

4. Alexander Hamilton, James Madison, and John Jay, *The Federalist Papers*, No. 59.

5. U.S. Constitution, Article IV, Section 4.

6. Akkhil Reed Amar, *America's Constitution: A Biography* (Random House, 2006), pp. 422–423.

7. Larry N. Gerston and Terry Christensen, *Recall! California's Political Earthquake* (Sharpe, 2004).

8. Data taken from Project Vote: http://www. projectvote.org/images/publications/ Felon%20Voting/felon_voting_laws_by_ state_Sept_11_2008.pdf.

9. The Council of State Governments, *The Book of the States 2007*, Vol. 39 (Author, 2007), pp. 293–295.

10. U.S. Census Bureau , *Statistical Abstract of the United States: 2001* (U.S. Government Printing Office, 2001), p. 26.

11. U.S. Election Assistance Commission, "The Impact of the National Voter Registration Act, 2005–06," http://www.eac.gov/assets/1/Page/ NVRA_Reports_and_Data_Sets_2006–2005.pdf

12. Cynthia Rugeley and Robert A. Jackson, "Getting on the Rolls: Analyzing the Effects of Lowered Barriers on Voter Registration," *State Politics and Policy Quarterly* 9(1): 56–78.

13. Benjamin Highton and Raymond E. Wolfinger, *Political Behavior* 20 (June 1998), pp. 94–97.

14. Raymond E. Wolfinger and Steven J. Rosenstone, *Who Votes?* (Yale University Press, 1980), p. 130.

15. R. Michael Alverez, Delia Bailey, and Jonathan N. Katz, "The Effect of Voter Identification Laws on Turnout," *Caltech/MIT Voting Technology Project*, working paper no. 57 (October 2007), www.vote.caltech.edu/media/documents/wps/ vtp_wp57.pdf.

16. U.S. Census Bureau, *Statistical Abstract of the United States: 2010*, Table 409, http://www .census.gov/compendia/statab/2010/tables/ 10s0409.pdf.

17. For a brief overview of the Voting Rights Act, see U.S. Department of Justice, Civil Rights Division, Voting Section, "Introduction to Federal Voting Rights Laws," www.usdoj.gov/crt/voting/intro/ intro.htm.

18. Barney Warf, "Voting Technologies and Residual Ballots in the 2000 and 2004 Presidential Elections," *Political Geography* 25 (June 2006), p. 533.

19. Election Data Services, Inc., *2006 Voting Equipment Study* (Election Data Services, 2006), p. 4.

20. Ibid.

21. Brennan Center Task Force on Voting System Security, *The Machinery of Democracy: Protecting Elections in an Electronic World* (Brennan Center for Justice, New York University School of Law, 2006).

22. R. Doug Lewis, "2006 Elections: Successful Implementation and Continuing Issues," *The Book of the States 2007* (Council of State Governments, 2007), pp. 277–279.

23. Paul S. Herrnson et al., *Voting Technology: The Not-So-Simple Act of Casting a Ballot* (Brookings Institution Press, 2008), pp. 91–110.

24. Ryan L. Claasen, David B. Magleby, J. Quin Monson, and Kelly D. Patterson, "At Your Service: Voter Evaluations of Poll Worker Performance," *American Politics Research* (forthcoming).

25. David B. Magleby, "Participation in Mail Ballot Elections," *Western Political Quarterly* 40 (March 1987), pp. 79–91.

26. Priscilla Southwell, "Five Years Later: A Re-Assessment of Oregon's Vote by Mail Electoral Process" (2003), and Paul Gronke, "Ballot Integrity and Voting by Mail: The Oregon Experience" (2005), both available at www.sos.state.or.us/executive/policy-initiatives/vbm/execvbm.htm.

27. The Early Voting Information Center at Reed College, "Absentee and Early Voting Laws: Summary Table (last updated, February 21, 2008)," www.earlyvoting.net/states/abslaws.php. Absentee ballots for all states are available at www.justvote.org.

28. Washington Secretary of State's Office Report available online at http://www.sos.wa.gov/ elections/absentee_stats.aspx.

29. Early Voting Information Center, "Absentee and Early Voting Laws."

30. Data taken from: http://elections.gmu.edu/ early_vote_2008.html.

31. Comment by Bryan Jones of the University of Washington, quoted in Neil Modie, "Obama Big Winner in Washington Caucus," *Seattle Post-Intelligencer*, February 10, 2008.

32. Lewis, "2006 Elections," pp. 284–285.

33. For information on the 2008 primaries and the relationship between party and the vote, see the exit poll data available at "Election Center 2008: Primaries and Caucuses," CNNPolitics .com, www.cnn.com/ELECTION/2008/.

34. Thomas M.Carsey, *Campaign Dynamics: The Race for Governor*, Chapter 8 (University of Michigan Press, Ann Arbor, MI, 2000).

35. Thomas M. Carsey and Gerald C. Wright. "State and National Factors in Gubernatorial and Senatorial Elections" (1998), *American Journal of Political Science 42*(3): 994–1002; see also James E. Campbell "Presidential Coattails and Midterm Losses in State Legislative Elections" (1986), *American Political Science Review 80*(1): 45–63.

36. National Conference of State Legislatures historical trends on ballot measures, http:// www.ncsl.org/default.aspx?tabid=20114# historical.

37. David B. Magleby, *Direct Legislation: Voting on Ballot Propositions in the United States* (Johns Hopkins University Press, 1984), Chapters 7–9.

38. David B. Magleby, "Campaign Spending and Referendum Voting," paper presented at the annual meeting of the Western Political Science Association, Albuquerque, NM, March 1994.

39. *Financing California's Statewide Ballot Measures: Receipts and Expenditures Through December 31,1998* (California Secretary of State, 1998), p. 2.

40. National Conference of State Legislatures, "Recall of State Officials" March 21, 2006, http://www.ncsl.org/default.aspx?tabid=16581.

41. California Secretary of State Kevin Shelly, www.ss.ca.gov/elections/elections_recall_faqs .htm#20.

42. See Gerston and Christensen, *Recall*.

43. California Voter Foundation, www.calvoter .org/voter/elections/archive/recall/index.html (accessed June 15, 2006).

44. National Conference of State Legislatures, "Recall of Local Officials," http://www.ncsl .org/Default.aspx?TabId=16540.

45. National Conference of State Legislatures, "Campaign Finance Reform: An Overview," February 5, 2008, www.ncsl.org/programs/ legismgt/about/campfin.htm.

46. U.S. Supreme Court ruling in *Citizens United* v. *Federal Election Commission* (2010).

47. Ian Urbina "24 States' Laws Open to Attack After Campaign Finance Ruling" *New York Times*, January 22, 2010, http://www.nytimes.com/ 2010/01/23/us/politics/23states.html.

48. Edward D. Feigenbaum and James A. Palmer, *Campaign Finance Law 2002* (U.S. Federal Election Commission, 2002), Chart 2-A. For more information on campaign finance laws, see www.fec.gov.

49. The Supreme Court decision is *Randall et al.* v. *Sorrell et al.*, No. 04–1528 (2006).

50. Secretary of State and Commission on Governmental Ethics and Election Practices, *2008 Candidate Guide: Running for Office in Maine*, pp. 39–41, mainegov-images.informe .org/ethics/pdf/2008_candidate_guide.pdf.

51. Other "clean money" states include Arizona, Connecticut, and Vermont, see www .publicampaign.org/where. For an assessment of the effects of two of these programs, see U.S. Government Accountability Office, *Campaign Finance Reform: Early Experiences of Two States That Offer Full Public Funding for Political Candidates*, GAO-03–453 (U.S. Government Accountability Office, 2003).

52. See remarks by Michael Malbin in *Rockefeller Institute of Government*, "Can and Should NYC's Campaign Reforms Be Extended to State Offices?" (Rockefeller Institute of Government, April 25, 2007).

53. Michael Malbin and Thomas Gais, *The Day After Reform: Sobering Campaign Finance Lessons from the American States* (Rockefeller Institute Press, 1998), pp. 65–70.

54. See Maine Citizens for Clean Elections, "Clean Election Supporters Call for Full Restoration of Clean Election Fund," www.mainecleanelections.org.

55. For example, see the North Carolina Voters for Clean Elections Web site, http://www.ncvce .org/index.php?page=ncjudicialprogram.

56. John F. Bibby, *Politics, Parties, and Elections in America*, 5th ed. (Wadsworth, 2003).

57. Mike Royko, *Boss: Richard J. Daley of Chicago* (Dutton, 1971).

58. Melvin G. Holli, *The American Mayor: The Best and the Worst Big-City Leaders* (Pennsylvania State University Press, 1999).

59. According to Todd Taylor, executive director, Utah Democratic Party, these requirements are intended to promote gender equity; personal communication, November 18, 1998.

60. The Web site for the National Republican Party is http://www.gop.com, and the Web site for the National Democratic Party is http://www.democrats.org/. State party links are available on these Web sites or are easily located with an Internet search of the party name and the state name of interest.

61. See Cornelius P. Cotter, James L. Gibson, John F. Bibby, and Robert J. Huckshorn, *Party Organizations in America* (Praeger, 1984).

62. Ronald E. Weber, ed., *American State and Local Politics: Directions for the21st Century* (Chatham House, 1999), p. 174.

63. U.S. Election Assistance Commission, "Voter Registration and Turnout 2000," www.eac.gov.

64. U.S. Department of Commerce, *Statistical Abstract of the United States: 2006* (October 2005), p. 264; and Greg McDonald, "Primary Turnout May Prolong Downtrend," stateline.org (accessed September 17, 2002).

65. Michael McDonald, United State Elections Project, http://elections.gmu.edu/voter_turnout.htm.

66. Donald P. Green and Alan S. Gerber, *Get Out the Vote* (Brookings Institution Press, 2004), p. 9.

67. For a discussion of coordinated campaigns, see Paul Herrnson, "National Party Organizations and the Postreform Congress," in Roger Davidson, ed., *The Postreform Congress* (St. Martin's Press, 1992), pp. 65–67.

68. See Cotter et al., *Party Organizations in America.*

69. New Jersey Election Law Enforcement Commission, *The 2005 Assembly Election: New Trends on the Horizon?* (Author, September 2006), p. 19.

70. Malbin and Gais, *The Day After Reform,* pp. 145–152.

71. New Jersey Election Law Enforcement Commission, *The 2005 Assembly Election: New Trends on the Horizon?* (September 2006), p. 19.

72. See Bruce E. Keith, David B. Magleby, Candice J. Nelson, Elizabeth Orr, Mark C. Westlye, and Raymond E. Wolfinger, *The Myth of the Independent Voter* (University of California Press, 1992), p. 52.

73. The Field Poll, "Voters Very Dissatisfied with State Budget Negotiations. Blame Davis and Both Parties in the Legislature. Three in Four Fear the State Is Seriously Off on the Wrong Track," www.field.com/ fieldpollonline/sub-scribers/RLS2074.pdf.

74. The Field Poll, "How Schwarzenegger's History and Characteristics Helps and Hurts Him in His Bid to Become Governor," www.field.com/fieldpollonline/subscribers/RLS2083.pdf.

75. Stephen Ansolabehere and James M. Synder, Jr., "The Incumbency Advantage in U.S. Elections: An Analysis of State and Federal Offices," March 15, 2002, web.mit.edu/polisci/research/representation/incumb_advantage_elj.pdf.

76. Malcolm E. Jewell and David M. Olson, *Political Parties and Elections in American States*, 3d ed. (Dorsey Press, 1988), p. 121; and William H. Flanigan and Nancy H. Zingale, *Political Behavior of the American Electorate,* 8th ed. (CQ Press, 1994), p. 195.

77. Flanigan and Zingale, *Political Behavior of the American Electorate*, 8th ed., (CQ Press, 1994), p. 171.

78. Thomas M. Carsey, *Campaign Dynamics: The Race for Governor* (University of Michigan Press, 2000).

79. James Sample, Lauren Jones, and Rachel Weiss, *The New Politics of Judicial Elections, 2006* (Justice at Stake Campaign, 2006).

80. Willis D. Hawley, *Nonpartisan Elections and the Case for Party Politics* (Wiley, 1973), pp. 81–82; see also Brian F. Schaffner, Matthew Streb, and Gerald Wright, "Teams Without Uniforms: The Nonpartisan Ballot in State and Local Elections," *Political Research Quarterly* 54 (March 2001), pp. 7–30.

81. Susan Welch and Timothy Bledsoe, "The Partisan Consequences of Nonpartisan Elections and the Changing Nature of Urban Politics," *American Journal of Political Science* 30 (February 1986), pp. 128–139.

82. Gerald C. Wright and Tracy Osborn, "Party and Roll Call Voting in the American Legislature," paper presented at the Midwest Political Science Association Meeting, Chicago, 2002.

83. Gerald C. Wright and Brian F. Schaffner, "The Influence of Party: Evidence from the State Legislatures" (2002), *American Political Science Review* 96(2): 367–379.

84. The major cases are: *Baker* v. *Carr* (1962), *Reynolds* v. *Sims* (1963), and *Wesberry* v. *Sanders* (1963).

85. Gary W. Cox and Jonathan N. Katz, *Elbridge Gerry's Salamander: The Electoral Consequences of the Reapportionment Revolution* (Cambridge University Press, 2002).

86. National Conference of State Legislatures, "2008 Partisan Composition of State Legislatures," www.ncsl.org/statevote/partycomptable2008.htm.

87. U.S. Census Bureau, *Statistical Abstract of the United States: 2010,* Table 400, http://www.census.gov/compendia/statab/2010/tables/10s0400.pdf.

88. Pamela M. Prah, "First Salvos Prepared for Statehouse Redistricting Battles," stateline.org, August 24, 2006, www.stateline.org/live/details/story?contentId=136505.

89. Bill Mears, "Texas Redistricting Reaches High Court," CNN, February 28, 2006, www.cnn.com/2006/LAW/02/28/scotus. texas/. The Supreme Court decision was *League of United Latin American Citizens et al.* v. *Perry, Governor of Texas et al.,* No. 05–204 (2006).

90. Kevin Duggan, "GOP Map Cast Aside," *Fort Collins Coloradoan,* December 2, 2003, http://coloradoan.com/news/coloradoanpublishing/Legislature2004/redistricting/120203_ruling.html.

91. The classic work here is V. O. Key, *Southern Politics in State and Nation* (Knoph, 1949; reprinted by the University of Tennessee Press).

92. Terrel L. Rhodes, *Republicans in the South: Voting for the State House, Voting for the White House* (Praeger, 2000), p. 88.

Chapter 5

1. National Conference of State Legislatures, http://www.ncsl.org/default.aspx?tabid=14843.

2. Ralph G. Wright, *Inside the Statehouse: Lessons from the Speaker* (CQ Press, 2005), p. 227.

3. For a useful look at Nebraska's unique legislature, see Jack Rodgers, Robert Sittig, and Susan Welch, "The Legislature," in Robert D. Miewald, ed., *Nebraska Government and Politics* (University of Nebraska Press, 1984), pp. 57–86.

4. *The Book of the States, 2009* (Council of State Governments, 2009), Table 3–3, p. 87

5. Peverill Squire and Keith E. Hamm, *101 Chambers: Congress, State Legislatures, and the Future of Legislative Studies* (Ohio State University Press), Table 4–1, p. 102.

6. Richard A. Clucas, "Exercising Control: The Power of State House Speakers," paper presented at the annual meeting of the Western Political Science Association, Los Angeles, March 1998; see also Malcolm E. Jewell and Marcia Lynn Whicker, *Legislative Leadership in the American States* (University of Michigan Press, 1997).

7. *The Book of the States, 2005* (The Council of State Governments, 2005), pp. 136–137.

8. Wayne L. Francis, *The Legislative Committee Game: A Comparative Analysis of 50 States* (Ohio State University Press, 1989).

9. *The Book of the States, 2009,* Table 3–23, p. 140.

10. Alan Rosenthal, *Legislative Life: People, Process, and Performance in the States* (Harper & Row, 1981), pp. 112–113.

11. See Peverill Squire, "Uncontested Seats in State Legislative Elections," *Legislative Studies Quarterly* 35 (February 2000), pp. 131–146.

12. Richard G. Niemi, Lynda W. Powell, William D. Berry, Thomas M. Carsey, and James M. Snyder, Jr., "Competition in State Legislative Elections, 1992–2002," in Michael P. McDonald and John Samples, eds., *The Marketplace of Democracy: Electoral Competition and American Politics* (Brookings, 2006).

13. Alan Rosenthal, "The Legislative Unraveling of Institutional Fabric," in Carl E. Van Horn, ed., *The State of the States,* 3d ed. (CQ Press, 1996), p. 118.

14. Gary F. Moncrief, Peverill Squire, and Malcolm E. Jewell, *Who Runs for the Legislature?* (Prentice Hall, 2000).

15. Frank Smallwood, *Free and Independent: The Initiation of a College Professor into State Politics* (Greene Press, 1976), p. 223.

16. The *Book of the States, 2007* (The Council of State Governments, 2007), p. 80.

17. See Sue Thomas, *How Women Legislate* (Oxford University Press, 1994); see also Lesley Dahlkemper, "Growing Accustomed to Her Face," *State Legislatures* (July–August 1996), pp. 37–45; and Kathleen Dolan and Lynne Ford, "Change and Continuity Among Women State Legislators" *Political Research Quarterly* 50 (March 1997), pp. 137–151.

18. "Former State Legislators in Congress," National Conference of State Legislatures, www.ncsl.org/statefed/fsl.htm.

19. For fascinating comparative data, see *Inside the Legislative Process: A Comprehensive Survey by the American Society of Legislative Clerks and Secretaries* (National Conference of State Legislatures, 1998).

20. Wayne L. Francis, *The Legislative Committee Game: A Comparative Analysis of 50 States* (Ohio State University Press, 1989).

21. Keith E. Hamm, Ronald D. Hedlund, and Nancy Martorano, "Measuring State Legislative Committee Power: Change and Chamber Differences in the 20th Century," *State Politics and Policy Quarterly* 6 (2006): 88–111.

22. Gerald C. Wright and Tracy Osborn, "Party and Roll Call Voting in the American Legislature," paper presented at the annual meeting of the 2002 Midwest Political Science Association, April 2002.

23. Boris Shor and Nolan McCarty, "The Ideological Mapping of American Legislatures," working paper, http://home.uchicago.edu/~bshor/research/votesmart.pdf.

24. Keith E. Hamm and Gary F. Moncrief, "Legislative Politics in the States," in Virginia Gray et al., *Politics in the American States*, 7th ed. (CQ Press, 1999), p. 184.

25. Anthony J. Nownes, Clive S. Thomas, and Ronald J. Hrebenar, "Interest Groups in the States" in Virginia Gray and Russell L. Hanson, eds., *Politics in the American States*, 9th ed. (CQ Press, 2008).

26. Lobbying strategies are outlined in Jay Michael and Dan Walters, *The Third House: Lobbyists, Power, and Money in Sacramento* (Berkeley Public Policy Press, 2001). Other lobbying realities are discussed in Tom Loftus, *Art of Legislative Politics* (CQ Press, 1994), Chapter 10; and Alan Rosenthal, *Drawing the Line: Legislative Ethics in the States* (University of Nebraska Press, 1996).

27. Thomas Frank, "Ex-Legislators Use Contacts," *The Denver Post*, July 5, 1996, p. 16A; see also Loftus, *Art of Legislative Politics*.

28. Joel A. Thompson and Gary F. Moncrief, eds., *Campaign Finance in State Legislative Elections* (CQ Press, 1998).

29. Frank Smallwood, *Free and Independent* (Greene Press, 1976), p. 165; see also Alan Rosenthal, *The Third House: Lobbyists and Lobbying in the States,* 2d ed. (CQ Press, 2001); and "State Legislators Mix Public and Private Business, Study Says," *New York Times,* May 21, 2000, p. 26.

30. David D. Kirkpatrick, "States Take Lead on Ethics Rules for Lawmakers," *New York Times,* January 1, 2007, p. A1.

31. Adam Nossiter, "New Louisiana Governor Pierces Brazen Style of Business as Usual," *New York Times,* February 28, 2008, p. A1.

32. Charles Mahtesian, "The Ethics Backlash," *Governing* (October 1999), pp. 39–41.

33. Quote appears in the documentary film by Paul Stekler, "Last Man Standing: Politics, Texas Style" (Midnight Films, 2004).

34. John E. Brandl, *Money and Good Intentions Are Not Enough: Or, Why a Liberal Democrat Thinks States Need Both Competition and Community* (Brookings Institution Press, 1998), p. 58.

35. Alan Rosenthal, "The Legislative Institution: In Transition and at Risk," in Carl E. Van Horn, ed., *The State of the States,* 2d ed. (CQ Press, 1993), pp. 136–137; see also Alan Ehrenhalt, "An Embattled Institution," *Governing* (January 1992), pp. 28–33; and Karen Hansen, "Our Beleaguered Institution," *State Legislatures* (January 1994), pp. 12–17.

36. Rosenthal, "The Legislative Institution," p. 144.

37. See, for example, Christopher Conte, "Laptop Legislatures," *Governing* (November 1999), p. 36.

38. "Size of State Legislative Staff: 1979, 1988, 1996, 2003, and 2009," National Conference of State Legislatures, http://www.ncsl.org/default.aspx?tabid=14843.

39. Carrie Koch, "A Room for a View," *State Legislatures* (May 1997), pp. 32–34.

40. http://www.pewcenteronthestates.org/uploadedFiles/Grading-the-States-2008.pdf.

41. Rich Jones, "The State Legislatures," in *The Book of the States, 1992–1993* (The Council of State Governments, 1992), p. 125.

42. Michael Janofsky, "Idaho Legislature Repeals Term-Limit Law, Undoing Voter Approved Measure," *New York Times,* February 2, 2002, p. A11; see also Wayne Hoffman, "The Battle Over Term Limits," *State Legislatures* (May 2002), pp. 25–29.

43. Janofsky, "Idaho Legislature," p. A11.

44. See Daniel B. Wood, "The Term-Limit Movement of the '90s Stalls," *Christian Science Monitor,* April 27, 2004, p. A1.

45. www.washingtonpost.com/wp-srv/politics/elections/2006/or.html.

46. See John M. Carey, Richard G. Niemi, and Lynda W. Powell, *Term Limits in the State Legislatures* (University of Michigan Press, 2000).

47. Thad Kousser, *Term Limits and the Dismantling of State Legislative Professionalism* (Cambridge University Press, 2005), p. 203.

48. Jack Quinn et al., "Redrawing the Districts, Changing the Rules," *The Washington Post National Weekly Edition,* April 1, 1991, p. 23.

49. Gordon E. Baker, *The Reapportionment Revolution* (Random House, 1966), p. 47.

50. *Baker* v. *Carr,* 369 U.S. 186 (1962).

51. *Wesberry* v. *Sanders,* 376 U.S. 1 (1964).

52. *Reynolds* v. *Sims,* 377 U.S. 533 (1964).

53. *Brown* v. *Thomson,* 103 S.Ct. 2690 (1983).

54. Gary W. Cox and Jonathan N. Katz, *Elbridge Gerry's Salamander: The Electoral Consequences of the Reapportionment Revolution* (Cambridge University Press, 2002).

55. *Shaw* v. *Reno,* 509 U.S. 630 (1993); *Abrams* v. *Johnson,* 138 L.Ed. 2d 285 (1997). For a summary of state and federal judicial cases on drawing legislative district lines, see *Redistricting Case Summaries from the '90s* (National Conference of State Legislatures, 1998); see also Ronald E. Weber, "Emerging Trends in State Legislative Redistricting," *Spectrum: The Journal of State Government* 75 (Winter 2002), pp. 13–15; and additional updates can be found at the National Conference of State Legislatures Web site, www.ncsl.org.

56. *League of United Latin American Citizens* v. *Perry,* 399 F. Supp. 2d 756 (2006); and *Davis* v. *Bandemer,* 478 U.S. 109 (1986).

57. See Spencer C. Olin, *California's Prodigal Sons: Hiram Johnson and the Progressives, 1911–1917* (University of California Press, 1968).

58. Teri Renner, "Local Initiative and Referendum in the United States," www.iandrinstitute.org/Local%20I&R.htm.

59. A comprehensive list is available in *The Book of the States, 2009,* pp. 343–347.

60. *The Book of the States, 2009,* p. 339.

61. John G. Matsusaka, "2008 Ballot Propositions" in *The Book of the States, 2009,* p. 337.

62. David B. Magleby, "Ballot Initiatives and Intergovernmental Relations," paper presented at the annual meeting of the Western Political Science Association, Los Angeles, March 1998, p. 2.

63. Ibid., p. 13.

64. See, for example, Eugene C. Lee, "The Initiative Boom: An Excess of Democracy," in Gerald C. Lubenow and Bruce E. Cain, eds., *Governing California* (Institute of Governmental Studies, University of California, 1997), pp. 113–136; see also David S. Broder, *Democracy Derailed: Initiative Campaigns and the Power of Money* (Harcourt, 2000). But see Zolton L. Hajnul, Elisabeth R. Gerber, and Hugh Louch, "Minorities and Direct Legislation: Evidence from California Ballot Proposition Elections," paper presented at the annual meeting of the American Political Science Association, Washington, D.C., September 1–3, 2000; see also Elisabeth Gerber, *The Populist Paradox* (Princeton University Press, 1999).

65. See Peter Schrag, *Paradise Lost: California's Experience, America's Future* (New Press, 1998); see also the decidedly negative appraisal offered by Richard Ellis, *Democratic Delusions: The Initiative Process in America* (University Press of Kansas, 2002).

66. David B. Magleby and Kelly D. Paterson, "Consultants and Direct Democracy," *PS: Political Science and Politics* 31 (June 1998), pp. 160–161; see also Broder, *Democracy Derailed.*

67. Daniel A. Smith and Caroline J. Tolbert, *Educated by Initiative: The Effects of Direct Democracy on Citizens and Political Organizations in the American States* (University of Michigan Press, 2004).

68. Thomas E. Cronin, *Direct Democracy: The Politics of the Initiative, Referendum, and Recall* (Harvard University Press, 1989).

69. Michael G. Hagen and Edward L. Lascher, Jr., "Public Opinion About Ballot Initiatives," paper presented at the annual meeting of the American Political Science Association, Boston, September 3–6, 1998.

Chapter 6

1. "Death Row Cases Should Be Reviewed, Justice Says," *Columbus Dispatch,* May 15, 2010.

2. *The Book of the States, 2009* (The Council of State Governments, 2009), p. 187.

3. Ibid., p. 176.

4. The National Governors Association (http://www.nga.org/) publishes a short biography of every current governor, available online at http://www.nga.org/Files/pdf/BIOBOOK.pdf.

5. National Governors Association Current List of Governors' Political Affiliations and Terms of Office, http://www.nga.org/Files/pdf/GOVLIST.PDF.

6. *Book of the States,* p. 176.

7. Ibid., p. 188.

8. *The Book of the States, 2009,* p. 188.

9. This story is adapted from Robert S. McElvaine, *Mario Cuomo: A Biography* (Scribner, 1988), pp. 337–338; see also the assessment of Governor Pete Wilson's turbulent first years as governor of California in Robert Reinhold, "The Curse of the Statehouse," *The New York Times Magazine,* May 3, 1992, pp. 27–28, 54, 58–59.

10. Paul Foy, "Utah Governor Defies No Child Left Behind Act," *Associated Press,* May 2, 2005.

11. Thad L. Beyle, "2004 Gubernatorial Elections," *Spectrum: The Journal of State Government* (Winter 2005), p. 12.

12. Thad L. Beyle, "Race to Spend Money," *State News* (January 2008), p. 14.

13. Thomas M. Carsey, *Campaign Dynamics: The Race for Governor* (University of Michigan Press, 2000), Chapter 8.

14. Beyle, "2004 Gubernatorial Elections," p. 12.

15. Charlie LeDuff, "The California Recall: The Governor-Elect," *New York Times,* October 9, 2003, p. A33.

16. See Thomas M. Carsey, *Campaign Dynamics: The Race for Governor* (University of Michigan Press, 2000), Chapter 6 for a detailed account of this race.

17. Economic conditions may be more important in gubernatorial elections in some states than in others. See Michael Ebeid and Jonathan Rodden "Economic Geography and Economic Voting: Evidence from the U.S. States," *British Journal of Political Science* 36, No. 3 (July 2006), pp. 527–547.

18. Thomas M. Carsey and Gerald C. Wright, "State and National Factors in Gubernatorial and Senate Elections," *American Journal of Political Science* 42(3) (1998): 994–1002.

19. Richard F. Winters, "The Politics of Taxing and Spending," in Virginia Gray, Russell Hanson, and Herbert Jacob, eds., *Politics in the American States: A Comparative Analysis,* p. 329.

20. Kathleen Gallagher, "Doyle Will Give Keynote Speech at Stem Cell Summit," *Milwaukee Journal Sentinel,* June 6, 2006.

21. Thad Beyle and Margaret Ferguson, "Governors and the Executive Branch" in Virginia Gray and Russell L. Hanson, eds., *Politics in the American States: A Comparative Analysis,* 9th ed. (CQ Press, 2008).

22. In some cases, a governor's style and strategy alienate legislators. See, for example, Charles Mahtesian's analysis of Minnesota's Jesse Ventura, "Can He Govern?" *Governing* (May 2000), pp. 36–42. In contrast, Governor Bruce Babbitt worked effectively even with a legislature controlled by the opposition party. See David R. Berman, *Arizona Politics and Government* (University of Nebraska Press, 1998), pp. 116–117.

23. For a lighthearted commentary by a member of Governor Pete Wilson's Electronic Commerce Advisory Council, see Stewart Alsop, "Helping the Governor Figure Out E-Commerce," *Fortune*, June 8, 1998, p. 269.

24. Ronald K. Snell, "Annual and Biennial Budgeting: The Experience of State Governments" (National Conference of State Legislatures, 2004), www.ncsl.org/programs/fiscal/annlbien.htm.

25. Kathleen Gray, "Granholm Stars in Her Own 'Kill Bill,'" *Detroit Free Press*, April 26, 2004, p. A1.

26. John Kennedy and Jason Garcia, "Governor's Veto Pen Leaves Heavy Mark," *Orlando Sentinel*, May 26, 2006.

27. Daniel C. Vock, "Governors Enjoy Quirky Veto Power," Stateline.org, April 24, 2007, www.stateline.org/live/printable/story?contentId=201710.

28. Cited in a profile of New York in *Governing* (February 1999), p. 66.

29. Thad L. Beyle, "Being Governor," in Carl E. Van Horn, ed., *The State of the States*, 3d ed. (CQ Press, 1996), p. 89.

30. But see Governor Tommy Thompson's defense of using frequent vetoes, *Power to the People: An American State at Work* (HarperCollins, 1996), and the view of one of his main critics in the Wisconsin legislature, Tom Loftus, *The Art of Legislative Politics* (CQ Press, 1994), Chapter 5. On the varied effectiveness of the line item veto as a tool for fiscal responsibility, see Glenn Abney and Thomas P. Lauth, "The Item Veto and Fiscal Responsibility," *Journal of Politics* 59 (August 1997), pp. 882–892. On how a governor's rash use of the line item veto can infuriate legislators, see Mahtesian, "Can He Govern?," p. 40.

31. Katie Zezima, "Obey Same-Sex Marriage Law, Officials Told," *New York Times*, April 25, 2004, p. A15.

32. Martha Derthick, "Where Federalism Didn't Fail," *Public Administration Review* (December 2007), p. 41; see also Kathleen Murphy, "Katrina Sets Record in State-to-State Help," Stateline.org/live/ViewPage.action?siteNodeId=136&languageId=1&contentId=53077 (accessed September 9, 2005).

33. *Perpich et al. v. Department of Defense*, 110 L.Ed. 312 (1990).

34. John Gramlich, "Governors May Regain Sole Control Over Guard," Stateline.org, December 17, 2007, www.stateline.org/live/printable/story?contentId=265258 (accessed September 17, 2010); see also Jennifer Nedeau, "National Guard Sacrifices Hit Home," Stateline.org, December 17, 2007, www.stateline.org/live/printable/story?contentId=211236.

35. "Governors Lose in Power Struggle Over National Guard," Stateline.org, http://www.stateline.org/live/details/story?contentId=170453.

36. Kavan Peterson, "Governors Shy from Clemency Power," Stateline.org, January 30, 2003, www.stateline.org/live/printable/story?contentId=15145.

37. Ryan Alessi and Jack Brammer, "Fletcher Pardons 9," *Lexington (Ky.) Herald-Leader*, August 30, 2005.

38. For background on this controversy, see Jonathan Alter, "The Death Penalty on Trial," *Newsweek*, June 12, 2000, pp. 26–34.

39. Willoughby, *The State of the States*, p. 137.

40. Kunin, *Living a Political Life*, p. 382.

41. Beyle, "The Governors," pp. 224–226.

42. Thomas H. Kean, quoted in Barbara Salmore and Stephen Salmore, *New Jersey Politics and Government* (University of Nebraska Press, 1998), p. 136.

43. Jesse Ventura, *I Ain't Got Time to Bleed* (Signet Press, 2000), pp. 296–297.

44. Beyle, "The Governors," pp. 224–226.

45. http://www.pewcenteronthestates.org/initiatives_detail.aspx?initiativeID=36072.

46. Alan Ehrenhalt, "Reinventing Government in the Unlikeliest Place," *Governing* (August 1993), pp. 7–8.

47. "Two New Agencies Launch Under Reorganization," *Associated Press*, August 31, 2004.

48. Jonathan Walters, "Fad Mad," *Governing* (September 1996), p. 49.

49. Dall Forsythe, ed., *Quicker, Better, Cheaper? Managing Performance in American Government* (Rockefeller Institute Press, 2001), especially Chapters 12–16.

50. Beyle, "Being Governor," p. 106.

51. See the discussion of Governor George W. Bush and his relationship with his lieutenant governor in Jonathan Walters, "The Taming of Texas," *Governing* (July 1998), p. 20; see also "The Future of the Texas Lieutenant Governor," *Comparative State Politics* (October 1995), pp. 21–24.

52. But see Charles N. Wheeler III, "Why Illinois Still Needs Lieutenant Governor's Position," *Illinois Issues* (September 1994), pp. 6–7.

53. Martha Derthick, "Federalism and the Politics of Tobacco," *Publius* (Winter 2001), p. 47.

54. For additional information on the Office of the Attorney General, State of California, visit www.caag.state.ca.us.

55. For Eliot Spitzer's career before he won the governorship, see Brooke A. Masters, *Spoiling for a Fight: The Rise of Eliot Spitzer* (Times Books, 2006).

56. See Thad L. Beyle, "Enhancing Executive Leadership in the States," *State and Local Government Review* (Winter 1995), pp. 18–35; and Thad L. Beyle, "The Governors," in Virginia Gray, Russell Hanson, and Herbert Jacob, eds. *Politics in the American States: A Comparative Analysis*, 7th ed. (CQ Press, 1999), pp. 191–231.

57. Lamar Alexander, *Steps Along the Way: A Governor's Scrapbook* (Nelson, 1986), p. 112. Similar views can be found in former Vermont Governor Madeleine M. Kunin's memoir, *Living a Political Life* (Vintage Books, 1995).

58. See Earl H. Fry, *The Expanding Role of State and Local Governments in U.S. Foreign Policy* (Council on Foreign Relations Press, 1998); see also, for example, Alan Johnson, "Taft Shows He's Up to the Job on Foreign Grounds," *Columbus (Ohio) Dispatch*, February 14, 2000.

59. *The Book of the States, 1998–1999* (The Council of State Governments, 1998), p. xxiii.

60. Professor Thad L. Beyle at the University of North Carolina at Chapel Hill tracks state polls on governors' job performances and finds that Democratic, Republican, and Independent governors alike all averaged approximately 60 percent public approval in the 1990s.

61. Alexander, *Steps Along the Way*, p. 141.

62. Thomas H. Kean, *The Politics of Inclusion* (Free Press, 1988), p. 248.

63. Scott Matheson with James Edwin Kee, *Out of Balance* (Peregrine Smith Books, 1986), p. 186; see also the reflections of another popular western governor in Cecil Andrus and Joel Connelly, *Cecil Andrus: Politics Western Style* (Sasquatch Books, 1998).

Chapter 7

1. National Center for State Courts, *Examining the Work of State Courts, 2006* (National Center for State Courts, 2005), p. 22.

2. The same Massey coal company owned the mine at which a major explosion took place in April of 2010 that killed 29 workers.

3. See Michael Solimine and James Walker, *Respecting State Courts: The Inevitability of Judicial Federalism* (Greenwood Press, 2000); and Matthew Bosworth, *Courts as Catalysts: State Supreme Courts and Public School Finance Equity* (State University of New York Press, 2001).

4. Lynn Mather, "Policy Making in State Trial Courts," in John B. Gates and Charles A. Johnson, eds., *The American Courts: A Critical Assessment* (CQ Press, 1991), pp. 119–157.

5. Patrick Schmidt and Paul Martin, "To the Internet and Beyond: State Supreme Courts on the World Wide Web," *Judicature* 84 (May–June 2001), pp. 314–325.

6. Robert F. Williams, "In the Supreme Court's Shadow: Legitimacy of State Rejection of Supreme Court Reasoning and Results," *South Carolina Law Review* 56 (Spring 1984), p. 353.

7. Harry P. Stumpf and John H. Culver, *The Politics of State Courts* (Longman, 1992), pp. 8–11.

8. Hans A. Linde, "Observations of a State Court Judge," in Robert A. Katzmann, ed., *Judges and Legislators: Toward Institutional Comity* (Brookings Institution Press, 1988), p. 118.

9. Philip L. Dubois, "State Trial Court Appointments: Does the Governor Make a Difference?" *Judicature* 69 (June–July 1985), pp. 20–21.

10. Charles H. Sheldon and Nicholas P. Lovrich, Jr., "State Judicial Recruitment," in John B. Gates and Charles A. Johnson, eds., *The American Courts: A Critical Assessment* (CQ Press, 1991), pp. 172–173.

11. See American Judicature Society, www.ajs.org/js/judicialselectioncharts.pdf.

12. Thurgood Marshall, in *Renne v. Geary*, 501 U.S. 312 (1991).

13. "Judges Say Political Influence Threatens Independence of Judiciary," *(Yankton, S.D.) Press and Dakotan*, www.pressandakotan.com/stories/101797/judges.html. [AU: Please check this link as it didn't open for me; also, is "*(Yankton, S.D.)*" correct as set?]

14. Adam Skaggs, "Buying Justice: The Impact of Citizens United on Judicial Elections," report for the Brennan Center for Justice, 2010, http://www.brennancenter.org/page/-/publications/BCReportBuyingJustice.pdf?nocdn=1.

15. Michael Scherer, "The Making of the Corporate Judiciary," *Mother Jones* (November 2003), p. 72.

16. *Republican Party of Minnesota v. White*, 536 U.S. 765 (2002).

17. William Glaberson, "Court Rulings Curb Efforts to Rein in Judicial Races," *New York Times*, October 7, 2000, p. A8.

18. See Justice at Stake Campaign, Brennan Center for Justice at New York University Law School, and National Institute on Money in State Politics, *The New Politics of Judicial Elections* (Justice at Stake Campaign, 2001); and American Bar Association, Standing Committee on Judicial Independence, *Public Financing of Judicial Campaigns: Report of the Commission on Public Financing of Judicial Campaigns* (American Bar Association, 2002).

19. *Wells v. Edwards*, 409 U.S. 1095 (1973).

20. *Chisom v. Roemer*, 501 U.S. 400 (1991); and *Houston Lawyers' Association v. Texas Attorney General*, 501 U.S. 419 (1991); see also Tracy Thompson, "The New Front in the Battle for Civil Rights: Judgeships," *The Washington Post National Weekly Edition*, December 18, 1989, p. 34.

21. J. W. Peltason, *The Missouri Plan for the Selection of Judges* (University of Missouri Studies, 1945). The plan was previously known as the Nonpartisan Plan for the Selection of Judges or the Kales Plan until it was called the Missouri Plan by this monograph.

22. Beth M. Henschen, Robert Moog, and Steven Davis, "Judicial Nominating Commissioners: A National Profile," *Judicature* 73 (April–May 1990), pp. 328–334.

23. Philip L. Dubois, "The Politics of Innovation in State Courts: The Merit Plan of Judicial Selection," *Publius* 20 (Winter 1990), p. 40.

24. Warren K. Hall and Larry T. Aspin, "What Twenty Years of Judicial Retention Elections Have Told Us," *Judicature* 70 (April–May 1987), pp. 340–347; and Susan B. Caron and Larry C. Berkson, *Judicial Retention Elections in the United States* (American Judicature Society, 1980).

25. Larry T. Aspin, "Trends in Judicial Retention Elections, 1964–2006," *Judicature* 90 (March–April 2007), p. 210; and "Evaluating the Performance of Judges Standing for Retention," *Judicature* 79 (January–February 1996), pp. 190–195.

26. Traciel Reid, "The Politicization of Retention Elections," *Judicature* 83 (September–October 1999), p. 68.

27. Thomas E. Cronin and Robert D. Loevy, *Colorado Politics and Government* (University of Nebraska Press, 1993), pp. 251–253.

28. "The Need for Judicial Performance Evaluations for Retention Elections," *Judicature* 75 (October–November 1991), p. 124.

29. Henry Weinstein, "Forum Airs Questions of Jurist Independence," *Los Angeles Times*, November 22, 1998, p. A18.

30. *The Book of the States, 2007* (The Council of State Governments, 2005), p. 256.

31. Jeffrey Shaman, Steven Lubet, and James Alfini, *Judicial Conduct and Ethics*, 3d ed. (Lexis, 2000), Sec. 15.07.

32. Jolanta Juskiewicz Perlstein and Nathan Goldman, "Judicial Disciplinary Commissions: A New Approach to the Discipline and Removal of State Judges," in Phil Dubois, ed., *The Analysis of Judicial Reform* (Lexington Books, 1982), pp. 93–106.

33. *Burch* v. *Louisiana*, 441 U.S. 130 (1979); and *Ballew* v. *Georgia*, 435 U.S. 223 (1978). See Reid Hastie, Steven D. Penrod, and Nancy Pennington, *Inside the Jury* (Harvard University Press, 1983), for a study showing that nonunanimous verdicts are more likely to bring convictions than those requiring unanimity. Federal courts often use juries of fewer than 12 for civil cases. For federal criminal trials, the Supreme Court still requires both the common-law jury of 12 and unanimous verdicts.

34. *Prosecutors in State Courts, 2005* (U.S. Department of Justice, Bureau of Justice Statistics, 2002), www.ojp.usdoj.gov/bjs/pub/pdf/psc05.pdf.

35. Robert H. Jackson, quoted in Jack M. Kress, "Progress and Prosecution," *Annals of the American Academy of Political and Social Science* (January 1976), p. 100.

36. William K. Muir, *Police: Streetcorner Politicians* (University of Chicago Press, 1977).

37. Charles E. Silberman, *Criminal Violence, Criminal Justice* (Random House, 1978), p. 303.

38. Jay Livingston, *Crime and Criminology* (Prentice Hall, 1992), p. 474.

39. Silberman, *Criminal Violence*, p. 218; see also David Cole, *No Equal Justice: Race and Class in the American Criminal Justice System* (New Press, 1999).

40. National Victims Constitutional Amendment Passage, www.nvcap.org/stvras.htm.

41. *South Carolina* v. *Gathers*, 490 U.S. 805 (1989); and *Payne* v. *Tennessee*, 501 U.S. 808 (1991).

42. *Felony Sentences in State Courts, 2002* (U.S. Department of Justice, Bureau of Justice Statistics, 2004).

43. Thomas M. Uhlman and N. Darlene Walker, "A Plea Is No Bargain: The Impact of Case Disposition on Sentencing," *Social Science Quarterly* 60 (September 1979), pp. 218–234; see also Malcolm M. Feeley, *The Process Is the Punishment* (Russell Sage, 1979).

44. Thomas Church, Jr., "Plea Bargains, Concessions and the Courts: Analysis of a Quasi-Experiment," *Law and Society Review* 14 (Spring 1976), p. 400. For a contrary view, see National Advisory Commission on Criminal Justice Standards and Goals, *Report of the Task Force* (U.S. Government Printing Office, 1979).

45. Church, "Plea Bargains," p. 400.

46. Jonathan D. Casper, *American Criminal Justice: The Defendant's Perspective* (Prentice Hall, 1972), pp. 52–53. Abraham S. Goldstein, *The Passive Judiciary: Prosecutorial Discretion and the Guilty Plea* (Louisiana State University Press, 1981), is critical of judges for not supervising plea bargains more actively.

47. *Santobello* v. *New York*, 404 U.S. 257 (1971).

48. Henry N. Pontell, *A Capacity to Punish* (Indiana University Press, 1985).

49. Lee Sechrest, Susan O. White, and Elizabeth D. Brown, eds., *The Rehabilitation of Criminal Offenders: Problems and Prospects* (National Academy of Sciences, 1979), pp. 3–6.

50. John Hagan and Kristin Bumiler, "Making Sense of Sentencing: A Review and Critique of Sentencing Research," in Alfred Blumstein et al., eds., *Research on Sentencing* (National Academy Press, 1983), Vol. 2; and Susan Welch, Michael Combs, and John Gruhl, "Do Black Judges Make a Difference?" *American Journal of Political Science* 32 (February 1988), pp. 126–135.

51. William B. Eldridge, "Shifting Views of the Sentencing Functions," *Annals of the American Academy of Political and Social Science* (July 1982), pp. 104–111.

52. The Supreme Court upheld these laws in *Ewing* v. *California*, 538 U.S. 11 (2003).

53. Data for this section comes from the Death Penalty Information Center, www.deathpenaltyinfo.org.

54. Bureau of Justice Statistics, "Prisoners in 2008," December 2010, Table 9, http://bjs.ojp.usdoj.gov/index.cfm?ty=pbdetail&iid=1763.

55. Eric Schlosser, "The Prison-Industrial Complex," *Atlantic*, December 1998, p. 52.

56. Bureau of Justice Statistics, "Probation and Parole in the United States, 2006," December 2007.

57. "One in 100: Behind Bars in America 2008," Pew Center on the States, February 2008, www.pewcenteronthestates.org/uploadedFiles/One%20in%20100.pdf.

58. William J. Sabol, Heather Couture, and Paige M. Harrison, *Prisoners in 2006* (Bureau of Justice Statistics, 2007).

59. Alison Lawrence, "State Sentencing and Corrections Legislation, 2007 Action, 2008 Outlook," National Conference of State Legislatures, January 2008, p. 4, www.ncsl.org/print/cj/07sentencingreport.pdf.

60. Barbara Fink, "Opening the Door on Community Corrections," *State Legislatures* (September 1984), pp. 24–31.

61. Lawrence, "State Sentencing and Corrections Legislation," p. 7.

62. Quoted in Associated Press, "ABA 'Public Jurist' Considers Reforms in Legal System," December 1993.

63. Franklin M. Zweig et al., "Securing the Future for America's State Courts," *Judicature* 73 (April–May 1990), pp. 297–298.

64. *The Book of the States, 2007*, p. 251.

Chapter **8**

1. The story is available online at http://www.npr.org/templates/story/story.php?storyId=122954677.

2. Employment data available at U.S. Census Bureau, "2006 Public Employment Data: Local Governments," ftp2.census.gov/govs/apes/06locus.txt.

3. *Hunter* v. *City of Pittsburgh*, 208 U.S. 161 (1907).

4. Brian Gill, Ron Zimmer, Jolley Christman, and Suzanne Blanc, *State Takeover, School Restructuring, Private Management, and Student Achievement in Philadelphia* (RAND Corporation, 2007), p. xi.

5. On the living wage, see Oren M. Levin-Waldman, *The Political Economy of the Living Wage: A Study of Four Cities* (Sharpe, 2004). One successful city campaign reform is found in New York City; for information on the New York City Campaign Finance Board and its programs, see www.nyccfb.info. Also see Rockefeller Institute, "Can and Should NYC's Campaign Finance Reforms Be Extended to State Offices," www.rockinst.org/search/SearchResults.aspx?bodytext=campaign%20finance&title=campaign%20finance. On charter schools and cities, see Paul S. Grogan and Tony Proscio, *Comeback Cities: A Blueprint for Urban Neighborhood Revival* (Westview Press, 2000), Chapter 9.

6. Richard L. Cole, John Kincaid, and Andrew Parkin, "Public Opinion on Federalism in the United States and Canada," *Publius* 32 (Fall 2002), Tables 1 and 7.

7. Data obtained from U.S. Census Bureau, "State and County Quickfacts," quickfacts.census.gov/qfd/.

8. An excellent overview of counties is Donald C. Menzel, ed., *The American County: Frontiers of Knowledge* (University of Alabama Press, 1996).

9. National Association of Counties, "An Overview of County Government," www.naco.org/Content/NavigationMenu/About_Counties/County_Government/A_Brief_Overview_of_County_Government.htm.

10. See County Executives of America, "Access Government: County Executives Map," www.countyexecutives.org/accessgov/countymap.htm.

11. For an assessment of the county performance in certain administrative and fiscal functions, see Katherine Barrett and Richard Greene, with Michele Mariani, "Grading the Counties 2002: A Management Report Card," *Governing* (February 2002), www.governing.com/gpp/2002/gp2intro.htm.

12. National Association of Counties, "An Overview."

13. Maine Municipal Association, http://www.memun.org/public/local_govt/government.htm.

14. See Amendment LXXXIX of the Massachusetts Constitution.

15. See this 1978 article in Time Magazine (http://www.time.com/time/magazine/article/0,9171,912178,00.html) and this 2004 article in U.S. News (http://www.usnews.com/usnews/news/articles/040322/22after.htm).

16. For a history of suburban development, see Rosalyn Baxandall and Elizabeth Ewen, *Picture Windows: How the Suburbs Happened* (Basic Books, 2000).

17. See Paul G. Lewis, *Shaping Suburbia: How Political Institutions Organize Urban Development* (University of Pittsburgh Press, 1996).

18. *Kelo* v. *City of New London,* 125 S. Ct. 2655 (2005).

19. National Conference of State Legislatures, "Eminent Domain," www.ncsl.org/programs/natres/EMINDOMAIN.htm.

20. National League of Cities "Cities 101," http://www.nlc.org/about_cities/cities_101/138.aspx.

21. Susan Welch, "The Impact of At-Large Elections on the Representation of Blacks and Hispanics," *The Journal of Politics* 52(4) (1990): 1050–76.

22. *Mobile* v. *Bolden,* 446 U.S. 55 (1980).

23. *Rogers* v. *Lodge,* 458 U.S. 613 (1982); and *Thornburg* v. *Gingles,* 478 U.S. 30 (1986).

24. For the experience of one mayor in a council–manager city, see the memoir by Cambridge, Massachusetts, Mayor Barbara Ackermann, *"You the Mayor?" The Education of a City Politician* (Auburn, 1989).

25. Kathy Hayes and Semoon Chang, "The Relative Efficiency of City-Manager and Mayor–Council Forms of Government," *Southern Economic Journal* 57(1) (1990): 167–177.

26. Richard C. Feiock, Moon-Gi Jeong, and Jaehoon Kim, "Credible Commitment and Council–Manager Government: Implications for Policy Instrument Choices," *Public Administration Review* 63(5) (2003): 616–625.

27. See James H. Svara and Associates, *Facilitative Leadership in Local Government: Lessons from Successful Mayors and Chairpersons in the Council–Manager Form* (Jossey-Bass, 1994).

28. See San Diego's official Web site, http://www.sandiego.gov/mayortransition/.

29. Center for American Women and Politics, Eagleton Institute of Politics, Rutgers, The State University of New Jersey, "Women Mayors in U.S. Cities 2009," http://www.cawp.rutgers.edu/fast_facts/levels_of_office/Local-WomenMayors .php.

30. Joint Center for Political and Economic Studies, "Black Big-City Mayors, 2002–2007," www.jointcenter.org/current_research_and_policy_activities/political_participation.

31. http://ncbm.org/2009/04/our-mission/.

32. See Earl H. Fry, *The Expanding Role of State and Local Governments in U.S. Foreign Affairs* (Council on Foreign Relations, 1998), especially Chapter 4.

33. U.S. Census Bureau, "Metropolitan and Micropolitan Statistical Areas," www.census.gov/population/www/estimates/metroarea.html.

34. U.S. Census Bureau, "Population and Percent Distribution by Core Based Statistical Area (CBSA) Status for the United States, Regions, and Divisions: 2000 and 2007," Population Division, Table 11, www.census.gov/population/www/estimates/metro_general/2007/CBSA-EST2007–11.xls.

35. U.S. Census Bureau, "Annual Estimates of the Population of Metropolitan and Micropolitan Statistical Areas: April 1, 2000 to July 1, 2007," Table 1.

36. The legal constraints on Baltimore, for example, are outlined in David Rusk, *Baltimore Unbound: A Strategy for Regional Renewal* (Abell Foundation/Johns Hopkins University Press, 1996).

37. These associations are particularly strong for children who live in very poor households during several years and when they are very young. See Jeanne Brooks-Gunn and Greg J. Duncan, "The Effects of Poverty on Children," *Future of Children* 7 (Summer/Fall 1997), pp. 55–71.

38. National Center for Children in Poverty, "Basic Facts About Low-Income Children," http://www.nccp.org/publications/pub_892.html.

39. U.S. Census Bureau, *Income, Poverty, and Health Insurance Coverage in the United States: 2005* (U.S. Government Printing Office, 2006), pp. 15–16.

40. D'Vera Cohn, "A New Millennium for America's Cities," *The Washington Post National Weekly Edition,* October 30, 2000, p. 34.

41. Joel Garreau, *Edge City* (Doubleday, 1991).

42. *Arlington Heights* v. *Metropolitan Housing Development Corp.,* 429 U.S. 252, 97 S.Ct. 555, 50 L.Ed.2d 450 (1977).

43. Updated information on which counties are included in Metropolitan Statistical Areas is published by the U.S. Office of Management and Budget and is available through the U.S. Census Bureau Web site at www.whitehouse.gov/omb/bulletins/fy2007/b07–01.pdf. Once the counties in an MSA are identified, the Census Bureau's "Governments Integrated Directory (GID)" Web site can produce a list of all governments within those counties, see harvester.census.gov/gid/gid_02/options.html. The latest data available, as of April 2008, are from the 2002 survey of governments. A complete survey of local governments is conducted every five years, so the next available survey will be for 2007.

44. David Rusk, former mayor of Albuquerque, makes this case well in *Baltimore Unbound* and in *Cities Without Suburbs,* 2d ed. (Woodrow Wilson Center Press/Johns Hopkins University Press, 1995).

45. See Suzanne M. Leland and Kurt Thurmaier, eds., *Case Studies of City–County Consolidation* (Sharpe, 2004); and Jered B. Carr and Richard C. Feiock, eds., *City–County Consolidation and Its Alternatives* (Sharpe, 2004).

46. Ellen Perlman, "Polite Tenacity," *Governing* (November 2000), pp. 34, 214.

47. See Myron Orfield, *Metropolitics: A Regional Agenda for Community and Stability* (Brookings Institution Press, 1997); and Manuel Pastor, ed., *Regions That Work: How Cities and Suburbs Can Grow Together* (University of Minnesota Press, 2000).

48. The metro government Web site is located at http://www.oregonmetro.gov/ and a link to the charter itself is located at http://www.oregonmetro.gov/index.cfm/go/by.web/id=629.

49. See E. J. Dionne, Jr., ed., *Community Works: The Revival of Civil Society in America* (Brookings Institution Press, 1998).

50. See David L. Kirp et al., *Our Town: Race, Housing, and the Soul of Suburbia* (Rutgers University Press, 1997); and Jonathan Harr, *A Civil Action* (Vintage Books, 1996).

51. See the recommendation often prescribed by a major proponent of regionalism, Neal R. Peirce, in Charles Mahtesian, ed., "The Civic Therapist," *Governing* (September 1995), pp. 24–27; see also Dreier, Mollenkopf, and Swanstrom, *Place Matters,* Chapter 7.

52. "The End of Urban Man? Care to Bet?" *The Economist,* December 31, 1999, pp. 25–26.

53. See the thoughtful recommendations in Robert J. Waste, *Independent Cities: Rethinking U.S. Urban Policy* (Oxford University Press, 1998); but also see Clarissa Rile Hayward, "The Difference States Make: Democracy, Identity, and the American City," *American Political Science Review* 97 (November 2003), p. 501.

Chapter 9

1. The report is archived by the National Commission on Excellence in Education at http://www2.ed.gov/pubs/NatAtRisk/index.html.

2. For more information on the study, see Amanda Ripley (2010), "Should Kids Be Bribed to Do Well in School?," *Time Magazine,* April 8, 2010, http://www.time.com/time/nation/article/0,8599,1978589-1,00.html.

3. U.S. Census Bureau, *Statistical Abstract of the United States: 2008* (U.S. Government Printing Office, 2008), Table 422, "State and Local Governments—Revenue and Expenditures by Function: 2004."

4. *Digest of Education Statistics, 2009,* "Total and Current Expenditures per Pupil in Fall Enrollment in Public Elementary and Secondary Education, by Function and State or Jurisdiction: 2006–2007," Table 183, http://nces.ed.gov/programs/digest/d09/tables/dt09_183.asp.

5. *Digest of Education Statistics, 2009,* "Number of Public School Districts and Public and Private Elementary and Secondary Schools: Selected Years, 1869–70 Through 2007–08," Table 86, http://nces.ed.gov/programs/digest/d09/tables/dt09_086.asp.

6. "Governors, State School Superintendents Propose Common Academic Standards" *The Washington Post,* March 11, 2010, http://www.washingtonpost.com/wp-dyn/content/article/2010/03/10/AR2010031000024.html?referrer=emailarticle.

7. See Gary Orfield and Chungmei Lee, *Brown at 50: King's Dream or Plessy's Nightmare* (Harvard Civil Rights Project, 2004); see also Gary Orfield, Susan E. Eaton, and the Harvard Project on School Desegregation, *Dismantling Desegregation: The Quiet Reversal of Brown v. Board of Education* (New Press, 1996).

8. "A New Diverse Majority: Students of Color in the South's Public Schools" Southern Education Foundation report, http://www.sefatl.org/pdf/New Diverse Majority.pdf.

9. "The Next Fight: Resegregation" *USA Today,* May 18, 2010, http://www.usatoday.com/news/opinion/forum/2010-05-19-column19_ST_N.htm.

10. Peter Harkness, "State and Localities: Test, but Verify," *CQ Weekly,* March 26, 2007, p. 882.

11. Quoted in "Statewide Student Tests," *State Legislatures,* February 2004, p. 33; see also Dewayne Matthews, "No Child Left Behind: The Challenge of Implementation," *The Book of the States, 2004* (The Council of State Governments, 2004), pp. 493–496; and June Kronholz, "Bush's Education Law Gets an Incomplete," *The Wall Street Journal,* September 1, 2004, p. A6.

12. William J. Mathis, "The Cost of Implementing the Federal No Child Left Behind Act: Different Assumptions, Different Answers," *Peabody Journal of Education* 80, No. 2 (2005), pp. 90–119.

13. Michael Sandler, "Commission Recommends Broad Changes to 2002 Education Law," *CQ Weekly,* February 19, 2007, p. 552. For a discussion of recommendations by state legislatures, see "Joint Statement of the National Conference of State Legislatures and the American Association of School Administrators on ESEA Reauthorization,"

National Conference of State Legislatures, www.ncsl.org/statefed/NCSLAASAJoint Statement.htm.

14. C. Eugene Steuerle, Van Doorn Ooms, George Peterson, and Robert D. Reischauer, eds., *Vouchers and the Provision of Public Services* (Brookings Institution Press, 2000); see also "Colorado Adopts Statewide School Vouchers," *State Legislatures*, July–August 2003, p. 7.

15. William H. Rehnquist, quoted in Richard Rothstein, "Failed Schools? The Meaning Is Unclear," *New York Times*, July 3, 2002, p. A14.

16. Jon Sarche, "Public School Vouchers Unconstitutional, Colorado Supreme Court Says," *Associated Press*, June 28, 2004.

17. See, for example, "Report Cards for the Knowledge Is Power Program," *U.S. News & World Report Online*, April 29, 2008, www.usnews.com/blogs/on-education/2008/4/29/report-cards-for-the-knowledge-is-power-program.html.

18. www.irvine.org/leadershipAwards/recipients/yvonneChan.shtml.

19. Diana Jean Schemo, "Study of Test Scores Finds Charter Schools Lagging," *New York Times*, August 23, 2006; see also the National Center for Education Statistics, U.S. Department of Education, *The Nation's Report Card: America's Charter Schools*, nces.ed.gov/nationsreport-card/pdf/studies/2005456.pdf.

20. Michael S. McPherson and Morton Owen Schapiro, "Funding Roller Coaster for Public Higher Education," *Science*, November 14, 2003, p. 1157.

21. "An Update on State Budget Cuts," Center on Budget and Policy Priorities, May 25, 2010, http://www.cbpp.org/cms/index.cfm?fa=view&id=1214.

22. Paula Pant, "U. Colorado Explores Options in Funding," *University Wire*, January 18, 2007.

23. Karin Fischer, "Colorado's 'Noble Experiment,'" *Chronicle of Higher Education*, July 15, 2005, p. 29.

24. See Christine Walton and Julie Davis Bell, "New Ways to Fund Higher Ed," *State Legislatures*, December 2003, pp. 28–31; see also John Buntin, "Setting Colleges Free," *Governing* (September 2003), pp. 18–22.

25. "Recipients and Families 1936–2001," Administration for Children and Families, www.acf.hhs.gov/news/stats/3697.htm.

26. R. Kent Weaver, *Ending Welfare as We Know It* (Brookings Institution Press, 2000).

27. On state policies, see Office of Family Assistance, Administration for Children and Families, U.S. Department of Health and Human Services, *Temporary Assistance to Needy Families: Sixth Annual Report to Congress* (Office of Family Assistance, 2004), Chapter 12.

28. See Rebecca Blank and Ron Haskins, eds., *The New World of Welfare* (Brookings Institution Press, 2001); Isabel V. Sawhill et al., *Welfare Reform and Beyond: The Future of the Safety Net* (Brookings Institution Press, 2002); and Carol W. Weissert, ed., *Learning from Leaders: Welfare Reform Politics and Policy in Five Midwestern States* (Rockefeller Institute Press, 2000).

29. Data on number of families on Temporary Assistance for Needy Families from the U.S. Administration for Children and Families, "TANF Families," Excel spreadsheet, April 8, 2008, available at www.acf.hhs.gov/programs/ofa/data-reports/caseload/2007/20074_caseloadreport.xls.

30. For an extensive review of studies on the effects of welfare reform, see Rebecca Blank, "Evaluating Welfare Reform in the U.S.," *Journal of Economic Literature*, December 2002, pp. 1105–1166.

31. Sharon Parrott and Arloc Sherman, "TANF at 10: Program Results Are More Mixed Than Often Understood," Center on Budget and Policy Priorities, August 17, 2006.

32. Peter Edelman, "The True Purpose of Welfare Reform," *New York Times*, May 29, 2002, p. A21.

33. See, for example, David Hage, *Reforming Welfare by Rewarding Work: One State's Successful Experiment* (University of Minnesota Press, 2004); and Courtney Jarchow and Jack Tweedie, "Welfare and Wedding Vows," *State Legislatures*, April 2003, pp. 24–28.

34. "Are unemployment benefits no longer temporary?". The Washington Post. March 9, 2010. http://www.washingtonpost.com/wp-dyn/content/article/2010/03/08/AR2010030804927.html.

35. Center on Budget and Policy Priorities, "Introduction to Unemployment Insurance" (updated April 16, 2010) http://www.cbpp.org/cms/index.cfm?fa=view&id=1466

36. "Issue Brief: Medicaid Redesigned: State Innovations in Health Coverage and Delivery," National Governors Association Center for Best Practices, March 27, 2008.

37. Dennis G. Smith, Janet G. Freeze, Susan N. Hill, and Lyn R. Killman, "The Future of Medicaid," in *The Book of the States, 2006* (The Council of State Governments, 2006), p. 491.

38. "Issue Brief: Leading the Way: State Health Reform Initiatives," National Governors Association Center for Best Practices, July 11, 2007; see also "Issue Brief: Medicaid Redesigned: State Innovations in Health Coverage and Delivery," National Governors Association Center for Best Practices, March 27, 2008.

39. David S. Broder, "States in Fiscal Crises," *The Washington Post National Weekly Edition*, May 27, 2002, p. 4

40. "Issue Brief: Medicaid Redesigned."

41. "Issue Brief: Leading the Way."

42. The program is detailed on the state's Web site at: http://www.mass.gov/?pageID=mg2subtopic&L=4&L0=Home&L1=Resident&L2=Health&L3=Health+Care+Reform&sid=massgov2.

43. "In Hawaii's Health System, Lessons for Lawmakers," *New York Times*, October 16, 2009, http://www.nytimes.com/2009/10/17/health/policy/17hawaii.html.

44. Law Enforcement Statistics, Bureau of Justice Statistics, www.ojp.usdoj.gov/bjs/lawenf.htm.

45. *Statistical Abstract of the United States: 2008* (U.S. Government Printing Office, 2008), Table 429, "State and Local Governments—Expenditures and Debt by State: 2004."

46. Data from the Bureau of Justice Statistics, "Local Police" link at http://bjs.ojp.usdoj.gov/index.cfm?ty=tp&tid=71.

47. Bureau of Justice Statistics, State-Level Crime Trends Database, http://bjsdata.ojp.usdoj.gov/dataonline/Search/Crime/State/RunCrimeStatebyState.cfm.

48. Jodi Wilgoren, "New Terror Alert Brings No Change in States' Security," *New York Times*, May 25, 2002, p. A11.

49. *Statistical Abstract of the United States: 2009* (U.S. Government Printing Office, 2008), Table 516, "Homeland Security Grants by States/Territories, 2007 and 2008," https://www.census.gov/compendia/statab/2010/tables/10s0516.pdf.

50. See Amy C. Hughes, "State Emergency Management: New Realities in a Homeland Security World," *The Book of the States, 2004*

(The Council of State Governments, 2004), pp. 485–488.

51. Larry Morandi, "Growing Pains," *State Legislatures*, October–November 1998, pp. 24–28.

52. www.communitygreens.org/ExistingGreens/existinggreens.htm.

53. Neal Peirce, "Walkability = Livability = Billions," *The Washington Post Writers Group*, December 16, 2007, www.citistates.com/peirce.

54. See Robert B. Albritton, "Subsidies: Welfare and Transportation," in Virginia Gray, Herbert Jacob, and Kenneth Vines, eds., *Politics in the American States: A Comparative Analysis*, 7th ed. (CQ Press, 1999); and E. J. Dionne, Jr., ed., *Community Works: The Revival of Civil Society in America* (Brookings Institution Press, 2000).

55. Colby Itkowitz, "Panel's Proposal to Raise Gas Taxes Finds Little Support on Capitol Hill," *CQ Weekly*, January 21, 2008, p. 209.

56. But see Michele Mariani, "Transit's High-Tech Route," *Governing* (May 2004), pp. 60–67; and Rob Gurwitt, "Connecting the Suburban Dots," *Governing* (October 2003), pp. 36–40.

57. Colby Itkowitz, "Mass Transit, Road Repair Vie for Federal Dollars," *CQ Weekly*, March 24, 2008, p. 772.

58. Darel Paul, *Rescaling International Political Economy: Subnational States and the Regulation of the Global Political Economy* (Routledge, 2005).

59. James C. McKinley, Jr., "For U.S. Exporters in Cuba, Business Trumps Politics," *New York Times*, November 12, 2007, p. A3.

60. For a discussion of the evolution of environmental policy in a particularly interesting place, see Charles O. Jones, *Clean Air: The Policies and Politics of Pollution Control* (University of Pittsburgh Press, 1973).

61. R. Steven Brown, "State Environmental Expenditures, 2005–2008," The Environmental Council of the States, March 2008.

62. Jeff Dale, "Realistic Redevelopment," *State Legislatures*, February 1999, pp. 28–31.

63. "States Leading the Way in Advancing Clean Energy," National Governors Association, May 6, 2010, http://www.nga.org/portal/site/nga/menuitem.6c9a8a9ebc6ae07eee28aca9501010a0/?vgnextoid=6611dfdd9b868210VgnVCM1000005e00100aRCRD&vgnextchannel=759b8f2005361010VgnVCM1000001a01010aRCRD.

64. Felicity Barringer and William Yardley, "Bush Splits on Greenhouse Gases with Congress and State Officials," *New York Times*, April 4, 2007, p. A1.

65. http://gov.ca.gov/press-release/8400/.

66. http://gov.ca.gov/press-release/12608/.

67. See Donald F. Kettl, "Federalism, Anyone?" *Governing* (February 2004), p. 14.

Chapter 10

1. "State Debt Woes Grow Too Big to Camouflage," *New York Times*, March 29, 2010.

2. Figures include full-time employees. Calculated from U.S. Census Bureau, "State and Local Government Employment and Payroll Data, 2008," http://www.census.gov/govs/apes/.

3. U.S. Census Bureau, "State and Local Government Employment and Payroll Data, 2008," http://www.census.gov/govs/apes/.

4. U.S. Bureau of Labor Statistics, "Employment Outlook: 2006–2016," *Monthly Labor Review* (November 2007), p. 7, www.bls.gov/opub/mlr/2007/11/art1full.pdf.

5. *Elrod* v. *Burns*, 427 U.S. 347 (1976).

6. "David Osborne and Ted Gaebler," *Reinventing Government: How the Entrepreneurial Spirit Is Transforming the Public Sector* (Addison-Wesley, 1992); see also "National Commission on the State and Local Public Service" ["Winter Commission"], *Hard Truths/Tough Choices: An Agenda for State and Local Reform* (Rockefeller Institute of Government, 1993).

7. Steven W. Hays and Jessica E. Sowa, "A Broader Look at the 'Accountability' Movement: Some Grim Realities in State Civil Service Systems," *Review of Public Personnel Administration* 26 (June 2006), pp. 107–108.

8. Jerrell Coggburn, "Personnel Deregulation: Exploring Differences in the American States," *Journal of Public Administration Research and Theory* 11, No. 2 (2001): 223–244.

9. J. Edward Kellough and Lloyd G. Nigro, "Pay for Performance in Georgia State Government: Employee Perspectives in Georgia Gain After 5 Years," *Review of Public Personnel Administration* 22 (Summer 2002), pp. 146–166; and Stephen E. Condrey, "Reinventing State Civil Service Systems," *Review of Public Personnel Administration* 22 (Summer 2002), pp. 114–124.

10. James S. Bowman, Marc G. Gertz, Sally C. Gertz, and Russell L. Williams, "Civil Service Reform in Florida State Government: Employee Attitudes 1 Year Later," *Review of Public Personnel Administration* 23 (December 2003), pp. 286–304.

11. Hays and Sowa, "A Broader Look," pp. 107–108.

12. Bowman et al., "Civil Service Reform," pp. 291, 294.

13. Kellough and Nigro, "Pay for Performance," pp. 151, 154–155.

14. Hays and Sowa, "A Broader Look," pp. 115–116; see also Condrey, "Reinventing State Civil Service Systems," pp. 119–121.

15. Coggburn, "Personnel Deregulation"; and Hays and Sowa, "A Broader Look," pp. 113–114.

16. Pamela Winston et al., "Privatization of Welfare Services: A Review of the Literature," report submitted to the Department of Health and Human Services, Assistant Secretary for Planning and Evaluation (Mathematica Policy Research, Inc., May 2002), pp. 3–6, www.mathematica-mpr.com/PDFs/privatization.pdf.

17. For a description of the enactment and early years of W-2, see Thomas Kaplan, "Wisconsin's W-2 Program: Welfare as We Might Come to Know It?," in Carol S. Weissert, ed., *Learning from Leaders: Welfare Reform Politics and Policy in Five Midwestern States* (Rockefeller Institute Press, 2000), pp. 77–113.

18. See http://www.dwd.state.wi.us/dwd/employers.htm.

19. See Wisconsin Department of Workforce Development, "Performance Standards for the 2006–2009 W-2 and Related Programs Contract," dwd.wisconsin.gov/w2/contracts/20062009/pdf/appendix_b1.pdf. For an update on Wisconsin's W-2 program in Milwaukee, see Karen Gardiner, Mike Fishman, Mark Ragan, and Tom Gais, "Local Implementation of TANF in Five Sites: Changes Related to the Deficit Reduction Act," final report prepared for the U.S. Administration for Children and Families, Office of Planning, Research, and Evaluation, March 31, 2008.

20. Winston et al., "Privatization," p. 11.

21. Robert T. Garrett, "Texas' Welfare Privatization Efforts Snagged," *The Dallas Morning News,* April 6, 2008, www.dallasnews.com/sharedcontent/dws/dn/latestnews/stories/040708dntexcallcenters.3b22a5b.html.

22. See Reason Public Policy Institute, a pro-privatization think tank, at www.privatization.org.

23. John Shannon, "The Deregulation of Fiscal Federalism," in Thomas R. Swartz and John E. Peck, eds., *The Changing Face of Fiscal Federalism* (Sharpe, 1990), p. 31.

24. U.S. Census Bureau, *Statistical Abstract of the United States: 2008* (U.S. Government Printing Office, 2000), Table 419.

25. Lucy Dadayan and Robert B. Ward, "State Tax Revenue Weakens Still Further, While Costs Rise Sharply," *State Revenue Report,* No. 71 (Rockefeller Institute Press, March 2008); and Donald J. Boyd and Lucy Dadayan, "State Revenue Flash Report: Sales Tax Declines in Most States," *Rockefeller Institute Fiscal Features* (Rockefeller Institute Press, May 1, 2008).

26. "State of the States 2010," Pew Center for the States, http://www.pewcenteronthestates.org/uploadedFiles/State_of_the_States_2010.pdf.

27. Don Boyd, "State Finances: Solid Recovery but Challenges Ahead," *The Book of the States, 2006* (The Council of State Governments, 2006), pp. 340–342.

28. U.S. Census Bureau, *State and Local Government Finances: 2006–2007,* Table 1, http://www2.census.gov/govs/estimate/07slsstab1a.xls.

29. For a recent discussion of state and local tax issues, see Katherine Barrett, Richard Greene, Michele Mariani, and Anya Sostek, "The Way We Tax: A 50-State Report," *Governing* (February 2003), pp. 11–40.

30. For a brief history of the property tax, see Dennis Hale, "The Evaluation of the Property Tax: A Study of the Relation Between Public Finance and Political Theory," *Journal of Politics* 47 (May 1985), pp. 382–404; see also C. Lowell Harris, ed., *The Property Tax and Local Finance* (Academy of Political Science, 1983).

31. Richard L. Cole, John Kincaid, and Andrew Parkin, "Public Opinion on Federalism in the United States and Canada in 2002," *Publius* 42 (Fall 2002), Table 4.

32. U.S. Census Bureau, *State and Local Government Finances: 2007,* http://www2.census.gov/govs/estimate/07slsstab2a.xls.

33. Calculations based on data from U.S. Census Bureau, *Statistical Abstract of the United States: 2008* (U.S. Government Printing Office, 2008), Table 428, www.census.gov/compendia/statab/tables/08s0428.xls.

34. See Roy Bahl, David L. Sjoquist, and W. Loren Williams, "School Finance Reform and Impact on Property Taxes," *Proceedings of the Eighty-Third Annual National Tax Association Conference, 1990* (National Tax Association, Tax Institute of America, 1991), pp. 163–171.

35. *Serrano* v. *Priest,* 5 Cal. 3d ed. 487, 96 Cal. Rptr. 601 (1971).

36. *San Antonio Independent School District* v. *Rodriguez,* 411 U.S. 1 (1973).

37. Michael A. Rebell, "Poverty, 'Meaningful' Educational Opportunity, and the Necessary Role of the Courts," *North Carolina Law Review* 85 (2007), p. 1501.

38. Michael A. Rebell, "Equal Opportunity and the Courts," *Phi Delta Kappan* 89 (February 2008), www.pdkintl.org/kappan/k_v89/k0802reb.htm.

39. For the most recent information on such litigation, see www.schoolfunding.info.

40. Calculation based on data from U.S. Census Bureau, *Statistical Abstract of the United States: 2008* (U.S. Government Printing Office, 2008), Table 441.

41. Suho Bae and Thomas Gais, "The Effectiveness of State-Level Tax and Expenditure Limitations (TELs)," *Rockefeller Institute Fiscal Brief,* April 15, 2007, www.rockinst.org/WorkArea/showcontent.aspx?id=11804.

42. "State Tax and Expenditure Limits, 2008," National Conference of State Legislatures, http://www.ncsl.org/default.aspx?tabid=12633.

43. "Time Series Chart of U.S. Government Spending, Local Spending on Education," usgovernmentspending.com, http://www.usgovernmentspending.com/downchart_gs.php?chart=20-local&state=US&local=s.

44. J. Richard Aronson and John L. Hilley, *Financing State and Local Governments,* 4th ed. (Brookings Institution Press, 1986), p. 138; see also U.S. Advisory Commission on Intergovernmental Relations, *Property Tax Circuit-Breakers: Current Status and Policy Issues* (U.S. Government Printing Office, 1975); and Steven D. Gold, "Circuit-Breakers and Other Relief Measures," in C. Lowell Harris, ed., *The Property Tax and Local Finance* (Academy of Political Science, 1983), pp. 119–132.

45. U.S. Census Bureau, *State and Local Government Finances: 2007,* http://www2.census.gov/govs/estimate/07slsstab1a.xls.

46. Calculations based on data in U.S. Census Bureau, *Statistical Abstract of the United States: 2008* (U.S. Government Printing Office, 2000), Table 439, www.census.gov/compendia/statab/tables/08s0439.xls.

47. Michael Mazerov, "Expanding Sales Taxation of Services: Options and Issues," *Center on Budget and Policy Priorities,* June 19, 2003.

48. Katherine Barrett and Richard Greene, "Growth and Taxes," *Governing* (January 2008), p. 24.

49. Based on 2005 data from U.S. Census Bureau, *Statistical Abstract of the United States: 2008,* Table 439. www.census.gov/compendia/statab/tables/08s0439.xls.

50. Ibid.

51. Ibid.

52. Pamela M. Prah, "States Scramble for Gambling Jackpot," Stateline.org, September 12, 2007, www.stateline.org/live/details/story?contentId=239294.

53. "For the First Time, A Smaller Jackpot," Fiscal Studies report from the Rockefeller Institute, September 21, 2009, http://www.rockinst.org/pdf/government_finance/2009-09-21-No_More_Jackpot.pdf.

54. Prah, "States Scramble."

55. Rockefeller Institute Press, forthcoming.

56. "For the First Time, A Smaller Jackpot," Fiscal Studies report from the Rockefeller Institute, September 21, 2009, http://www.rockinst.org/pdf/government_finance/2009-09-21-No_More_Jackpot.pdf.

57. Ibid.

58. U.S. Census Bureau, *State and Local Government Finances: 2007,* http://www2.census.gov/govs/estimate/07slsstab1a.xls.

59. Ibid.

60. U.S. Census Bureau, *Statistical Abstract of the United States: 2010,* Table 420.

61. Suho Bae and Thomas Gais, "Fiscal Report: K–12 Education Spending by State and Local Governments," *Rockefeller Institute Policy Brief,* June 25, 2007; see also U.S. Census Bureau, "Public Education Finances, 2007," July 2009, http://www2.census.gov/govs/school/07f33pub.pdf.

62. Kathryn A. Foster, *The Political Economy of Special-Purpose Government* (Georgetown University Press, 1997); and Robert L. Bland and Wes Clarke, "Budgeting for Capital Improvements," in Roy T. Meyers, ed., *Handbook of Government Budgeting* (Jossey-Bass, 1999), pp. 653–677.

63. U.S. Census Bureau, *Statistical Abstract of the United States: 2010* (U.S. Government Printing Office, 2008), Table 434, https://www.census .gov/compendia/statab/2010/tables/ 10s0434.pdf.

64. Data on state and local government finances for these and other years are available at U.S. Census Bureau, *State and Local Government Finances,* www.census.gov/govs/www/ estimate.html.

65. James W. Fossett and Courtney E. Burke, *Medicaid and State Budgets in FY 2004: Why Medicaid Is So Hard to Cut* (Rockefeller Institute Press, July 2004), www.rockinst.org/ WorkArea/showcontent.aspx?id=6592.

66. Lucy Dadayan and Robert B. Ward, "State Tax Revenue Weakens Still Further, While Costs Rise Sharply," *State Revenue Report* (Rockefeller Institute Press, March 2008), pp. 10–12, www.rockinst.org/WorkArea/ showcontent.aspx?id=14556.

67. Declan McCullagh, "More States Propose Internet Sales Taxes" CNET News, March 8, 2010, http://news.cnet.com/8301-13578_3-10465658- 38.html.

68. U.S. Census Bureau, *Statistical Abstract of the United States: 2010* (U.S. Government Printing Office, 2010), Table 665, https://www.census .gov/compendia/statab/2010/tables/ 10s0665.pdf.

69. Yesim Yilmaz et al., "Measuring Fiscal Disparities Across the U.S. States," *Assessing the New Federalism: Occasional Paper No. 74* (Urban Institute, 2006); and The Lewin Group and the Rockefeller Institute of Government, *Spending on Social Welfare Programs in Rich and Poor States,* final report prepared for the Department of Health and Human Services, Assistant Secretary for Planning and Evaluation (DHHS/ASPE, 2004).

70. Yilmaz et al., "Measuring Fiscal Disparities," p. 24; and Lewin and Rockefeller, *Spending,* p. 24.

71. See "Grading the States, 2008," *Governing* (March 2008).

72. Lawrence M. Mead, *Government Matters: Welfare Reform in Wisconsin* (Princeton University Press, 2004).

73. Peter Harkness, "Management Matters," *Governing* (April 7, 2008), www.governing .com/articles/0804hark.htm.

CREDITS

Photo Credits

CHAPTER 1: 6: Tony Avelar/The Christian Science Monitor/Getty Images; **9:** Damian Dovarganes/AP Photo; **12:** Johnny Crawford/The Image Works; **13:** nagelstock/Alamy; **15:** Aaron D. Allmon II/U.S. Air Force via Getty Images; **16:** *(top)* Carl D. Walsh/Aurora; **16:** *(bottom)* Joe Raedle/Getty Images; **18:** Michael Smith/Newscom; **20:** Jonathan Nourok/Getty Images; **21:** Thomas Wright/ University of Florida/IFAS/AP Photo; **22:** Dream Pictures/Getty Images; **24:** Alex Wong/Getty Images; **25:** Ed Kashi/Corbis; **26:** Yael Swerdlow/AP Photo

CHAPTER 2: 32: Rich Pedroncelli/AP Photo; **36:** *(left)* Bill Ross/Corbis; **34:** *(center)* Richard T. Nowitz/Corbis; **34:** *(right)* Alamy; **36:** Alamy; **37:** Stan Honda/AFP/Getty Images; **40:** Alamy; **41:** Julia Malokie/AP Photo; **43:** David Greedy/Getty Images; **46:** James D. Wilson/Woodfin Camp & Associates; **48:** Chicago Tribune/MCT/Landov

CHAPTER 3: 52: Elise Amendola/AP Photo; **573:** Elaine Thompson/AP Photo;

CHAPTER 4: 68: Tracy A. Woodward/The Washington Post/Getty Images; **70:** Library of Congress; **73:** McCain Library and Archives, University of Mississippi; **75:** Marcio Jose Sanchez/AP Photo; **77:** AP Photo; **78:** Bill Pugliano/Getty Images; **84:** Eric Engman/Getty Images; **86:** Charlie Neibergall/AP Photo; **88:** Sue Ogrocki/AP Photo

CHAPTER 5: 94: Tom Olmscheid/AP Photo; **97:** Aurelia Venture/Newscom; **100:** Joshua Lott/Reuters/ Landov; **108:** Harry Cabluck/AP Photo

CHAPTER 6: 116: John Zich/AFP/Getty Images; **118:** Courtesy Scott Merrick; **119:** *(top)* John Froschauer/AP Photo; **119:** *(bottom)* John L. Russell/AP Photo; **120:** David Kohl/AP Photo;

127: Damian Dovargenes/AP Photo; **129:** *(top)* Chitose Suzuki/ AP Photo; **129:** *(bottom)* Gerald Herbert/AP Photo; **133** Raleigh News Observer/MCT/Landov

CHAPTER 7: 138: Teri Stratford/Six-Cats Research Inc.; **141:** Billy E. Barnes/Photoedit; **144:** Tony Freeman/ Photoedit; **145:** Photo by Robert Laughon Jr.; **148:** Tony Gutierrez/AP Photo; **149:** Scott T. Baxter/Photodisc/Getty Images

CHAPTER 8: 156: David McNew/Getty Images; **162:** Farrell Grehan/Corbis; **169:** Corbis; **171 both:** Ross D. Franklin/AP Photo; **172:** *(top)* Richard Cummins/Superstock; **172:** *(bottom)* Chris Hondros/Newscom; **174:** Justin Lane/ epa/Corbis; **176:** Ethan Hyman/The News & Observer; **177:** Farrell Grehan/Corbis

CHAPTER 9: 182: © Samantha Contis; **185:** Bob Daemmrich/Alamy; **187:** Sarah L. Voisin/The Washington Post via Getty Images; **188:** Byron Purvis/AdMedia/Newscom; **190:** Chicago Tribune/MCT/Landov; **194:** Tim Boyle/ Getty Images; **198:** Kevin R. Morris/ Corbis; **199:** Craig Lassig/Corbis; **202:** Ronen Zilberman/AP Photo

CHAPTER 10: 206: Charles Cherney/AP Photo; **215:** AP Photo; **217:** Mark Humphrey/AP Photo; **219:** Charles Rex Arbogast/AP Photo; **220:** Mark Wilson/Getty Images; **221:** Aric Crabb/Bay Area News Group/The Contra Costa Times/AP Photo; **222:** Bloomberg via Getty Images

Text Credits

CHAPTER 1: 10: From "Obama More Popular Abroad Than at Home, Global Image of U.S. Continues to Benefit" July 2010, by Pew Global Attitudes Project. Copyright (c) 2010 by Pew Global Attitudes Project, a project of the Pew Research Center. Reprinted with permission. **3:** From GETTING CURRENT:

RECENT DEMOGRAPHIC TRENDS IN METROPOLITAN AMERICA by William H. Frey, Alan Berube, Audrey Singer and Jill H. Wilson. Copyright (c) 2010 by William H. Frey, Alan Berube, Audrey Singer and Jill H. Wilson. Reprinted by permission of The Brookings Institution.

CHAPTER 4: 74: From "Voting Technologies and Residual Ballots in the 2000 and 2004 Presidential Elections" by Barney Warf in POLITICAL GEOGRAPHY, June 2006. Copyright (c) 2006 by Barney Warf. Reprinted by permission of Elsevier. **89:** From THE YOUTH VOTE IN 2008 by Kirby and Kawashima-Ginsberg. Copyright (c) by Kirby and Kawashima-Ginsberg. Reprinted by permission of CIRCLE.

CHAPTER 5: 98: "Legislators' Occupations in all States" by National Conference of State Legislators. Copyright (c) 2010 by National Conference of State Legislators. Reprinted with permission. **107:** "Legislators' Occupations in all States" by National Conference of State Legislators. Copyright (c) 2010 by National Conference of State Legislators. Reprinted with permission.

CHAPTER 6: 122: From "Governors and the Executive Branch" by Thad Beyle and Margaret Ferguson in POLITICS IN THE AMERICAN STATES: A COMPARATIVE ANALYSIS, 9e, ed. Virginia Gray and Russell L. Hanson. Copyright (c) by Thad Beyle and Margaret Ferguson. Reprinted by permission of CQ Press.

CHAPTER 8: 163: "Map of St. Louis." Copyright (c) 2007 by East-West Gateway Council of Governments. Reprinted with permission.

CHAPTER 10: 213: From "How the Recession Might Change States" by Pew Center on the States, February 2010. Copyright (c) 2010 Pew Center on the States. Reprinted with permission.

INDEX

242

COURSE EXAM

Chapter 1: American Federalism
Explain federalism in America, and analyze the relationship between the federal and state and local governments.

1. Define federalism and explain the ways governments at different levels can share power in different kinds of federalism.

2. Which one of the following is NOT an advantage of federalism?
   a. It checks the growth of tyranny.
   b. It encourages experimentation.
   c. It allows unity without uniformity.
   d. It encourages holding elected officials accountable through a division of power.
   e. It keeps government closer to the people.

3. What is the difference between delegated or express powers and implied powers? List some of both types.

4. A decentralist would agree with which one of the following statements?
   a. For the sake of national well-being, more power should be given to the federal government.
   b. Any question about whether the states have given a particular function to the central government or have reserved it for themselves should be resolved in favor of the states.

Chapter 2: State and Local Politics
Identify the range of policy programs administered by state and local governments, and analyze the influences on state and local politics.

9. Explain the theory of pluralism in local politics.

10. Citizens have the greatest trust in which of the following levels of government?
    a. National
    b. State
    c. Local
    d. Intra-state
    e. The amount of trust is roughly the same for all levels

11. Which of the following is NOT a central concern for state and local governments?
    a. Inner city poverty
    b. Education
    c. Health care
    d. A strong military
    e. Environmental regulation

12. What are some of the factors that restrain newspapers from holding local officials accountable?

Chapter 3: State Constitutions
Compare and contrast the U.S. Constitution with state constitutions.

13. What does it mean to say that a constitution is like a straitjacket, and what factors lead to straitjacket constitutions?

c. The devolution revolution should be defeated.
   d. Presidents Abraham Lincoln and Franklin Roosevelt had a correct understanding of the balance in power between the states and federal government.
   e. The national government is an agent of the people, not the states.

5. Which of the following is one of the three types of federal grants currently given?
   a. Welfare grant
   b. Income equalization grant
   c. Categorical-formula grant
   d. Revenue sharing grant
   e. Education grant

6. Historically, how had federalism been used to retain slavery, segregation, and discrimination? Provide arguments for and against retaining federalism given these patterns. Are there examples of states having laws today that treat people differently?

The Big Picture

7. Compare and contrast the originalist approach to interpreting the U.S. Constitution with the adaptive approach.

8. Explain how the system of federalism addressed the framers' concerns over the power of the new federal government.

14. Which of the following is NOT a way that state constitutions can be amended?
    a. Legislative proposal
    b. Revision commission
    c. Constitutional initiative petition
    d. Constitutional convention
    e. U. S. Supreme Court decision

15. Explain why some states might require supermajorities to change their state constitutions.

16. If a state supreme court rules that a U.S. constitutional provision outlining the rights of gun owners is more limited than previously believed, this would be an example of:
    a. Judicial interpretation
    b. New judicial federalism
    c. Strict constitutionalism
    d. Constitutional literalism
    e. None of the above

Chapter 4: Parties and Elections in the States
Assess the importance of parties and elections at the state level.

17. An election that is held to fill a vacant office or address a one-time issue is called a:
    a. General election
    b. Primary election
    c. Recall election
    d. Provisional election
    e. Special election

18. According to the Constitution, who is primarily responsible for determining who may vote?
    a. Congress
    b. The federal courts
    c. State governments
    d. Town councils
    e. The electoral college

19. Explain the meaning of the term *office block ballot*. Does it typically encourage a straight ticket vote or a split ticket vote?

20. Explain the difference between a *closed primary* and an *open primary*.

21. Following the national census, state legislatures are constitutionally required to realign congressional district boundaries to make them equal in population. This is called:
    a. Reapportionment
    b. Redistricting
    c. Disclosure
    d. Voter mobilization
    e. Electoral adjustment

Chapter 5: State Legislatures
Describe the functions of state legislatures and evaluate their responsiveness to the people.

22. Which of the following traits would NOT be typical of a state legislator?
    a. White
    b. Male
    c. Lawyer
    d. Lower income
    e. All of these traits are typical

23. Which of the following is an example of an elected official acting as a trustee?
    a. Voting for a canal because his or her neighbors all support it
    b. Voting for a tax increase even though her or his constituents all strongly oppose it
    c. Voting for an immigration bill after being pressed by friends
    d. Voting for the new seatbelt law because it is popular
    e. All of the above

24. What are the pros and cons of term limits?

25. Which of the following is an example of malapportionment in legislative districts?
    a. Drawing a district that excludes all Democrats
    b. Excluding all African Americans from a district
    c. Drawing a district that is not contiguous
    d. Neighboring districts that vary greatly in population
    e. All of the above

26. What is direct democracy and what are its strengths and weaknesses?

Chapter 6: State Governors
Explain how governors use their formal and informal powers to influence public policy.

27. Which of the following is NOT true of a typical state's governor?
    a. The executive power is fully vested in him or her
    b. Has the power to make appointments
    c. Has the power to veto legislation
    d. Commands the state National Guard
    e. Can pardon or grant clemency to criminals

28. Explain what a line item veto is.

29. Which one of the following is typically second in command to the governor?
    a. Attorney general
    b. Lieutenant governor
    c. Secretary of state
    d. Treasurer
    e. Senate president

30. What are some of the challenges facing current governors?

Chapter 7: Judges and Justice in the States
Describe the judicial system at the state level, and evaluate the differences across the states in judicial selection and sentencing.

31. Describe the functions of the three main kinds of state courts—minor courts, trial courts, and appellate courts.

32. Which of the following is NOT one of the ways that state judges are chosen?
    a. Appointment by the governor
    b. Election by the legislature
    c. Popular election
    d. Appointment by the president
    e. The Missouri plan

33. Explain how a *retention election* works.

34. An *information affidavit* is a certification that there is enough evidence to justify bringing named individuals to trial. Who is responsible for submitting an information affidavit?
    a. Judge
    b. Trial jury
    c. Public prosecutor
    d. Grand jury
    e. Public defender

35. Explain how an *assigned counsel system* works.

36. Describe three proposals for reforming the state judicial system.

Chapter 8: Local Governments and Metropolitics
Identify the functions of local governments, including counties, cities, towns, and special districts.

37. Explain why New England town meetings are the most complete demonstration of direct democracy in the United States.

38. What is the informal definition of a *metropolitan area*?
    a. A large city
    b. A large city and its suburbs
    c. The suburbs surrounding a large city
    d. A large city and its suburbs, as well as neighboring towns that use the same public transportation systems

39. Why is the concept of *eminent domain* controversial?

40. A *township* is a level of local government beneath the county that is primarily used in which region of the United States?
    a. Northwest
    b. Southwest
    c. Northeast
    d. Southeast

41. List and describe three strategies for governing metropolitan regions.

Chapter 9: Making State and Local Policy
Evaluate the importance of state and local governments in implementing policy.

42. In the United States, the responsibility for administering public education is constitutionally reserved to:
    a. The federal government
    b. State governments
    c. Private individuals
    d. All of the above
    e. None of the above

43. Explain the term *voucher*.

44. On what Constitutional grounds are some states challenging the recent national health care reform law, and on what Constitutional grounds does the the federal government respond?

45. Explain three general purposes for enacting and enforcing zoning laws.

46. Give two examples of how states are taking the lead in setting responsible environmental policy.

Chapter 10: Staffing and Financing State and Local Governments
Describe the challenges for state and local governments in organizing resources, raising funds, and managing expenditures.

47. Public employment that is structured so that selection and promotion depend primarily on political patronage is called:
    a. The spoils system
    b. The merit system
    c. Outsourcing
    d. Competitive bureaucracy
    e. Professional civil service

48. Which of the following is the states' largest source of revenue?
    a. Sale of state properties
    b. Federal grants
    c. Charges for government services
    d. Taxes
    e. Tuition at state universities

49. Explain why property taxes are often controversial.

50. A tax graduated so that people with higher incomes pay a larger fraction of their income than people with lower incomes is called a(n):
    a. Excise tax
    b. Value-added tax
    c. Progressive tax
    d. Sales tax
    e. Severance tax

51. Why do states differ in fiscal capacity (the economic resources they can tax)?

The Big Picture

52. What are the arguments for and against higher salaries for state legislators?

53. Explain the four different ways in which state judges are selected.

54. Explain the arguments for and against giving state governors the power of the line item veto.

ANSWERS

1. Federalism is a constitutional arrangement in which power is distributed between a central government and subdivisional governments, called states in the United States. The national and subdivisional governments both exercise direct authority over individuals. The ways that governments at different levels can share power include:
   - Dual federalism: a limited list of powers are given to the national government, and the rest are reserved to the states.
   - Cooperative federalism: stresses intergovernmental relationships in delivering governmental goods and services.
   - Marble cake federalism: a mixed set of responsibilities where all levels of government engage in a variety of issues and programs (as opposed to dual federalism).
   - Competitive federalism: all levels of government compete with each other over ways to put together packages of services and taxes.
   - Permissive federalism: the states' share of power depends on the permission and permissiveness of the national government.
   - New federalism: the power of the federal government is limited in favor of the broad powers reserved to the states.

2. D

3. Delegated, or express, powers are powers explicitly given to the national government through statements in the Constitution. Implied powers are powers inferred from the express powers that are given to Congress in the Constitution. Express powers include the powers to declare war and to create post offices, while implied powers include the power to create banks.

4. B

5. C

6. State and national governments have disagreed often on civil rights and civil liberties issues. Thus, even when the national government outlawed slavery, segregation, and discrimination, states in which these new laws were not popular did not enforce these federal laws. Federalism also can create inconsistent laws among states that can create problems for people moving between states or for expanding businesses. Despite these potential problems, federalism has many advantages, including decentralization of power, and preventing the growth of tyranny. It also encourages experimentation in lower levels of government that might be adopted elsewhere. Finally, it keeps government closer to the people so that it can better engage more citizens in the governing process. There are laws today permitting same-sex marriage or civil unions in some states and not others.

7. Those who use an originalist approach to constitutional interpretation read the document literally and understand the words to mean what they meant at the time they were ratified. The adaptive approach is one through which the Constitution is seen as an evolving document that should be understood in light of society's norms and values.

8. The framers wanted a central government strong enough to address their concerns over the economy and international relations, but they also wanted government that was responsive to the diverse needs of state citizens. Federalism does both by providing the benefits of a strong central government balanced by smaller state governments that are closer to the people.

9. A theory of government that holds that open, multiple and competing groups can check the asserted power of any one group.

10. C. Polling shows that citizens are most trustful in local government.

11. D. Military strength is a concern of the federal government.

12. Owners of newspapers are often friends with local officials, and they recognize that speaking well of their town and officials is ultimately to their benefit if it brings expansion.

13. "Constitutions as straitjackets" refers to constitutions being very detailed; hence they are like straitjackets imposed on the present by the past. Constitutions become more detailed as amendments are passed, often in an attempt to reign in the power of corrupt legislators.

14. E. The Supreme Court has no power to directly enact an amendment on a state constitution. Their rulings may in effect change state law but their rulings do not amend constitutions.

15. Some states may be concerned that their constitutions are too easily changed. Amendments that only garner a bare majority might not be in the best interest of the state. With a higher bar for amending the document, groups would be forced to appeal to a greater segment of the state's population.

16. A. Judicial interpretation is a method by which judges modify the force of a constitutional provision by reinterpreting its meaning.

17. E

18. C

19. An office block ballot is a ballot on which all candidates are listed under the office for which they are running. This type of ballot typically encourages a split ticket vote.

20. A closed primary is a primary election in which only persons registered in the party holding the primary may vote. An open primary is a primary election in which any voter, regardless of party, may vote.

21. B

22. D. The typical state legislator is financially well-off.

23. B. All other answers involve the legislator acting in response to constituent pressure.

24. Having term limits prevents professional politicians serving in the legislature, but it leads to an amateur legislature and gives increased power to lobbyists.

25. D. Malapportionment refers to having districts with unequal populations.

26. It refers to the initiative process where citizens are able to place issues directly on a state-wide ballot. It brings the political process closer to the people, but it can be

manipulated by special interests and uninformed citizens.

27. A. In contrast to the president, governors typically have to share executive power with other officers.

28. Line item veto is the right of an executive to veto parts of a bill approved by a legislature without having to veto the entire bill.

29. B

30. Governors are expected to be the state's chief policy maker, shaper of the state budget, savvy political party leader, chief recruiter of the best available advisers and administrators, and inspiring leader who renews public confidence in state programs.

31. Minor trial courts handle minor violations of state and local laws and, in some cases, the preliminary hearings for more serious offenses. Major courts are typically courts of general jurisdiction hearing civil and criminal cases. Appeals courts handle challenges to outcomes of trial courts.

32. D

33. A sitting judge runs *uncontested* for reelection: Voters simply vote in favor or against keeping her or him in office.

34. C

35. An arrangement whereby attorneys are provided for people accused of crimes who are unable to hire their own attorneys. The judge assigns a member of the bar to provide counsel to a particular defendant.

36. Efforts to reform state courts include some that focus on increasing judicial quality, improving professional administration, and developing alternative methods to resolve disputes.

37. Voters participate directly in making rules, passing new laws, levying taxes, and appropriating money.

38. B

39. Eminent domain is controversial because it places individual landowners' interests at odds with state and local governments' interests. It allows the government to take private land for public purposes, even when the landowner does not give consent, as long as the owner is paid the fair market value. Many people have different views of what important public purposes would justify governments exercising this power.

40. C

41. Strategies to govern metropolitan areas include annexation, agreements to furnish services, public authorities, special districts, regional coordinating and planning councils, city-county consolidations, and federated government.

42. B

43. Money provided by the government to parents for payment of their children's tuition in a public or private school of their choice.

44. Some states challenge the federal government's efforts at health-care reform as exceeding their authority under the commerce clause and infringing on the states' power under the Tenth Amendment. Proponents argue that the federal government has regulatory authority due to its impact on interstate commerce and to provide for the general welfare.

45. For the local government to coordinate services and land use; to stabilize property values; to maintain standards of sanitation; to maintain public safety; to improve quality of life in the community.

46. States have become active in protecting the environment through waste management, controlling auto emissions, and promoting responsible energy use and sustainability.

47. A

48. D

49. Property taxes bear little relationship to a taxpayers' income or other measures of their ability to pay. Real property cannot always be easily converted into money with which to pay the tax. Exemptions sometimes create situations where two taxpayers with similar property pay different tax rates. Assessments may or may not reflect the actual market value of the property. Most property taxes require a lump-sum payment that could be difficult for some taxpayers to meet.

50. C

51. States differ in average personal incomes. Average personal income is often correlated with consumption and property values, which affect the amount of money a state can raise through sales taxes and property taxes. States also have different amounts of natural resources, which affect the amount they can collect in severance taxes.

52. Opponents of raising state legislators' salaries argue that professional politicians do not necessarily do a good job. Proponents argue that legislators work longer hours on more complicated and demanding work than most citizens realize.

53. State court judges are determined in several ways throughout the U.S. including gubernatorial appointment, election by the state legislature, popular election, and merit-selection plans.

54. Some argue that a line item veto would give governors unchecked power that could frustrate the will of the legislature. Others argue this power is needed to check legislatures which are including more and more legislation in their appropriations bills.